LLERENA FRIEND

Sam Houston

The Great Designer

AUSTIN · UNIVERSITY OF TEXAS PRESS

International Standard Book Number 0-292-78422-8
Library of Congress Catalog Card Number 54-13252
Copyright 1954 by Llerena B. Friend
All rights reserved
Printed in the United States of America

Texas History Paperback, 1969
Third Paperback Printing, 1985

Requests for permission to reproduce material from
this work should be sent to Permissions, University of
Texas Press, Box 7819, Austin, Texas 78713-7819.

To Sue Stringer
in grateful remembrance

Published in cooperation with
The Texas State Historical Association

Foreword

U NDER A SIMILAR TITLE and in only a slightly different form, this biography of Sam Houston was prepared as a doctoral dissertation in history at the University of Texas. The study was suggested by Professor Eugene C. Barker, who thought that a Houston biography might well utilize the eight-volume compilation of *The Writings of Sam Houston* done under a grant of the Bureau of Research in the Social Sciences at the University of Texas. Edited by Drs. Barker and Amelia Williams, the *Writings*, plus the unpublished correspondence which accrued as they were prepared, have facilitated immeasurably the task of presenting the story of a public figure who wrote and spoke extensively over a full and lengthy life span. Particularly helpful were Miss Williams' identifications and biographical sketches which were a part of the editorial work.

Because of the abundance of Houston material, published and unpublished, factual and legendary, it was necessary to choose a point of emphasis. My effort has been to show Houston's place in national politics, including only such local history as was necessary to delineate his position in the American scene. His experiences in Tennessee and Arkansas, including his friendship with Andrew Jackson, his sojourns with the Indians, his early military career, his political services to Tennessee, and his contact with frontiersmen, were background and preparation for his Texas career. I have not been able, had it been my wish, to prove that Houston came to Texas as Jackson's tool to win the area for the United States or that he was involved in a capitalist conspiracy to speculate in Texas lands as a corporation lawyer. The Texas revolution was inevitable, with or without Houston.

The victory at San Jacinto established Houston as the symbol of Texas heroism and as a candidate for the presidency of the Republic of Texas. During his presidency, Texas political groupings crystallized into pro-Houston and anti-Houston factions, and by the end of his second term interest centered on his attitude towards annexation. With union accomplished, he became United States senator from Texas in 1846 and held that post until March, 1859. As a senator he played an active part in Democratic party politics until 1854, when he offended Texas Democrats and the South generally by his opposition to the Kansas-Nebraska Bill. After 1855 he was virtually a lame duck congressman. Serenely oblivious of that fact, he established himself as a symbol of strong Unionism. In a nation torn by sectionalism, that Unionist stand did not suffice to win for him the presidency of the United States, although his name was mentioned for chief executive from 1848 to 1860. When Abraham Lincoln was elected in 1860, Texas seceded, despite Houston's opposition, and Houston was forced from the governor's office when he refused to take the oath of allegiance to the Confederate States of America. Declining a federal offer of troops to keep himself in office and Texas in the Union, he lived for three more years, loyal to Texas and her best interests as he saw them.

Houston as frontiersman and soldier has been the personification of much of the romantic in American history. Everybody is acquainted with the "buckskin hero from Tennessee," but questions concerning him tend to relate to his life with the Indians, his marital problems, and his conviviality, and to ignore his work as a practical politician and a statesman.

Houston was devoted in his family relationships—as son, brother, uncle, and cousin. Courtly and courteous to all women, he was a solicitous husband and a loving father. He wanted comfort and security for his family, but wealth for its own sake had small attraction for him. In his lifetime Houston was a man who inspired violent dislike or great devotion. While striving for impartiality, I confess that I have been unable to resolve many of the apparent contradictions in his life and actions; but I can only conclude that his life was one of integrity, loyalty, and patriotism and that, in the words of his grandson, his "consuming passion was to be of service to the nation which had given him birth."

Acknowledgments

IF RESEARCH BE THE SELECTION of bones of information from one stack to reassemble them in another mound, my first acknowledgment of gratitude must be to librarians and archivists who assisted in the digging for materials which they considered neither dead nor dry. My work was facilitated by co-operation far beyond the line of duty by the staffs of the Library of the University of Texas, the Archives Division of the Texas State Library, and the Manuscripts Division of the Library of Congress. Mr. Francis L. Berkeley, Jr., curator of manuscripts in the Alderman Library of the University of Virginia; Miss Pauline Cone of the Manuscripts Department of Duke University Library; Mr. Robert W. Bingham, director of the Buffalo Historical Society; and Dr. George W. Pierson of Yale University have also been helpful in making research materials available.

My obligation to the Daughters of the Republic of Texas is great. They gave not only encouragement but material assistance through the award to me for two years of the Clara Driscoll Scholarship for Research in Texas History. The scholarship provided my opportunity to work for a time at the Library of Congress.

Mr. D. C. Arthur granted permission to quote from his M.A. thesis. Oxford University Press, the Arthur H. Clark Company, Barnes and Noble, Doubleday and Company, the Ohio Historical Society, Longmans, Green and Company, the Broadman Press, Appleton-Century-Crofts, Alfred A. Knopf, the Carnegie Institution of Washington, the Department of History of Randolph-Macon College of Ashland, Virginia, A. C. McClurg and Company, and the American Historical Association have been generous in granting permission to quote from their publications.

Dr. Herbert Gambrell of Southern Methodist University dealt kindly with the manuscript and gave unlimited permission to repeat what his *Anson Jones* had to say of "Old Sam." Similarly, Mr. Marquis James said to quote "whatever you read from *The Raven*." And I read it often and at length and it was good. Dr. Barnes Lathrop's keen reading eye assisted in eliminating some of the errors; for those that are gone I am grateful. Dr. J. H. Bennett, Jr., took time off from pursuing English history on the home ground to cut for Sam's sign in British newspapers and documents. I am thankful as well to family and friends and fellow students who bent a willing ear and often queried, "Have you seen . . . ?"

In Maryville, Tennessee, Mrs. Charles Timmons and Miss Inez Burns were gracious as hostesses and have been encouraging correspondents. Mrs. Madge W. Hearne and Mr. Temple Houston Morrow, grandchildren of General Houston, have been interested and generous to supply material.

My deepest obligations are to Dr. Walter Prescott Webb, who gave the work a name and motivated its publication, and to Dr. Eugene Campbell Barker, who suggested the topic, directed the dissertation, reread the manuscript and pared it, and without whom it could not have been.

LLERENA FRIEND

University of Texas
May, 1954

x

Contents

Sam Houston

The Great Designer

The Tennessee Background

IN JUNE, 1831, Matthew Maury was on a steamboat at White River Landing near the mouth
of the Arkansas River when a jolly boat picked up a passenger who had
been waiting on shore with two dogs at his feet and a gun on his shoulder. Wearing an old straw hat and a hunting shirt of coarse calico, the
new passenger carried Indian knapsacks and buffalo skins in lieu of a
traveling bag. He was introduced to Maury as General Sam Houston,
formerly governor of Tennessee. After dinner, Houston joined the
Maury party to take wine, and in the long and lively conversation which
followed he discoursed on the Indians in Arkansas, the value of an
abundance of unoccupied land in holding the United States together,
how he thought the United States should acquire the Pacific Northwest,
and how he, if he could get capitalists to join him, would establish a
government on the Columbia River.

Maury recorded the meeting in his journal with the comment that Houston "gave no symptoms of that general knowledge & information which the imagination would consider indispensable in a Governor of a State." The reflections to which Houston's conversation gave rise in Maury's mind included—

The extension of civilization

The American fondness for emigration

The ill adaptation of a republican government to a densely settled country? or otherwise?

The operation of universal suffrage in making such a man as Houston Governor of a State.[1]

Maury was not the only traveler moved by conversation with Houston to philosophical musings on popular sovereignty and the workings of the American political system. Six months later, on December 27, 1831, Alexis de Tocqueville and Gustave de Beaumont, on a tour of the western part of the United States after inspection of American penal institutions, met Houston, also at the mouth of the Arkansas, and again boarding a steamboat. Only a week before, Tocqueville had noted in his diary: "When the right of suffrage is *universal*, and when the deputies are paid by the state, it's singular how low and how far wrong the people can go." Tocqueville queried his fellow passengers as to Houston's identity, and at first regarded the former governor as the personification of the "unpleasant consequences of popular sovereignty." After the men had met and conversed, the Frenchman made a diary entry called "Indians." The notes included some Houston biography, with a comment on his apparent physical and moral energy, and a long list of questions and answers on Indians: their religion, government, concepts of justice, and the position of women in the tribes, as well as the government policy toward Indians.[2]

Both diarists commented on the abrupt end of Houston's political career in Tennessee; both spoke of the tragic termination of his marriage; both mentioned his life among the Indians; both were stirred to wonder about the system of government in which this man could have held high elective office. Both would doubtless have been more surprised could they have glimpsed his political future: twice president of a republic, thirteen years a United States senator, and several times a potential candidate for the presidency of the United States. What was there

[1] Matthew Maury Papers. Matthew Maury was the son of James Maury, consul to Liverpool.

[2] From *Tocqueville and Beaumont in America* (607–15), by George Wilson Pierson, copyright 1938 by Oxford University Press, Inc.

4

in his background and what were to be his accomplishments that would make the republic of which he was president known nationally and internationally as "Sam Houston's Texas," that would make him a conspicuous, even a distinguished, member of the Senate, that would cause his name to be synonymous with the spirit of the American Southwest? Was he a statesman with intellectual qualities? Was he an opportunist shrewd enough to turn opportunity to advantage, or did he deliberately aim to achieve high position in Texas as a steppingstone to higher position in the United States? Having helped make Texas independent, did he plan to keep it independent and extend its area to the Pacific Ocean to rival the United States? Did he design the exploitation of the urge of manifest destiny to establish a protectorate over Mexico and so divert American attention to expansion south to the Isthmus of Darien that secession and civil war might be averted?

In what was said about him, even if never in what he directly said himself, there are affirmative answers to every question. He was reputed to have plotted to win Texas from Mexico; those who considered him, perhaps erroneously, an opponent of the annexation of Texas to the United States said that he designed the establishment of a rival republic; when he was almost seventy, his enemies were convinced, and some of his friends hoped, that he was contriving a Mexican protectorate. And while his shrewd and active brain pondered choices for a presidential cabinet or planned an Indian conference, his nimble fingers designed a heart, a crucifix, or a winding spool to present to some admiring woman in the Senate gallery or to send home to Texas to his wife.

The fifth son of Samuel Houston, a brigade inspector and later major in the Virginia Militia, and Elizabeth Paxton Houston, Sam Houston was born near Timber Ridge Church, in Rockbridge County, Virginia, on March 2, 1793. Intermittently between 1801 and his father's death in 1806, Sam attended the school held in the story-and-a-half school building that had once housed Liberty Hall Academy.[3] In 1807 the widow moved her nine children to East Tennessee and located in Blount County, west of Maryville, on a branch of Baker's Creek. Having no taste for farming, young Sam was put to work in the general store in Maryville. His aptitude for clerking was apparently no stronger than for planting, and he disappeared across the Tennessee River to live with the Cherokee Indians for a year. He was back in Maryville in September, 1810, when he was fined for disorderly conduct for beating a drum

[3] C. Edwards Lester, *The Life of Sam Houston: The Only Authentic Memoir of Him Ever Published,* 19; Oren F. Morton, *A History of Rockbridge County, Virginia,* 189–90.

so loudly as to disturb the court. He did not pay the fine but disappeared for another year among the Indians, who adopted him into the tribe and gave him the name of "the Raven."[4]

After three years with the Cherokees, a sort of prolonged holiday broken by infrequent visits home and some scouting of Tecumseh in 1811, Houston was in debt. Not finding any job to his liking, he opened a school which he taught, apparently successfully and to financial advantage, between May and November, 1812. His tuition charge was eight dollars per term, paid one-third in corn, one-third in cash, and one-third in cotton domestic.[5] Years later, giving advice to his son on how to take advantage of school in the "seed time of life," Houston lamented in the traditional paternal fashion, "Oh, if I had only enjoyed an education of one year, I would have been happy."[6] His total classroom experience which had equipped him to be a schoolmaster in 1812 had probably not exceeded a year. John Reynolds, later a governor of Illinois, described Houston as "an agreeable young man whom all respected" when they were supposed to have been classmates, about 1809, in Isaac Anderson's academy.[7] Anderson, like Houston a native of Rockbridge County, Virginia, had a school located six miles east of Knoxville and known variously as Grassy Valley Academy and Union Academy. It would seem more likely that Sam attended Porter Academy, which began operating in Maryville about 1808.[8] He was proficient in spelling and liked to read, although his choice of books was limited. According to Lester, he left the academy in anger because he was not allowed to study the classics in Latin and Greek. A second exposure to the classroom found him interested in military tactics only. Perhaps his teaching experience revealed certain educational deficiencies, for he gave up his instructor's role to go back to the academy to be uninspired by mathematics.[9]

In March, 1813, he enlisted as a private in the Thirty-ninth Infantry for service in the war with England. He was promoted to ensign on July 29, 1813, and was commissioned a third lieutenant on December 31, 1813.[10] The lieutenant colonel of his regiment was Thomas Hart Benton. The Thirty-ninth marched into Fort Strother on February 3, 1814,

[4] Marquis James, *The Raven: A Biography of Sam Houston*, 16–20.
[5] Lester, *Life of Sam Houston*, 26.
[6] Amelia W. Williams and Eugene C. Barker (eds.), *The Writings of Sam Houston*, VIII, 33. Hereinafter cited as *Writings*.
[7] John Reynolds, *My Own Times, Embracing Also the History of My Life*, 119.
[8] Inez Burns of Maryville to Llerena Friend, November 18, 1953; Lucius Salisbury Merriam, *Higher Education in Tennessee*, 231–32.
[9] Lester, *Life of Sam Houston*, 21–22; James, *The Raven*, 29.
[10] Thomas H. S. Hamersly, *Complete Regular Army Register of the United States for One Hundred Years, 1779–1879*, 521.

6

and there Lieutenant Houston met General Andrew Jackson, who from that time on was to have a deciding influence on his life. Jackson commended the young officer for his coolness and courage in the Battle of Tohopeka or Horseshoe Bend late in March of 1814. Severely and permanently wounded in the engagement, Houston was cared for at Fort Williams for a time and then went home to recuperate. He was promoted to second lieutenant on May 20, 1814.

After a view of Washington, burned by the British, and a rest with friends and relatives at Lexington, Virginia, he was back in Tennessee by March, 1815. He decided to remain in the army, applied for a commission, and on May 17, 1815, was transferred to the First Infantry, garrisoned at New Orleans. His trip south, by skiff to Natchez and steamboat on to New Orleans, was made in company with Edward Douglas White, who had just graduated from the University of Nashville.[11] The gaiety of life in the Crescent City was marred by the necessity of an operation on his wounded shoulder and by a quarrel with the War Department over the date of his commission as lieutenant.[12] He was sent to New York for his health and was then furloughed home before being transferred to the Southern Division of the army, commanded by Andrew Jackson, with headquarters at Nashville.

Houston was detailed on duty in the adjutant's office at Nashville in January, 1817.[13] On May 1 he was promoted to first lieutenant. Doubtless he and his general discussed current Tennessee topics and reminisced of Horseshoe Bend and took up Indian problems, particularly Cherokee resentment of a treaty of 1816, by which some of the chiefs had ceded land in the Cherokee Nation in East Tennessee for territory west of the Mississippi. Return J. Meigs wrote Jackson from the Cherokee agency of the desirability of having regular troops present to prevent disorders at an approaching Indian conference and implied that intruders had returned to the Indian lands because Lieutenant Houston was no longer in the area.[14]

Until the fall of the year Houston remained in Nashville, making certificates of military equipment drawn by personnel of the First Infantry and varying his professional activities with letters from Jesse Beene in Knoxville advising him to marry "the princess of E.T." On July 22, 1817,

[11] Lester, *Life of Sam Houston*, 38.

[12] James, *The Raven*, 38–39; Houston to Crawford, February 16, 1816, *Writings*, I, 6.

[13] Josephus Conn Guild, *Old Times in Tennessee, with Historical, Personal, and Political Scraps and Sketches*, 262; Lester, *Life of Sam Houston*, 40.

[14] Meigs to Jackson, May 24, 1817, John Spencer Bassett (ed.), *Correspondence of Andrew Jackson*, II, 296.

he joined the Cumberland Masonic Lodge at Nashville.[15] Appointed subagent to the Cherokees on October 28, 1817, he returned to his old friends to live their life, fulfill government promises to the tribe, and help equip them for moving west. Finally he accompanied a delegation of the tribe to Washington for a conference with Secretary of War John C. Calhoun. The Indians apparently fared better than did their agent at the hands of Calhoun. The Secretary reprimanded the Lieutenant for appearing in Indian dress and later informed him that he had been accused of complicity with slave smugglers. The smugglers, angered at the subagent's action in preventing smuggling of Negroes from Florida into the West, had trumped up the charges. Houston cleared himself with the War Department and with President James Monroe but resigned his commission on March 1, 1818. His resentment against Calhoun was never to diminish and was to be evident many times in the future: when Calhoun was vice-president, when both men were members of the Senate, and even after Calhoun's death.[16]

His military career temporarily ended, Houston accompanied the Cherokees back to Tennessee, resigned his subagency, and in June, 1818, went to Nashville to study law in the office of Judge James Trimble. He renewed his contacts with the young men about town who, during the summer of 1817, had suggested that Noah M. Ludlow build and manage a theater in Nashville. It was not until July, 1818, that Ludlow became stage manager for the short-lived Dramatic Club of Nashville. Wilkins Tannehill, cashier of a Nashville bank, was treasurer, and John H. Eaton managed "out-door business." Judge Trimble's legal apprentice was the member described as "the *largest,* if not the most gifted with dramatic ability." General Jackson and Felix Grundy were honorary members. Houston played only a fair Glenvalon in John Home's tragedy of *Douglas;* he improved for his second role, that of Chevalier St. Franc in *Point of Honor.* Ludlow decided to exploit a "rich vein of comic humor" by casting the Lieutenant in an afterpiece, *We Fly by Night,* as a drunken porter who appears in two "short but 'all fat' " scenes. It took connivance with Eaton, priming of the audience, and careful soothing of the red-wigged and red-nosed actor to persuade him to go on stage and subject himself to possible ridicule. The audience applauded, and the newspapers praised. Ludlow said that he had "never met a man who had a keener sense of the ridiculous . . . nor one who could more readily assume the ludicrous or the sublime."[17] As recounted by Ludlow, the story

[15] Andrew Jackson Papers, Series I, Reel 69; James, *The Raven,* 40.
[16] Lester, *Life of Sam Houston,* 40; James, *The Raven,* 45.
[17] N. M. Ludlow, *Dramatic Life as I Found It,* 166.

is revealing. Houston, to the end of his days, eschewed a situation which would cause him to be ridiculed. At the same time, he forever acted a part, and his world was his stage on which he displayed that versatility in the switch from the ludicrous to the sublime.

He telescoped an eighteen-month law course into six months, was admitted to the bar, and began his practice at Lebanon, where he rented an office from Isaac Galladay, local merchant and postmaster, who extended credit and introductions. Houston's law practice and his popularity both increased, and he was appointed adjutant general by Governor Joseph McMinn, but election to the office of attorney general took Houston from Lebanon to Nashville in October, 1819.[18] He was serving as prosecuting attorney in July, 1820, when he became an active member of the Tennessee Antiquarian Society, devoted to education and general literature in addition to antiquities and history, the first learned society in the region.[19]

The prosecutor's post was not sufficiently lucrative for a young man on the way up, so Houston resigned it to go into private practice. The Nashville *Whig* for December 26, 1821, carried the announcement: "Sam Houston attorney at Law. Having removed to an office second below A. Kingsley's Esq. on Market Street, can be found at all times where he ought to be."[20] He could also be found at the Nashville Inn and among the officers of the Tennessee Militia, who, in the fall of 1821, elected him major general of the Southern Division of the militia. After a two-year correspondence with Calhoun, he finally secured all of the money due him from the government at the time he resigned from the army, and in May, 1822, Jackson wrote James Gadsden of his pleasure in the settlement of the account of the "noble-minded Houston," whom he expected to be "returned for Congress" at the next election.[21] For his part, Houston was a member of the Tennessee junto supporting Jackson and wrote the General that the Tennessee Senate had recommended him for the presidency, so that he was before the eyes of the nation with "nothing to fear, but everything to expect."[22] Houston prophesied the end of the caucus system in order that the next president would be the "People's choice." Thirty-eight years later, it was not to be the caucus

[18] Guild, *Old Times in Tennessee*, 262, 275–76.

[19] Guy Miles, "The Tennessee Antiquarian Society and the West," East Tennessee Historical Society *Publications, No. 18* (1946), 286. While he was president of the Republic of Texas, Houston was elected to honorary membership in the Copenhagen Antiquarian Society. *City Gazette* (Austin), January 19, 1842.

[20] "Historical News and Notices," *Tennessee Historical Quarterly*, V (1946), 286.

[21] *Writings*, I, 10–12; *Correspondence of Andrew Jackson*, III, 162.

[22] Houston to Jackson, August 3, 1822, *Writings*, I, 13.

but the convention that he would advocate abolishing as a presidential nomination device with Houston himself advanced as the "People's choice."

Houston took time off at the holiday season to be one of the managers for a Masonic ball at the Nashville Inn, but in January, 1823, he was reporting to the "noble old Chieftain" on political possibilities." Supported by William Carroll, the new governor of Tennessee, and by Jackson, he wrote Joseph McMinn in March that as yet he had no opposition for Congress but would be on the alert should any opposition arise. In August he was elected to the United States House of Representatives from the Ninth Tennessee District. In Washington he joined Mark Lewis and Felix Grundy in working for Jackson's nomination, sent underlined copies of Niles' Register to influential friends at home, and learned more intimately the workings of national politics. On January 22, 1824, he made his maiden speech in support of the recognition of Greek independence. In general, he supported in the House the measures which Jackson approved in the Senate." He performed various services for his constituents, secured vital statistics and made recommendations to office, tried to secure patronage, and plugged in his correspondence: "Jackson is gaining and will be next President."" He joined Eaton and twenty-two other congressmen in canvassing the members of Congress to be able to report that 181 and possibly more of the 261 members considered the caucus for nomination of the president inexpedient." The four potential nominees were Jackson, Henry Clay, William H. Crawford, and John Quincy Adams. Adams recorded in his diary on June 3, 1824, that Houston had assured him that he had a high regard for all the candidates except Crawford."

When Congress adjourned, Houston transferred his activities to Nashville, resumed his law practice after an illness, predicted that "Old Hickory" would win in the South and West, and planned a trip to South Carolina. From Morganton, North Carolina, in November, 1824, he wrote his cousin John H. Houston in Washington that he would not room at Mrs. Wilson's when he returned to Washington—for special reasons which he would explain later."

²² Ibid., III, 1; Houston to Jackson, January 19, 1823, ibid., I, 15.
²⁴ Supporting Recognition of Greek Independence, ibid., 21–24; James, The Raven, 53.
²⁵ Writings, II, 2–6; Houston to R. W. Williams, February 4, 1824, Andrew Jackson Donelson Papers.   ²⁶ James Parton, Life of Andrew Jackson, III, 26.
²⁷ Charles Francis Adams (ed.), Memoirs of John Quincy Adams, Comprising Portions of His Diary from 1795 to 1848, VI, 372.
²⁸ Houston to John H. Houston, August 28 and November 4, 1824, Writings, V, 1;

Those plans for new living quarters in Washington and Jackson's plans to move into the White House in March, 1825, were all to go awry. In the 1824 election, Jackson received a plurality of the electoral votes, but no candidate had a majority and the election was thrown into the House of Representatives. Crawford had suffered a stroke and was out of the race. Clay, the most popular man in Congress, could control enough votes to determine the presidency. Houston assured the Ohio delegation, which favored Clay, that in the event of Jackson's election, Clay could "have anything he pleased." The indifference with which his overtures were received was background for the Jackson supporters' cry of "bargain and corruption" when Clay threw his influence to Adams and then became secretary of state in the Adams cabinet.[29] Before the vote was taken on February 9, 1825, Houston wrote a constituent that he was in constant attendance at the House but could not tell how the election would go because the Clay men were silent as the tomb. He added that he planned to be married in March or April.[30] But not only did Old Hickory fail to become president; Houston's ancient enemy Calhoun became vice-president. The election over, Houston went to President Monroe's on February 26, 1825, to represent General E. P. Gaines at a distribution of medals. All of the representatives and generals read written answers except Houston and another orator, Daniel Webster.[31]

In Congress, Houston was classifying himself as an "internal improvement" man by voting for the Western National Road, for incorporation of the Chesapeake and Delaware Canal, and for Virginia's incorporation of the Chesapeake and Ohio Canal.[32] In the line of constituent interest, he obtained a midshipman's warrant for Matthew Fontaine Maury.[33] Whether or not Houston turned author and pamphleteer in 1825 is not certain, but many contemporaries thought that a book on Jackson, a campaign document printed in New York by P. M. Davis and titled *A Civil and Military History of Andrew Jackson*, was written by Houston

---

VII, 1. The special reasons were doubtless his plans to be married in the spring of 1825. See James, *The Raven*, 55, and Houston to John H. Houston, June 30, 1825, *Writings*, V, 3.

[29] George Ticknor Curtis, *Life of James Buchanan*, I, 514 n.

[30] Houston to A. M. Hughes, January 22, 1825, *Writings*, I, 24.

[31] *Memoirs of John Quincy Adams*, VI, 512.

[32] *Register of Debates in Congress, Comprising the Leading Debates and Incidents of the Second Session of the Eighteenth Congress*, I, 259, 334, 668.

[33] Diana Fontaine Maury Corbin (comp.), *A Life of Matthew Fontaine Maury*, 14. Thirty-five years later Maury was to send Governor Sam Houston of Texas the latest information on military techniques for use with his Texas regiment.

Matthew Fontaine Maury is not to be confused with the Matthew Maury mentioned earlier.

and published anonymously "lest the noted friendship between Jackson and himself might impair its force in the minds of captious critics."[34]

Congress adjourned, Houston started south, hoping still to carry out those plans of marriage for March or April. He had corresponded frequently enough with Miss M—— to know that letters from Cheraw, South Carolina, would pass to Washington, and the reverse, in four days. He stopped in Raleigh, North Carolina, to check on his horses there and then went on to Cheraw. Something happened to the plans. To his cousin he explained that he had not provided a home in Washington and would not want to leave "Madam" alone in the capital while he would have to be busy in Tennessee campaigning for re-election. Furthermore, friends wrote him of "*personal* difficulties" in Tennessee and urged him to "come home in a single situation." In Cheraw he was retained in a law case with a thousand-dollar fee. He and his fiancée agreed to postpone their wedding, and he assured her and her family that he would be back in South Carolina in November. Because of those personal difficulties or personal inclinations, he evidently was not "back on this track in the fall" and continued longer "in the full enjoyment of the sweets of single blessedness."[35]

At the end of his first term in Congress, Houston prepared a message summarizing the accomplishments of the Congress, with particular emphasis on measures of benefit to the West, and bringing to his constituents' attention the need of a system of electing the president which would not allow the selection of one candidate when another man was the popular choice.[36] Apparently his constituents were satisfied with his stewardship, and he had no difficulty in being re-elected to Congress. His "personal difficulties," closely interwoven with his political activities, got him into a "difference" with Major John Eaton, growing out of a quarrel with General Gibbs. All three men were Masons, and a committee of Masons was appointed in July, 1825, to investigate the matter. As he departed for Harrodsburg Springs, Kentucky, in August, Houston wrote Jackson that his enemies were on the watchtower and that he could see the machinations of Felix Grundy behind the affair. Judge John Catron also wrote Jackson of the difficulties and expressed the hope that during the five weeks Houston was to be in Kentucky he could be kept

[34] Augustus C. Buell, *History of Andrew Jackson: Pioneer, Patriot, Soldier, Politician, President*, I, 26; James, *The Raven*, 56.

[35] Houston to John Taylor, March 26, 1825, Manuscript Department, Duke University Library; Houston to John H. Houston, March 12, April 20, and June 30, 1825, *Writings*, V, 2–3; VIII, 1.

[36] To the Freemen of the Ninth Congressional District, March 3, 1825, *Writings*, III, 1–7.

quiet and would publish no handbills. Jackson assured Houston of his friendship for both him and Eaton and, possibly to forestall any handbills, suggested that Houston profit by the old adage, "O that mine enemy would write a Book."[37] Back from Kentucky, Houston asked the Grand Master of the Tennessee Grand Lodge to call a joint meeting of the two Nashville lodges to settle his differences with Gibbs, "referring to alleged slanderous expressions said to have passed between them as to the reputation of Major Eaton." The Grand Lodge, in October, adopted resolutions exonerating both parties.[38]

Houston was back in Washington for the opening of Congress in December, 1825, and wrote Clay to request appointment of some of his Knoxville constituents to print the laws of the United States. The following January he wrote a friend that he was making himself "less frequent in the Lady World" and must "attend more to politics and less to love."[39] In pursuance of that resolution, he made a speech on the Congress of Panama, not a profound commentary on foreign policy, but one move in the delaying tactics directed against sending delegates to Panama and concocted to oppose Adams' foreign policy.[40] The next political move was to have repercussions. In March, Houston recommended to the President that B. Y. Curry be appointed postmaster at Nashville to replace the Adams appointee, John P. Erwin, a son-in-law of Henry Clay. Houston characterized Erwin as an eavesdropper, a man of questionable moral character, who could not command public confidence in Nashville. News of the letter traveled rapidly to Tennessee and prepared a warm welcome and more personal problems when Houston got home. While Congress held in the long session, he continued to make political capital for the Jackson party. He used a debate on the militia claims of Massachusetts as an opportunity to criticize Adams' home state and the treasonable tendencies of the Hartford Convention of 1814 in contrast to the patriotism of Jackson. In its tone of sarcasm and ridicule of Massachusetts for refusing to let its militia cross the state line during the war and then later requesting federal pay for that militia, the speech was a fore-

[37] Houston to Jackson and Catron to Jackson, August 8, 1825, Jackson Papers, Series, I, Reel 33 (Vols. LXV–LXVI, 1824–26); Jackson to Houston, August 11, 1825, *Correspondence of Andrew Jackson*, III, 290.
[38] Houston to W. Tannehill, September 26, 1825, and to John Bell and others, October 4, 1825, *Writings*, IV, 2–3; John Frizzell, *Proceedings of the Most Worthy Grand Lodge, F. and A.M., of the State of Tennessee, from Its Organization*, I, 166–68.
[39] Houston to Clay, December 9, 1825, *Writings*, IV, 3; Houston to W. J. Worth, January 24, 1826, *ibid.*, I, 28.
[40] Speech on the Congress of Panama, February 2, 1826, *ibid.*, I, 28–40.

runner of Houston's speeches as president of Texas and United States senator. It was prophetic of his future also in its proclamation of love of Union and observance of the Constitution.⁴¹ Perhaps as token of political approval, Secretary of War James Barbour, of Virginia, named the Tennessee congressman to the Board of Visitors for West Point. Houston served with Jared Sparks, George Ticknor, and Colonel J. G. Totten on that board in June, 1826, when young Robert Edward Lee ranked third in his class at the Point.⁴²

The Gibbs-Eaton-Houston feud was still smoldering in Tennessee, and Houston accused Felix Grundy of being the man who wished him destroyed. Trouble from Erwin, who remained in the Nashville postmastership, was to be expected too; and Houston, who had been practicing with pistols in anticipation of challenges when he returned home, wrote a potential post-mortem letter to state that it was attachment to Jackson and to principle that had won him enemies.⁴³ If necessary, even his obituary must be Jackson propaganda.

When Houston got back to Nashville, Erwin sent him a challenge through a professional duelist who signed himself John Smith, T. Houston's second refused the communication on the grounds that Smith was not a native of Tennessee; but when William A. White interfered, Houston agreed to receive a challenge from White, and the affair developed into an academic point of honor. For a week Houston practiced for the duel under Jackson's tutelage; then he wounded White in the encounter of September 22, 1826. He was indicted for assault by a Kentucky grand jury, the duel having been fought on the Simpson County plantation of Sanford Duncan near the state boundary line, but he was never arrested.⁴⁴

Houston was soon to be able to repay Jackson's courtesy as tutor. In October, Jackson wrote him that Secretary of the Navy Samuel L. South-

⁴¹ Houston to Adams, March 18, 1826, *ibid.*, IV, 4; Speech on Militia Claims, March 25, 1826, *ibid.*, I, 40–62.
⁴² Douglas Southall Freeman, *R. E. Lee: A Biography*, I, 61; R. E. Lee to A. M. Lea, March 1, 1860, Governors' Letters.
⁴³ Concerning Expected Trouble with Felix Grundy, May 27, 1826, *Writings*, I, 63–64. Felix Grundy was a Jackson leader, who, although he personally preferred Clay or Calhoun, wanted to increase Tennessee prestige by making the Tennessee hero president and took over management of affairs in the Tennessee Legislature to that end. He was defeated when he ran for Congress in Houston's place in 1827 but was selected to take Eaton's place in the Senate in 1829, when Eaton went into Jackson's cabinet. Grundy and Houston were later friends. See Joseph Howard Parks, *Felix Grundy, Champion of Democracy*, 166–73.
⁴⁴ Answer to a Toast at Telico, Tennessee, July 13, 1827, *Writings*, I, 113–14; James, *The Raven*, 64–66.

ard had criticized Jackson's defense of New Orleans and had said that the city had been saved only by the direction of James Monroe. Houston was instructed to call on Southard as soon as he reached Washington, present a letter from Jackson, demand an answer, and send that answer to Jackson. Houston conferred with the junto in Washington and delayed delivery of the caustic letter until further correspondence with Jackson. In that exchange he advised Jackson to use a mild tone, asked to be allowed to make the demand on Southard himself, and counseled delay.[45]

It was no wonder that a man who could restrain and advise Jackson could look to higher political rewards in Tennessee. Houston had played with the idea of the governorship in 1825; early in 1826 he decided to run, and both John Bell and Grundy announced for his seat in Congress. While Houston was finishing out his term, Jackson wrote him that harmony pervaded the entire state, that the current in the western district had changed, and that he would win by an overwhelming majority but that he must make a swing over the state in the spring.[46] In reply Houston could write Jackson that matters were "surely favorable to a change in the administration," and that John Randolph of Roanoke, John Floyd of Virginia, and DeWitt Clinton of New York were his friends, as well as Martin Van Buren, who would support him "in all good *faith*." In the House the Congressman worked for a bill to pay Willie Blount, one of his opponents in the gubernatorial race, for services in the War of 1812 and made a speech on patronage in the guise of contracts for public printing, which gave him an opportunity to criticize Clay as secretary of state and Adams as both a poet and a minority president. While he was negotiating for the purchase of fine horses from John Randolph, he continued to represent Jackson in correspondence with Southard and to blame Southard's course on advice from Adams' cabinet.[47] Before he left Washington in March, 1827, Houston arranged to have a tri-weekly Philadelphia paper sent him in Nashville; he wanted to keep abreast of national politics while he was electioneering. From Maryville he wrote John Houston that he was making stump speeches, and asked the cousin

[45] Jackson to Houston, October 23, 1826, *Correspondence of Andrew Jackson*, VI, 485–86; Jackson to Houston, November 22 and December 15, 1826, *ibid.*, III, 319, 324–25; Houston to Jackson, December 13, 1826, *Writings*, I, 65–66.

[46] Norman L. Parks, "The Career of John Bell as Congressman from Tennessee, 1827–1841," *Tennessee Historical Quarterly*, I (1942), 231; Jackson to Houston, November 22, 1826, *Correspondence of Andrew Jackson*, III, 319.

[47] Houston to Jackson, January 5 and 15 and February 15, 1827, and Houston to Southard, February 15, 1827, *Writings*, I, 69–109.

to call on John C. Rives and Duff Green to be sure that copies of his speeches were sent on to Nashville for political ammunition. He was confident of his own election by a large majority.[48]

Opponents in the canvass were Willie Blount, who received only a few scattered votes, and Newton Cannon, whom Houston had defeated for adjutant general in 1821. Backed by Jackson and by former Governor William Carroll, who was not eligible to run in 1827 and who, according to some authorities, had Houston elected merely to hold his own place during a two-year interim, Houston won easily. *Niles' Register* for September 8, 1827, reported that the votes as received up to press time were 42,433 for Houston and 31,290 for Cannon.[49]

Houston was inaugurated governor of Tennessee in the First Baptist Church at Nashville on October 1, 1827. His brief inaugural address stressed the obligation of upholding the United States Constitution at the same time that it emphasized the duty of the state to guard against infraction of state sovereignty by the federal government.[50] Two weeks later he sent his message to the Legislature. It discussed public improvements as a legitimate field of state jurisdiction and recommended engineers to work out a state-wide plan of development, including transportation. Anticipating the Tennessee Valley Authority by almost a century, he spoke of the desirability of a canal to surmount the obstacle of Muscle Shoals and give an outlet to the south for products from East Tennessee. The message advocated a system of disposing of the public domain to provide for permanent homes, rather than merely securing the highest possible price, and suggested that funds derived from the sale of the public domain be used for general education and internal improvements. The Governor hoped for a speedy solution to the contested boundary line between Tennessee and Kentucky and commended the permanent school fund established for common schools.[51] The message may not have been a brilliant state paper, but it was direct, practical, and democratic.

---

[48] Houston to James A. Jones, March 14, 1827, *ibid.*, IV, 9; Houston to John H. Houston, April 8, 1827, *ibid.*, VII, 1–2.

[49] Buell, *History of Andrew Jackson*, II, 186; *Niles' Register*, XXXIII (September 8, 1827), 18. In that same poll, two of the new Tennessee congressmen were Pryor Lea and David Crockett. They too were to go to Texas. John Bell, another new member, was to be Houston's rival for the presidential nomination in 1860. Still another new member was James K. Polk, who was to be president of the United States when Houston went to the Senate in 1846.

[50] Walter Rowe Courtenay, "The Tennessee Sesquicentennial Sermon: God Walked These Hills," *Tennessee Historical Quarterly*, V (1946), 353; Inaugural Address as Governor of Tennessee, *Writings*, IV, 9.

[51] To the Legislature of Tennessee, October 15, 1827, *Writings*, I, 115–21.

It hardly seemed in character with a description applied to Houston a few days before by Tench Ringgold in a letter to James Monroe in which he said Houston had been described to him as "a blustering bullying man & *not* in the *confidential confidence* of General Jackson."[52]

Confidential confidant of Jackson or not, the Governor helped entertain the General at a public dinner at the Nashville Inn on Christmas Eve of 1827 and two days after Christmas joined the Jackson party on the steamer *Pocahontas* bound for a victory celebration of the Battle of New Orleans. It was a gay trip punctuated with speeches to the crowds assembled at the piers of the river towns. Mrs. Jackson calmed the General, who threatened to shoot at the vessels which crowded too close, and she told James A. Hamilton, representing New York—and Martin Van Buren—that he must select a becoming bonnet for her. William B. Lewis, A. J. Donelson, Robert Armstrong, and Houston constituted an anti-Calhoun faction, and their conversation probably revolved around an old letter from James Monroe to Calhoun concerning Calhoun's criticism of Jackson's conduct in the Florida campaign, a letter that was to result in the Jackson-Calhoun split in 1830.[53]

At the battlefield the Governor of Louisiana met the honor delegation for the ceremonies; then the city of New Orleans had its celebration on January 9, 1828. Houston and Hamilton slipped away from the speeches of the public dinner to look in on a quadroon ball in progress in the same building.[54]

It was a pleasant and profitable excursion, politically and personally. Hamilton installed Van Buren in Jackson's good graces; seeds of distrust of Calhoun were planted; and Houston revived old acquaintances and gained favor with more ladies, including Mrs. Nathan Morse. When he got back to Nashville, he fulfilled a promise made in New Orleans to send her a lock of Jackson's hair.[55]

Then he mixed his state executive responsibilities with more maneuvering for the presidential campaign of 1828, reprimanded Chapman Johnson for a speech made in the anti-Jackson convention in Virginia, and vindicated the conduct of Tennessee troops at the battle of Horseshoe Bend. Johnson's answer, denying any intent to belittle Houston or the Tennessee Militia, published in the Nashville *Republican* and *Niles'*

[52] Ringgold to Monroe, October 10, 1827, James Monroe Papers.
[53] Marquis James, *The Life of Andrew Jackson*, 470; Parton, *Life of Andrew Jackson*, III, 315; James A. Hamilton, *Reminiscences of James A. Hamilton; or, Men and Events, at Home and Abroad, during Three Quarters of a Century*, 66–69.
[54] Hamilton, *Reminiscences*, 72.
[55] Houston to Mrs. Morse, January 30, 1828, *Writings*, VI, 1.

Register, was not satisfactory to Houston, and the entire resulting correspondence was good political propaganda.[56]

John Floyd, on the opposite side of the Virginia political fence, wrote Houston to advise Jackson to use a "studied and guarded course" since every breath he drew was noticed, denounced Clay as a "bargaining dog" and the instigator of opposition in Indiana and New York, and stated that his friends felt that Houston, because of his "friendship and intimacy with General Jackson, . . . could signify our wishes in the most delicate manner."[57] Floyd's letter ended with a statement of his gratification at seeing Houston in the governor's chair in Tennessee and the hope that he would "long continue to enjoy the confidence of *the people*, the *true source of power*."

As governor, Houston's recommendations had been conservative and his administration successful. He had, more or less as a protégé of Carroll, carried on the sound business principles which Carroll had instituted. The state banks had all been examined and had been required to resume specie payments; a United States branch bank had been established in Nashville in 1827. So popular was he indeed that Carroll began to fear lest his protégé might not be satisfied with one term. The two men were opponents for the governorship in 1829, and Tennessee politics did get entangled. Jackson, who had won the presidential election in 1828 and on March 4, 1829, would assume his office, wanted to support Houston. But he was also Carroll's friend, and a movement was developing in Tennessee to send whoever was defeated in the governor's race to the Senate. Jackson was eager for Felix Grundy to have the senatorship.[58] The solution to the dilemma was to be most unexpected.

True, the Governor's career had not been one of unmixed success. In October, 1828, he was tried on two charges before the Masonic Lodge. The judgment against him for impeaching the integrity of Brother John Erwin was reversed, but that for fighting a duel with Brother White was confirmed, and Cumberland Lodge, No. 8, of Nashville suspended him for twelve months for political dissensions.[59] There were, however, interests more appealing than lodge meetings. With the James K. Polk family

[56] *Ibid.*, I, 123–28; *Niles' Register*, XXXV (October 25, 1828), 139.
[57] Floyd to Houston, March 15, 1828, Jackson Papers, Series II, Reel 2.
[58] James Phelan, *History of Tennessee: The Making of a State*, 296; John Trotwood Moore (ed.), *Tennessee, the Volunteer State*, I, 399; Gabriel Hawkins Golden, "William Carroll and His Administration, Tennessee's Business Governor," *Tennessee Historical Magazine*, IX (April, 1925), 21; Powell Moore, "The Political Background of the Revolt against Jackson in Tennessee," *East Tennessee Historical Society Publications, No. 4* (January, 1932), 48–50.
[59] George L. Crocket, Notes.

Houston often visited the Hermitage and picked flowers in Rachel Jackson's garden. As frequently as possible he went to Gallatin to visit in the home of Colonel John Allen, who was pleased to entertain the Governor. In November, Houston wrote his cousin that he might be married in a few weeks.[60] Then his prospective happiness was dimmed by his old commander's grief. Houston was chief pallbearer when Mrs. Jackson was buried in her Hermitage garden on Christmas Eve of 1828.[61]

On January 22, 1829, the marriage ceremony between Houston and Miss Eliza Allen of Gallatin was performed by Dr. William Hume, one of Houston's fellow members of the Antiquarian Society. The match seemed a good one and a political boon to the groom, despite the discrepancy in eighteen and thirty-six years. The couple established residence at the Nashville Inn, and the *Banner and Whig*, on January 30, carried the announcement that the Honorable Samuel Houston was a candidate for re-election. William Carroll's candidacy had been announced on January 21. The campaign was soon under way; on March 23, J. P. Clark wrote from Nashville to A. J. Donelson: "I think Houston will beat Carroll—they have commenced their canvass & from this out will be busy—It is a poor business for men high in office to be thus trudging about. I wish to God we had more Jacksons to put such things down."[62]

A few weeks later, Houston's cousin Robert L. Caruthers wrote Donelson that Grundy would have a good chance for the Senate unless Houston should be defeated for governor and want the place. Caruthers continued: "The contest will be pretty close in middle Ten. but Houston will get a small majority unless I am extending myself by my partiality. If I be right in this opinion there can be no doubt about the general result. The politicians & people here almost unanimously desire that the contest be avoided by Carroll's getting the appointment in the army vacated by Genl. Scott's resignation."[63]

The contest was avoided, not by Carroll's becoming a brigadier general, but by his becoming governor without opposition. While Caruthers was writing optimistically of political victory, Houston was experiencing tragic and humiliating defeat in his personal life. An almost incoherent letter to his father-in-law indicates that some misunderstanding with his wife would have to be treated as if it had never occurred. Evidently he

[60] Houston to John H. Houston, November 10, 1828, *Writings*, II, 10–11.
[61] Tom W. Campbell, *Two Fighters and Two Fines: Sketches of the Lives of Matthew Lyon and Andrew Jackson*, 423.
[62] Clark to Donelson, March 23, 1829, Donelson Papers.
[63] Caruthers to Donelson, April 8, 1829, *ibid.*

had been reassured of the affection of "the only earthly object dear to me," and he wrote that his future happiness could exist only "in the assurance that Eliza & myself can be happy & that Mrs. Allen & you can forget the past." His last sentence to the father was a plea to "let me know what is to be done."[64] Complete adjustment and reconciliation could not be effected, and Houston took his wife home to her family. His private world had crashed about him, and he jerked the foundation from under his political career when he wrote his resignation as governor of Tennessee on April 16, 1829.[65] Three pages in his public life had been turned: state's attorney, congressman, governor.

[64] Houston to John Allen, April 9, 1829, *Writings*, I, 130.
[65] Resignation as Governor, *ibid.*, 131.

The Indian Interlude

HOUSTON'S UNEXPECTED SEPARATION from his wife and his sensational retirement from the governorship stunned his friends, the state of Tennessee, and the national capital. When his friends insisted that he must explain the separation or sacrifice himself, he refused to explain and wrote his letter of resignation in which he said that, "overwhelmed by sudden calamities," he thought it "more respectful to the world" that he retire. Colonel Charles J. Love had written Jackson the day before the resignation that Houston would leave the state immediately for the Arkansas Territory to reside among the Indians.[1] While rumors and scandal mounted and reports came from Gallatin, the Allen home place, that he had been burned in effigy, Houston remained in Nashville for a week. There, according to

[1] Love to Jackson, April 15, 1829, *Correspondence of Andrew Jackson*, IV, 23.

21

Niles' Register, troops had to be called out to prevent another effigy burning. A mob did gather and threaten violence.[2]

Emily Drennen reflected genuine interest and sympathy along with normal feminine curiosity when she wrote to Emily Austin Perry at Potosi, Missouri Territory:

There is a dreadfull stir in the country and town about our governor—he was married two months ago and is now parted from his wife. There is a thouseand diferent tails afloat. He has resined, and poor fellow is miserable enough. I never can believe he has acted ungentlemanly untill I see him and know the trouth from himself for he was a man so popular I know it must be some thing dreadfull or he never would have left her. He is very sick and has been ever since. As soon as he gets well enough he intends leaveing the country never to return. He is comeing to see us before he leaves town and then I will know the trouth. And what is more astonishing none of her connection has been near. If he was in fault I should think some of them would resent it. He never has said any thing to any one not even his brother about her. I suppose he has toald the particulars to his most intimate friends for none of his friends blame him so when you here the repoarts about him you may know they are not so. He has a good menny enemies and a great menny friends. He says time will show who is to blame. The reason he does not tell. I expect you are tyered of this but I feel so interested.[3]

A friend of the Allen family later wrote that Houston affected to be insane, "put on the white-tanned skin of a pied heifer, and actually wore it on the streets of Nashville until he left the State forever."[4] According to close friends, he remained in seclusion, almost dazed, and locked himself in his room after Dr. Hume and Obadiah Jennings of the Nashville Presbyterian church, because of the state of public feeling, refused his request to be baptized.

A psychiatrist would doubtless interpret this evidence of remorse as indicative of a guilt complex. Years passed and time did not show who was to blame, although many besides Mrs. Drennen were "so interested." The explanation that has received the widest credence is that the Governor had gone to a political meeting but, finding that it had been postponed, had returned home early and found his wife weeping as she read some letters. Impulsive and jealous, and humiliated by the knowledge that he had not been able to supplant another man in her affections, he exclaimed, "Eliza, I would not permit you to be my slave so will return

[2] *Niles' Register,* XXXVI (May 23, 1829), 198.
[3] Emily Drennen to Emily Perry, n.d., 1829, James F. Perry Papers.
[4] Henry A. Wise, *Seven Decades of the Union: The Humanities and Materialism,* 148.

you to your family." He felt that only one person's happiness need be sacrificed and that Eliza would secure a divorce and marry her former fiancé. Doubtless he said harsh things which caused him bitter regret and accounted, along with his own dramatic temperament, for his distrait demeanor.[5]

On April 23, Houston's long-time friends Sheriff Willoughby Williams and Dr. John Shelby accompanied him to the packet *Red Rover*, on which he took passage under an assumed name. At Clarksville two men of the Allen family came aboard, and Houston asked them to publish in the Nashville papers that he would return to Tennessee to kill anyone who questioned Mrs. Houston's honor.[6] In company with an Irishman named H. Haralson, he then sailed down the Cumberland and the Ohio to Cairo, where they secured a flatboat to go to Memphis, and from there continued down the Mississippi and up the Arkansas River. Rumors evidently had preceded him. On May 11 young Charles Noland wrote from Little Rock to his father, William Noland, in Virginia:

> Governor Houston arrived here three days since on his way to join the Indians—Merciful God! is it possible that society can be deprived of one of its greatest ornaments, and the United States of one of her most valiant sons, through the dishonor and baseness of a woman? He converses cheerfully, made a great many inquiries after you. He will stay this winter with the Cherokees and probably will visit the warm spring . . . this summer. He wishes to go to the Rocky Mountains, to visit that tract of country between the mouth

[5] Lester's *Life of Sam Houston* describes the marriage as "unhappy as it was short" because of circumstances "about which far more has been conjectured than known by the world." Conjecture continued through Houston's lifetime and maybe even more freely after his death. Newspaper stories purporting to tell the "true story" of the marriage and the separation have confused Dr. William Elmore Douglas, whom Eliza Allen Houston later married, with the young man to whom she was supposedly engaged when she decided or was persuaded to marry Governor Houston. Conflicting accounts relate that Houston was induced, and that he could not be induced, to give an explanation of his divorce to the Lea family before his second marriage. Descendants disagree as to how much he confided to Margaret Lea Houston. A seemingly plausible story which appeared in the Dallas *News* for April 4, 1892, recounts that Houston realized that Eliza did not love him, and doubted the wisdom of his engagement, but was so enchanted by the beauty and accomplishments of Judge Allen's second daughter that he was overconfident and ignored what he later learned—that Eliza loved someone else and was overpersuaded by relatives and friends to marry the Governor of Tennessee. Despite the best and most honorable intentions of both, the uncongenial situation grew increasingly unbearable until it culminated in the separation. An article entitled "Some Unwritten History Regarding a Tennessee Tragedy—an Impression Corrected," in the Temple (Texas) *Times*, June 7, 1901, names Will Tyree as Miss Allen's former fiancé, "a poor but promising young lawyer who went to Missouri to build up a practice, intending to return and marry." Tyree died in Missouri of tuberculosis.

[6] James, *The Raven*, 79–84.

of the Oregon and California Bay. He came with his rifle on his shoulder. General Jackson will certainly persuade him to come back from the woods.[7]

Reverting to his youthful custom of seeking refuge in the woods with the Cherokees, Houston did maintain his ties with his "Old Chief," to whom he described himself as an unfortunate and unhappy man but not a man without honor or one who could brook the idea that Jackson would suppose him capable of any act that would injure or involve his country. He promised that while in the Indian country, acting in an individual capacity, he would report information that might benefit Jackson's administration, would try to keep peace between Indians and whites, and, as of old, would report any injustices done the Indians by their agents.[8]

Immediately after he wrote to the President, Houston proceeded by way of Louisburgh and Fort Smith to Webbers Falls on the Arkansas in the Cherokee Nation. There he was welcomed by Oo-loo-te-ka ("He Who Puts the Drums Away"), better known to the whites as John Jolly, the chief with whom he had lived as a youth and whom he called his "Indian Father." At his wigwam, according to Jolly, his son the Raven walked straight and caused his father's heart to rejoice.[9]

At Oo-loo-te-ka's home Houston donned Indian attire, picked up threads of former friendships, and listened in on Cherokee councils while the chieftains pondered the problem of the red man's future. While there, he received Jackson's answer to his letter from Little Rock. Jackson's reaction to his protégé's plight had been expressed in a note to John G. McLemore: "I have this moment heard a rumor of poor Houston's disgrace. My God, is the man mad?" To Houston himself he expressed astonishment and grief to know that he was an exile from his country and lamented: "What reverse of fortune! How unstable are all human affairs."[10]

Cherokee affairs were unstable too; members of the tribe in Georgia had been ordered to the West, and the chiefs wondered if the white man's treaty of 1828 would remain unfulfilled as had previous treaties with the Cherokees. They worried about continued war against tribes to

[7] Charles Fenton Mercer Noland to William Noland, May 11, 1829, Lewis Berkeley Papers. (Photographic copy in Archives Collection, University of Texas Library.)
[8] Houston to Jackson, May 11, 1829, *Writings*, I, 132–34.
[9] Jolly to Jackson, December 3, 1829, Grant Foreman, *Indians and Pioneers: The Story of the American Southwest before 1830*, 268 n.
[10] Jackson to McLemore, April ?, 1829, *Correspondence of Andrew Jackson*, IV, 21; Jackson to Houston, June 21, 1829, Henderson Yoakum, *History of Texas, from Its First Settlement in 1685 to Its Annexation to the United States in 1846*, I, 307.

the west or peace and possible alliance with some of those tribes, particularly the Osages. The celebration of welcome for Houston at John Jolly's wigwam at the mouth of the Illinois was to be followed by a meeting of the Cherokee Grand Council, but before the council met, Haralson and Houston had ridden into the Osage country to Six Bull River to interview Auguste Pierre Chouteau. With Chouteau they visited the Osage agency and the American Fur Company trading post at Three Forks. There Houston heard the Indian complaints against John Hamtramck, the agent. As a result, when the former subagent and former governor reached Fort Gibson, he wrote Secretary of War John Eaton to outline the desirability of peace with the Pawnees and the Osages and to recommend Auguste P. Chouteau as the agent for negotiating treaties and distributing presents. If Chouteau were appointed, then Houston would like to accompany him, not in an official capacity, but to "recreate" his mind.[11] The letter to Eaton traveled to Washington with a letter from the full council of the Creek Nation to President Jackson complaining of the activities of their agent, David Brearly. Houston had established himself as friend of the Cherokees, the Osages, and the Creeks; he was prompt in carrying out his promise of information on Indian affairs.

Less than two weeks later he was at Bayou Ménard as Chief Jolly's personal representative at a Cherokee council and hastened to write to Colonel Matthew Arbuckle at Fort Gibson of Cherokee plans for a war against the Pawnees and Comanches. He warned of possible Indian concentration on the frontier and of the likelihood of further delay in persuading the tribes remaining east of the Mississippi to remove to the West. He suggested an order from the Secretary of War, extralegal if necessary, prohibiting the Cherokees from making war on other tribes unless the act was the result of united council, cautioned of the danger of removing United States troops, stated the need for a definite boundary between the Creeks and the Cherokees, and pointed out the necessity of fulfilling treaty obligations. For himself he asked nothing except that his letter remain confidential lest its contents cause "heart burning" toward him.

From the Cherokee council he went on to Fort Smith and at the agency there listened to the complaints of the Choctaw tribe. Those also he described to the Secretary of War.[12]

---

[11] James, *The Raven*, 104–11; Houston to Eaton, June 24, 1829, *Writings*, I, 134–36.

[12] Houston to Arbuckle, July 8, 1829, and to Eaton, July 22, 1829, *Writings*, I, 136–40.

In his eight weeks of travel in the Arkansas and Oklahoma area in the heat of summer Houston had contracted malaria. He cut short his visit with the Choctaws to return to Jolly's wigwam, where for over a month he was desperately ill and received solicitous care from his Indian brothers.

Permanent residence in Arkansas was not part of Houston's plan. As soon as he was able to write, he assured Jackson that he had been considering locating in Arkansas but that there was no field for distinction in the territory, that it was fraught with factions, and that wealth could be obtained only by fraud and perjury. Natchez, he thought, might be a better place to locate. There he was well acquainted and could rally Tennesseans round him. He went on to tell of his interest in politics and of his hopes for the Jackson administration in the United States, "for I must ever love that country."[13] Thoughts of the Rockies apparently were forgot. He loved his own country, but he became a citizen of another nation, a nation as far as legal recognition was concerned. On October 21, 1829, because of his former services to the Indians and because of their "confidence in his integrity and talents," he was granted the privileges of a citizen of the Cherokee Nation, with the condition that he observe Cherokee law.

That same month he was present when Major E. W. DuVal paid the Cherokee annuity, not in gold, but in certificates of indebtedness, meaningless and worthless paper to the Indians—paper that quickly changed from Indian hands to the hands of white men who knew its value.[14]

Speculation in certificates, sale of liquor to the Indians by government agents themselves—these and other matters Houston thought might well be reported directly to the administration. Furthermore, he might create a business opportunity for himself by securing the contract to supply rations for the tribes who were soon to be moved to the West under the Indian Removal Act.[15] Dressed as an Indian and accompanied by Walter Webber and John Brown, Houston slipped away to Washington in the role of Cherokee ambassador with a letter of commendation from Jolly to Jackson expressing the hope that the "Great Father" would "take him by the hand and keep him as near to his heart as I have done." As the steamer bearing up the Mississippi drew opposite the Tennessee bluffs, the former governor of the state composed a poem. In his nostalgia for the things he had renounced, he wrote his old friend John Overton to thank the Judge for sustaining him in his "moments of awful agony" and

[13] Houston to Jackson, September 19, 1829, *ibid.*, 140–43.
[14] James, *The Raven*, 125–27; *Writings*, I, 143–44.
[15] Foreman, *Indians and Pioneers*, 284.

said that if he stopped in Tennessee on his return trip, he would tell him the object of his visit.[16]

Houston reached Fredericktown, Maryland, on January 11, 1830, and sent a note to John H. Houston inviting him to dinner at Brown's Hotel in Washington on January 12. John Houston took his cousin to his heart, even as did Jackson. The President was in the middle of a quarrel with Calhoun, a quarrel based partly on a letter written by William Crawford which stated that Calhoun, as secretary of war in 1818, had advocated punishing Jackson for his conduct in the Florida War, and partly on Calhoun's—or Mrs. Calhoun's—failure to recognize socially Mrs. John Eaton, the former Peggy O'Neal. He was doubtless more than ever glad to welcome an old Calhoun foe into the fray.

Houston took care of his Indian obligations first. Then he had John Van Fossen, a New York financier, enter their joint bid for the Indian ration contracts. Thirteen bids were made, ranging from eight to seventeen cents per portion. The Houston–Van Fossen bid was thirteen cents. Eaton, after advertising for bidders and receiving the bids, did not award the contract to the lowest bidder, first on the grounds that the thirty-day wait had been too brief to allow bids from Illinois to arrive. Finally he made no contracts at all because the treaties for the Indian removal had not been ratified and the rations would not be needed.[17] Two years later the question of the amount of the bids and Eaton's delaying tactics in the whole affair were to be the basis of charges of fraud and corruption against Eaton and Houston, with implications that Jackson was a party to the deception.

Houston left Washington before any decision was made and temporarily forgot ration contracts while he went back to Tennessee. The Carroll faction was apprehensive lest he had come to re-enter politics. The Allen family was disturbed lest Eliza return to him. In Gallatin, Sumner County citizens met and appointed a committee to draw up a report to express their opinion of the private virtues of Mrs. Houston and say whether or not her character had been injured by the separation from her husband. The committee's report was submitted to the papers for publication, but not until Houston, even though delayed by illness, was gone again. When he finally read a newspaper account of the Gallatin meeting, he wrote Jackson, pointing out errors in the committee report and expressing his confidence that the people of Tennessee would elect him again should he present himself for office. Two days later he wrote William B. Lewis that he thought he could beat Carroll for gover-

---

[16] Houston to Overton, December 28, 1829, *Writings*, I, 144–45.
[17] *Ibid.*, 147–48, 149 n.

nor if he would return to Tennessee. To Jackson he promised a report, "so soon as I reach home," on whether or not the Mexican troops had reached the United States border.[18]

"Home" perhaps had a new connotation for Houston in the summer of 1830. With or without marriage ceremony, but with propriety in the light of Cherokee custom, he formed an alliance with Tiana Rogers Gentry, half-sister of his friends John and James Rogers, and established her at his Wigwam Neosho, a log house on the Neosho River above Fort Gibson where he conducted a store.

On his way back from the East, Houston had written Eaton asking appointment as sutler at Fort Gibson. When he reached the fort, he discovered that there was no vacancy at the post but that there was much rumor of his attempt to secure the Indian ration award. He indicated to Eaton that he was going to write articles for the *Arkansas Gazette* to air the entire Indian situation and reported the likely swindling from the Cherokees of the fifty-thousand-dollar claim due them under the last treaty. Writing under the names of "Tah-lohn-tus-ky" and "Standing Bear," Houston subsequently published five articles detailing charges against various Indian agents and expressing his usual sympathy with the Indians. Various individuals denied the charges and attacked Houston.[19]

While the duel in print was in progress, Houston received a boatload of stores for his trading post. He asked Colonel Arbuckle to send officers to examine his supplies, particularly to prove his refusal to sell whiskey to the Indians. He had other business deals in mind too, for he wrote John Van Fossen that he was about to make a purchase of Salt Springs.[20] But new wife, or new business, or prospects of Salt Springs could not bring complete oblivion of the past. Perhaps the "personalities" in the derogatory letters against him had made a deeper thrust than he admitted. Whatever the motivation, on December 7, 1830, he wrote a long letter to William Hall, to whom he had addressed his letter of resignation as governor and who had automatically, as speaker of the state Senate, succeeded him as governor. He felt that he must point out to Hall the errors in the Sumner County charges of the summer before. He also told Hall of the threats made against him if he should return to Nashville and of attacks made against Jackson for receiving him in Washington.

---

[18] Houston to Jackson, May 18, 1830, and to Lewis, May 20, 1830, *ibid.*, 149–52.
[19] *Ibid.*, 152–85; *Arkansas Gazette*, August 14, 1830, and Supplement to *Arkansas Gazette*, October 20, 1830 (typescript in Houston Unpublished Correspondence, I).
[20] Houston to Arbuckle, July 21, 1830, and to Van Fossen, August 22, 1830, *Writings*, I, 185–87.

This letter to Hall, with its statement of facts and charges of persecution, he gave permission to have published. That was a sort of trial balloon to see how the wind blew in Tennessee politics.[21] Hall did not take advantage of the permission. Instead, Nashville had attacked Houston from another angle, publication of the story of connivance between Houston and Eaton on the rations contracts.[22]

Rebuffs in the old home and malicious rumors in his new abode were too much. Houston almost knew despair. He drank, and drank too much, he lost face with the Indians, he quarreled with his foster father. In his restlessness and desperation he dreamed of making money in a salt works, of going to the Rockies, of returning to Tennessee politics. Perhaps he dreamed of Texas. In the spring of 1831 he was a candidate for a seat in the Cherokee council and was defeated. Chagrined, he talked of abandoning the Cherokees to go to the Choctaw country.[23] But first he must go back to Tennessee.

His defeat in Cherokee politics was still stinging when he joined a steamer at Montgomery and on board ship fell into conversation with Matthew Maury, who recorded among Houston's comments on the Indians: "They steal from friend & foe, & tho' they were so friendly & so trusting to Genl. Houston, that they would not sign their treaty with the United States without consulting him, they sought all occasions of stealing his horses." Maury recorded that he continued to pass the bottle and Houston continued to talk:

My opinion . . . is that the U.S. can only hold together so long as there is an abundance of rich unoccupied wild land for settlers; because as soon as the population is at all dense we shall fall to pieces. I would run a line on the parallel of 33 or 34 to the Pacific Ocean, & say all north of it belongs to the U.S.; it would embrace Santa Fe & N. California, but we could easily get them by conquest or treaty, & I would have the U.S. establish a fort & settlement at the mouth of the Columbia. And by God Gentlemen (said he, striking the table) if they don't do it, & if I can get some capitalists to join me, I would easily collect 2 or 300 volunteers on the Western frontiers, & I would proceed to establish a colony myself at the mouth of the Columbia; . . . I should get plenty of settlers, & from our great distance we could & would maintain an independence of any power on earth.[24]

The "Great Designer" had plans; he had capitalists in mind. Could it be that his design would fit an area nearer to Arkansas than the Columbia River?

[21] Houston to Hall, December 7, 1830, *ibid.*, 188–93.
[22] *Ibid.*, II, 12–15.   [23] Foreman, *Indians and Pioneers*, 285–86.
[24] June, 1831, entry in Maury Papers.

In Tennessee he was not well received. Doubtless he drank too much and caused embarrassment to his friends. Exiled to the wilderness himself, it seemed to him appropriate to have his portrait painted—as Marius among the ruins of Carthage. He even issued a proclamation authorizing "all *scoundrels whomsoever* . . . to accuse, defame, calumniate, slander, vilify, and libel me to any extent, in *personal* or *private* abuse." To the author of the most ingenious lie he proposed to give on next All Fools' Day a copy of the *Kentucky Reporter,* bound in sheep, or the *United States Telegraph,* bound in dog. Those were two of the newspapers which had carried articles unfriendly to him. Bitterly he ended his proclamation: "Given under my hand and private seal (*having no seal of office*) at Nashville in the State of Tennessee."[25]

Back he went to his Neosho Wigwam and wrote his cousin that his business was going well enough. In September he returned to Tennessee to bury his mother. On November 19 he was once more at Cantonment Gibson and wrote to Lewis Cass to recommend Thomas Anthony as subagent to the Osages. He asked Cass to excuse him for taking the liberty of making the recommendation to him rather than to the War Department, for "tho' I possess the most perfect *confidence* and *respect* for the present administration, I feel some delicacy in soliciting any favor or benefit in behalf of any person."[26] This reluctance to ask favors may have been a factor in his not being a member of the Cherokee delegation with which he started back to Washington, via New Orleans, in December, 1831.

In January, 1832, Houston was in the familiar surroundings of Brown's Indian Hotel in Washington. He entertained old friends and cultivated new ones, including some New York financiers, whom he may have met through Van Fossen. To further those connections he went to New York and, on March 27, wrote a letter to James Prentiss, the first of a long series of letters concerning Houston's possible representation of New York capitalists who wanted to speculate in Texas lands. The first letter did not concern Texas but was an effort to interest Prentiss in Houston's land titles in a section of southeast Tennessee where gold had been discovered.

Back in Washington by April 3, Houston read in the *National Intelligencer* a speech made by Representative William Stanbery of Ohio on March 31. In the speech, which was critical of the Jackson administration, Stanbery had asked: "Was the late Secretary of War [Eaton] removed in consequence of his attempt fraudulently to give to Governor

[25] Proclamation, July 13, 1831, *Writings,* I, 196.
[26] Houston to Cass, November 19, 1831, Sam Houston Papers.

Houston the contract for Indian rations?" Houston immediately wrote to Stanbery and demanded to know if the *Intelligencer* had quoted him correctly.[27] He had wanted to challenge the Representative in the House but had been dissuaded by James K. Polk. With the preliminaries staged for a challenge to a duel, Stanbery began to carry a weapon. On the evening of April 13, Houston, armed only with a cane, accosted the Representative and gave him a beating. The "most daring outrage and assault" made headlines in the Washington papers, and Duff Green's *United States Telegraph*, anti-Jackson and pro-Calhoun, played up Houston as a Jackson favorite and lamented that "tactics of the Nashville school were to be transferred to Washington and that the voice of truth was to be silenced by the dread of the assassin."[28]

Stanbery wrote to Andrew Stevenson, speaker of the House, that he had been "attacked, knocked down by a bludgeon, and severely bruised and wounded, by Samuel Houston" and requested that the Speaker put the matter before the House. Over Polk's protest, the House voted 145 to 25 to arrest Houston. After the arraignment, Houston employed Francis Scott Key as his attorney and appeared two days later to plead not guilty to assaulting Stanbery as outlined in the arraignment—that is, for words spoken in the House in debate—for which, under the theory of constitutional immunity of the lawmakers, the Congressman could not be held responsible. Rather, said Houston, he was angered by the article in the *Intelligencer,* had asked Stanbery for an explanation, and under provocation of great excitement, had beaten the Representative with a cane. He denied that his act constituted contempt of the House or a breach of privilege of a member of the Congress.[29] With the plea of not guilty, the trial before the House was set to begin on April 19 and dragged on for a month. The papers played up the affair, and letters from Washington, particularly those of Jackson's enemies, embroidered the theme with salacious details. John Floyd of Virginia, who had been pro-Jackson and had befriended Houston only four or five years earlier, was bitter against Jackson by 1832. On April 20 he made a long entry in his diary summarizing the background of the story in erroneous and abusive language reflecting on Houston, the President, and others who had incurred his disapproval. Ten days later he made another entry:

News from the City of Washington informs us that the President is outrageously abusive in all his conversations of every member of Congress who

[27] Houston to Prentiss, March 27, 1832, and to Stanbery, April 3, 1832, *Writings,* I, 197–99.
[28] Quoted in James, *The Raven,* 164–65.
[29] *Writings,* I, 202–203.

31

differs with him in opinion about any measure, and openly bullies all who do not acquiesce in his declarations that the assault upon Stansberry [*sic*] a member of Congress, by Houston for words spoken in debate is correct. He, Jackson, says that he wished there were a "dozen Houstons" to beat and cudgel the members of Congress.[30]

Niles' Register, on April 28, commented that it was inserting the proceedings of the trial for the record only, since the facts were uninteresting and everybody had become fatigued with the subject. The *Register* could see no propriety in the course the affair had taken; the House had nothing to do with the Stanbery charge against Eaton and should have restricted itself to preserving its own independence, not allowing strangers, for real or supposed grievances, to assault members, "lest *the whole concerns of the people become submitted to the* DOMINION OF FORCE." The *Register* regretted to add "that some things have transpired which give it a *character* that no one could have anticipated—save in a total prostration of the rights of the representatives of the people."[31]

Houston anticipated nothing more unpleasant than the discussion and publicity. He wrote Prentiss that he was playing the part of a patient man, although he did not feel composed. He considered himself the representative of the "liberty & reputation of every American citizen." Others also assured Prentiss that Houston would "not suffer much harm by any doings of Congress."[32]

Because Key was ill, the defense did not present its final plea until May 7. On the night before, Houston and his friends, including Polk, Speaker Stevenson, Bailey Peyton, and Felix Grundy, met and planned and drank in Houston's room. Polk, whom Houston described as "a victim of the use of water as a beverage," left early; the others were not so wise, and Houston was not at all sure the next morning that he would be able to array himself in his new suit, provided by Jackson, and appear in the House.[33]

By high noon, the hour appointed for the hearing of the trial on "breach of privilege," Speaker Stevenson was able to call the crowded House to order, and Houston was able, following Key's speech, to appear, in splendid attire and with perfect composure, in a long speech in his own defense. He emphasized his respect for the rights and privileges of

[30] Charles H. Ambler (ed.), *Life and Diary of John Floyd*, 178–79, 181.

[31] *Niles' Register*, XLIII (April 28, 1832), 153.

[32] Houston to Prentiss, May 1, 1832, and Prentiss to Houston, May 4, 1832, *Writings*, I, 203–206.

[33] James, *Life of Andrew Jackson*, 624; A. W. Terrell, "Recollections of General Sam Houston," *Southwestern Historical Quarterly*, XVI (1912/13), 123.

the House of Representatives, based partly on his own pride in having been a member of that House. His personal associations there, however, were to be no extenuation of the offense of a man "of broken fortune," crushed by adversity, whose only pride lay in sustaining the laws of his country. He cited the testimony of witnesses to the affray that he had not been armed, and insisted that his anger had not been aroused by Stanbery's speech in Congress but by the charge of fraud in the columns of the *Intelligencer*. Houston discussed the constitutional and legal aspects of trying a private citizen, not by his peers, but by the House that was a party to the accusation. Whatever the decision of the court should be, he would "bow to the very shadow of the authority of the House," so long as his resistance could be construed as contempt of the "representatives of the people of the Union," but the privileges asserted by the House should be defined for the security of the citizens. For the administration, then in the bitter struggle with Congress over the bank bill, he threw in the sentence: "If I apprehended the subversion of our liberties, I should look not to the Executive but to the Legislative Department." Houston quoted Greek and Roman and British history—and Shakespeare. He accused government counsel of showing disrespect to his attorney; he emphasized again and again his ever respectful deportment to the House. Pointing to the American flag, he ended his speech by declaring that so long as it should wave, the rights of American citizens should be preserved "safe and unimpaired."[34]

The House, after a four-day debate, found Houston guilty and sentenced him to be reprimanded by the Speaker, but it also allowed him, through intervention of William S. Archer of Virginia, on May 14, to incorporate a protest in the House *Journal*. Speaker Stevenson's reprimand alluded to the character and intelligence of the former congressman and forbore more "than to pronounce the judgment of the House, which is that you . . . be reprimanded at this bar by the Speaker, and . . . I do reprimand you accordingly." Stanbery could but wonder if Jackson's friend had not made capital of the occasion, both for himself and the administration; the reprimand sounded more like commendation than reproof.

The Ohioan then moved that a committee, with himself a member, be appointed to investigate the proof of the charge of fraud in the contracts for Indian rations. For six weeks more the proceedings went on, with many witnesses called and with Houston conducting his own defense. Duff Green's *United States Telegraph* pronounced Houston's guilt in

---

[34] Houston's Defense, *Writings*, I, 207–25.

advance; Francis P. Blair's *Globe*, the administration organ, defended Houston. By a divided vote the committee reported that Eaton and Houston were acquitted of all imputation of fraud. Stanbery had two other anti-Houston processes under way. The resolution to exclude him forever from the lobby of the House failed, but a trial on a criminal indictment for assault resulted in a fine of five hundred dollars and costs.[35] Judge William Cranch of the District of Columbia Court imposed the fine on June 28, "tough enough" as Houston opined, though it would not delay him in Washington as it did not have to be paid until the next winter. The fine was never paid. The court never attempted to collect it. In July, 1833, Houston asked his cousin what had happened about the fine and suggested: "Get that remitted by the Old Chief." Back in Washington in the spring of 1834, Houston memorialized the President to remit the fine, and the remission was granted on July 3, 1834.[36]

During those "trial days" in the summer of 1832, Houston was practically a member of Jackson's family—and official family. He made recommendations for office, including that of Richard Pearse for the consulate at Matamoros and Charles A. Clinton as commissioner to France, and wrote to Lewis Cass recommending the presentation of medals to tribes west of the Mississippi River and suggesting that he himself would be willing to be accountable for their delivery.[37] The Pearse endorsement had repercussions, for the nomination was at first approved and was then suspended because of Pearse's difficulties with General Thomas Dickens Arnold, a long-time enemy of Jackson. Arnold, in 1832 a member of Congress from Tennessee, made a speech condemning Houston, for which Morgan A. Heard threatened to shoot Arnold and then attacked him, after the current fashion, with a club. John Floyd recorded the story as an inevitable aftermath of the administration attitude on the Stanbery affair, and concluded his entry of May 16, 1832: "Jackson has encouraged these attacks upon the members, and Stansberry [*sic*] has so said in his place in the House and pledged himself to prove it if the House would grant an investigation, but the servile, contemptible House refused an inquiry into so flagitious an outrage upon the people, the dignity of the country and the purity of the principles of the Constitution."[38] Jackson's own comment was reported to have been: "After a few more

[35] James, *The Raven*, 170–72; Lester, *Life of Sam Houston*, 59–61; *Writings*, I, 245–46.

[36] Lester, *Life of Sam Houston*, 61; Parton, *Life of Andrew Jackson*, III, 385; *Writings*, I, 289; V, 6.

[37] Houston to Prentiss, April 8 and June 16, 1832, *Writings*, I, 201, 241; Houston to Cass, June 19, 1832, Houston Papers.

[38] Ambler, *Life and Diary of John Floyd*, 187–88.

examples of the same kind, members of Congress would learn to keep civil tongues in their heads."[39]

The events of the summer of 1832 had put the erstwhile exile back into the American political scene. As Houston said to George W. Paschal in Texas over twenty years later: "I was dying out, and had they taken me before a Justice of the Peace and fined me ten dollars for assault and battery, they would have killed me. But they gave me a national tribunal for a theatre, and set me up again."[40]

On July 10, just before he left Washington, Houston published an article in the *Globe* as a final summary of his participation in the bidding on the Indian ration contracts and as a last bitter denunciation of Stanbery, of whom he said: "His vices are too odious to merit pity and his spirit too mean to deserve contempt."[41] On his way west, he stopped at Cincinnati; his quarrel with the Congressman from Ohio was probably part of the background for the note which appeared in *Niles' Register* on August 4, 1832: "It was recently 'announced in the bills of the day,' with all 'the pomp and circumstance' due on such occasions, that Gen. *Houston* was invited to attend the theatre at Cincinnati, and had accepted the invitation—Offence was taken at this proceeding and a 'row' followed, which broke up the performances of the theatre before they were half through."[42]

Before his departure from Washington, in line with his recommendation to Cass of distribution of medals to the Plains Indians, Houston had been commissioned by Jackson to go to the Indians in the West, and while in Nashville he received his passport. It described him as six feet, two inches in height, with brown hair and light complexion.[43] Houston wrote Prentiss on August 18 that he planned to go to the Hermitage to see Jackson before his departure for Texas. A change must soon take place in Texas, he said. "The people look to the Indians on Arkansas as auxiliaries, in the event of a change—So I will pass that way and see my *old friends*."[44] On September 16, he set out for Texas via Fort Gibson and Auguste Chouteau's house on Grand River, where he met Washington Irving. Charles Noland, who earlier in the summer had thought of accompanying him to Texas, wrote: "Houston reached this place a few

---

[39] *Statues of Sam Houston and Stephen F. Austin Erected in Statuary Hall of the Capitol Building at Washington*, 29.
[40] George W. Paschal, "Last Years of Sam Houston," *Harper's New Monthly Magazine*, XXXII (1865/66), 631.
[41] To the Public, July 9, 1832, *Writings*, I, 250–57.
[42] *Niles' Register*, XLII, 404.
[43] *Writings*, IV, 11; Grant Foreman, *Pioneer Days in the Early Southwest*, 200.
[44] *Writings*, I, 264.

days since in fine spirits—his destination—Texas. The unsettled state of things there together with the flattering prospect that Austin will succeed, has a tendency to make grants there somewhat more valuable."[45]

As the story goes, when Houston left the Cherokee country, he was accompanied by Elias Rector, then the United States marshal in Arkansas, who gave him a razor, a horse, and some money. To Rector he said: "I accept your gift, and mark my words, if I have good luck, this razor will sometime shave the chin of the President of a republic." Or, as another version of the story has it: "Elias, remember my words. I will yet be the President of a great Republic. I will bring that nation to the United States, and if they don't watch me closely I will be the President of the White House yet."[46]

The Great Designer, if the stories be true, was revealing something of the outline of his pattern for conquest. But at Fort Towson, on December 2, 1832, just as he got ready to cross Red River into Mexican territory, he was looking both ways when he reported to his cousin that he had received news that his friends had announced his name as candidate for governor of Tennessee, and that if he lived he would be back in March or April to see how the land lay, and he thought he would run. His Texas business was "of importance to his pecuniary interest." His health and spirits were good, he said, his habits were sober, and his heart was straight.[47]

[45] C. F. M. Noland to William Noland, October 14, 1832, Berkeley Papers.
[46] *Statues of Sam Houston and Stephen F. Austin,* 31; Paschal, "Last Years of Sam Houston," *Harper's New Monthly Magazine,* XXXII (1865/66), 631.
[47] Houston to John H. Houston, December 2, 1832, *Writings,* VI, 1–2.

Opportunist in Texas

W<small>HAT WERE</small> "the springs of action in his mind"? How did he hope in Texas "to grace his name for after ages to admire"?

On July 31, 1833, Sam Houston wrote to John H. Houston from Hot Springs, Arkansas:

> You want to know "what the Devil I am going to do in Texas"? Part, I will tell you, and the balance you may guess at. I will practice law, and with excellent prospects of success. . . . With two other Gentlemen (who furnish the capital) I have purchased about 140,000 acres of choice land; in which I am equally interested—Besides this I own, and have paid for 10,000 [acres] that is, I think, the most valuable land in Texas. Several minor matters I am engaged in, and if I enjoy health I must make well out of them.[1]

[1] *Writings,* V, 5–6.

Before and since that time the question has continued to be: What the devil was Sam Houston doing in Texas? For the part he told was too little and the balance he left to guess at provided too much field for conjecture. That he was interested in land speculation is certain—so was every other man who came to early Texas—but that he actually owned land in Texas prior to the grant from Stephen F. Austin in 1832 is uncertain. Much of the motivation of the whole frontier movement was to secure cheap land and hope that by improvements and increased population its value would grow. As Houston himself once expressed it: "Your feelings will become attached to the land; it will imbue your hearts; you will catch the contagion of the frontier settler; you will not be able to escape it. You may escape the small pox, but you can never escape the contagion of land loving."[2]

Despite the statement in the "Only Authentic Memoir" that his intention was "to become a herdsman, and spend the rest of his life in the tranquillity of the prairie solitudes,"[3] the evidence is that in 1833 Houston's case of land fever was slight. It is those "several minor matters" in which Houston said he was engaged that have occupied the speculations of those who have sought to explain Houston's motives for removing to Texas.

For example, the Anglo-American settlement of Texas, the winning of Texas independence, and the events culminating in the annexation of Texas were contemporary with the development of abolition sentiment in the United States. Abolitionist propaganda explained the westward movement into Texas as a deliberate plot of slaveholding interests to expand slave territory. Enemies of "King" Andrew Jackson—and numerous enemies there were—found what was to them plausible evidence that Jackson sent Houston to Texas to revolutionize the area and steal it from Mexico for the United States.

John Quincy Adams belonged in both the abolition and the Jackson-hating categories. As a member of Congress in 1838, Adams converted resolutions of the Legislature of Massachusetts protesting against the annexation of Texas into a springboard to bring up the Texas question as a means of removing the gag on slavery topics. At length he dominated debate in the House and charged the United States government with fomenting war against Mexico for the purpose of annexing Texas. Firmly convinced of the deceitfulness of the Jackson and Van Buren administrations, he went on in his speech to introduce documents which, to

[2] Speech on the Boundary of Texas, *ibid.*, V, 34.
[3] Lester, *Life of Sam Houston*, 64.

him, and to a long succession of partisan American historians, proved that Sam Houston was one of the chief agents of that duplicity.[4]

Adams was not the first to advance the thesis that Houston was a deliberate schemer for the conquest of Texas. The story had been abroad since 1829; it was being "proved" as the thesis of research students after 1929. The Portsmouth (New Hampshire) *Journal* of July 2, 1836, reprinted from the Memphis *Enquirer* a fanciful, even fantastic, story of a supposed friendship between Houston and General Antonio López de Santa Anna and of their contemplated conquest of Texas and Mexico.[5] That Memphis reporter possessed a real imagination when he made Santa Anna, instead of Jackson, Houston's partner in a great design.

Horace Greeley, in his *American Conflict*, written in 1865 to give his interpretation of the causes, incidents, and results of the "Great Rebellion," gave traditional abolitionist argument. He quoted a Little Rock paper as predicting that it would soon hear of Houston's raising his flag in Texas, for "Houston and other restless spirits . . . were pushing into Texas expressly to seize upon the first opportunity to foment a revolution, expel the Mexican authorities, and prepare the region for speedy Annexation to this country."[6]

Belief in Houston-Jackson collaboration was not restricted to abolitionists or to those who lived north of Mason and Dixon's line. Henry A. Wise of Virginia wrote in 1872 that Jackson, the deep- and far-seeing politician, made especial use of Houston and planned to employ United States troops to aid the Texas Revolution by claiming the Neches and not the Sabine River as the western boundary of the United States. Houston, in command of the Texas Army in 1836, was to retreat to join troops under General E. P. Gaines, ordered to Texas soil by Jackson, and only the insubordination of Texas troops who forced the battle at San Jacinto "prevented the success of deep laid plans."[7] J. F. H. Claiborne, writing in 1880, said that Jackson's "enlarged views" as to the legitimate western boundaries of Louisiana were well known and that it was generally believed that he had not exerted his power to prevent citizens of the United States from joining Houston's rebels in Texas.[8] According to

[4] *Speech of John Quincy Adams . . . on the Freedom of Speech and Debate,* 103–104.

[5] Typescript in Houston Unpublished Correspondence, I.

[6] Horace Greeley, *The American Conflict: A History of the Great Rebellion in the United States of America, 1860–64,* I, 150.

[7] Wise, *Seven Decades of the Union,* 149.

[8] *Mississippi as a Province, Territory, and State, with Biographical Notices of Eminent Citizens,* 431.

Henry Bruce's biography of Houston, published in 1891, "Houston went forth to Texas with a conditional authorization from Jackson, 'Good luck to you in any case; recognition if you succeed.'"[9] Marquis James, in his scholarly biography *The Raven,* could only hint at Houston's motive. Baffled in his effort to decipher Houston's actions, James commented that it was doubtful that Houston himself knew in 1829 where he was heading, but that his first thought was "to do something grand"—"to capture an empire and lay it at his old Chieftain's feet."[10]

Richard R. Stenberg, in a doctoral dissertation titled "American Imperialism in the Southwest," presented his findings to prove the Texas schemes of Jackson and Houston, although he was forced to agree that Houston had not entered into the causes of the Texas Revolution. According to Stenberg, Houston managed to get himself made commander of the army but was "too dictatorial and too secretive to carry out his plans" and the Battle of San Jacinto retarded his scheme of "reincorporation" because it precluded annexation without Congressional vote.[11] Another version of the same theme is included in the memoirs of Houston's pastor of many years later. Whether Houston told his minister the truth about his military objectives in 1836, or whether Dr. Burleson chose the story as a justification of Houston's retreat across Texas before San Jacinto, will probably never be known; but according to Burleson there was a secret agreement that in case of necessity the Texans should retreat to the Sabine, where they would be joined by four thousand deserters from the United States Army under Gaines. The combined forces would then repulse the Mexicans, march to the Rio Grande, and demand that Texas independence be granted or Mexico would be invaded. "A grander campaign was never planned."[12]

Stenberg's statement that Houston, to secure money for his schemes, sought financial help from New York speculators in Texas lands[13] is in only partial accord with Elgin Williams' view that the Texas Revolution and the annexation of Texas were a capitalist conspiracy to insure financial returns on a huge speculative venture, with Houston in the role of corporation lawyer for the Galveston Bay and Texas Land Company.[14]

So much for what "they say" about why Houston betook himself to

---

[9] *Life of General Houston,* 80.

[10] Pp. 115, 173.   [11] Pp. 261–63.

[12] Georgia J. Burleson (comp.), *The Life and Writings of Rufus C. Burleson, D.D., Ll.D., Containing a Biography of Dr. Burleson by Harry Haynes,* 565.

[13] Richard R. Stenberg, "The Texas Schemes of Jackson and Houston," *Southwestern Social Science Quarterly,* XV (1934/35), 239.

[14] *The Animating Pursuits of Speculation: Land Traffic in the Annexation of Texas,* 67.

Texas. What did Houston say? He said nothing directly. He probably approved or inspired the explanation given by his Huntsville neighbor and attorney, Henderson Yoakum, who said in his *History of Texas* in 1855 that Houston had two objects: "to act as a confidential agent of the government of the United States in looking into the condition and disposition of the Indian tribes . . . and to examine into the character of the country, with a view to its value to the United States should they purchase it. His second object was that of an agent for claimants of lands."[15]

Perhaps it was psychologically impossible for Houston to be direct or explicit. Certainly, if he went to a foreign country with the deliberate plan to manipulate addition of a part of that country to another, whether or not he was acting under presidential order, he had need for caution in his remarks and in what he wrote. Only by implication can his writings be construed to say that he had actual plans for an empire in Texas. In many later episodes in his career it is equally difficult to say conclusively what he had in mind. Possibly the only solution is to list the events as they occurred, pick out his own words, however obscure, that seem to have a bearing on the problem, and let the reader make his own interpretation.

Houston may have conceived himself to be a speculator in Texas lands as early as 1822, when he was an original shareholder in the Texas Association of Tennessee, which applied to the Mexican government for permission to settle a colony in Texas. Robert Leftwich, agent for the association, secured a grant in his own name in April, 1825, and the area designated came to be known as the Leftwich Grant and ultimately as the Sterling C. Robertson Colony. Because of changes in the Mexican immigration laws and conflicting land grants, the Robertson Colony was involved in lengthy litigation and controversy.[16] Far removed from the scene of action, stockholders in Tennessee regarded the enterprise as a speculation and seemed to expect to be absentee owners of the land to which they assumed each shareholder was entitled.

Before 1832, Houston seems to have had little concern with the association or its problems. He did know of the desirability of Texas land from his lawyer friend, William H. Wharton of Nashville, who had gone to Texas in 1827, and who by 1829 was suggesting that Houston visit Texas. Sometime before February, 1830, Houston met one of the Texas *empresarios*, David G. Burnet, who had been in and out of Texas since 1813. Their correspondence seems to indicate that Burnet outlined to

[15] I, 308.
[16] Eugene C. Barker, *The Life of Stephen F. Austin, Founder of Texas, 1793–1836: A Chapter in the Westward Movement of the American People*, 329–73.

Houston his hopes for his own contract in Texas and discussed the possibility of negotiating loans in New York. After they conferred in Baltimore, Houston wrote Burnet a letter of introduction to his old friend James Alexander Hamilton, with the explanation that Burnet's "business to your City is on the subject of making a settlement upon a Grant in Texas. The scheme, I think well of, and if I were so situated that I could embark in it, I would assuredly do so with sanguine expectation of success."[17]

By the spring of 1832, Houston had decided to make a change in his situation. The association with Burnet may have been the background for the correspondence with James Prentiss of New York which began on March 27, 1832, and continued until the last week in April, 1834. There apparently was other pertinent correspondence, but it has not been located. Some thirty letters in the Prentiss Papers in the Archives Collection of the University of Texas Library seem to throw some light on Houston's plans to speculate on the Leftwich Grant, on hopes for land grants on the Rio Grande, on Houston as a prospective agent of the Galveston Bay and Texas Land Company, and on some great plan which Houston had for Texas—with or without his Cherokee Indians. Although their emphasis is on land, the Prentiss letters contain phrases and allusions which obscure the land issue as much as they illuminate it and give some plausibility to the theory of Houston's designs on Texas. Because the puzzling correspondence is relatively unknown, it is necessary to follow it at some length.

Houston and Prentiss met in New York and talked about harmonizing their views and interests. In April, Houston wrote that it would be necessary to go to Texas to secure reliable intelligence. He planned to go there in the spring or summer, but he could leave for the West immediately if the interested parties in New York wished him to go as agent of their company.[18] On April 15, Prentiss wrote that the state of affairs in Mexico was calculated to advance his and Houston's views and that Houston

---

[17] Houston to Hamilton, March 16, 1830, David G. Burnet Papers.

[18] Houston to Prentiss, April 8, 1832, *Writings*, I, 200–201. The company was the Galveston Bay and Texas Land Company, organized in New York on October 16, 1830, to act as agent for, and to exploit the *empresario* contracts of, David G. Burnet, Joseph Vehlein, and Lorenzo de Zavala, under which a total of twelve hundred families were supposed to be settled in Texas. The capitalists wanted to sell stock in the company and also to sell land scrip valued at five or ten cents an acre. The scrip did not convey title, but most Americans considered it a deed. The first immigrants sent to Texas by the company had trying times when they arrived; but after the repeal of the Immigration Law of April 6, 1830, the company secured extension of time for the fulfillment of the contracts and continued its work of attracting colonists. See Barker, *Life of Stephen F. Austin*, 144, 321–24.

should make ready for a rapid movement.[19] But on April 13, Houston made his attack on Stanbery and all movement was out of the question for three months. On May 1, he wrote Prentiss that as soon as he got through the trial he would come to New York to arrange matters and "set out for the *land of promise*." While he waited impatiently in Washington, Prentiss asked him to delay there until he could obtain opinions on dispatches being sent from Mexico to the government by Anthony Butler.[20] As Houston, perforce, had to remain in Washington to contest the series of Stanbery charges, the Galveston Bay Company decided to delay sending an agent to Texas until after they checked with John T. Mason, their confidential agent, who was due from Mexico by June 10; but Prentiss assured Houston that there was little doubt that the company would still desire him to go to Texas and inquired whether or not he had a good man to accompany him. Prentiss also wanted a progress report on buying shares in the Leftwich Grant.[21]

On June 1, Houston and Prentiss drew up an agreement. Houston was to go to Texas and purchase shares in the Leftwich Grant, the profits growing out of the agency on that grant to be divided equally between Houston and Prentiss. Money for purchase of the Leftwich Grant was to be realized from sale of certificates for land in the Juan Domínguez Grant, in which Houston was to become an equal owner. Houston was not to obligate himself for any payment of over $500 without Prentiss' consent and was to advise Prentiss of his progress in negotiations. Finally, Houston was not to admit any third person to share in the speculation. Houston's notes made to Prentiss totaled $8,502.90.[22] On June 4,

[19] Prentiss to Houston, April 15, 1832, *Writings*, I, 204.

[20] Houston to Prentiss, May 1, 1832, and Prentiss to Houston, May 4, 1832, *Writings*, I, 203–206. Anthony Butler became the United States chargé d'affaires to Mexico in 1829 and was instructed by President Jackson to negotiate, if possible, the purchase of Texas from Mexico. The attempt to purchase was a fruitless negotiation, which Butler may possibly have prolonged from personal interest because he owned scrip (totaling a million acres) in the Arkansas and Texas Land Company and the Galveston Bay and Texas Land Company, neither of which was then recognized by Mexico. To realize on his investment, Butler had to persuade Mexico to recognize the companies and, in case of cession of Texas to the United States, to be sure that the United States would recognize the company titles. In 1835, Prentiss authorized Butler to try to buy Texas from Mexico for the company for ten million dollars and to get the political jurisdiction transferred to the United States. See Eugene C. Barker, "The Private Papers of Anthony Butler," *The Nation* (June 15, 1911), 601.

[21] Prentiss to Houston, May 18 and 24, 1832, *Writings*, I, 225–27.

[22] Agreement between Houston and Prentiss, *ibid.*, 228–30. The Juan Domínguez Grant was a colonization contract made on May 6, 1829, by which Domínguez was to settle two hundred families in an area of northeast Texas and present Arkansas, including the twenty border leagues prohibited to foreign settlement. Domínguez, a

Houston had returned from New York to Washington, when Prentiss wrote a detailed explanation of his objective in their contract and discussed the comparative values of the scrip mentioned in the agreement. He enclosed in his letter maps and pamphlets descriptive of the lands and titles and assured Houston that if he were not satisfied with the bargain he could decline it and return the scrip, even that of the Domínguez Grant, which Prentiss considered an actual sale. In reply Houston asked for more explicit information about taking someone with him to Texas, assured the banker that he would be an equal partner in possible profits, and promised to do whatever Prentiss wished, so long as matters were handled as promptly as possible. For a "companion of intelligence, of means, and of first rate moral and physical courage," Houston proposed Charles F. M. Noland, an old friend of Little Rock days, now at home in Virginia. He assured Noland, "But if we should live, our wealth must be boundless."[23]

Houston's letter of June 12, reassuring Prentiss that he was "close" and positively would not dispose of any scrip in the Washington area, crossed a Prentiss letter of June 13, which reported that the company had the funds ready and could raise a little extra for a traveling companion but that the members preferred Houston to delay for a talk with John T. Mason. The financier went once more into the terms of their agreement, emphasizing the liberality of his proposals and disclaiming any desire to pressure Houston into a speculation which might prove costly. Prentiss was jubilant because the *empresario* grants of John Charles Beales had been extended for six years and Beales had agreed to secure the grant for the Arkansas and Texas Land Company. Again he insisted that Houston purchase as much as possible of the Leftwich Grant. Houston answered that he hoped matters would soon be arranged so that he might be off. "Indeed," he wrote, "I must and will be off soon—if I have to walk to some large water course, and make a raft to float upon!"[24] Impatient, and busy preparing the defense for the charges against him, Houston

---

native Mexican and a colonel in the Mexican Army, had been given the grant partially on the grounds that his location on the frontier would afford security to the country. See Mary Virginia Henderson, "Minor Empresario Contracts for the Colonization of Texas, 1825–1834," *Southwestern Historical Quarterly*, XXXII (1928/29), 20–21.

No families were introduced into the area by Domínguez, and one can but wonder why and how an officer in the Mexican Army could or would transfer to an American banker title which he did not actually have until fulfillment of the contract.

[23] Prentiss to Houston, June 4, 1832, and Houston to Prentiss, June 9, 1832, *Writings*, I, 232–35; Houston to Noland, June 10, 1832, *ibid.*, VII, 2–3.

[24] Houston to Prentiss, June 12 and 16, 1832, and Prentiss to Houston, June 13, 1832, *ibid.*, I, 237–42.

wrote that he had no time to look into the matter of the scrip, which seemed fair enough to him, and agreed that a grant for the navigation of the Rio Grande would take well. He felt that Mason's presence was not essential, particularly since matters in Mexico and Texas were so "fluctuating" that Mason's information would be out of date. Houston had, he told Prentiss, promised Noland fifty thousand acres out of his share of the land, and added that he wanted no bother as to that promise, for "my word is my only capital." By June 17, Houston confidentially showed Samuel P. Carson the agreement on the Leftwich Grant and wrote Prentiss to ascertain whether Carson might become interested in his share.[25]

At long last, on July 12 Houston left Washington and on the eve of his departure wrote both to Prentiss and to Daniel Jackson, a New York banker and member of the Galveston Bay Company. He warned them of too much dependence on Mason and of potential trouble from Anthony Butler. He reported that his friend Noland had been deterred from going with him because of the delay. He promised that he would see what he could do at Nashville about the Leftwich Grant and would return the scrip unless he saw some means of disposing of it to advantage. He assured his friends that if their project to send him to Texas fell through he would have to go on his own account, but that he would bear them no ill will nor use to their disadvantage any information given him. And the project fell through. By the end of July, Prentiss wrote that he could not secure the funds for Houston's trip to Texas, where "the field is now open for a great work . . . and you must go and reap the harvest." With a cholera epidemic in New York the last hope of raising the money seemed to disappear. Houston could not dispose of scrip in Nashville, where businesses were failing. When he received no funds from New York, he left the scrip with his cousin Robert H. McEwen and asked Prentiss to return his notes. His final letter to Prentiss voiced a slight complaint that the land matter had delayed him two months—he hoped the delay was not induced by "disingenuousness."[26]

The chances are that Houston was too busy with his Indian conferences and with beginning his establishment in Texas to write to Prentiss during 1833. When he met the financier in New York in March, 1834,

[25] Houston to Prentiss, June 17, 20, 27, and 28, 1832, *ibid.*, 242–50.

Carson arrived in Texas from North Carolina, via Mississippi, in 1836, signed the Texas Declaration of Independence, was secretary of state for Texas for two months, and then was sent to seek United States recognition of Texas independence.

[26] Houston to Prentiss, July 10, August 18, September 11, and 15, 1832; Houston to Jackson, July 12, 1832; Prentiss to Houston, July 31 and August 18, 1832, *Writings*, I, 257–66.

Prentiss again proposed retaining him as agent for the Galveston Bay Company, and negotiations were continued by letter. Houston had been to Texas; he was positive in his reply. He was not, nor had he ever been, employed by any person or company interested in Texas lands. He asked no such job, nor was he anxious to be counsel for any company. To secure his services a company would have to advance him not land scrip but cash—two thousand dollars in the beginning and one thousand dollars each six months. He concluded his letter: "I should not feel bound to be subservient." To his own chagrin, Prentiss could not secure the fee to retain Houston as counsel. He made suggestions on location of fifty sitios of land in their joint account, hoped Houston could be compensated for the disappointing outcome of his dealings with the Galveston Bay Company, and said he still expected the company to employ Houston after he returned to Texas.[27]

Did Houston make his contacts with the New York bankers in the hope of securing the money to go to Texas for reasons over and beyond representing their land interests? Did Prentiss know what his other, his real, objective was? Perhaps. In the letters of the two men there are phrases that could be convincing to one seeking conviction. In his reply to Prentiss' question whether he had gained any intelligence in Washington on "your project," Houston wrote vaguely of the future independence of Texas. On June 16, 1832, he forwarded to Prentiss from his old Tennessee friend, John A. Wharton, then practicing law in New Orleans, a letter in which Wharton spoke of Branch T. Archer, who was forecasting the conquest of Texas. Wharton wanted Houston's help in securing a passport to Texas, which "does undoubtedly present a fine field for fame, enterprise, and usefulness."[28] To Prentiss, Houston said that Wharton's letter made it look "as tho' we ought to be in *some* haste" and offered to go by Richmond, Virginia, to see Dr. Archer "if it should be desired by you, & friends." Here seems to be a dovetailing of land speculation with fighting in Texas "next fall" and "fame and enterprise." The correlation of ideas seems also to be expressed by a Prentiss comment on the price of land: "In case of Sales the purchase[r] values lands in pro-

---

[27] Houston to Prentiss, March 28 and April 11, 1834, and Prentiss to Houston, April 1, 11, and 15, 1834, *ibid.*, 283–87.

[28] Wharton to Houston, June 2, 1832, *ibid.*, 230–31.

In 1833, John Wharton joined his brother William H. Wharton in Texas. In the same year Houston was a delegate to a convention at San Felipe which framed a constitution for Texas statehood separate from Coahuila, and over which William H. Wharton presided. In 1835, Branch T. Archer was to preside over the Consultation at San Felipe which elected Houston commander in chief of the Texas Army.

portion as he considers the probability of possessing them under the Mexican Government or that of the United States of N.A. Knowing all the circumstances that can make these lands more or less valuable you can judge of the expediency of retaining those I lately sold you or not as you please."[29]

Houston was well aware that there were possibilities of change in ownership of the Texas domain, even reporting the plan concocted by one man of obtaining grants to Texas land from the King of Spain on the ground that it never did belong to Mexico anyhow. For himself he said:

I never can entertain but one opinion in relation to this subject. You know what *that is,* and I need say nothing more upon it! Delay may produce the following consequences to the Grantees. England may seek to derive Title thro the King of Spain, or it may obtain a lien from the Mexican Government, when in either event it would render it a bone of contention between England and the U. States. Whichever power should succeed, would claim it by conquest, and the Grantees, would be compelled to accept terms, and not dictate them! There is a better plan!!![30]

This note on the grantees' dictating terms does not sound like the words of a man sent by the president of his country to secure the land for that country. How unfortunate for the historian that he thought he need say nothing more of his opinion and the "better plan"! Houston asserted that, candidly, he was not solicitous about the land because he "looked to other matters," but thought it might be well to have enough scrip "to form a pretext when I get there, for moving about, and in locating." Prentiss was satisfied, even if Houston's purchase of land was but means to an end, and replied: "The more conflict the more I am convinced of the expediency and practicability of our plans as lately understood by us." Other company members, however, "not knowing the importance of our objects," were unwilling to contribute what they considered "excessive and unnecessary for any proper purpose." Evidently Prentiss did not share all that he knew about Houston's plans with his fellow financiers, who considered Houston's terms, plus funds for a traveling companion, a little exorbitant for a mere agent. To add to the mystery—mayhap the intrigue—Prentiss sent Houston a cypher to be used in their further correspondence.[31] Truly matters must be kept secret.

A Houston comment to Prentiss in regard to young Noland as a com-

---

[29] Prentiss to Houston, June 4, 1832, *ibid.,* 232–33.
[30] Houston to Prentiss, June 9, 1832, *ibid.,* 234–35.
[31] Prentiss to Houston, June 13, 1832, *ibid.,* 237–40.

panion is cryptic and possible of two interpretations: "I have told him that my business was to watch, and secure the interest of the *Grantees!* but he does not know what I am to get."[22] Just what was he to get—millions of acres of land—or something more? And what did he mean when he wrote that his route to Texas would be oppressive and that from the time he landed at the mouth of White River he would have to travel express, sometimes day and night? Was it just the heat of an Arkansas-Oklahoma-Texas summer that made him anticipate so much speed, or would there be those in the area who might try to apprehend him? Further, what did he mean by: "Nothing on earth, can be gained by Genl. Mason's arrival, here, as respects the part, which I may have to act in Texas—Of this be *confident!*"[23] Was that part to be something completely aside from the land in which Mason, as confidential agent, was interested? And again, concerning information from Mason, he commented, "If you will recollect I always regarded *this* matter as one some what extraneous of the object of my trip to Texas." That Prentiss knew the object we conclude from a promise to him: "So soon as I arrive at any conclusion positively about the land, you shall know it, as well as all other matters: for really I have no motive, for with-holding one Single view, from you which may appertain to the whole subject."[24]

By the middle of August, 1832, Houston was regretting a bit that he was not in Texas at the time of the disturbances at Anahuac and Velasco but agreed that it probably was best that he was not on hand. Changes in Texas were imminent; he had been requested to come; he had better go see his Indian friends, for "the people look to the Indians on Arkansas as auxiliaries, in the event of a change."[25]

The implication about the Indians is just enough to tantalize, not enough to satisfy. Equally tantalizing is a comment as ambiguous as the following:

Should changes take place in Texas: It will not be in my power to act for the Companies, or to interfere as I am bound to go off, without any thing to shew, that I ought to act, and for those who wish to act effectually there, they must act prudently.

My hopes were ardent in the prosperity of that country, but they are less so at this time—You know that "hope deferred, maketh the heart sick!"[26]

[22] Houston to Prentiss, June 16 and 17, 1832, *ibid.*, 240–43.
[23] Houston to Prentiss, June 20, 1832, *ibid.*, 243–45.
[24] Houston to Prentiss, June 27 and 28, 1832, *ibid.*, 246–50.
[25] Houston to Prentiss, August 18, 1832, *ibid.*, 263–64. A memorandum on the back of this letter reads: "It may be necessary to act forthwith in Texas, or it may be impolitic to act in 12 months."
[26] Houston to Prentiss, September 11, 1832, *ibid.*, 264–65.

Before Houston could go to New York during the last of March, 1834, Prentiss had urged him to confide all that he "dared trust to James Prentiss." How much he "trusted" in their conferences is not known. He was given an important map, which he forgot in the bar at the City Hotel and had to have Prentiss send on to him in Washington under Felix Grundy's frank. He evidently did not tell company representatives enough to exact a retaining fee, but told Prentiss enough to have him write on April 1 that "all things in Texas appear so dark and doubtful to those who know less than you and I."

The two of them soon knew of the repeal of the law of April 6, 1830, a repeal which would further American immigration and the prospects of the Galveston Bay Company; but by April 20, Houston wrote Prentiss: "Now as to Texas, I will give you my candid impressions—I do not think that it will be acquired by the U. States. I do think within one year that it will be a Sovereign State and acting in all things as such. Within three years I think it will be separated from the Mexican Confederacy, and remain so forever."[37] Houston concluded his letter: "You may reflect upon these suggestions—They are not pleasant to me, but you may file them, and see how well I *prophesy.*" Undeniably he was correct on the time schedule for independence, if not the perpetuity of that independence. Was it the separation of Texas from Mexico that would be unpleasant to him or the idea of Texas' remaining independent? If the correct interpretation is that Texas' remaining independent was distasteful, and Houston is consistent, then that would be an affirmative answer to the later question of whether or not he favored annexation. But in a matter as mercurial as Houston statements, no assumption or interpretation is safe. Only four days after prophesying perpetual separation from Mexico he wrote:

You need not hope for the acquisition (if ever) by this Government of Texas during the Administration of Genl. Jackson—If it were acquired by a Treaty, that Treaty would not be ratified, by the present Senate—!!!

Texas will be bound to look to herself, and to do for herself—This present year must produce events, important to her future destiny. I *think*, greatly beneficial to her prosperity. I deprecate the necessity,—and however favorable the result, may be for her—Still if Mexico had done right, we cou'd have travelled on smoothly enough.

Many suppose that such events will be sought for by us, but in this their notions will be gratuitous, I assure you! The course that I may pursue, you must rely upon it, shall be for the true interests of Texas, (as I may believe)

[37] *Ibid.*, 289–90.

and if it can be done, as it ought to be; to preserve her integrity to the Confederacy of Mexico.[38]

The first paragraph quoted above is a remarkable prophecy of events of 1836–37 and 1844–45. It and the statement that Texas must look to herself apparently absolve Jackson from connection with any scheme. The third paragraph declares those persons wrong who say Houston sought to produce the changes, for his course was to preserve Texas within the Mexican confederation. Had his few months in Texas wrought a change in attitude, or had something happened to change his relations with Jackson?

What other evidences are there to indicate that interest in land was incidental to some other objective?

Houston originally left Nashville for Arkansas Territory in April, 1829. On May 11, from Little Rock, he wrote Jackson promising to check on Indian affairs as they concerned the administration. His letter contained a puzzling reference to a rumor "that I meditated an enterprise calculated to injure, or involve my country," and indicated that Houston was hurt by an intimation that Jackson disapproved his plans as injurious to the United States.[39] Who had told Jackson what? When the General had last seen Houston, in January, 1829, he had rejoiced with his friend in his approaching marriage and in the promise of his political career in Tennessee. Now, on June 21, he answered the exile's protest as to the purity of his motives:

It has been communicated to me that you had the *illegal enterprise* in view of conquering Texas; that you had declared you would, in less than two years, be *emperor* of that country, by conquest. I must have really thought you deranged to have believed you had such a wild scheme in contemplation; and particularly, when it was communicated that the physical force to be employed was the Cherokee Indians! Indeed my dear sir, I cannot believe you have any such chimerical, visionary scheme in view. Your pledge of honor to the contrary is a sufficient guaranty that you will never engage in any enterprise injurious to your country, or that would tarnish your fame.[40]

Had Jackson received his information from the Donelsons? Andrew Jackson Donelson was with the President in Washington acting as his private secretary. It might be reasonable to assume that what the secretary knew his chief would know. On June 11, 1829, A. J. Donelson received a letter from his brother Daniel S. Donelson reporting that he had sent to the brother in Washington several letters concerning the rupture

[38] Houston to Prentiss, April 24, 1834, *ibid.*, 291.
[39] *Ibid.*, 132–33.   [40] Yoakum, *History of Texas*, I, 307.

between Houston and his wife. Daniel Donelson had decided that Houston was not deranged with jealousy but was obsessed with what he described as his "grand scheme" for revolutionizing Texas. In March, 1829, Donelson recounted, Houston told him that William Wharton had gone to Texas as Houston's agent to foment the revolution from Mexico and would notify Houston when "everything was properly arranged." Houston's desertion of his wife, Donelson decided, was planned as a justification for his leaving the United States.[41]

If there be truth in Donelson's conjecture, it surely must be that Houston's great unhappiness in his marriage and his realization that it must end in disaster had put the Texas idea into his tortured mind by March, after his marriage the last of January, 1829. He had been urged to visit Texas by John A. Wharton and Leonard Groce before October, 1829, but just how long before is not evident.[42] It seems impossible that a former congressman, a popular governor, and a likely candidate for the presidency would give up everything to gamble on the outcome of a revolution in Texas, as remote as that eventuality seemed in 1829.

If we accept this hypothesis, we can believe that, once possessed of the Texas theme, Houston decided to exploit it. Such seems to be the evidence in an account written by Z. N. Morrell many years after the fact. According to Morrell, Houston confided in his friend McIntosh, a deacon of the Baptist church in Nashville, that he would renew his contacts with the Cherokees, intending with their aid and with emigration from Tennessee and elsewhere to establish "a little two-horse republic" of which he would be the first president.[43]

Other persons had heard rumors. Houston's old colonel, Thomas Hart Benton, wrote him in Arkansas requesting him to call on Benton for any services he might wish. He sent Houston editorials on the southwestern boundary, to be printed in Arkansas papers, and closed his letter: "This subject [the boundary], and the public lands, are the two *levers* to move public sentiment in the West. If you have ulterior views your *tongue* and *pen* should dwell incessantly upon these two great topics."[44]

Another curiously circumstantial incident, which suggests a hoax, began in February, 1830. Houston was at the time staying at Brown's Indian Hotel, on the same floor as Dr. Robert Mayo, evidently a well-known Washington character of the time. According to a report which

[41] Stanley F. Horn (ed.), "Holdings of the Tennessee Historical Society," *Tennessee Historical Quarterly*, III (1944), 349–51.
[42] Yoakum, *History of Texas*, I, 308 n.
[43] *Flowers and Fruits in the Wilderness; or, Forty-Six Years in Texas and Two Winters in Honduras*, 20.
[44] Benton to Houston, August 15, 1829, *Writings*, I, 140.

Mayo made to Jackson in November, 1830, the two men had long conversations which developed into sufficient intimacy for Houston to suggest that Mayo go to Texas, telling the Doctor of the advantage of the Indian settlements beyond the Mississippi as a steppingstone to Texas and describing his own adoption of Indian costume and habits as a cloak for an expedition that he was organizing against Texas to be timed for about February, 1831. At Jackson's request, according to Mayo, the Doctor repeated the report to Jackson on December 2, 1830, in a letter in which he summarized the Houston confidences and his own attempts to gain more information on the scheme, including his acquaintance in the summer of 1830 with a man named Hunter, supposedly a recruiting agent for Houston, who revealed to Mayo the secret alphabet used in correspondence between recruiting agencies established throughout the United States. Mayo said that Hunter told him of steamboats already chartered to convey troops to Texas, where, after Houston had accomplished a military conquest, he could be superseded by a civilian government.[45]

Five days after receiving the Mayo letter, Jackson delivered his second annual message to Congress and, in regard to Mexican relations, said that Mexico's unfounded suspicions of the United States had been removed with the consequent "establishment of friendship and mutual confidence." Then three days after his message he wrote to William S. Fulton, secretary of Arkansas Territory, outlining the information concerning Houston as given him by Mayo. Jackson told Fulton that, notwithstanding the circumstantial manner in which the story had come to him, he believed the information erroneous. However, because he so detested the idea of such a filibustering expedition, he hoped to get at the truth of the matter and asked Fulton to watch affairs in Arkansas and keep him advised.[46]

This Mayo-Jackson-Fulton correspondence has posed "whodunit" problems in research. In the spring of 1837, as Jackson prepared to retire from the presidency, he cleared his desk of accumulated papers and returned to Dr. Mayo the December 2, 1830, letter concerning Houston. By mistake, says John Spencer Bassett, editor of the Jackson correspondence, he put in the same envelope with the Mayo letter a copy of his own letter of December 10, 1830, to W. S. Fulton. The independence of Texas was recognized by the United States on March 3, 1837, and annexation was under discussion. Houston had become president of

---

[45] Robert Mayo, *Political Sketches of Eight Years in Washington*, 118–22.
[46] Jackson to Fulton, December 10, 1830, *Correspondence of Andrew Jackson*, IV, 212–14; Mayo, *Political Sketches*, 125.

Texas. No wonder Mayo was interested when he got his letter back, plus Jackson's letter to Fulton. Apparently Mayo had become bitterly anti-Jackson, perhaps from being ignored in 1830, but whatever his motive, he turned the letters over to John Quincy Adams.

No more perfect propaganda could have fallen into the hands of that arch abolitionist and Jackson-hater. Adams asked the State Department for all correspondence with Mexico relating to American neutrality in 1830, particularly the letter to Fulton. The State Department could not locate the file; Jackson consulted his own Executive Record Book and found a memorandum. He wrote to Fulton, by 1838 senator from the new state of Arkansas, and asked for a copy of the letter, suggesting that perhaps the files of the correspondence might be in the War Department since the Indians were involved.[47] Fulton replied that his letters were in Arkansas, but stated his recollection of the contents of the December 10 letter and said that he had made personal and confidential investigations and had found no proof that Houston or anyone else was, in 1831, organizing any expedition against Mexico.[48] In July, 1838, in his Texas speech on the subject of the right of petition, Adams introduced the Mayo-to-Jackson and the Jackson-to-Fulton letters of 1830 as proof of Jackson's knowledge of designs on Texas. Adams thought that Jackson had written his letter to Fulton but decided not to use it in order to leave Houston unhampered in his projects, declaring the letter that Mayo got back in 1837 the original and not a copy. The original letter was finally found in Arkansas in February, 1839. In the meantime, Adams had made his charges, and Jackson, furious, had accused Mayo of stealing the letter to Fulton. Francis P. Blair, in his Washington *Globe*, had written editorials on Adams' attack on Jackson; Mayo sued Blair for libel, and Blair had to secure depositions from Jackson concerning the entire affair.[49]

But to go back to events before Mayo got the Fulton letter and started the abolition hornets buzzing. Two months after Jackson received his original information from Mayo in 1830, the President wrote to Anthony Butler to commend him for his success in placing relations between Mexico and the United States on such an amicable basis. The President reported to his minister that there was reason to fear that a project was on foot by which adventurers from the United States were to act in concert with disaffected Mexican citizens to seize Texas. Because it

[47] Jackson to Martin Van Buren and Jackson to Fulton, January 23, 1838, *Correspondence of Andrew Jackson*, V, 529–33.
[48] Fulton to John Forsyth, March 6, 1838, *ibid.*, 540 n.
[49] Blair to Jackson, April 26, 1839, *ibid.*, VI, 10–13.

might be difficult for Mexico to understand the limited power of the American executive to avert such an occurrence, Jackson suggested that, in order to counteract potential Mexican jealousy, Butler should mention the matter and assure Mexico that the government would take every possible step to thwart the plot and punish the conspirators. Butler might also use the incident to demonstrate the necessity for a prompt decision on a definite boundary between the United States and Mexico.[50]

Houston, in Arkansas, was not doing anything to arouse Fulton's suspicions, even if he did talk to strangers such as Maury about collecting volunteers to establish a colony on the Columbia River. When he finally got back to Washington in 1832, he was not treated by Jackson as a conspirator to be punished for plotting to steal land from a friendly neighboring country. Other persons might not call it theft, but a splendid undertaking. John Van Fossen, for example, with whom Houston had tried to work out the partnership on the Indian ration contracts, wrote Houston to that effect.[51]

Houston went to Texas with his War Department commission to hold parleys with the nomadic Indian tribes. He was in Texas in December, 1832, and January, 1833, and reported to Jackson from Louisiana in February, 1833. He attended the Texas convention at San Felipe in April, 1833, and, after a time in Arkansas, wrote on October 4, 1833, that he had established residence at Nacogdoches.

In the fall of 1833, Mexican diplomatic agents in Washington, including young Agustín de Iturbide, son of the former emperor of Mexico, and José María Tornel, Mexican minister in Washington, protested to the United States government that the President of the United States was conniving with Houston to take Texas, and Tornel left the capital in anger.[52] Jackson wrote Butler on October 30, 1833, that the slanders of Iturbide and Tornel had no foundation in either his own acts or his views and that their statement of his intimacy with Houston was not true. Furthermore, said the President: "The very opposite would have been nearer the fact, for we have had, ever since the intimation of his being regarded as unfriendly to the existing government of Mexico, a secret agent watching his movements and preparing to thwart any attempt to organize within the United States a military force to aid in the revolution of Texas."[53]

[50] Jackson to Butler, February 15, 1831, ibid., IV, 243–45.
[51] Van Fossen to Houston, August 3, 1832, quoted in William Carey Crane, Life and Select Literary Remains of Sam Houston of Texas, 48–49.
[52] Stenberg, "American Imperialism in the Southwest," 240.
[53] Correspondence of Andrew Jackson, V, 221. This statement about no intimacy

Had Houston's Texas schemes gone so far as Mayo declared and Mexico feared, surely there would have been knowledge of recruiting officers. No volunteers were found on the border. Houston went to Texas alone. Justin H. Smith, in his study of the annexation of Texas, states: "Only gross partisanship can find proof in this mere collection of circumstances and guesses that the President of the United States was a hypocrite, a liar, and virtually an oath-breaker."[54]

What the devil was Sam Houston doing in Texas?

He was there to make a living and a name for himself. His separation from his wife had shattered his personal life and his political future. Timed with that shock was an invitation to Texas. The retreat to Arkansas was but an interlude in which he grasped at tempting possibilities —the Rocky Mountains, or the Columbia River, or a location in Oregon for trade with the East Indies.[55] He went back to Tennessee and he went back to Washington, but the old stage sets did not fit the new drama in which he must play. Texas was adjacent and offered a chance, political and financial. A political change was inevitable there, and he had political experience which he might use to advantage, but in what direction he was not sure. Above all he was an opportunist. Burnet gave him some ideas on how money might be made. The negotiations with the land company were incidental. Financial backing would help, but he was destined for Texas in any case, and his commission to treat with the Indians was a good letter of introduction.

---

with Houston seems a little extreme, but perhaps it was all in the name of diplomacy. Stenberg, convinced that Jackson was a party to Houston's schemes, believes that Jackson did not actually write his letter of warning about Houston to Fulton until 1833, when he became alarmed at Mexican repercussions and wrote the letter, carefully labeling it "copy" although it was really the original. Whether young Iturbide got his information from Houston directly, as Butler states in a letter to Houston on December 15, 1845 (*Correspondence between Col. Anthony Butler and Gen. Sam Houston*), or whether the Mexican agents arrived at their conclusions from Washington rumors combined with reports in 1833 that Jackson planned to claim the Neches and not the Sabine River as the western boundary of the United States, is not certain. See Prentiss to Houston, March 8, 1834, *Writings*, I, 280, and Richard R. Stenberg, "Jackson's Neches Claim, 1829–1836," *Southwestern Historical Quarterly*, XXXIX (1935/36), 255–74.

[54] *The Annexation of Texas*, 25–26.
[55] Fred Wilbur Powell, "Hall Jackson Kelley, Prophet of Oregon," *Quarterly of Oregon Historical Society*, XVIII (March, 1917), 43.

General Houston

Houston rode south and west from Red River to San Felipe, Austin's colonial capital on the Brazos, where, on December 24, 1832, he applied, as a married man, for a grant of land within the coastal border leagues on the bayou called Karankawa "Bay." The grant was approved; Seth Ingram was ordered to make the survey in the bounds of Stephen F. Austin's third colony, and title to a league of land was issued on January 9, 1833. Meantime, Houston proceeded along the Camino Real to Bexar, where he met Comanche chiefs who promised to visit the United States Indian commissioner at Fort Gibson in about three months. Houston left a medal of General Jackson to be taken to the principal chief. When he reached Natchitoches, Louisiana, on February 13, 1833, he reported to Commissioner Ellsworth that it might be fairly late in May before the Comanches arrived at the fort. He found, he said, that

56

the Pawnees were carrying on trade with the Northwest Fur Company, whose influence extended to the Brazos and Colorado rivers in Texas. On the same day he wrote to Jackson, with the merest comment on his Indian business and considerable detail on information secured in Texas that was calculated to forward the President's views touching the acquisition of Texas by the United States—a measure desired, Houston thought, by nineteen-twentieths of the people in Texas. Mexican troops had been expelled from Texas, and the people were determined to form a separate state government and might, unless order was restored, break off from Mexico. In her need for money, Texas might have to appeal to England, and Houston had been given to understand that the British legation had a controlling influence over Anthony Butler, the American chargé in Mexico.[1] Where he got his information Houston did not say.

He knew of the convention scheduled to be held at San Felipe in a few weeks, and at Nacogdoches he was encouraged to establish his residence in Texas and allow his name to be advanced as a candidate for election to that assembly.[2] He may possibly have gone directly back from Natchitoches to Nacogdoches to campaign for that election, for on March 1 he was chosen one of the five delegates from Nacogdoches. From April 1 to April 13, 1833, he attended the San Felipe Convention, where he helped elect to the presiding office William H. Wharton instead of Austin, a victory for the more radical, or so-called "war party," eager for a showdown with Mexico. In the convention, Houston introduced a resolution protesting Mexico's encroachment on Indian lands and was chairman of the committee which framed the constitution for the proposed state of Texas, if separated from Coahuila. He opposed Branch T. Archer on the banking clause inserted in the constitution and secured the provision that no bank or banking institution or any other moneyed corporation should be chartered under the constitution.[3] In

[1] Houston to Ellsworth and Houston to Jackson, February 13, 1833, *Writings*, I, 272–76.

[2] Lester, *Life of Sam Houston*, 64–65.

[3] Yoakum, *History of Texas*, I, 312. The antibanking clause is Article 30 of the General Provisions of the *Constitution or Form of Government of the State of Texas*. Evidently Houston was vocal enough in the convention. The papers of Washington D. Miller contain a page and a half of notes on why Mexican troops were expelled from Texas, the lack of law in the Mexican confederation, and the thesis that Mexican plans made without the consent of Texas were not binding upon Texas. On the back of the document is this memorandum: "The above notes were written in April 1833 in reference to a convention to form a state Govt. at San Felipe—notes made for speech & delivered—constitution formed & sent to Mexico by Gen. Austin who was imprisoned."

that controversy he was Jackson's disciple. The convention completed the constitution, addressed a memorial to the Mexican government, and chose Austin, Wharton, and J. B. Miller as delegates to present the memorial, the constitution, and other resolutions. Austin, as it turned out, was the only commissioner who went to Mexico.

Sometime between January and July, 1833, Houston made at least one more trip to San Antonio. To Secretary of War Lewis Cass he explained that he did not return to Bexar to escort the Comanche chiefs to Fort Gibson for fear of antagonizing Mexico, since that country was extremely jealous of the United States and might conclude that the object of a treaty with the Indians would include furnishing arms to make the tribesmen a more formidable menace to Mexico. To explain further his failure to meet the Indians, Houston told Cass that he feared he might have his charges scalped on his hands if he led the Comanches through hostile country. He suggested that if Jackson really wanted a Comanche delegation to visit the United States, it might be well to secure permission through the Mexican minister and have an official escort.[4]

Houston was not alone in offering the government information on the Indians. Albert Pike, on March 16, 1833, also wrote to Cass, reporting the Comanches divided into two bands and commenting: "Governor Houston . . . will effect nothing with the Comanches. He goes to treat with the southern portion of them who are already friendly—he will never meet one of the northern portion from whom is our only danger, and even should he do so he would be immediately scalped."[5]

On May 28, 1833, Houston went to Fort Gibson to make his report to the Indian commissioners but found them absent. Trouble from his old wound was aggravated by the horseback trip across Texas, and he was so ill that he went to Hot Springs to recuperate. It was late July before Houston sent his accounts to the War Department for settlement. The department objected to the account, questioning his mission as special agent and saying that the charges were higher than those usually allowed. Houston demanded a "just and liberal" compensation assured by the President and commented parenthetically that had he known how arduous and hazardous the trip would be, he would not have undertaken it.[6]

From Hot Springs he wrote enthusiastic letters concerning Texas,

[4] Houston to Cass, July 30, 1833, *Writings*, II, 15–17.
[5] Reprinted by permission of the publishers, The Arthur H. Clark Company, from Grant Foreman's *Pioneer Days in the Early Southwest*, 202.
[6] Houston to Robb, October 4, 1833, *Writings*, II, 18–19.

"the finest portion of the Globe that has ever blessed my vision!" Later he promised his cousin John, "will . . . be time enough to interest you in its fate & mine." To Jackson he apologized for delay in writing but excused himself for lack of materials and "the risk which my letters must have run." He reported that the people in Texas would be satisfied with nothing less than a constitution and just laws, congratulated the President for his scotching of nullification in South Carolina, reported on inefficiency at Fort Gibson, and observed: "The Government has some efficient officers engaged in the business of emigration in this quarter—Maj. Armstrong, and Col. Rector—The former you know well, and I can assure you the latter will do his duty, whenever it is assigned to him."[7] Was Jackson's interest in increasing the volume of emigration or in scrutinizing those who emigrated?

Houston returned to Texas by way of Crow's Ferry and Natchitoches and resumed his law practice in Nacogdoches, where he began his friendship with the Adolphus Sterne and Henry Raguet families, particularly Miss Anna Raguet, aged seventeen. On November 30, 1833, he applied for a divorce from Eliza Allen Houston, basing his petition on the length of time since the separation in 1829 and the impossibility of a reunion. The petition, presented by Jonas Harrison, contained a diatribe on the "false wisdom and hypocritical piety" of established attitudes on divorce and an essay on the opportunity Texas possessed to be indifferent to ancient jurisprudence and to attract the independent of all nations with an enlightened and liberal policy. It would be interesting to know whether it was Harrison or Houston who concocted the strange medley of ideas in the petition, particularly since it was only a few weeks until Houston, as Samuel Pablo, was baptized in the Catholic faith, with Eva Rosine Sterne, wife of Alcalde Adolphus Sterne, as his godmother.[8]

With his fine horse and his courteous manner he excited the curiosity of the ladies in the family parties he met as he rode to San Augustine to try a law case or visit Philip Sublett. There were reports that Governor Houston said there would be a war in Texas before long and that he meant to figure in it.[9] Sometimes he penetrated deeper into the Texas interior than the Redlands area, perhaps to visit the Whartons or to seek information on Austin's activities in Mexico and the prospects of separate statehood. The Christmas season found him back in San Felipe,

---

[7] Houston to John Houston, July 31, 1833, *ibid.*, V, 5–6; Houston to Jackson, July 31, 1833, Jackson Papers, Series I, Reel 43.

[8] Divorce Petition, *Writings*, I, 277–79; James, *The Raven*, 203–204.

[9] *Quarterly of the Texas State Historical Association*, I (1897/98), 228.

and William B. Travis made a diary entry for December 15, 1833: "Genl. Houston in town."[10]

In the early part of the next year Houston again started east. He may have stopped for a conference with the Creeks and Cherokees at Fort Gibson, where Horace and Hannibal Bonney met a buckskin-clad white man, "over six feet in height," heading a body of five hundred warriors."[11] From the military post he proceeded by way of Cincinnati and Tennessee to Washington, where he spent the months of March and April, except for short visits to New York. He petitioned Jackson, on April 20, 1834, for the remission of his fine in the Stanbery assault case; Jackson remitted the fine, as "excessive," on July 3, 1834, but that may have been after Houston's departure for the West. In May, 1834, Benjamin Hawkins, a Creek Indian and Houston's friend and partner in various trading and mining enterprises, reported that Houston had planned an Indian conference on either the Brazos or the Trinity River in Texas on June 20, 1834. Later in 1834 the Creeks attempted to buy lands north of Nacogdoches from a New York land company, Hawkins being one of the agents. The American settlers and the Cherokees were opposed, and the project was abandoned, probably after September, 1835, when the vigilance committee at Nacogdoches designated Houston to prevent the introduction into Texas of Indians from the United States.[12]

Wherever Houston was during the summer of 1834, he was reported to have been in the United States capital in the fall and to have boasted to Junius Brutus Booth that he was meant to "revel in the Halls of the Montezumas." By December, 1834, other reports located him some twenty miles from the Texas border at Washington, Arkansas. An Englishman named G. W. Featherstonhaugh reminisced of his visit in that Arkansas community:

I was not desirous of remaining long at this place. General Houston was here, leading a mysterious sort of life, shut up in a small tavern, seeing nobody by day and sitting up all night. The world gave him credit for passing these, his waking hours, in the study of *trente et quarante* and *sept a lever;* but I had been in communication with too many persons of late, and had seen too much passing before my eyes, to be ignorant that this little place was the rendezvous where a much deeper game than faro or *rouge et noir* was playing. There were

[10] Diary of William Barret Travis, August 20, 1833–June 26, 1834, p. 5.
[11] Varina Howell Davis, *Jefferson Davis, Ex-President of the Confederate States of America: A Memoir by His Wife*, I, 156–57.
[12] Foreman, *Pioneer Days in the Early Southwest*, 205–19; Yoakum, *History of Texas*, I, 328.

many persons at this time in the village from the States lying adjacent to the Mississippi, under the pretence of purchasing government lands, but whose real object was to encourage the settlers in Texas to throw off their allegiance to the Mexican government.[13]

In the winter and early spring of 1835, Houston was busy practicing law in Nacogdoches and San Augustine and was at times himself a defendant in civil actions in the alcalde's court. On February 11, 1835, he and Nathaniel Robbins were the witnesses when Thomas Jefferson Rusk took his oath of allegiance to the Mexican government. On April 21, 1835, exactly one year before San Jacinto, his own character certificate, as Samuel Pablo Houston, a man of good character and without family, was signed by Juan M. Dor.[14] That same day Houston applied for a headright in the David G. Burnet Colony, receiving title on May 5.[15]

In the meantime, Austin was in prison in Mexico, and division of opinion between conservative and war-minded elements in Texas was widening. A convention called to meet at Bexar in November, 1834, had not materialized, and the central committee designated to look after public interests recommended quietude in Texas. In January, 1835, the centralists won control of the Mexican Congress; Santa Anna came into power and opposed the admission of Texas as a state but held out some hope that he would organize the area as a territory, an alternative objectionable to Texas. The state government of Coahuila and Texas had passed a land law which opened Texas to gigantic speculation and alarmed the colonists. A quarrel between Saltillo and Monclova over the location of the state capital resulted in Santa Anna's approving Monclova. With the revival of the customhouse at Anahuac and sending of customs officials to Anahuac and Brazoria, the scene was set for further trouble. Texas affairs remained generally peaceful, however, until the early summer of 1835, when Martín Perfecto de Cós ordered the arrest of William B. Travis and R. M. Williamson for agitation against the government, particularly against the customs officer at Anahuac. Moseley Baker, fearing that Cós was headed for Texas to establish military rule, sent Houston documents concerning recent governmental activities in Mexico and Texas and, in August, 1835, visited Houston at Nacogdoches. There Houston advised Baker to keep quiet and reported that the war

[13] G. W. Featherstonhaugh, *Excursion through the Slave States from Washington on the Potomac to the Frontier of Mexico*, II, 161.
[14] Nacogdoches Archives, LXXVI, 187, 188, 206, 208; LXXVII, 43.
[15] *Writings*, I, 296.

party was unpopular in East Texas and that the *ayuntamiento* at Nacogdoches had even forbidden the election of delegates to a convention.[16] Houston, on September 11, 1835, as a member of the Committee on Vigilance and Safety of the Nacogdoches Department, joined with the six other members of the committee in notifying President Jackson that Benjamin Hawkins was attempting to introduce some five thousand Creek Indians into Texas in violation of an article of the Treaty of Amity and Commerce between the United States and Mexico. On September 15, the same committee, with Frost Thorn as president and Thomas J. Rusk as secretary, appointed Houston to take the necessary steps to deter Hawkins.[17] This action, in the light of Houston's friendship with Hawkins and his supposed instrumentality in enticing the Indians to Texas, seems somewhat anomalous. One explanation might be that Houston wanted Cherokee Indians, not Creeks, or at least that he did not want trouble between Creeks and Cherokees. Perhaps his residence in Nacogdoches and his realization of the unprotected condition of the frontier made him oppose the Indian incursion. Mayhap he showed to his Nacogdoches friends one hand and to his Indian friends the other. According to Foreman, he was again making plans for locating Creeks in Texas in 1837.[18]

Austin returned to Texas from his Mexican imprisonment on September 1, 1835. At Brazoria, a week later, he declared himself in favor of the holding of a consultation, and public opinion began to crystallize. Sentiment had changed sufficiently in Nacogdoches for a mass meeting on September 14 to discuss the advisability of holding a consultation. Houston was chairman of the mass meeting.[19] He was convinced, by October 5, that war in Texas was inevitable and wrote Isaac Parker that volunteers from the United States would receive liberal bounties of land if they joined Texans to support the Mexican Constitution of 1824 and put down the centralist usurper. As courier, Parker gave wide circulation in the United States to the Houston letter and to the news that Cós had arrived in Texas with four hundred troops.[20] On October 6, Houston was nominated commander in chief of the troops of the Department of Nacogdoches. In that capacity, on October 8, he issued a proclamation for volunteers, ordered organization of the troops into companies of fifty

[16] Moseley Baker to Houston, October, 1844 (typescript in Archives Collection, University of Texas Library).
[17] Houston and others to Jackson, September 11, 1835, *Writings*, I, 299–301; Yoakum, *History of Texas*, I, 328 n.
[18] Foreman, *Pioneer Days in the Early Southwest*, 206.
[19] Louis Wiltz Kemp, *Signers of the Texas Declaration of Independence*, 178.
[20] Houston to Parker, October 5, 1835, *Writings*, I, 302.

under elected officers, and declared: "The morning of glory is dawning upon us. The work of liberty has begun."[21]

The Consultation met at Columbia on October 16 and 17, 1835, and then moved to San Felipe for a session from November 1 to November 14. Houston, as a delegate from Nacogdoches, took an active part in the proceedings. He served on the select committee on Indian relations, moved a resolution of thanks for the volunteers arriving from New Orleans, recommended resolutions of thanks to Austin, James Bowie, and James W. Fannin for their activities in behalf of Texas at Bexar, and commended the General Council for its able discharge of duties. On November 3 he was selected the Nacogdoches representative on the committee appointed to make declarations of the causes that impelled the Texans to take up arms.[22] The resulting Declaration of November 7, 1835, in setting up a state government under the Mexican Constitution of 1824, was a conservative move designed to win support of Mexican liberals and give Texas time to recruit troops and resources. While the declaration was in preparation, Gail Borden, Jr., wrote from San Felipe to Austin, then in command of the Texas Army outside of San Antonio: "Had a conversation with Genl. Houston today—I believe he has the interest of our country at heart. He made the best speech yesterday I ever heard; the whole tenour of it went to harmonize the feelings of the people and to produce unanimity of sentiment."[23]

The provisional government set up by the Consultation consisted of a legislative body, called the General Council, and a governor. Henry Smith was made governor. On November 12, on motion of Merriweather W. Smith, the body elected Houston major general of the Texas Army, and Houston made an eloquent address of thanks.[24] His first action as general was to offer James W. Fannin the post of inspector general. Then, constantly emphasizing the words *munitions* and *discipline*, the

---

[21] *Ibid.*, 303–305.

[22] *Telegraph and Texas Register*, November 7, 1835.

[23] Borden to Austin, November 5, 1835, Eugene C. Barker (ed.), *The Austin Papers*, III, 238.

[24] Kemp, *Signers of the Texas Declaration of Independence*, 178. According to Moseley Baker, the Consultation's election of Houston was unexpected and unpopular to the degree that the volunteer army could hardly believe it. According to Mirabeau B. Lamar, the Consultation would have elected Austin governor rather than Smith had it not been for Houston's opposition. That opposition was supposedly based on the fact that Austin, on November 3, wrote the Council to get some general of high military standing and integrity in the United States—one who would have the confidence of the people in Texas—since Houston had declared he would not have the command. See Baker to Houston, October, 1844, cited in n. 16 above, and C. A. Gulick, Jr., and others (eds.), *The Papers of Mirabeau Buonaparte Lamar*, VI, 173. Hereinafter cited as *Lamar Papers*.

commander set up headquarters at San Felipe for organization of the army. From one friend he solicited cash, for with that Texas could never be conquered by the Mexicans; to another he wrote that 3,500 volunteers would be accepted; from the government he asked immediate organization of the army, appointment of officers, establishment of bounties, attractions to volunteers, and contracts for supplies. He urged the governor to appoint army officers soon, declaring that union and confidence and a generous support of the army would achieve success but that his military responsibility would be diminished in the same degree in which proper means were withheld from him.[25]

On December 8, 1835, Houston appointed Almanzon Huston quartermaster general and sent him a list of equipment to be bought in New Orleans: lead, tomahawks, flour, brogans, soap, tobacco, and whiskey. The commander doubtless recalled his old days in the quartermaster's department at Nashville. On December 11 he requested a judge advocate general to be appointed to his staff, and by December 12 he was able to issue a proclamation listing bounties to be given for military service and calling for five thousand volunteers.[26] Governor Smith made favorable reports on Houston's bold and manly appeal and wrote Leonard Groce that in his speech on the fall of Bexar and the death of Ben Milam, Houston was "felicitous quite beyond himself."[27] The Governor, on December 12, was asked to order Houston to Washington-on-the-Brazos to recruit the army. D. C. Barrett became judge advocate general, and Wyatt Hanks, although he had made personal remarks against Houston and as chairman of the military committee had blocked army organization, was appointed army sutler on January 9, 1836. Frustrated in his organization of the regular army, Houston was further hampered by the General Council's creation of too many independent military units: a corps of rangers, a militia, an auxiliary volunteer corps, a legion of cavalry, and an "Army of Reserve."[28] He left San Felipe for Washington on December 23, 1835, and remained there until January 8, 1836. He reported a dull Christmas season and no fun on New Year's—"miserably cool and sober."

[25] Houston to Fannin, November 13, 1835; to Anderson Hutchinson, November 30, 1835; to Thomas Hughes, December 4, 1835; and to Henry Smith, December 6, 1835, *Writings*, I, 305–13.

[26] Houston to D. C. Barrett, December 11, 1835, and to the Citizens of Texas, December 12, 1835, *Writings*, I, 314–18; Houston to Almanzon Huston, December 8, 1835, *ibid.*, IV, 12–14.

[27] Smith to Groce, December 24, 1835, James Harper Starr Papers, No. 738.

[28] Ralph W. Steen, "Analysis of the Work of the General Council, 1835–1836," *Southwestern Historical Quarterly*, XLI (1937/38), 330–42.

What was happening meantime to the Texas Army? A volunteer force had won the Battle of Gonzales on October 2, 1835. After Austin took command at Gonzales, he and the volunteers moved towards San Antonio on October 12. Austin remained in command until November 24, when Edward Burleson was elected to succeed him. Austin, William H. Wharton, and Branch T. Archer were sent by the provisional government as commissioners to secure aid in the United States: a loan, a navy, supplies, sympathy, troops, and possibly annexation. The army under Burleson had skirmishes at Mission Concepción and an encounter with the Mexicans called the "Grass Fight"; then, sparked by Ben Milam, a relatively small detachment got into San Antonio, conducted a siege from December 5 to December 10, 1835, captured the city, and forced Cós to capitulate and agree to withdraw Mexican troops from Texas. Goliad had already been captured; for a time there were no Mexican troops on Texas soil.

Instead of using the respite for organization, training, and discipline against the inevitable Mexican invasion, the Texas Army practically evaporated, and the Texas government deteriorated. Many of the soldiers had to return home to see about their families. Other troops at Bexar were persuaded by F. W. Johnson and Dr. James Grant that offense was the best defense and that co-operation with north Mexican liberals also opposed to Santa Anna, particularly an invasion of Mexico and seizure of Matamoros, was the proper course for Texas. The weakness and indefinite organization of the Texas provisional government not only made it incapable of decisive action but split it into irreconcilable factions. Smith, bitterly anti-Mexican, even to so-called "liberal" Mexicans, was opposed to the Matamoros Expedition, as was Houston. The Council approved the move on Mexico. Eventually the Council deposed Smith and named J. W. Robinson acting governor in his place, but Smith refused to surrender the governorship. The harassed commander in chief, without a staff, without supplies, without clear-cut demarcation between volunteers and regulars, had his problems further complicated. When he learned that Colonel J. C. Neill had been left to hold Bexar with only eighty men, some sick and all without supplies, Houston wrote to Smith in despair: "What will the world think of the authorities of Texas? Prompt, decided, and honest independence is all that can save them."[29] Austin had also arrived at a belief in "honest independence" and on January 7, 1836, wrote Houston from New Orleans: "I can only say that, with the information now before me, I am in favor of an immediate

---

[29] Houston to Smith, January 6, 1836, *Writings*, I, 333.

declaration of independence."³⁰ It was almost two months, however, before a Texas convention was scheduled to meet.

Houston left Washington-on-the-Brazos to join the army on January 8, 1836, arrived at Goliad on January 14, and the next day addressed the soldiers there to urge the severing of any last links with Mexico. He sent Bowie back to Bexar with orders to blow up the Alamo and destroy the post, for Neill had warned that a Mexican army was advancing into Texas. Hugh Love was sent to Nacogdoches to raise an auxiliary force of friendly Indians. Houston went on to Refugio but found the officers absent and no supplies available. When Francis W. Johnson arrived at Refugio with the news that the Council had deposed Smith and made James Fannin the actual head of the army, Houston wrote Smith that the powers granted Fannin, plus Fannin's assurances to his troops that they would be paid with enemy spoils, made the Matamoros campaign a piratical and predatory war destined for inevitable failure. Houston's action at Goliad and Refugio reduced the size of the force willing to proceed on the Mexican expedition, and M. Hawkins wrote J. W. Robinson that "the whole army is delighted with Houston who met the shock of disorganizers at La Bahia, with firmness and success."³¹

By January 30, 1836, Houston was back at Washington. Two days later he was defeated as a delegate from Nacogdoches to the convention scheduled to meet at Washington in March and declare independence, but he was elected a delegate from the Refugio district.³² His place as a delegate secure, he turned his attention to Indian matters. On November 13, 1835, the Consultation declared that the Cherokee Indians had derived just claims to land from Mexico and pledged the Texas public faith to support that claim. The General Council, on December 17, appointed Houston, John Forbes, and John Cameron to treat with the Cherokee and associated bands. Back from Refugio, Houston was granted a furlough from the army and by February 5, 1836, was in Nacogdoches when he wrote the Cherokee chief, John Bowl, that Henry Rueg, the political chief at Nacogdoches, requested the Indian representatives to come in for a conference. On his way to the Indian parley, Houston met William Fairfax Gray, by whom he sent a memorandum back to Governor Smith.³³ At Bowl's village, Houston and Forbes and eight chiefs made

³⁰ *Austin Papers*, III, 298–99.
³¹ Hawkins to Robinson, *Lamar Papers*, I, 307.
³² Kemp, *Signers of the Texas Declaration of Independence*, 178; *Lamar Papers*, V, 375.
³³ William Fairfax Gray, *From Virginia to Texas, 1835: Diary of Col. Wm. F. Gray Giving Details of His Journey to Texas and Return in 1835–1836 and Second Journey to Texas in 1837*, 100.

a treaty which provided for firm and lasting peace between the provisional government and the Indians, set aside land in northeast Texas as tribal property to be governed by tribal law, and provided for the establishment of Indian agencies. The *Telegraph and Texas Register* wrote that the commission which effected a permanent and good understanding with the Indians did their country a service deserving the gratitude of every citizen.[34]

On February 29, W. F. Gray was at Washington-on-the-Brazos, where the delegates to the convention were arriving hourly and where he recorded: "Gen'l Houston's arrival has created more sensation than that of any other man. He is evidently the people's man, and seems to take pains to ingratiate himself with everybody. He is much broken in appearance, but has still a fine person and courtly manner."[35]

When the convention met, on March 1, 1836, in an unfinished building in the raw new town on the Brazos, Santa Anna's army was besieging fewer than two hundred men under Travis at the Alamo, and José Urrea's troops were advancing on the force at Goliad. On March 2, Houston's forty-third birthday, the independence of Texas was declared, and that afternoon Houston issued a proclamation of the enemy occupation of Bexar and called on the citizens of Texas to rally. On March 4, on motion of James Collinsworth, Houston was appointed major general of the Army of the Republic of Texas, regular, volunteer, and militia. He was to take immediate command, to organize the army, and to retain command until suspended by order of a *de facto* government under a constitutional provision.[36] On March 6, before he could sign the Declaration of Independence, Houston left the convention en route to San Antonio, the day that the Alamo fell. He had opposed a motion of Robert Potter that the convention adjourn to march to relief of the Alamo, arguing that the government must be organized in order to win outside respect and conduct an efficient defensive war.[37]

The *Telegraph and Texas Register* gave the commander a vote of confidence.

No general has ever had more to do. At this time, like the turn out last fall, our citizens are rushing to the field without any other officer than a captain. We believe, however, that an organization will be speedily effected under the direction of Genl. Houston, whose experience renders him eminently qualified in the discharge of so arduous a duty; and it is hoped, that every officer and

[34] *Writings*, I, 355–60; *Telegraph and Texas Register*, February 27, 1836.
[35] Gray, *From Virginia to Texas*, 121.
[36] Second Commission as Commander in Chief, *Writings*, I, 361.
[37] Lester, *Life of Sam Houston*, 90–91.

private will contribute every aid in promoting that organization so indispensable to our very existence. And we trust that our citizens at home will not presume to give orders to our army in the field, or lay out plans for the commander-in-chief. Let us suppose that *he,* on the spot, knows better the plan of attack than those in the chimney corner.[38]

Houston's plan of attack—or whether or not he had a plan of attack—has forever since remained a question of controversy. This book does not propose to consider Houston as a military strategist. He was in command at San Jacinto; the battle was won; Mexico was defeated. From that day forward, so far as the majority of Texans were concerned, he was "Old Sam Jacinto" himself. The hero of San Jacinto became a hero in the United States and a veritable legend. As the shadows lengthened, the legend grew. A hundred years after San Jacinto, Sam Houston was the personification of Texas valor in the war of independence.

The convention remained in session until March 17, writing a constitution and setting up an ad interim government to direct the Republic until the Constitution could be adopted and a regular government organized. The convention elected David G. Burnet president and Lorenzo de Zavala vice-president, and a cabinet was organized.

When Houston reached Gonzales, he found some 374 men ready to fight—psychologically ready, but with few arms, inadequate provisions, and little ammunition. At Gonzales he learned that the Alamo had fallen and that the Mexican Army was moving eastward. Decided to retreat, he reached the Colorado River with 600 men by March 17; on March 28, he was at the Brazos. As the army moved east, so did the populace, in the tragic "Runaway Scrape." And the government fled with the people —from Washington to Harrisburg and thence to Galveston Island. When Houston condemned the government for retreating, President Burnet reproved the General: "You must fight. . . . The salvation of the country depends on you doing so." Houston wrote Secretary of War Rusk on March 29: "I consulted none—I held no councils-of-war. If I err, the blame is mine."[39]

Houston, on March 11, ordered Fannin to fall back from Goliad to Guadalupe Victoria, but Fannin delayed to wait for some one-third of his men who had been detailed to warn citizens in the Refugio area. That detachment was killed or captured by José Urrea, who, on March 19, surrounded Fannin and his men on Coleto Creek and forced a surrender. Under order of Santa Anna, the Fannin command was massacred

---

[38] *Telegraph and Texas Register,* March 12, 1836.
[39] Rupert Norval Richardson, *Texas, the Lone Star State,* 132–33.

at Goliad on Palm Sunday, March 27, 1836. Houston's army was the only military unit left for Santa Anna to dispose of. From his camp west of the Brazos, Houston reported to Burnet: "I have not shrunk from any responsibility, nor will my situation allow me." Were he in striking distance, he would attack the enemy, who were on the Colorado, cautious and doing little scouting. "San Felipe," he said, "was *burned* down, tho' not by orders. It will lessen their inducements to march upon the place." He was grateful for the presence of Secretary of War Rusk and assured the President: "There will be no collision betwixt us for I am assured that we have a common object, and that is to save Texas, and repel the enemy."[40]

The Mexican troops followed Houston across the Brazos at San Felipe and proceeded east to burn Harrisburg after they arrived there too late to catch Burnet and his government. By April 20, Santa Anna was camped on the left bank of the San Jacinto River with Buffalo Bayou before him. Houston's army had crossed the Brazos on April 12 and 13 and then turned south toward Harrisburg. With some 900 troops as against 1,300 to 1,500 Mexicans, he crossed south of Buffalo Bayou and faced Santa Anna. After a preliminary skirmish on April 20 and a morning of relative inactivity on April 21, the Texans, on the afternoon of April 21, made an attack and in less than half an hour, according to Houston's official report, captured 730 prisoners and killed 630 of the enemy. Nine Texans were killed and 34 were wounded. On April 22, Santa Anna was captured.[41]

That Houston's indecision before San Jacinto and the direction of his march up to April 19 were determined by the presence of United States troops on the Sabine River seems to be substantiated by a letter of April 7, written from his camp west of the Brazos, to Henry Raguet in Nacogdoches: "Don't get scared at Nacogdoches—Remember old Hickory claims Nachez [the Neches] as 'neutral Territory.'"[42] General E. P. Gaines, commanding the United States troops in the Southwest, had received word at Natchitoches, Louisiana, on April 13, 1836, of a concentration of Indians and some Mexicans in the Nacogdoches area and had requisitioned additional troops and advanced to the Sabine, but had orders not to cross that stream. Samuel P. Carson, who had been sent to solicit American aid, wrote Houston on April 14 to retreat, if necessary,

---

[40] Houston to Burnet, April 6, 1836, Burnet Papers. Quoted in part in A. M. Hobby, *Life and Times of David G. Burnet, First President of the Republic of Texas,* 28.

[41] Rupert Norval Richardson, *Texas, the Lone Star State,* 134–35.

[42] *Writings,* I, 400.

as far as the Sabine unless he was sure he could defeat the enemy or was compelled to fight. At the Sabine, said Carson, he would have plenty of volunteer troops. After receiving news of the Texas victory at San Jacinto, Gaines wrote Houston on April 25 that he would "extend . . . any act of kindness in my power, not incompatible with the laws governing the conduct of neutrals." He offered some advice: "An old soldier of your acquaintance has often taken occasion to say to young officers who were liable to be rendered inefficient by the very natural exultation which usually follows the achievement of a signal victory—*be vigilant*—be magnanimous, be just, be generous to the vanquished foe—but above all be vigilant!"[43]

To the charge that insubordination of Houston's men forced the Battle of San Jacinto, there is a possible answer in Houston's letter from Harrisburg to Henry Raguet, just two days before the battle: "We go to conquer. It is wisdom growing out of necessity to meet the enemy now; every consideration enforces it. No previous occasion would justify it. The troops are in fine spirits, and now is the time for action."[44]

After the victory at San Jacinto, Houston was the idol of the army. He remained at the battlefield until May 5, incapacitated by a shot which had shattered his right leg above the ankle. To Anna Raguet he sent the laurels of victory. On April 22, towards nightfall, the captured Santa Anna was brought to him and proposed an armistice. On April 25, Houston wrote his official report of the battle for President Burnet, appending a list of the officers and men engaged, with a commendation of their "daring intrepidity and courage." For the Secretary of War, the General prepared a memorandum of points which, to his mind, should have weight in any treaty made with Santa Anna. These points included recognition of Texas independence as the *sine qua non*, Texas limits to extend to the Rio Grande, indemnity for Texan losses, retention of Santa Anna as a hostage until ratification of the terms by the Mexican government, withdrawal of Mexican troops from the limits of Texas, restoration of property, cessation of all hostilities, and sending of agents to the United States to secure that country's mediation in affairs between Mexico and Texas.[45]

In accordance with the armistice, Santa Anna had ordered Vicente Filisola to retire to Bexar and José Urrea to fall back to Victoria. On May 14, 1836, at Velasco, the public and the secret treaty negotiated with

[43] Thomas Jefferson Rusk Papers, May 2, 1836.

[44] Houston to Raguet, April 19, 1836, *Writings*, I, 413.

[45] Houston to Burnet, April 25, 1836, and to Rusk, May 3, 1836, *Writings*, I, 416–20, 425.

Santa Anna incorporated many of the terms of the Houston memorandum. Houston himself was not at Velasco. He bade his officers farewell on May 5 and transferred active command to Rusk; then, ordered by his physician to go to New Orleans for medical care, he was a somewhat unwelcome passenger on the vessel *Yellow Stone* as it conveyed the ad interim government and Santa Anna from the battlefield to Galveston. Six years later John A. Quitman recalled some of the details of the boat trip.

I well recollect a long conversation which took place between you and the President Santa Anna, in which I also participated, on our way up the Buffalo, at the time of the change of your encampment from San Jacinto. By your invitation I had a seat in the boat which conveyed you and the dictator to the new camp. After some compliments upon you and your brave men, he remarked that he was now persuaded that Texas, if reconquered by the power of Mexico, could never be retained; that the cost of such an attempt to Mexico would greatly exceed the value of the acquisition; that it would be policy in Mexico to suffer an independent nation to grow up between her and the great grasping power of the United States, and that, should his influence ever prevail in Mexico, he would urge the recognition of the independence of Texas; that all must be sensible that such was the true policy of Mexico, and that no obstacle could be thrown in the way but what might grow out of national pride.⁴⁸

From Galveston, Santa Anna was taken to Velasco for signing of the treaties. The public treaty provided for the cessation of hostilities, restoration of property, and retirement of Mexican troops beyond the Rio Grande. The secret treaty was based on Santa Anna's promise to use his influence to obtain the recognition of Texas independence if he were allowed to return to Mexico. He was to order the troops to leave Texas, and to prepare the Mexican government to receive commissioners for the negotiation of differences, recognition of independence, and a treaty of limits and commerce.

In accordance with these terms, the Texas government, on June 1, 1836, had Lorenzo de Zavala and Bailey Hardeman ready, as commissioners, to embark with Santa Anna on the *Invincible* for Vera Cruz. Mounting public opposition to Santa Anna's return to Mexico was augmented with the arrival from the United States of new volunteer troops, who joined in protest against release of the dictator and forced Burnet to require his transfer from the vessel to Quintana. The very men who had

⁴⁸ Quitman to Houston, April 7, 1842, quoted in J. F. H. Claiborne, *Life and Correspondence of John A. Quitman*, I, 193–94.

71

fought Mexicans on the principle of opposition to military dictatorship had now subordinated Texas civil government to the military. The government was powerless to enforce the Treaty of Velasco, and Mexico was given grounds to repudiate it; Santa Anna remained a prisoner.

Meanwhile, Houston was refused passage to New Orleans on a Texas naval vessal and had to go on a trading schooner, the *Flora*. From the *Flora* he wrote to the troops and to the new volunteers, urging obedience to the constituted authority and to the laws of the country. He arrived in New Orleans on May 22, 1836, and, after an operation on his leg, was cared for in the William Christy home. By June 1 he was able to sit up for a time each day and acknowledged an invitation to a public dinner with the statement that, even had his health permitted a festive occasion, he would not have felt like participating in one so long as Texas was not completely independent and free of Mexican soldiers.[47] While recuperating, he was able to transact a little business. Doubtless his expenses were sufficient that he was glad, at long last, to be employed by a land company as its attorney. John T. Mason, also in New Orleans, on June 4, 1836, wrote to Samuel Swartwout in New York:

> I wrote to you yesterday a long letter advising you that I had advanced to Genl. Houston $2000, as the advocate and agent for our land business in Texas, and gave you in detail my reasons therefor. . . . Our Surveys are all in the district between the Neches, Sabine & Red Rivers & will be embraced within the U. States if the Neches be declared the boundary. I had this in view in directing the location. . . . I think Houston will be able to get us a commissioner from the next Congress without waiting for a general land law & a regular land office—His power in Texas will be very great, & he has now a double motive in interest & friendship to give us.[48]

Mason was not the only person who was sanguine about Texas prospects. Judge John Catron wrote Andrew Jackson that he understood that Houston was going to recover from his wounds, and said of Texas: "I know not on Earth, and never have heard of, so small a community so well able to take care of itself."[49]

Houston may not have been so certain of Texas' ability to take care of itself without his presence. He left New Orleans the middle of June and by June 26 arrived at Natchitoches, where Dr. Robert Irion met him to dress his wounds. As the Houston entourage neared the Sabine River on

[47] *Writings*, I, 428–30.
[48] Mason to Swartwout, June 4, 1836, Samuel Swartwout Papers.
[49] Catron to Jackson, June 8, 1836, *Correspondence of Andrew Jackson*, V, 401.

July 2, Houston sent Sumner Bacon with a message to Richard Dunlap of Knoxville, Tennessee, that he had heard that Mexican troops were in Texas and that Dunlap should come to Texas by the quickest route.

For the traditional Fourth of July barbecue, Houston was visiting Philip Sublett and Sublett's father-in-law, Elisha Roberts, in San Augustine and was welcomed home by such Redlanders as James Bullock, Alexander Horton, Donald McDonald, and Jonas Harrison—the last dressed in brown homespun and a slouch hat as he made the welcome address, eloquent and logical, to which Houston, on crutches, replied "in his happiest manner."[60] In the midst of festivities he was planning to dispatch men to the army, if they were "useful and essential," and cautioned Henry Raguet not to mention that his wound was worse. On July 10, 1836, Houston ordered Dr. Alexander Ewing to army headquarters to organize the medical department.[61]

Houston had addressed the Ewing order to Rusk, but by July 1, Burnet and his cabinet had appointed Mirabeau B. Lamar to replace Rusk as commander of the restive Texas Army, a force greatly augmented by volunteers, short of rations, and with no visible Mexicans to fight. The army refused to accept Lamar as its general, and that despite the fact that T. Y. Buford wrote Lamar from Nacogdoches on July 11 that the Redlanders were highly pleased with his appointment.[62]

High among army grievances was the fact that Santa Anna was still a prisoner at Columbia, for the military not only wanted to have a trial and execute the General but threatened to arrest Burnet and his cabinet and give them a military trial also. Burnet then attempted diversionary tactics by making the army an offensive force and encouraging an expedition against Matamoros. On July 26, 1836, Houston informed Rusk that he had heard of the plan to try the dictator and take him to Goliad for execution but that he could not credit the rumor for it was so contrary to the true policy of Texas—a violation of the rules of civilized warfare, a disregard of national character, and a hazard to Texans held prisoner in Mexico. Santa Anna, "living and secured beyond all danger," might be of incalculable advantage to Texas in her crisis. On August 8 he again wrote to Rusk to say that he could see nothing to be gained from an expedition to Matamoros, which would be both impolitic and hazardous. On the contrary, he felt that Texas policy was "to hazard nothing" and urged: "Let us act on the defensive. If the Enemy chooses let them run

[60] Memoirs of John Salmon Ford, I, 12.
[61] *Writings*, I, 433–34.
[62] Buford to Lamar, June 11, 1836, *Lamar Papers*, I, 415.

the risk. A wise man will wait for the harvest, and prepare the reapers for it when it comes."[53]

The Houston defensive policy had its admirers in Kentucky, even if it was not without its critics at home. Joseph Ficklin wrote to Austin from Lexington that

the military feeling of the state would be most favorable for Texas if your affairs were as they were last winter. . . . The removal of *Houston* is one among the heaviest blows—The objections to Houston can *not* equal the confidence the world has in him, and the very circumstance of dismissing him proves a want of fitness in the authorities of the Country which must do the greatest injury. . . . The world is too ready to consider Texas like all new countries rash and cruel in its measures. The death of *St. Anna* would ruin your country. . . . The caution of *Houston* makes him worth all the untried men in your armies— many men may possess equal or even superior talents and still be unfit to command.[54]

Rusk, in the field with the army, wrote Houston that all the favorable tides in their affairs had been neglected and that his only hope was that the Lord would have mercy to save Texas from the enemy and the "mighty operations" of its own great men. He thought every act of the cabinet was predicated on the destruction of the army, but gave assurance: "They calculated no doubt that I would be fool enough for the sake of fame or vanity to risk all upon the hazardous attack, but in this they mistake. I have no disposition to sacrifice myself much less the Country by any fool hardy risk."[55]

The two generals were also exchanging comments on the approaching elections for officials for the Republic to replace the ad interim government. Rusk wrote:

I shall always feel under many obligations to you for your repeated evidences of friendship for me and particularly do I feel flattered that you should think me worthy of filling the Presidential Chair, but my age precludes me from running. This is an important office, not only so far as the credit of our Country is concerned abroad, but all important so far as our defence against our enemies is concerned. I would rather vote for you than any other man in the country, but we cannot spare you from the army. And as I have seen now two attempts by those holding the reigns [*sic*] of government to destroy you, I feel particularly anxious to see some man in the executive chair who will co-operate with you in the measures of defence for the country and would like

[53] Houston to Rusk, July 26 and August 8, 1836, *Writings*, I, 434–35, 436–39.
[54] Ficklin to Austin, August, 1836, *Austin Papers*, III, 426–27.
[55] Rusk to Houston, August 11 and 15, 1836, T. J. Rusk Papers.

to hear from you on this subject before the election, for the man who will in my opinion co-operate with you in the proper measures for our defence . . . I shall vote for for President."

A postscript on Rusk's August 15 letter to Houston commented: "Smith and Austin are the only Candidates out as yet for President. Smith outruns Austin here." Henry Smith was generally regarded as the candidate of the Wharton faction as opposed to the Austin faction; but Austin and Wharton, while serving as commissioners to the United States, had discarded old differences to become fast friends, and Austin actually entered the presidential race at the request of Wharton and Archer. Many newcomers to Texas did not know Austin; old and new alike had heard of "Old Sam Jacinto." At a mass meeting at the Mansion House in San Augustine on August 15, Sublett nominated Houston for president and Rusk for vice-president of the Republic." Six hundred names were signed to a communication from Columbia on August 23, declaring: "General Sam Houston is nominated as a Candidate for the Presidency. . . . No man in Texas stands so high in the United States and in Europe." That communication, published in the *Telegraph* on August 3, carried a postscript: "A Handbill, published at Brazoria, denies that Gen. Houston is a candidate, and charges the bringing of him out to a few of Austin's friends. This is not the fact—men of both parties have nominated him, and expresses have been sent to every part of Texas with the news. The people have a right to require the services of General Houston, and if elected he will serve; and that he will be elected his friends entertain no doubt."

On August 30 the *Telegraph* carried an extract from a Houston letter: "You will learn that I have yielded to the wishes of my friends in allowing my name to be run for President. The crisis requires it or I would not have yielded." The same issue of the paper carried a letter signed "Voter" which was a plea for Austin's election on the ground that, while Houston stood well as a military man and was entitled to honors of the highest order, the war was not over and Houston's services were needed in the field.

Houston, apparently, was more concerned with military campaigns than with campaigning for office. On August 29, 1836, he called on East Texas counties to organize their militia to repel a threatened Indian invasion until General Gaines could send reinforcements. Houston also authorized Daniel Parker to build a fort on the Indian frontier and or-

⁵⁶ Rusk to Houston, August 9, 1836, Houston Unpublished Correspondence.
⁵⁷ *Telegraph and Texas Register*, August 30, 1836.

dered Martin Lacey to take over the Neches Saline and work it while trading with the Indians—trading in all things except lead and liquor.[58]

Presidential candidate Austin wrote to his brother-in-law, James F. Perry, instructions for building Austin a house on the premise that he was not likely to reside in an executive mansion: "These arrangements are made on the supposition that I shall not be elected—Houston will, I am told, get all the east, and Red river now—Many of the old settlers who are too blind to see or understand their interest will vote for him, and the army I believe will go for him, at least a majority of them—So that I have a good prospect of some rest this year."[59]

Smith, more popular with the army than Austin was, refused to campaign and supported Houston, but his name remained before the people. Austin's campaign was a defensive battle against accusations, some of which were expressions of long-time discontent: that he had been implicated in the land speculations in Monclova in 1834–35 which allowed the sale of eleven hundred leagues of Texas land; that he had been unmilitary in his discipline of the army; that he was responsible for saving Santa Anna; that he had been opposed to Texas independence; and that he had not spent profitably his time as commissioner. Houston came in for criticism too: that his conduct had been cowardly in the San Jacinto campaign; that he had assumed honors to which he was not entitled; and that he was intemperate in the use of alcohol.[60]

In the election held on September 5, 1836, Houston received 5,119 votes; Smith, 743; Austin, 587; other candidates received 191 scattered votes. Rusk had withdrawn as a candidate for vice-president, and Lamar was elected to that office.

Two days after the election Houston wrote to his cousin Robert Mc-Ewen back in Nashville. He did not mention the fact that he was probably to be the president of a republic—but forwarded Santa Anna's saddle and bridle, purchased for Houston by a friend. The gifts, an evidence of grateful affection, went to the cousin with the statement that if he did not wish to keep them, he might give the bridle and saddle with its gold stirrups to General Jackson or to Dr. John Shelby.[61]

In the first few months of his presidency, when the life of the new republic was precarious in all respects, and particularly in respect to Mexican threats to make that life short, the new executive was essentially the

---

[58] *Writings*, I, 445–47.

[59] Austin to Perry, September 2, 1836, *Austin Papers*, III, 428.

[60] Nina Covington, "Presidential Campaigns of the Republic of Texas of 1836 and 1838" (M.A. thesis, University of Texas, 1929), 28–41.

[61] Houston to McEwen, September 7, 1836, *Writings*, II, 25.

commander in chief. He gave orders to the War Department concerning the army, but more often he dealt personally with army problems. His letters to Albert Sidney Johnston, to whom he wrote in December, 1836, to hasten to take his post as brigadier general "for the interest of Texas," reveal him as a general concerned with the stomach and the morale of his troops. When he heard, to his "boundless mortification and regret," of the duel between Felix Huston and Johnston, he sent two doctors with medicines for Johnston and exhorted: "Let harmony in camp be inculcated and by all means prevent duelling in the future!" When there were reports of troops "acting badly" in San Antonio, he wrote: "Let this be stopped and I *command most positively* that all ardent spirits in Bexar and on the frontier be *instantly destroyed and spilled on the ground.*" He was infuriated with stories of inadequate guards and wasted supplies, and summed up his concern: "My anxiety has been intense and must continue so until I can see the country tranquil."[62]

With recognition of Texas by the United States and the realization that Mexican threats were chiefly verbal, a degree of tranquillity was achieved. Houston could give up the role of commanding general to devote time to other problems of the President of Texas.

[62] Houston to Albert Sidney Johnston, December 22, 1836, and January 26, March 1, 21, 31, and April 8, 1837, William Preston Johnston and Albert Sidney Johnston Papers.

Houston's Republic

THE AD INTERIM GOVERNMENT of Texas existed from March 16 to October 22, 1836. The same election which made Houston president also adopted the Constitution, which provided that the first president should serve two years, that the presidential term thereafter should be three years, and that the president might not succeed himself. Houston's first term lasted from October 22, 1836, to December 10, 1838. During that administration there were sessions of the First and Second Congresses, and Houston's term overlapped the Third Congress between November 6 and December 10, 1838. From November 11, 1839, to February 5, 1840, and again from November 2, 1840, to February 5, 1841, he represented San Augustine in the House of Representatives of the Fourth and Fifth Congresses during Lamar's presidency. The second Houston administration, December 12, 1841, to December 9, 1844, encompassed the Sixth, Seventh, and

Eighth Congresses and the first seven days of the Ninth Congress. Houston was therefore directly concerned with each session of the Congress of the Republic, even when that concern was sending veto after veto to a legislative body with which he might be violently at odds. It was not merely idle verbiage when the Republic came to be known abroad as "Mr. Houston's Texas," especially after C. E. Lester published *Sam Houston and His Republic* in 1846. The designation was jeered but ruefully admitted by Houston's bitterest enemies. In March, 1847, Lamar, in commenting to Burnet on the Lester book—and on Houston as a "demented monster" and a "bloated mass of iniquity"—wrote: "*His* republic! That is true; for the country literally belongs to him and the people [are] his slaves. I can regard Texas as very little more than *Big Drunk's* big Ranch."[1]

The First Congress convened at Columbia on October 3, 1836, and Houston arrived at the capital six days later. Although the date for installation of the new government was set for the second Monday in December, Burnet, at outs with Congress, resigned on October 22, 1836, and that afternoon at four o'clock Houston took his oath of office and delivered his inaugural message. Lamar later recalled, as Burnet's friend and Houston's foe, that Houston was so anxious to take office that Burnet's friends in Congress advised the incumbent to retire or be pushed out. "That little month Houston could not wait; nor could the hungry expectants brook delay, who were looking forward for presidential favors."[2]

The inaugural speech, extempore according to H. S. Thrall, proclaimed: "Futurity has locked up the destiny which awaits our people. ... A country situated like ours is environed with difficulties, its administration is fraught with perplexities."[3] Then the President set about establishing a framework of government for that struggling new country which occupied a "place somewhere in the background of the family of nations,"[4] working without even an authentic copy of the Constitution and with government archives in the form of loose papers indiscriminately tossed together in an old trunk.[5]

In submitting his first cabinet nominations to the Senate on October 26, Houston stated that, with total disregard to personal preference, he had selected the men whose talents he thought best suited to furtherance

---

[1] *Lamar Papers*, IV, Part I, 165.
[2] *Ibid.*, I, 528.
[3] Inaugural Address, October 22, 1836, *Writings*, I, 449.
[4] E. T. Miller, *A Financial History of Texas*, 18.
[5] Homer S. Thrall, "Sam Houston," *Round Table*, IV (July, 1892), 108.

of the interests of the country: Austin as secretary of state, Henry Smith as secretary of the treasury, Thomas J. Rusk as secretary of war, and S. Rhoads Fisher as secretary of the navy. The portfolio of attorney general was declined by James Collinsworth, and that place went to James Pinckney Henderson. Austin accepted his position on condition that he might retire should his health and situation require his resignation, and wrote to his cousin Mary Austin Holley: "I am happy to inform you that everything is going on well. All the temporary excitements of the past have entirely subsided—Houston goes into office under favorable auspices and harmony and union is the order of the day."[6]

The outstanding problems which had to be solved by the administrations of the Republic included establishing the machinery of government; financing that Republic with an exhausted treasury which had neither money nor credit; coping with the Indian problem; disposing of the one significant asset of the country, its public lands; establishing a system of public education; providing military defense against Mexico, which, while unable to make good its threats to reconquer Texas, never recognized the Republic and always constituted a menace; and securing recognition of other nations. While those problems were in process of solution, the population grew from about thirty thousand in 1836 to some one hundred thousand in 1846, a population "not timid in any of its governmental undertakings."[7]

At the beginning of the first Houston administration, Smith presided over an empty treasury. The public debt contracted during the Revolution amounted to about $1,250,000 and was to grow larger, for, even though the poverty of the government was embarrassing, expenses of the first administration amounted to almost $2,000,000. A tariff produced the greatest amount of revenue; tonnage dues, port fees, a direct property tax, poll taxes, business taxes, and land fees were imposed but netted little income. In consequence the government issued paper money in the form of promissory notes, which depreciated, by the summer of 1838, to sixty-five cents on the dollar. The Lamar administration saw a vast increase in spending and a widening difference between income and expenditure. Tariff duties were lowered to practically a free-trade basis; direct taxes and license taxes, both difficult to collect, were paid in depreciated currency. New non-interest-bearing treasury notes, called "redbacks," were issued in 1839, 1840, and 1841, and by November, 1841, had depreciated to fifteen cents on the dollar. Lamar's aggressive policy

---

[6] Austin to Houston, October 31, 1836, and to Holley, November 7, 1836, *Austin Papers*, III, 444, 452.
[7] Miller, *Financial History of Texas*, 18.

towards Mexico and the Indians added to the public debt, which by the end of his term amounted to some $7,000,000. Houston practiced drastic economy during his second presidency, abolishing offices, paring wages, and restricting military expenses to the support of a few ranger companies. Exchequer bills replaced other paper money but depreciated in value despite their limited issue. During the last part of Houston's second term and during the Anson Jones administration, revenue and expenditure were almost balanced, but no interest could be paid on the public debt, which by 1846 was about $12,000,000.[8]

The estimated area of Texas at the beginning of the Republic was 242,594,560 acres, chiefly unoccupied and unclaimed.[9] Despite Houston's vetoes, the Congress passed a comprehensive land-office act and provided for the opening of the land offices which had been closed by the Permanent Council and the Consultation. Little of the 180,000,000 acres of public land could be sold, even at fifty cents an acre, because so much land was given away in continuing the policy of granting free land to immigrants as well as paying for military services in bounties and donation grants.[10] Issuance of fraudulent land certificates was a contributing cause of the contest in East Texas between the "Regulators" and the "Moderators" which began in 1839, broke into open warfare in 1842, and was finally put down by Houston's calling out the militia to suppress both factions in 1844.[11] The policy of pre-empting land for settlers began on December 21, 1838, with the granting of 160 acres to settlers along the military road from Red River to the Rio Grande on condition of cultivation for two years. Grants made in 1841 for settlement along the military road required five years' occupation.[12] The Homestead Exemption Act of 1839, which provided immunity for a citizen's homestead and tools against seizure for debt, was passed to encourage colonization and guarantee to the settlers equipment essential for living. Acts providing for endowment of public education passed during the Lamar administration set aside four leagues of land for each county for primary schools and fifty leagues to establish two universities.

Laws passed in December, 1836, called for a chain of blockhouses,

[8] Rupert Norval Richardson, *Texas, the Lone Star State*, 149, 155, 160; Ralph W. Steen, *History of Texas*, 179–83.

[9] Miller, *Financial History of Texas*, 51.

[10] Rupert Norval Richardson, *Texas, the Lone Star State*, 146; Steen, *History of Texas*, 183–84.

[11] Yoakum, *History of Texas*, II, 438–40; Proclamation against the Regulators, January 31, 1842, *Writings*, II, 459–61; To the Texas Congress, December 4, 1844, *ibid.*, IV, 397.

[12] Miller, *Financial History of Texas*, 52–53.

forts, and trading houses to protect the frontier from Indian depredations. By keeping troops out of the Indian country, Houston managed to avoid serious Indian difficulties, despite Cherokee threats after the Texas Senate refused to ratify the treaty, made during the Revolution, granting that tribe permanent title to their lands. The beginning of the Lamar administration found the Indians restless from the continued white encroachment, and the Lamar policy of expulsion or extermination resulted in driving the Cherokees from Texas after the Cherokee War of 1839. Campaigns against the Comanches continued until the close of 1840. Lamar's policy had been effective; Houston's appears to have been more successful and less costly. Houston's defense of his Indian friends was to be a source of much newspaper comment and of bitter debate in the Texas Congress.[13]

The abrupt end of the Texas Revolution came while many volunteer troops were en route to Texas and others were yet being recruited. With continued rumors of Mexican invasion and threats of Indian hostilities, Congress passed much defense legislation, and Houston displayed great personal concern with army movements. As invasion threats diminished and the President was without funds to pay an army, particularly an army composed predominantly of adventurers and soldiers of fortune restlessly clamoring to fight Mexico, Houston was more interested in disposing of the troops he had than in raising more. This he did in 1837 by "a judicious system of furloughing," described by Francis Lubbock as "one of the most marked evidences of statecraft I have ever known."[14] However judicious the move, it antagonized many soldiers and some of the army officers and was one of the causes of unfavorable criticism of Houston.

In 1841, Lamar dispatched the Texan Santa Fe Expedition, and in retaliation Santa Anna, again heading the Mexican government, sent a Mexican army under Rafael Vásquez to Texas in March, 1842. San Antonio, Goliad, and Refugio were captured before the Mexicans retired. Houston, now in his second term, declared a state of emergency, proclaimed a blockade of Mexican ports, and ordered the Texas government moved to Houston. The Republic had no standing army, but the militia flocked to San Antonio. Congress assembled on June 27, 1842, and voted to declare war on Mexico, but it had nothing except land for meeting the expenses of a war, and Houston vetoed the declaration giving

---

[13] *Ibid.*, 21; Rupert Norval Richardson, *Texas, the Lone Star State,* 155.

[14] C. W. Raines (ed.), *Six Decades in Texas or Memoirs of Francis Richard Lubbock, Governor of Texas in War Time, 1861–63: A Personal Experience in Business, War, and Politics,* 74–75. Hereinafter cited as Lubbock, *Six Decades in Texas.*

him dictatorial powers. His delay in calling Congress, his proclamation of April 25, 1842, against self-appointed agents' raising troops in the United States, his refusal to reveal his military plans, and his veto of the bill for offensive war the day before Congress adjourned—all supplied fuel for his opponents.[15] A comment in a report to the Senate on July 18, 1842, on insubordination and mutiny among foreign volunteers elicited a bitter letter from Jeremiah Clemens to the effect that the executive had offered to those volunteers in return for efficient services not only no supplies but "wanton, unprovoked, unmanly insult, added to gross injury and injustice."[16]

In contrast, Andrew Jackson had only the highest commendation for his military protégé when he wrote to approve the veto of the war bill, by which "you have saved the country, and yourself from disgrace."[17]

In September, 1842, General Adrian Woll and a Mexican army again captured San Antonio, and again the Texas Militia gathered. Alexander Somervell, on October 3, was ordered by Houston to take command of the Texas troops and advance to the Rio Grande. After taking Laredo in December, 1842, the Texans were disbanded and ordered home on the grounds that no invasion of Mexico should be attempted without a more adequate force. Some three hundred of the militia, eager for a punitive expedition into Mexico, organized themselves under W. S. Fisher, crossed the Rio Grande, and were captured at Mier on December 26, 1842. Their long confinement in Perote Prison before they were released through the intervention of the United States minister to Mexico, Waddy Thompson, and British diplomatic agents caused much bitterness against Houston, who disclaimed any governmental responsibility on the grounds that the men went on the expedition to Mier without orders. Antiadministration newspapers in 1843–44 carried abuse and slander against Houston, abuse which culminated in Thomas Jefferson Green's *Journal of the Texian Expedition against Mier*, published in 1845. Whether or not Houston's efforts to secure the release of the Mier prisoners through diplomatic channels were the best possible means to be employed, he was powerless to use military assistance because of lack of finances.[18]

Houston's policy with regard to the Texas Navy also won him enemies. Contracted for during the first Houston administration, the seven-

[15] To the House of Representatives, July 22, 1842, *Writings*, III, 116–24.

[16] Clemens to Houston, August 6, 1842, Houston Unpublished Correspondence, III.

[17] Jackson to Houston, August 17, 1842, *Writings*, III, 124–25.

[18] Houston to Elliot, January 24, 1843, *ibid.*, 299–303.

vessel fleet was delivered during Lamar's term and was commanded by Edwin Ward Moore. In the summer of 1840 three of the Texas ships aided the rebels in Yucatán in revolt against Mexico, and in September, 1841, part of the Texas Navy was rented to Yucatán to harass Mexican shipping. While the vessels were at New Orleans for repairs, Houston proclaimed a blockade of Mexican ports and ordered Moore to use the fleet to enforce the blockade. Unable to pay for the repairs at New Orleans, Moore could not obey the instructions, and it was not long before Houston issued secret orders for the sale of the fleet. Moore, who had previously quarreled with the President over navy administration and funds, slipped the vessels away to Yucatán, with the result that Houston declared the commander and his men pirates and ordered them back to Texas for trial. Moore was acquitted, but the quarrel and the trial, all aired in detail in Texas and New Orleans newspapers, added to the criticism directed at Houston, the "Talleyrand of the Brazos."[19]

In foreign relations, as in Indian policy and in finances, the two Houston administrations were in striking contrast to the Lamar administration sandwiched parenthetically between them. One of the first problems facing Houston was the disposal of Santa Anna, who, even before Houston's inauguration, proposed that he be permitted to go to the United States to interview the American government on the diplomatic issues of annexation. Houston had scant hope of the General's beneficent influence on negotiations in Washington, but he probably thought the erstwhile dictator might have a nuisance value in disturbing Mexican politics. As W. B. Lewis quoted Jackson to Houston: "He *said he had no doubt but it was the best thing the Government of Texas could do, as it would give the Mexicans employment at home, instead of making war upon their neighbors.*"[20]

The Texas Senate demanded copies of all correspondence concerning Santa Anna, finally decided that the President was vested with the custody and disposal of prisoners of war, and ultimately acquiesced in Houston's decision to send Santa Anna under escort to Washington, D.C. Houston's letters of introduction of Santa Anna to Jackson and to Daniel Webster were dated November 20, 1836.[21]

[19] For a detailed study of the Texas Navy see Jim Dan Hill, *The Texas Navy in Forgotten Battles and Shirtsleeve Diplomacy.*

[20] Lewis to Houston, October 27, 1836, New York Public Library (photostatic copy in Archives Collection, University of Texas Library).

[21] E. W. Winkler (ed.), *Secret Journals of the Senate of the Republic of Texas, 1836–1845,* 13–14, 21; C. H. Van Tyne (ed.), *The Letters of Daniel Webster, from Documents Owned Principally by the New Hampshire Historical Society,* 209.

After several interviews with President Jackson, Santa Anna returned to Mexico to seclusion and a brief unpopularity and retirement. Although Mexico refused to recognize the Treaties of Velasco or the independence of Texas and continued to threaten invasion, the threats remained in the rumor category—a fact highly advantageous to a Texas without an army and sufficiently busy with domestic concerns. Then the Lamar administration, thinking· in terms of a Texas extended to the Pacific Ocean, reversed Houston's passive policy towards Mexico and began an active effort to secure Mexican recognition of Texas by combining diplomacy with feints of the Texas Navy against Mexican shipping and ports and use of the navy to aid the Yucatán Rebellion. Finally Lamar, despite the refusal of the Texas Congress to authorize such a move, sent out the Texan Santa Fe Expedition to establish title to the area of New Mexico east of the Rio Grande and claimed by the Republic of Texas as within its jurisdiction. The survivors of that captured expedition were confined in prison in Mexico when Houston began his second term. In retaliation for the attempt to establish title over Santa Fe, Mexican troops invaded Texas twice in 1842, with the resulting tragedy of the Mier Expedition. However many calls he issued for troops to allay the panic of Texas citizens, Houston apparently never felt any real fear of Mexican invasion and was determined to keep the situation in the status of, in modern parlance, a "cold war." In the spring of 1843 he authorized an expedition against Mexico, but that Snively Expedition, sent to intercept trade between Missouri and Santa Fe, was frustrated not by Mexicans but by the United States Army.

The Republic of Texas made a trade convention with Great Britain in 1838, and in 1839 secured recognition from France and a French commercial treaty. In 1840, England made three treaties with Texas: one concerning commerce and navigation, one agreeing to mediate with Mexico for independence, and one giving Great Britain greater liberty in efforts to suppress the foreign slave trade. The Netherlands and Belgium also recognized the Texas Republic. After the Woll invasion of 1842, Houston sought to persuade the governments of Great Britain, France, and the United States to require Mexico either to recognize Texas or to make war by "official" rules. Nothing came of his efforts.

In 1843, Santa Anna sent James W. Robinson home from prison to Texas bearing an offer of peace on condition of Texas recognition of Mexican sovereignty. Houston had not the slightest intention of accepting any such offer but thought that publication of the Santa Anna proposition might help to secure liberation of the Texas prisoners in Mexico

85

while he bargained for time.[22] On June 15, 1843, therefore, he proclaimed a truce with Mexico, an action which his enemies chose to interpret as accedence to Santa Anna's demands. The opposition to the truce was simultaneous with attacks on the President for his charges against Moore, his inconsistency with regard to the army, his alleged subservience to the British, and his reported views in favor of the abolition of slavery. Uncommunicative himself, Houston must have been doubly appreciative of the few words of approval that he received, such as a letter from Francis Lubbock commending him on his policy towards Mexico and expressing faith in his achievements.[23]

To carry out conditions of the truce, Houston, on September 4, 1843, ordered release of any Mexican prisoners held in Texas in return for Santa Anna's release of the Mier prisoners. George W. Hockley and Samuel M. Williams were appointed commissioners to Mexico to work out terms of an armistice, but before the armistice could be arranged, Mexico was antagonized by the news of the full-swing negotiations in Washington, D.C., for an annexation treaty and threatened the United States with a declaration of war if annexation took place. The Texas commissioners finally signed an armistice on February 18, 1844, but since the document referred to the Republic as a "department of Mexico," Houston ignored it. As he wrote to Isaac Van Zandt and J. P. Henderson: "I did not deem it necessary to take any action upon the agreement signed by our Coms. further than to reject it silently."[24]

As soon as Mexico heard of the rejection of the annexation treaty by the United States Senate, Santa Anna made abortive plans for another raid into Texas and, on June 19, 1844, had Adrian Woll notify Houston that hostilities between Texas and Mexico were resumed, partially because of the "perfidious conduct of the said inhabitants of Texas towards Mexico" in regard to the armistice.[25] The Mexican dictator finally liberated the last of the Mier prisoners on September 16, 1844. During the Anson Jones administration, England and France made final desperate efforts to prevent the annexation of Texas to the United States by securing a Mexican treaty for Texas guaranteeing her independence on condition that she should never unite with the United States. Texas chose annexation and not the treaty.

So much for government problems during the period of Mr. Hous-

[22] W. D. Miller to J. W. Robinson, August 23, 1848, Washington D. Miller Papers.
[23] Lubbock to Houston, July 14, 1843, Houston Unpublished Correspondence, IV.
[24] Houston to Van Zandt and Henderson, May 10, 1844, *Writings*, IV, 318.
[25] Yoakum, *History of Texas*, II, 434.

ton's Republic. The time of that Republic also brought decided changes in Houston's living conditions and personal life.

When the Republic set up its official housekeeping, its officers were provided poor accommodations at Columbia: an unfurnished house of two rooms for the Congress, and unfinished and unfurnished houses for the President and his cabinet.[26] For an honor guest such as General Felix Huston (whom Houston entertained while he secretly sent the General's army on furlough) the President gave up his bed and slept on the floor.[27]

From Columbia, Houston wrote Anna Raguet to send poetry for her appraisal, verses that promised to obey her every mandate and lay the laurels of victory at her feet.[28] In the same letter he intimated that the seat of government would soon be moved to Groce's Retreat, but the Retreat was not chosen, and Houston wrote Miss Anna that he would have to accept the city of Houston as the capital. As for himself, he wanted to go to Nacogdoches to see if his tenants had built him comfortable cabins and perhaps "look out for a 'spare rib' to appropriate to myself."[29] He was still at Columbia, however, when the first anniversary of the Declaration of Independence was celebrated at Washington-on-the-Brazos with a procession of citizens from Roberts' Hotel to Gray's "new building" for a dinner and ball. Robert M. Stevenson, vice-president of the celebration, presented a toast: "Uncle Sam's big corn field and his son Sam's cotton patch, May they soon be united in one big plantation." Stephen R. Roberts proposed a toast to "Sam Houston: the man who is contented to be called Sam, and who has proved a Sam's-son to the enemies of Texas."[30]

Between April 12 and April 17, 1837, the capital was moved to Houston. The next month John James Audubon, the ornithologist, visited the new town on the bayou and recorded in his diary his visit in the Governor's Mansion, a two-room log cabin with a "dogtrot." "His Excellency," dressed in "velvet coat and trousers trimmed with broad gold lace," was a considerate host.[31]

One of the members of the staff who worked with Houston in those primitive surroundings was Yale graduate Dr. Ashbel Smith, who was

[26] Thrall, "Sam Houston," *Round Table*, IV (July, 1892), 110.
[27] Gray, *From Virginia to Texas*, 218.
[28] Houston to Anna Raguet, January 1, 1837, *Writings*, II, 29–32.
[29] Houston to Anna Raguet, January 29, 1837, *ibid.*, 43–44.
[30] *Telegraph and Texas Register*, March 21, 1837.
[31] Quoted in Alfred M. Williams, *Sam Houston and the War of Independence in Texas*, 246–47.

persuaded by James Pinckney Henderson to transfer from North Carolina to Texas and who, on June 7, 1837, was nominated by Houston as surgeon general of the Texas Army. Years later his fellow physician, John H. Bauer, reminisced to Smith of those days when "we worked in Genl. Houston's house in Houston until early morning—stripped of all clothing except our shirts."[32] Dr. Smith was a member of Phi Beta Kappa, which celebrates its Founders' Day on December 5. It may have been more than coincidence that December 5, 1837, was the day chosen for the organization of the Philosophical Society of Texas, of which Smith and Houston were both charter members. Two weeks later, also in the Capitol Building, Houston presided at the organization of the Grand Lodge of Texas.[33]

Not all of the President's acquaintances and visitors were so kindly in their descriptions as was Audubon. Erasmus Manford visited the new capital, "a moral desert—a hell on earth," where "vice of most every name and grade reigned triumphantly"—and dined with Houston in "the log cabin where he boarded." Manford described the executive as "a good talker but an awful swearer."[34] W. D. Redd ridiculed the President's martial strides and "gaudy" and "peculiar" attire in "black silk velvet, gold lace, crimson vest, cravat, and silver spurs."[35] Lamar heard in July, 1837, that already Houston was a "lively village, almost as large as Brazoria," and this report of the man for whom it was named: "I saw the President going to the ball in a superb suit of black velvet lined with white satin, and a large hat ornamented with waving plumes! The English consul Crawford in citizens clothes was walking along side of him; and the great speculator Allen was on the other."[36]

It was of this "great speculator," John Kirby Allen, promoter of Houston city, that the President had teasingly written Anna Raguet: "My friend, Major Allen, says that in consideration of your charms and your kind consideration of his capacity, that the most splendid Lot in Houston is Deeded to you! 'I guess' some day he may get it back, most elegantly improved! It must be so if Miss Raguet shou'd adorn the premises."[37]

Houston's letters to Miss Raguet, half-serious and half-whimsical, continued until her marriage in April, 1840, just a month before his own

[32] Bauer to Smith, July 11, 1844, Ashbel Smith Papers.
[33] *Telegraph and Texas Register*, March 17, 1838.
[34] Erasmus Manford, *Twenty-five Years in the West*, 53.
[35] Redd to Lamar, May 23, 1837, *Lamar Papers*, I, 552–54.
[36] LeRay de Chaumont to Lamar, July 14, 1837, *ibid.*, 562.
[37] Houston to Anna Raguet, May 20, 1837, *Writings*, II, 100.

second marriage. That he told her much of his own family and background is revealed in his reports to her concerning his sisters and nieces and nephews. That he had confidence in her discretion and judgment is indicated in his complaints to her concerning conditions in the army and the government. His fondness for her was well known, and bachelors in East Texas reported to him periodically on social life in Nacogdoches with Miss Anna the center of attraction, and Houston teased her about those bachelors much as he had about Allen. On one occasion Jacob Snively wrote to the General of the numerous candidates for the lady's hand—including a future Congressional colleague, David S. Kaufman—but discounted their success with "the brightest and loveliest star of Texas" as against "the Conqueror who gave our banner to the breeze."[38]

To what degree Houston himself was a candidate for Miss Anna's hand it is hard to determine from his letters. That he proposed marriage to her is indicated in one letter in which he disclaimed any intention to address her at a time when he was not satisfied that his divorce from Eliza Allen Houston was legal, and he enclosed a copy of the court order for the divorce.[39] Two weeks later he wrote her of his sadness at the news of the death of one of his sisters, regretted that Anna had had a tumble from a horse named Whalebone, which he had given her, reported that Dr. Irion was chafing at a delay in Houston, and added: "I don't say that he is courting—but—he has some matters on hand of importance—He is a noble Gentleman!!!"[40] Almost every letter from Houston to Anna Raguet contained mention of Robert Irion, often with the ending: "Dr. Irion sends all love." After the Doctor and Miss Raguet were married, the friendship continued, and Houston and his wife, Margaret Lea, were frequent visitors in the Irion home. Houston sent his and his wife's best love to the Irion family in May, 1841, and wanted to know if he still had no namesake. The first Irion son was named Sam Houston.

The bachelor Republic was not without its social life, even if the town of Houston had to do without Miss Anna. The first annual celebration of San Jacinto Day was held there, elaborate invitations bringing guests by horseback from fifty or sixty miles around. The party from Harrisburg, including Houston, the Francis Lubbocks, and the

---

[38] Snively to Houston, November 22, 1837, Houston Unpublished Correspondence, II.

[39] Houston to Anna Raguet, June 4, 1838, *Writings*, II, 244–45.

[40] Houston to Anna Raguet, June 19, 1838, Houston Unpublished Correspondence.

Moseley Bakers, arrived by rowboat. Houston escorted Mrs. Baker to lead the grand march to the strains of "Hail to the Chief." The festivities were temporarily marred when two of the young ladies, the Misses Cooper, learned that their brother had been killed by Indians somewhere on the Colorado. After the dance, the party went to Ben Fort Smith's Hotel, two large rooms of pine poles, to sup on "turkey, venison, coffee cakes, and sparkling wine" under an improvised wooden chandelier." The next year the ball was held in the new upper story of the hotel. Dilue Rose Harris, recording the event in her reminiscences, recalled her chagrin when the President kissed her and called her a "pretty little girl."

Mrs. Harris also noted that the President often attended the theater in Houston, no doubt recalling his own amateur Thespian career. On one occasion he calmed disorderly conduct at the theater. And when the leading man in the theatrical company died and left his family destitute, Houston moved to a boardinghouse and turned over his mansion to the widow and three children."

When Congress recessed for three days in May, 1838, many of its members accompanied the President and Vice-President to Galveston on the steamboat *Friend* for a tour of the navy yard. In the evening the ball at the Biggs Hotel was "graced by the presence of the beautiful and intelligent of the softer sex."" Part of Houston's bill for the Galveston trip, as receipted by J. A. Biggs and Brother, included dinner for sixty-three, $315, and "Liquor at the Bar for Company," $33."

For many years, Houston, as was true of many of his contemporaries, drank to excess, frequently until he was physically helpless. Striking in physique, outstanding in accomplishment, he was equally conspicuous in that weakness, and his political enemies took every opportunity to point out the failing. That he struggled against it is shown in the remarks of his friends. He must have made a New Year's resolution in 1838, for a visitor to Texas wrote back to Virginia:

Whilst I remained in Houston I called on the President, found him in good health, and perfectly sober. He told me he had resolved and was determined to stand to it: not to "touch, taste, or handle the unclean thing," until the first

" O. F. Allen, *The City of Houston from Wilderness to Wonder*, 6.
" "Reminiscences of Mrs. Dilue Harris," *Quarterly of the Texas State Historical Association*, VII (1903/1904), 215, 217, 219.
" *Telegraph and Texas Register*, May 5, 12, 1838.
" Hotel Bill for General Sam Houston and Company, May 5, 6, 1838, Rosenberg Library, Galveston.

of January next. I am in hopes that he will refrain from intoxication for the short term of one year, which will do credit to himself, and be a fine thing for the Republic of Texas.[45]

J. Wilson Copes was able to report the resolution still in effect when he wrote to Ashbel Smith some two weeks later: "The President is now in fine health and has not tasted strong drink since you left."[46]

It may have been partially on the basis of the Copes letter, and certainly on the basis of his own affection for Houston, that Dr. Smith wrote a letter for the New Orleans *True American* which was reprinted in the *Telegraph and Texas Register*. In reply to what he called calumnies against his President, Smith declared:

He has been represented as an imbecile in body and intellect:—a moral and physical wreck. Never was calumny more false. His health has certainly been impaired by privations and exposures; but he possesses at this moment more physical force—despite his severe attack of the congestive fever last summer,— than ninety-nine able bodied men out of one hundred; and he is still capable of enduring fatigue, privations, and watching in a most extraordinary degree. As regards his mind, he is still in the pride of his intellect. . . . His bearing is that of the most lofty and princely courtesy; and he is singularly endeared to his personal friends: and despite all that has been said to the contrary, I believe him the most popular man in Texas. The statements of his being a madman and cutting tall antics before high Heaven and man, are utterly and gratuitously false.

When Smith was in Virginia en route home to Texas, he wrote the President to report on his purchase of medical supplies, on his entertainment by Martin Van Buren, on the seeming impossibility of annexation, and on the impermanence of falsehoods circulated by Houston detractors.[47]

Back in Texas the President was holding firm to his resolve; he wrote to Anna Raguet in May that he and a friend were reformed: "Neither gets 'tight'!"[48] He needed to be sober, not only for his official responsibilities but for the other social demands made upon a popular public man. On October 11, 1838, at a called meeting of the Milam Guards at

[45] W. T. Brent to J. H. Brent, January 23, 1838, Houston Unpublished Correspondence, II.
[46] Copes to Smith, February 4, 1838, Ashbel Smith Papers.
[47] *Telegraph and Texas Register*, February 24, 1838; Smith to Houston, March 22, 1838, Ashbel Smith Papers.
[48] Houston to Anna Raguet, May 15, 1838, *Writings*, II, 228.

Houston, he was invited, along with Dr. Smith, Lamar, George W. Hockley, A. S. Thruston, and Robert Barr, to become an honorary member of the corps.[49] Whether or not he was able to maintain his temperance resolution throughout 1838 is not known. Such a resolution must have been put to a severe strain in a community in which public dinners for visiting celebrities were featured by the abundance of the toasts drunk. Former President Houston was one of the distinguished guests present at such a dinner for Dr. Jack Shackelford on February 4, 1839, when five regular and twenty-five volunteer toasts were offered. After the toast to Houston, he gave his own toast to Shackelford: "Honor to the brave!"[50] Two weeks later Houston "offered a resolution favorable to the cause of temperance" at the first temperance meeting held in the city of Houston, February 18, 1839.[51]

Houston's first term as president ended on December 10, 1838. The Rev. William Y. Allen wrote from Galveston to Anson Jones, then in Washington, D.C., to describe the Lamar inauguration as "quite a pageant":

Sam. Houston made quite a racy speech; he stood up for his prerogative, objurgated the last Congress for not sufficiently respecting it, and entreated the present Congress to treat his successor better. You know, perhaps, that he and the present Congress have been in a *snarl* most of the present session. The old chief has a good many friends yet, I think. . . .

At the ball which wound up the *grand affair* 'tis said there was some excess of riot, and some shameful spreeing, towards the breaking of the day.[52]

Forty years later, Allen described the Houston valedictory with other details:

A great crowd had assembled to witness the inauguration of Lamar as the second President of the Republic. It was expected by his friends that his inaugural would be a politico-oratorical production, as he had the reputation of being a fine writer and a poet. . . . Houston, knowing something of Lamar's nervousness, took occasion to make an exaugural, reviewing at great length his administration, and, by the time he was done, Lamar had become so nerv-

[49] William Kerley, F. R. Lubbock, and J. M. Eldredge to Ashbel Smith, October 12, 1838, Ashbel Smith Papers.
[50] *Telegraph and Texas Register*, February 13, 1839.
[51] *Ibid.*, February 20, 1839.
[52] Anson Jones, *Memoranda and Official Correspondence Relating to the Republic of Texas, Its History and Annexation*, 139–40. Hereinafter cited as *Republic of Texas*.

ous that he could not read his inaugural, and had to commit it to his private secretary, Algernon Thompson, to be read to an exhausted audience.[53]

The newspaper reporter covering the event described the "immense concourse" of spectators in front of the Capitol, told that Houston described his office as a "pillow of thorns," and ended the news item:

After he had concluded, he cordially saluted General Lamar and invited him to the chair of state, which he then relinquished with dignity and complacency. The President and Vice-President having been duly installed into office, the secretary of the Senate proceeded to read the inaugural address of the President, who was unable, on account of indisposition, to deliver it in person.[54]

Out of public life for the first time since the outbreak of the Texas Revolution, Houston returned to private law practice and on January 8, 1839, formed a partnership with John Birdsall in Houston.[55] He appointed George W. Poe to be his agent during an anticipated absence in the United States and wrote Anna Raguet that his plans for departure from Texas were delayed by business and "city making." The city making was helping plan the details of laying out the projected city of Sabine, to be located at the mouth of the Sabine River. Houston, Philip A. Sublett, John S. Roberts, and George W. Hockley were among the stockholders in the city development company.[56] Because of the press of private business Houston declined a farewell dinner and ball offered him by the citizens of Houston, but he did attend a "frolic" on the British Bark *Ambassador* on February 25, 1839.[57]

News of the traveler was not all from the friendliest sources. From New Orleans, Memucan Hunt wrote Lamar that Houston had received little or no attention there, and the report was that "his coat was burned off him whilst he was drunk on his journey here and that he was seen proceeding to his lodgings on the day of his arrival (the weather being very warm) wrapped up closely in a large cloak!"[58] In Mobile the former Texas president had a better reception; he made two speeches and

---

[53] W. S. Red, "Allen's Reminiscences of Texas, 1838–1842" (written at Rockville, Indiana, August 18, 1879), *Southwestern Historical Quarterly*, XVIII (1914/15), 295.

[54] *Telegraph and Texas Register*, December 12, 1838.

[55] Terms of Partnership, January 8, 1839, *Writings*, II, 308.

[56] Houston to Anna Raguet, February 8, 1839, *ibid.*, 310; *Telegraph and Texas Register*, May 14, 1839.

[57] S. M. Williams to Anson Jones, March 11, 1839, Jones, *Republic of Texas*, 145.

[58] Hunt to Lamar, May 31, 1839, *Lamar Papers*, III, 7.

"created quite a sensation."[59] While he was in Alabama, he visited the stock farm of Hickman Lewis, from whom he was later to buy blooded horses, paid for in scrip of the city of Sabine, and was entertained in the home of William Bledsoe. There Emily Antoinette Lea Bledsoe introduced General Houston to her sister Margaret Lea.[60]

Houston spent much of the summer of 1839 with Andrew Jackson in Tennessee and from Nashville sent back "truly welcome tidings" to young Margaret Lea, who wrote to him on July 17, 1839: "My answer must be taken as strong evidence [that the tidings were welcome], for it is the first I have ever addressed to any gentleman." The courtly manners and natural charm of the visitor from Texas had left a lasting impression on the twenty-year-old Alabama beauty, who wrote him that, although surrounded by childhood friends, she could not be quite happy because "there are those absent whose station within my heart remains unfulfilled." And to that absent one she confided that she had gazed upon "*our* emblem, *the star of my destiny*," and had been inspired to write some poetry which she would not send him lest he call her a "romantic star-struck young lady." Her family, she stated, planned to visit Texas the following October, but they would not consider her going to the Republic until its former president had visited her home at Marion.[61] Houston returned to Alabama in late July or early August and secured Margaret's promise to be his wife.

Back in Texas, a Sam Houston party was being organized to oppose Lamar in the Texas Congress, and Houston's red brother, Chief Bowl, was killed in the Cherokee War. Although a presidential election was two years in the offing, Henry Thompson, to illustrate the close tie between Indian wars and politics, had written Lamar that Bowl's capture would knock Houston out of the next presidency. Thompson proved no prophet. And while Houston was yet absent, his friends at San Augustine elected him representative from that county for the next Congress.[62] They either did not listen to, or cared little about, the reports which came back to Texas of Houston's activities in Tennessee. Perhaps they did not count Memucan Hunt a disinterested party when he wrote Ashbel Smith that he had heard from reliable sources that Houston had been drunk almost every day while in Nashville and that his name would be out of the question. From Jackson, Mississippi, Henry S.

[59] D. H. Daves to Ashbel Smith, May 10, 1839, Ashbel Smith Papers.
[60] Contract with Lewis, August 30, 1839, *Writings*, II, 313–14; James, *The Raven*, 307–308.
[61] Margaret Lea to Houston, July 17, 1839, Houston Unpublished Correspondence.
[62] *Telegraph and Texas Register*, September 11, 1839.

94

Foote reported in the same tenor that "civilities" extended Houston were for the Texas cause alone and that his oratory was disappointing, while his egotism and vanity brought ridicule.[63] It may have been wishful thinking when W. J. Jones wrote to Lamar that "if [Anthony] Butler and old Ben [Fort Smith], the African, is beaten, you have nothing to fear from old Sam—He will drink too much of the ardent to injure you —He will kill himself."[64] But Houston did not kill himself, and Lamar was assured of political death when the Congressional elections in the fall of 1839 returned only ten of the men who had been elected with him in 1838.

On his return to Texas, Houston delayed in Nacogdoches only long enough to deliver a bitter denunciation against the expulsion of the Cherokees and then started west. At LaGrange, on September 20, he borrowed fifty dollars from O. B. Hill and made a note for payment on Christmas Day. Lamar established his government at Austin, the new capital, on October 17, 1839, and the Fourth Congress convened on November 11. That day a cavalcade escorted by three colonels rode out to meet the hero of San Jacinto; Anson Jones presided over a dinner for two hundred persons held in Houston's honor on November 13. Forty-three toasts were offered. Houston's sentiment was "Texas—if true to herself, she can be false to no one!" And the toast to Houston was phrased: "The soldier and the statesman: we have tried him once and we will try him again."[65]

The East Texas congressman wrote Anna Raguet that Austin was the most unfortunate site upon earth for a seat of government, that eating was scarce, that there was no society to enjoy, and that he did not visit "court."[66] He expressed his sentiments to Congress on December 2 and 3, 1839, in a speech which declared that the people of East Texas had been defrauded in the location of the capital and ridiculed the government as a speculator in the sale of city lots. In that speech and in many others delivered during the session, he defended the claims of the Cherokees and condemned white perfidy in failure to recognize Indian treaty rights and in encroachment on Indian lands. Feelings ran even higher in Congress when Burleson sent to Hugh McLeod Chief Bowl's hat as part of the plunder of the Battle of the Neches and requested that McLeod present the hat to Houston. Houston exploded in

[63] Hunt to Smith, September 5, 1839, Ashbel Smith Papers; Foote to Lamar, November 20, 1839, *Lamar Papers*, V, 326.
[64] Jones to Lamar, August 23, 1839, *Lamar Papers*, III, 79.
[65] Herbert Gambrell, *Anson Jones, the Last President of Texas*, 181–82; Austin *City Gazette*, November 27, 1839.
[66] Houston to Anna Raguet, December 10, 1839, *Writings*, II, 322.

an hour-and-a-half speech on January 8, 1840, his attack on the Indian policy and on Lamar and Vice-President Burnet eliciting a sarcastic reply from William H. Jack. The *Telegraph* commented that Houston's conduct "excited the grief and shame of his friends, and the just reproach and scorn of his enemies." The intense party feeling soon degenerated into personal animosities, with all political factions merging into two—Houston and anti-Houston.[67] By January 10, 1840, the presidential campaign of 1841 was well under way, and Henry Thompson, in Houston, was writing to Lamar that "Genl. Houston is the whole talk for your successor here and at Galveston."[68] The *Telegraph*, tongue in cheek, proclaimed that Houston could not be a candidate without "subjecting himself to the charge of perjury," since his valedictory and subsequent speeches had declared that he would not receive an office which had been but a "pillow of thorns." And the paper of Dr. Francis Moore, Jr., and Jacob W. Cruger continued: "We cannot believe, therefore, that he will be so regardless of his reputation and *personal quiet,* as to consent again to engage in a political race, where every step will but plunge him deeper and deeper in the mire of public disgrace."[69]

A letter from George W. Hockley shows the other side of the picture. Hockley was getting ready for the Washington's Birthday dinner and sent his general three toasts with the request that Houston pick the one to be used: "To the mother of Sam Houston," "To the *memory* of the mother of Sam Houston," or "Houston—He whose very battle field is holy ground which breathes of Nations saved not worlds undone."[70]

By March, 1840, the *Texas Sentinel* in Austin began a series of articles to throw light on the official conduct of the "honorable" member of Congress from San Augustine, and Henderson was writing Smith from San Augustine that Houston must hurry home as soon as possible and run for Congress again.[71] Houston himself was in Galveston, ill, and declaring that he would not be a candidate for the presidency. Rumor had it that he was in the island city to await his bride-to-be.[72] Actually, he was not waiting for his bride but was probably paying court to her

[67] *Texas Sentinel,* January 15, 1840; *Telegraph and Texas Register,* February 5, 1840; Memoirs of John Salmon Ford, II, 213.

[68] *Lamar Papers,* III, 304.

[69] *Telegraph and Texas Register,* February 5, 1840.

[70] Hockley to Houston, February 20, 1840, Houston Unpublished Correspondence, II.

[71] *Texas Sentinel,* March 4, 1840; Henderson to Smith, March 30, 1840, Ashbel Smith Papers.

[72] Francis Moore, Jr., to Lamar, March 9, 1840, and James Love to Lamar, March 15, 1840, *Lamar Papers,* III, 349, 354.

mother, Mrs. Nancy Lea, before he left Texas for Alabama to claim the daughter. Margaret had written to her mother to describe her trousseau: "I have made me a white satin dress, a purple silk, and a blue muslin."[73]

Houston and Margaret Lea were married in the home of her brother, Henry Lea, at Marion, Perry County, Alabama, on May 9, 1840. His friends and his enemies discussed matrimony and politics simultaneously. One of Smith's correspondents declared that Houston would "sweep the field" for the presidency if he did not break down physically —and proceeded in the same letter to comment that with a wife in Tennessee it was impossible for Houston to marry—"and fortunate it is so." Hockley lamented Houston's unmended political fences and voiced his trepidation concerning romance: "This marriage I fear is his death warrant—i.e., *if it ever occurs*. Even so far as it has now progressed I shall only believe it when I hear that it has been perfected."[74] Hockley was commenting "after the fact."

Barnard E. Bee was also pessimistic: "I see with great pain the marriage of Genl. Houston to Miss Lea! I had hoped it would never have been consummated—in all my intercourse with life I have never met with an individual more totally disqualified for domestic happiness. . . . I suppose his chance for the Presidency is good—no matter what occurs."[75] Smith himself refrained from prophecy when he explained why he could not go to Alabama as Houston's groomsman: "He urged me warmly to accompany him and I was willing enough, but alas the unsentimental obstacle to my going—though a very popular one. I had no funds—and I knew the Old Chief had none."[76]

The *Telegraph and Texas Register* made brief note of the wedding and then took occasion to make politics when it quoted in full an "Original Ode," sung to the tune of "The Old Oaken Bucket" by a group of young ladies at a party given the Houstons the evening after their marriage. The last verse began:

> Our Washington's name has been hallowed in story,
>   As founder of Freedom's retreat in the West.
> Another has risen to share in his glory—
>   The Texian Patriot—our own honored guest!

[73] Margaret Lea to Nancy Lea, April 25, 1840, Houston Unpublished Correspondence.
[74] Hockley to Smith, June 1, 1840, Ashbel Smith Papers.
[75] Bee to Smith, June 5, 1840, *ibid.*
[76] Smith to Radcliff Hudson, June 1, 1840, *ibid.*

The *Telegraph* was blunt in its comment that it did not consider the comparison "deserved."[77]

The Houstons probably reached Texas in June. At any rate, Houston delivered an oration at the old Capitol in Houston on July 6, and on July 25 made a speech at Henry Corri's Theater on the occasion of the beginning of construction of the Houston and Brazos Railroad.[78] Ashbel Smith had no complaint that Houston was a dull city as long as the Old Chief and his lady were there, and noted changes in his friend:

His health is excellent, as good or *better than* I have ever seen it. He indulges in no conviviality with his friends—but strange to say is a model of conjugal propriety. I had dreadful misgivings as to the propriety of his taking this step—thus far I have been most agreeably disappointed. His health and ways are infinitely mended. Will it last? I always hope for the best.[79]

The bride and her groom, whom Bee called "a courteous . . . but never a *domestic* man," went to East Texas the last of July. They were entertained in the best of pioneer tradition at San Augustine and at Nacogdoches, and the young bride, more than twenty-five years younger than her husband, must have had many adjustments to make—some of them to what may have been frontier humor. John Salmon Ford's memoirs include the story of a Nacogdoches encounter between the Houstons and N. D. Walling:

Walling inquired, "Mrs. Houston, have you been in Shelby County?" The reply was in the negative. "You ought to go there, Madam. Gen. Houston has forty children in Shelby County." At this announcement the lady looked rather confused. Walling added, "—that is, named after him." Gen. Houston remarked: "Friend Walling, you would oblige me very much by connecting your sentences more closely."[80]

While Margaret was ill with fever on the Redlands trip, the General was a model of kindness, and Smith reported that he had been perfectly temperate for two months. Hockley also was cheered: "All agree that if permanent reformation *can* be effected his estimable wife will succeed in doing so. God grant it."[81] And the estimable wife did succeed,

---

[77] *Telegraph and Texas Register*, July 1, 1840.
[78] Henry Gillett to Smith, July 6, 1840, Ashbel Smith Papers; William Ransom Hogan, *The Texas Republic: A Social and Economic History*, 74.
[79] Smith to Bee, July 27, 1840, Ashbel Smith Papers.
[80] Memoirs of John Salmon Ford, II, 216.
[81] Smith to Bee, September ?, 1840; Hockley to Smith, August 17, 1840, Ashbel Smith Papers.

although it was long before Houston's enemies could be persuaded of the reformation. When they had been married some five months, Houston wrote to his wife, while she was visiting the Bledsoes and he was alone practicing law in San Augustine, that he hoped she heard no more slanders of him. "It is the malice of the world to abuse me, and really were it not that they reach my beloved Margaret, I would not care one picayune—but that you should be distressed is inexpressible wretchedness to me! . . . If you hear the truth you never shall hear of my being on a 'spree.' "[82]

On September 7, 1840, Henry W. Augustine and Houston were elected from San Augustine to the Fifth Congress. The election demonstrated Texas political techniques and tensions of the period. The four candidates in the race were Houston, Augustine, Joseph Rowe, a former speaker of the House, and an attorney named W. D. Duffield. At the first term of district court after the election, Houston moved that Duffield be disbarred because he had used pressure on an election judge, John T. Rawls, to make false returns and had himself forged a return of the votes polled in one of the San Augustine precincts. Duffield's rebuttal charged that Houston had so manipulated the election as to hold back and combine votes to concentrate them for Augustine. Duffield further contended that intimidation had been used to secure Rawls's statement that Duffield had been guilty of forgery, and that Houston had introduced the motion for disbarment while the grand jury was sitting on the Duffield case in order to have a prejudicial effect on that jury. Houston's motive, as claimed by Duffield, was twofold: a desire for revenge because Duffield had made a speech condemning eleven-league land grants in the border leagues and the hope of securing a portion of Duffield's lucrative law practice. Duffield closed his answer with a particularly personal assault on Houston:

This respondent views as a peculiar hardship . . . attempts to deprive him of the means of an honorable support for himself and his family and that too by an individual who has no home, who has never known the charms of that word but who has been content to receive from his friends a precarious existence by domiciling himself at their homes and receiving from their hands the gifts which generosity and benevolence might dictate to them.[83]

Duffield was suspended. Thomas J. Rusk was his attorney when he peti-

[82] Houston to Margaret Lea Houston, September 23, 1840, *Writings*, II, 352–53.
[83] *Sam Houston v. W. C. Duffield*, District Court, San Augustine, Fall Term, 1840, given in D. C. Arthur, "The San Augustine Collection in the Library of Texas Technological College" (M.A. thesis, Texas Technological College, 1931), 16.

tioned for a new trial to set aside the order on the grounds that he had been denied due process of law.

On October 13, 1840, Houston was at Nacogdoches on his way west. He was delayed by illness at Washington-on-the-Brazos and wrote Hockley to reserve a room for him in Austin. Adolphus Sterne, on November 25, heard a report that Houston was dead. Some of his fellow members of Congress probably regretted that the report was merely rumor when the Representative from the Redlands renewed his attack on land speculators and his arguments in behalf of the Cherokee Land Bill. The rumor almost became fact on December 10, when S. W. Jordan would have killed Houston with an ax but for Sterne's interference.[84] Undaunted, Houston continued his argument on the Cherokee bill the next day before a crowded House. When his long speech was interrupted by a motion to grant Lamar leave of absence from the Republic and have Burnet perform the duties of president, Houston changed the tenor of his speech to a condemnation of Burnet and defeated the Senate amendment for raising Burnet's salary.[85]

The presidential campaign, so long in the discussion stage, was officially open. Two days before the adjournment of the Fifth Congress Houston described to Anthony Butler the "useless extravagance and the most unprincipled profligacy" of the administration.[86] Then he left the Austin scene of hectic debate over eleven-league grants and the Franco-Texienne Bill to join his wife, who had been seriously ill at Houston.

A public dinner was given Houston at Galveston on Texas Independence Day. On April 5, 1841, the citizens at San Augustine, headed by Kenneth L. Anderson, W. R. Scurry, and S. W. Blount, offered him a similar honor. He was nominated for the presidency at a Harris County meeting in early April, made a speech at San Augustine on April 19, and on San Jacinto Day spoke at the Old Stone Fort at Nacogdoches. On May 19, 1841, the *Telegraph and Texas Register* declared for Burnet, calling Houston "a noble wreck of humanity—great even in ruins." However caustic the *Telegraph* might be, it never equaled the *Texas Sentinel* in bitterness of attack on Houston. His own description of Burnet as a "hog thief" was one of the milder terms of the campaign. The *Red-Lander*, the Austin *City Gazette*, and the *Colorado Gazette and Advertiser* were the chief pro-Houston organs. At Cedar Point, Houston busied himself writing a series of articles against Burnet. The

---

[84] Harriet Smither (ed.), "Diary of Adolphus Sterne," *Southwestern Historical Quarterly*, XXXI (1927/28), 78, 80.

[85] *Telegraph and Texas Register*, December 20, 1840.

[86] Houston to Butler, February 2, 1841, *Writings*, II, 365–66.

Houston letters, signed "Truth," were bitter, but they could not equal in invective and slander the letters prepared by Burnet, possibly with the aid of Lamar, and signed "Publius" and "Texian." Friends on both sides entered the writing contest, and A. C. Allen, contributing under the signature of "Clodhopper," boasted that he gave Judge Burnet "little particular hell."[87]

The depreciated currency and bad financial condition in Texas probably damaged both factions. Houston was desperately pressed for money. He asked for a loan of $60 or $80 from Samuel M. Williams; and when he ordered a buggy from the firm of McKinney and Williams, he stressed the fact that he would have to pay "on time." To an old friend in Tennessee he sent his regrets that he could not repay a loan of $500 and offered property to cover the note. To further explain his situation to his Tennessee correspondent, he said that two Negro boys, for whom he had recently paid $2,100, had run away to Mexico, and that although he had $25,000 due him, he would not be able to collect enough to pay a fourth of his land tax.[88]

Campaign issues of the 1841 contest, aside from personalities, were the Franco-Texienne Bill, advocated by Houston, to establish French settlers on the frontier; claims to eleven-league grants of land, both Houston and Burnet being accused of securing such grants; retrenchment measures; protection of the frontier; and removal of the seat of government from Austin. The summer of 1841 grew warmer, with political "scandal, newspaper palavering, and electioneering at fever heat." Houston was at Nacogdoches on election day, September 6, 1841, when he received 7,508 votes and Burnet 2,574 votes for the presidency. Edward Burleson defeated Memucan Hunt for the office of vice-president.[89]

Washington County citizens celebrated the victory with a dinner for the Houstons—"*thirteen* barbecued hogs and two thundering big beeves well roasted with lots of honey, *taters*, chickens and goodies in general." But "strange to say," according to E. H. Winfield, "it was a cold water *doins*," for the Old Chief did not touch or handle the "smallest drop of the ardent during his stay in this county."[90] On September 28, 1841, Houston was back in Nacogdoches for a meeting to honor him as

[87] Allen to Smith, July 19, 1841, Ashbel Smith Papers.

[88] Houston to Williams, July 30, 1841, *Writings*, II, 370; Houston to W. F. Harding, July 17, 1841, Houston Unpublished Correspondence, II.

[89] Conn D. Catterton, "The Political Campaigns of the Republic of Texas of 1841 and 1844" (M.A. thesis, University of Texas, 1935), 83.

[90] Henry Gillett to Smith, September 17, 1841, and Winfield to Smith, September 22, 1841, Ashbel Smith Papers.

president-elect, but many of his constituents resented his attacks on them in Congress as "land thieves and robbers" and as less brave than Chief Bowl; so they also used the occasion to invite Lamar to a public dinner—but set the date for the following March 2 or April 21.[91] By the time Houston made another speech at Nacogdoches, October 20, most of the bitterness on all save the Cherokee question had subsided, and Charles Chevallier invited all of the local dignitaries to a party for the Houstons before they left to visit Dr. Irion.[92]

Between speeches at Crockett and at Houston, the President-elect planned his policy and selected his cabinet. On October 21, 1841, he asked Washington D. Miller to resume the post of private secretary; on November 24, he named Anson Jones to be his secretary of state. An administrative organ, the *Daily Bulletin*, began publication in Austin on November 27 and reported activities of the Sixth Congress, which then had been in session for three weeks. As the debate in Congress over the retrenchment bill progressed, Robert Potter made the caustic comment that "there was an idea in vogue that this was a two-horse government, and he thought they would soon have it regulated, so as to work with one mule."[93]

About the time Houston left Margaret in East Texas and started towards the capital, the Houston *Morning Star* ran an article to the effect that A. M. Tomkins and others were compiling a biography of "the distinguished patriot," to be published in New York—"a work for whose appearance," said the *Star*, "we wait with impatience." The *Daily Bulletin* copied the article with the note: "After this, from the Telegraph concern, our name is Haines—'We've seen the Elephant!'"[94]

In Austin the committee for the reception of the President-elect held frequent meetings at the Bexar Exchange, arranged to have him escorted into the capital by the Travis Guards, and planned a "plentiful collation" at the Eberly House, where he was to reside. Whether because of her health or because of primitive conditions in Austin, or because of the protracted discussion over the location of the seat of government, Mrs. Houston did not go to Austin. The inauguration ceremony there took place amid "salvos of artillery and general rejoicing" on December 13, 1841, at the rear of the Capitol Building on West Eighth Street

[91] *Telegraph and Texas Register,* October 27, 1841.
[92] Smither, "Diary of Adolphus Sterne," *Southwestern Historical Quarterly,* XXXII (1928/29), 177, 256–58.
[93] Austin *Daily Bulletin,* December 1, 1841.
[94] *Ibid.*

under a canopy erected for the occasion. Lamar declined to make a valedictory.[95]

Josiah Gregg was one of the audience of about a thousand persons who listened to the inaugural speech, a part of which Gregg considered good enough, but he thought the speaker would have done better not to have been his own eulogist. Nor did Gregg approve the presidential attire of linsey-woolsey hunting shirt, pantaloons, and an old wide-brimmed white fur hat, which "demonstrated more vanity than if he had appeared in an ordinary cloth suit."[96]

The inaugural ball in the Senate Chamber went off merrily with Houston and Burleson present the greater part of the time; "various persons of distinction participated in the dance, and visitants from all parts of the country."[97]

The next day the President attended a convocation of Royal Arch Masons to consider the propriety of forming a grand chapter in the Republic.[98] Three days later Hockley described to Dr. Smith the splendor of the inauguration and ended his letter with a cryptic comment: "Some members talk of a journey for the purpose of spending the Christmas holidays at Bexar. . . . Would they not be surprised to find the archives on their way to Houston when they return?"[99]

Houston had consistently objected to Austin as the seat of the government. One can but wonder if he left his wife in East Texas because he expected his absence to be brief. It was to be a full year, however, before he could use the Mexican invasion of San Antonio as an excuse for the abandonment of Austin. Then his attempt to transfer the government by moving the archives resulted in the so-called "Archive War," but it had been a year filled with discussion of and bickering over the move. At the beginning of his term, however, the President was busy accepting office calls between one and six in the afternoon only, being occupied with business before and after those hours.[100] There is no record of his attending Lamar's ball on December 22, a function for which the hall was decorated with a "transparency" on which was inscribed, "An honest man the noblest work of God," and a mirror gilded with the words, "We hope for your return."[101]

[95] Frank Brown, "Annals of Travis County and the City of Austin from the Earliest Times to the Close of 1875," VIII, 27–28.

[96] Maurice Garland Fulton (ed.), *Diary and Letters of Josiah Gregg*, I, 109–10.

[97] *Daily Bulletin*, December 14, 1841.   [98] *Ibid.*, December 25, 1841.

[99] Hockley to Smith, December 17, 1841, Ashbel Smith Papers.

[100] *Daily Bulletin*, December 30, 1841.

[101] *Ibid.*, December 23, 1841.

On December 27, the anniversary of St. John the Evangelist, Companion Houston began the exercises of the Masonic procession by reading the invocation:

> Before Jehovah's awful throne,
> Ye nations bow with sacred joy,
> Know that the Lord is God alone:
> He can create and he destroy.[102]

At the moment, Sam Houston's nation was beset with difficulties, but the *Morning Star* expressed faith in his ability and stressed the identity of Texas and Houston interests.[103]

Houston remained in Austin until the adjournment of the first session of the Sixth Congress on February 5, 1842; then, leaving Miller in charge of the executive office, he rode muleback from Austin to Houston in "two hours less than four days" and surprised Margaret by his early arrival. Under just what circumstances he left Austin is not known, but on February 8, Adolphus Sterne recorded in his diary: "A rumor is afloat that Gel Houston is dead, hope it is not so as we surely would be in a wors fix than we are now (so far as *a President* is concerned)."[104]

Miller sorted the executive mail, forwarded newspapers from the United States, and wrote almost daily reports of capital affairs. He described Austin as quite dull on February 16, but on March 6 he reported to the President the Mexican invasion and seizure of San Antonio and expressed the hope that the archives would not be moved until the true character of that invasion was better known. On March 10, 1842, Houston ordered Hockley to have the archives moved to the city of Houston by way of Caldwell.[105] Hockley suspended the order; local citizens sent a petition in protest; and the militia converging at San Antonio under Edward Burleson, who "loved his country more than he feared the President's displeasure," chafed at not being allowed to pursue the Mexicans to the Rio Grande.[106] Meanwhile, as Miller informed Smith, "the President moves coolly and deliberately in the execution of his plans."[107] Samuel Whiting of Austin was neither cool nor coherent when he wrote to Lamar:

[102] *Ibid.*, December 24, 1841.

[103] *Morning Star* (Houston), December 30, 1841.

[104] Smither, "Diary of Adolphus Sterne," *Southwestern Historical Quarterly*, XXXIII (1929/30), 161.

[105] Miller to Houston, February 16 and March 6, 1842, Miller Papers; Houston to Hockley, March 10, 1842, *Writings*, II, 495–96.

[106] Edward Burleson, To the Public, April 6, 1842, Ashbel Smith Papers.

[107] Miller to Smith, April 6, 1842, *ibid.*

Old *Sam Burnet & David G. Houston* have played the Very Devil here, I have been puzzled to determine which of the two is the d——st Rascal. It appears to me that poor Texas in the choice of the two worthies with Corn crib Moore has closed her doomedest. We are holding on to the Archiv[e]s like death to dead negro & are determined they shall not be taken from here 'till ordered by a higher power that [than] Sam Houston.[108]

When Houston wrote to Secretary of the Treasury William Henry Daingerfield that Margaret was ill and was leaving May 1 for a brief visit in Alabama, he said that she was reluctant to go lest he "take a fancy for the Rio Grande and 'dodge' her until the war with Mexico is ended." His own chief fear was the impetuosity of the people.[109] He put Mrs. Houston on the boat at Galveston and returned to Houston to commission special agents to raise troops in the United States. He cautioned Burleson of the need for order and civil rule, asked George W. Terrell to have Joseph Durst and Leonard Williams attend to keeping peace among the Indians, and finally called for a special session of Congress to meet at Houston on June 27, 1842. James Reily wrote Secretary of State Anson Jones, who was personally critical of the presidential policy, that calling Congress was impolitic and that the excitement in Texas was damaging the cause of the Republic in the United States.[110]

The President was having difficulty pleasing everybody. Although some of the western members talked of refusing to attend the Congressional session at Houston, a quorum arrived by the day designated, and the President's message to Congress on the morning of June 27 emphasized the insecurity of the public records and stressed the importance of establishing the government at a point convenient for the speedy and efficient transaction of public business. The message apparently put the burden of decision upon Congress. Then the executive left for Galveston to meet his wife but there learned that she had been detained in Alabama by illness.[111] Upon his return to Houston, he spent a warm July giving the House an estimate of the number of troops needed for a campaign against Mexico; explaining that he had tried to ameliorate the condition of the Santa Fe prisoners but had no appropriations for the purpose; ordering a Congressional election to be held on September 5; and assuring the Senate that volunteer aid was expensive and useless. Despite the hope, as expressed by Henderson, that Congress would not

[108] Whiting to Lamar, April 5, 1842, *Lamar Papers*, IV, Part I, 5.
[109] Houston to Daingerfield, April 27, 1842, *Writings*, III, 37–40.
[110] Jones, *Republic of Texas*, 169–70.
[111] Joseph Waples to Anson Jones, July 3, 1842, *ibid.*, 192.

advise an invasion of Mexico and that "the 'Old Chief' will have it his own way—fortunately for the country"[112]—the Congress did pass a bill for offensive war. Houston vetoed the measure on July 22, 1842. James Morgan reported the veto to Dr. Smith: "There was some little excitement caused by that veto, which has pretty much died away, and 'Old Sam' is more popular than ever I believe."[113]

The popularity was spotted, and some of the disaffection spread even among Houston's closest friends, including Hockley, who, on September 1, 1842, because of Houston's vacillation in defense, his attacks on the army, and his plans to sell the steamer *Zavala,* wrote a bitter letter of resignation as secretary of war and marine. Houston accepted the resignation with the comment that Hockley was a true friend and a prime officer.[114] The men later picked up the threads of the old friendship, though perhaps not on the terms of former intimacy. It was Houston's trait and misfortune to seem to antagonize, almost deliberately, those who were his best friends. As Ashbel Smith described the characteristic: "He exhibited a propensity which to his friends seemed unaccountable and injudicious: it was to make enemies of persons who were desirous of friendly relations with him. He acted on one of Talleyrand's strange maxims, 'Would you rise, make enemies.' "[115]

Elections for the Seventh Congress were held on September 4, 1842, and two days later Richardson Scurry, one of the administration stalwarts in Congress, advised the President that the new membership from the east would not be able to compete with that from the west. If Houston would not go to Austin, Scurry thought he should convene Congress at Washington, as a sort of compromise, because "it is useless to bite off the nose to spite the face as the convening of Congress at Houston would be."[116]

The face was spited, so far as the *Daily Gazette* in Austin was concerned. Furious at the change in the location of the capital, the editor of that paper wrote: "As we have expended some thousands in puffing Sam Houston into office under false promises, and the only reward we have yet received from him has been his curses, we will expend what

[112] J. P. Henderson to Smith, July 18, 1842, Ashbel Smith Papers.

[113] To the House of Representatives, July 22, 1842, *Writings*, III, 116–24; Morgan to Smith, August 20, 1842, Ashbel Smith Papers.

[114] Hockley to Houston, September 1, 1842, and Houston to Hockley, September 2, 1842, *Writings*, IV, 136–43.

[115] Ashbel Smith on Houston, n.d., Ashbel Smith Papers.

[116] Scurry to Houston, September 7, 1842, Houston Unpublished Correspondence, III.

spare means we have to give the public his character in its true light."[117]

There may have been other factors than the "spirit of compromise" which determined the move to Washington. As early as January, 1842, Houston had reported to the Senate that the proprietors of the town of Washington had proposed to provide free transportation for government properties and to furnish offices for the administration and suitable buildings for the Congress, all without cost, if the capital were removed to that place.[118] When the city of Houston made no proposal to provide such facilities for the government, the President sent "Uncle Buck" Pettus to verify the Washington proposition. The Washington city fathers, led by Judge John Lockhart, agreed to furnish offices free if the dilapidated buildings on the Brazos could be made tenable, and private families planned to accommodate the government employees, since the town had only one hotel. The Houston family, W. D. Miller, and M. C. Hamilton, War Department clerk, were to live with the Lockharts.[119]

On September 10, 1842, Houston wrote W. Y. McFarland that he might have the men at Washington send six wagons and teams to Houston to move the public property of the government to Washington because of "inconveniences and insecurity" and "want of mails" at Austin. The Adrian Woll invasion of San Antonio on the very next day could but emphasize the insecurity of a capital on the western frontier. Houston had not heard of the invasion when he revoked the blockade of the ports of eastern Mexico on September 12, but by September 20 he had received an express from San Antonio and commanded Gail Borden, Jr., to have the Galveston defenses in good order.[120]

J. W. McCown was in charge of the wagon train which moved the government from Houston to Washington. The President rode beside the train on his pacing mule Bruin, and "when the wagon train had passed beyond the limits of the corporation, Old Sam . . . stopped the train and pronounced a curse on that people and stomped the mud off his feet."[121]

The President reached Washington on October 2 and, as soon as he could turn to correspondence, ordered Alexander Somervell to concen-

[117] Quoted in *Telegraph and Texas Register*, September 14, 1842.
[118] To the Senate, January 13, 1842, *Writings*, III, 430.
[119] Jonnie Lockhart Wallis and Laurance L. Hill, *Sixty Years on the Brazos: The Life and Letters of Dr. John Washington Lockhart*, 95–96.
[120] Houston to Borden, September 20, 1842, *Writings*, IV, 146.
[121] "Historical Sketch of Washington County," *The American Sketch Book*, IV (1878), 207.

trate troops on the southwest frontier and to rely for aid on John C. Hays. Official correspondence for the next few months indicated more concern with the Indian situation than fear of Mexico.

On October 8, 1842, Houston ordered Thomas William Ward, land office commissioner, to make arrangements for moving the archives to Washington. Determined Austin citizens then empaneled a grand jury with Samuel Whiting, editor and publisher, as foreman, and that body presented an indictment against the President of the Republic, "not as a nuisance but as guilty of MORAL TREASON."[122] Ward had to report that the messenger bearing the presidential orders had been seized and his horse's mane and tail shaved, and that the chest of archives buried under the quartermaster general's store had been taken by William Cazneau, who was to represent Travis County in the next Congress, and placed under guard.[123] Finally, on December 10, Houston issued orders to Thomas I. Smith and Eli Chandler to remove the archives. On December 30, with twenty men to assist, they had almost finished loading the documents when Angelina Eberly fired a shot which set off the alarm. Mrs. Eberly had lost one business when San Felipe was burned; she did not intend to lose the congressmen and other officials who were the best customers at her Austin hostelry. Smith and his men were surrounded at Kenney's Fort on Brushy Creek in Williamson County; the Archive War was over on December 31, 1842, and the archives remained in Austin.[124] Houston washed his hands of the responsibility when he sent a message to the House on January 10, 1843, saying that the representatives of the people had failed to sustain him and that he felt acquitted from his trust. "Whatever of evil may befall the nation from the loss or destruction of its archives," he said, "must *fall upon the people*—but not by the agency of their President," who no longer felt it "his duty to use any exertions for their preservation."[125]

A special session of the Seventh Congress had been called, on October 15, to convene at Washington on November 14, 1842, but the western members refused to make a quorum until Houston, on November 21, issued a second proclamation calling the regular session to meet on December 5. A quorum was finally secured on December 1, and the President delivered his message in person. Secretary Miller reported

[122] *Telegraph and Texas Register*, October 19, 1842.
[123] Ward to Houston, October 30, 1842, Houston Unpublished Correspondence, III; *Telegraph and Texas Register*, November 9, 1842.
[124] Hope Yager, "The Archive War in Texas" (M.A. thesis, University of Texas, 1939), 67.
[125] To the House of Representatives, January 10, 1843, *Writings*, III, 287–88.

to Ashbel Smith that he thought it possible that nothing would be done and that the session would break up in a row without making any appropriations for the ensuing year. Smith's cousin Henry Gillett, operating his Union Academy near the temporary capital, was also pessimistic and reported that Houston was the target for all to shoot at, for "they wish the honors he enjoys but have neither ability nor patience to take the necessary steps."[126]

Not all the shooting was done in Texas. The New Orleans *Bee* called Houston's December message to Congress a "very feeble document" and his comments upon the Mexican invasions "such as might have been expected from an Executive whose vacillating and quibbling conduct . . . at once disgusted the citizens of his own state and mortified every friend of Texas in other countries."[127] On January 10, that Congress, according to Gillett "one of the weakest that was ever assembled in any nation," had as yet done little for the country, for "they are continually sparring at they know not what themselves."[128] Meantime, the President sent them a message on the deplorable condition of the navy, proclaimed a treaty with the Netherlands, submitted a treaty of amity with the United States, vetoed a bill for protection of the frontier, and on January 16, 1843, the day that Congress adjourned, ordered Auditor Charles Mason not to audit the accounts of members of that body for the time they were "absent by desertion from their duties."[129] Such could be interpreted as economy. With Congress out of the way, the President busied himself disposing of the navy and arranging for an Indian council to be held at Washington on April 14, 1843.

Domestic concerns called for executive attention also. Houston's office was a one-story, one-room affair, previously tenanted by William McFarland. W. D. Miller usually occupied the one chair in the room while Houston reclined on a couch to dictate his letters and messages. During their first months in Washington the Houstons lived at the home of Judge John Lockhart. The Judge's wife was of pioneer stuff but was "strong for the niceties of the old life" and could not but be exasperated by the President's habit of spitting on her clean porch when, "by exerting no undue energy and exercising a bit of consideration, he could have expectorated over the rail." She was probably much more exasperated

---

[126] Gillett to Smith, November 25, 1842, and Miller to Smith, December 8, 1842, Ashbel Smith Papers.
[127] Quoted in *Telegraph and Texas Register*, January 4, 1843.
[128] Gillett to Smith, January 10, 1843, Ashbel Smith Papers.
[129] Houston to Mason, January 16, 1843, *Writings*, III, 298.

when, during his wife's absence to visit her mother and sister at Grand Cane, he fell from grace, imbibed too much Madeira wine, and had his servant chop off the posts of a fine old bed.[130]

Nancy Lea joined her daughter and son-in-law in the winter of 1842, and the family moved to a cottage on the outskirts of Washington to set up housekeeping with "everything as plain as could well be, for the general said that he and the government were too poor to indulge in any unnecessary luxuries."[131] Houston had William Bryan at New Orleans buy his household necessities, including everything from a double barouche to two sets of guitar strings. The furnishings were to include a neat workstand, pitchers and bowls, three or four bolts of furniture fringe, "fine Callico (handsome)," with "Vines, Flowers, or any figure of taste" but no "Turkey Gobblers, Peacocks, Bears, Elephants, wild Boars, or Stud Horses." The list of supplies included a bolt of dimity and one of "Linnen *Diaper for Towels*."[132] Whatever Houston's intent may have been in emphasizing that the diaper cloth was for towels, word went to Ashbel Smith in Europe that appearances indicated that the presidential family was soon to be increased.[133] Sam Houston, Jr., was born on May 25, 1843. The father wrote his British friend Captain Charles Elliot in reply to a congratulatory message: "Mrs. H. and the boy are doing well. He is stout, and I hope will be useful to his kind. May he be anything but a loafer, an agitator, or in other words, a demagogue."[134]

Just which agitators and demagogues the President had in mind at the moment would be difficult to ascertain, for he was sustaining attacks from all quarters, particularly from the west, where a convention was scheduled for July 17 to condemn the executive for actions in general and the Mexican armistice and removal of Commodore Moore in particular. Only six delegates actually attended the meeting at LaGrange,[135] but the outcroppings of public meetings and the incessant newspaper jibes—possibly combined with new paternal problems—made Houston write Smith:

We cannot be harassed, any longer! I am weary. In a few days, I expect to set out for Bird's Fort, on the Trinity to meet various Indian Tribes in council. Nothing but the health of my family will prevent me from the visit as I hope

[130] Wallis and Hill, *Sixty Years on the Brazos*, 28, 119, 156.
[131] *Ibid.*, 119.
[132] Houston to William Bryan, January 24, 1843, *Writings*, III, 304–305.
[133] Gillett to Smith, March 10, 1843, Ashbel Smith Papers.
[134] Houston to Elliot, June 15, 1843, *Writings*, IV, 211.
[135] *Telegraph and Texas Register*, August 2, 1843.

at this time. Mrs. H. is indisposed seriously today, but I am happy to *inform* you her boy is quite well!!!![136]

Mrs. Houston and the "rascal," who was, according to Miller, "a living miniature of his father,"[137] spent the late part of the summer of 1843 with Mrs. Lea and Mrs. Bledsoe, while the President went to confer with his Indian friends in what turned out to be an unprofitable council on the upper Trinity. One wonders whether his regalia for that council was the same that he had donned for the Indian conclave at Washington-on-the-Brazos earlier in the year. His ordinary attire in Washington was his hunting shirt of linsey-woolsey checks, trousers of Osnaburg, russet shoes without strings, and his smoky-colored broad-brimmed hat with "fur nap half an inch long," but for the Indians he had worn a flaming red silk robe that was a gift from the Sultan of Turkey.[138]

En route to the Trinity, Houston made a speech at Crockett on August 4, 1843, wherein he "almost pledged himself to the people of Texas if they would give him a majority of the next Congress, that he would have peace between Texas and Mexico, and, on a satisfactory basis."[139] But the abortive armistice with Mexico was not a basis for a satisfactory peace, and the Eighth Congress opposed him on every issue: on the sale of the navy, on the tariff, on the removal of the seat of government, and on his silence on annexation policy. As a result, he vetoed a long list of bills between January 10 and February 5, when the Congress adjourned. That adjournment Gillett described as "the most praiseworthy act of the whole session."[140] The President, convinced that "no collection of mankind, from Adam down, . . . was more corrupt," anticipated a cool reception for the congressmen from their constituents and hoped for better representation next time.[141] When, in a speech at the Presbyterian church in Houston, he characterized the Congress as the "most base, ignorant, and vicious legislative assembly since the Rump Parliament," the *Telegraph* countered that the executive forgot that the "most drunken, ignorant, & despicable creatures of Congress were among his own supporters."[142]

Vituperation and recrimination widened the breach between Houston and anti-Houston factions as the summer of 1844 generated extra

[136] Houston to Smith, July 2, 1843, *Writings*, III, 418.
[137] Miller to Smith, July 21, 1843, Ashbel Smith Papers.
[138] Wallis and Hill, *Sixty Years on the Brazos*, 120.
[139] *Telegraph and Texas Register*, September 13, 1843.
[140] Gillett to Smith, February 21, 1844, Ashbel Smith Papers.
[141] Houston to T. W. Ward, March 14, 1844, *Writings*, IV, 279.
[142] *Telegraph and Texas Register*, April 17, 1844.

heat in the presidential campaign in which Anson Jones and Edward Burleson were the opposing candidates. While the incumbent remained officially silent about his preference, public comment in general and newspaper publicity in particular named Jones as the heir apparent, and the anti-Houston *Telegraph* turned its attack on the "servile" Secretary of State.

Advocates of annexation were bitter at both Houston and Jones for their policy of increasing friendliness with England and France. Barnard Bee wrote Jones that he presumed that, as president, Jones would send Ashbel Smith to France and Houston to England, for "he would be delighted with that wonderful country, and make a decided impression there." Jones endorsed the Bee recommendation: "I should like to oblige Gen. Houston, but cannot trust him so far from home."[143]

Finally, on August 5, 1844, Houston broke his silence on politics and committed himself in favor of Jones in a letter which pointed out Burleson's lack of co-operation as vice-president. As for Jones, the President enumerated the events in their long association and declared:

He has concurred in my policy and with distinguished ability he has conducted the foreign relations of the govt. and I have confidence that if the choice of the people should devolve the duties of President upon him, he would consult the true interests of the country, and that he would endeavor to carry out the policy which he might conceive would best promote its honor and prosperity.[144]

On August 25, 1844, Christian F. Duerr recorded in his diary that Houston had "gone east to electioneer for Anson Jones for the presidency & for himself for a seat in Congress from San Augustine or some other eastern county." Duerr apparently guessed wrong about Houston's again considering a seat in Congress. The President of Texas was so eager for annexation that he hoped there would not have to be any further Congressional sessions. He was occupied with the problems of the Regulator-Moderator affair in Shelby County and with a prolific correspondence on annexation. As he committed his legal business to O. M. Roberts, he wrote: "I have been so much employed in public concerns, that my private affairs are and have been woefully neglected."[145] Tucked into official correspondence with his close friends were comments on his family: "Mrs. Houston . . . bids me say to Madam, 'Sam has no less than four

---

[143] Jones, *Republic of Texas*, 389.
[144] Houston to Black *et al.*, August 5, 1844, *Writings*, IV, 357.
[145] Houston to Roberts, March 19, 1844, Letters to Oran M. Roberts, Oran M. Roberts Papers, III, Part I (1844–61).

teeth,' and I say, 'Sam's mother has recovered from her ecstasy at the discovery of his first tooth.' "[146] By the last of September he was writing his wife at Grand Cane to "tell Sam I will try and get an antelope skin for him" and reporting in the same letter, "Dr. Jones, I suppose, is elected by some 1700 votes."[147]

The Ninth Congress met on December 2, 1844. Two days later Houston delivered his last annual message to a Texas Congress; at Anson Jones's inauguration on December 9, he made his valedictory. Jones's biographer emphasizes the "polite and distant note" on which one administration ended and the other began.[148]

The retiring president remained in Washington a few days and then joined his family in Liberty County, "gratified that my probation has passed." He wrote to the new president as the Christmas holiday approached:

It was, indeed, a joyous meeting, and strange to say, I find my mind falling back into a channel, where the current flows in domestic peace and quiet, without one care about the affairs of Government, and only intent upon domestic happiness and prosperity. . . . That you may not only be successful, but more glorious in your administration than any predecessor, is my ardent wish and desire.[149]

Officially, Houston's connection with the Republic of Texas was ended. Still his every movement, especially as regarded annexation, was to be watched and reported, so that Texas newspapers continued to devote much space to Houston. His enemies in Congress could not resist a parting shot as that body took up the old and bitter problem of locating the capital. Cazneau of Travis again condemned Houston's action in removing the government as illegal tyranny. James W. ("Smoky") Henderson and W. R. ("Dirty Shirt") Scurry defended Houston's action. When a bill was passed directing Jones and his cabinet officials to move to Austin, Houston's political friends entered a protest in the House *Journal* on December 23, 1844.[150]

At Bastrop, on Christmas Day, with weather fine but a heavy track, another sort of contest featured the name of Sam Houston. The subscription price for entering the sweepstakes for colts and fillies two years old was two bales of cotton. A. D. Hunt's Hail Storm took the race from Red

[146] Houston to James Reily, March 18, 1844, *Writings*, IV, 280.
[147] Houston to Margaret Lea Houston, September 28, 1844, *ibid.*, 373.
[148] Gambrell, *Anson Jones*, 369.
[149] Houston to Jones, December 21, 1844, *Writings*, IV, 408–409.
[150] Memoirs of John Salmon Ford, II, 304.

Rover, Mary Bowles, and Big Drunk. All of the entries had been sired by the same horse—Sam Houston.[151]

Almost a decade had passed since the establishment of Mr. Houston's Republic. It had been a decade of change for the nation and for the man, a period characterized by uncertainty and threats and alarms for both; but both had survived and had come to the end of the period with relative security and serenity. In the era described as one of "rampant individualism," Houston had received an undue measure of both criticism and praise.

[151] LaGrange *Intelligencer*, January 2, 1845.

More Coy than Forward:
Diplomacy of Annexation

O N FEBRUARY 21, 1846, Houston and Thomas
J. Rusk were elected United States sena-
tors from Texas. Houston took his seat in the Senate on March 30; on
April 15 he made his maiden senatorial speech. In debating the Oregon
question, he used the discussion of the United States' relations with Eng-
land on that issue as a springboard to review the whole process of the
annexation of Texas so that he might "correct any errors that may exist
on this subject before they are received as history by the public mind."
In describing annexation, he said, "Texas was more coy than forward."
Six years later, the Senator lectured in Philadelphia on the "Trials and
Dangers of Frontier Life," giving a running summary of the history of
Texas and of annexation and emphasizing his own and Andrew Jackson's

part in the events. "I am very glad," he said, "that the misfortune of annexation happened to us."[1]

These two remarks are typically Houston. They bear on the questions of whether Houston worked skillfully to bring about annexation, even coquetting with England or with the United States to that end, or whether he sincerely opposed annexation and was not being facetious in his use of the word "misfortune" as applied to the union. There were those persons in Texas who thought that he did his best to defeat the measure in the face of the overwhelming desire of the great mass of people in Texas for annexation. Ashbel Smith, who, as Texas representative in England and France, helped formulate Houston's foreign policy and who perhaps knew the Old Chief more intimately and over a longer period of time than did any other person, said on this subject:

General Houston was not considered to be very ardent for annexation—nor was he. In my opinion his *own* judgment—and in him judgment was preeminently calm and thoughtful, his very bursts of tempestuous passion were premeditated—his own judgment was opposed to annexation. . . . No man ever loved the American union, the United States, with more intense affection than Houston. He had poured out the blood of his youth like water in its battles. But he had grave doubts whether the welfare of Texas or of the United States would be promoted by their union under one common government.

And again Smith said:

In my opinion his strong judgment preponderated in favor of separate independence. In 1836, he voted for annexation . . . he did not then think that the people of Texas were capable of sustaining an independent government. Time rolled on, he believed Texas capable of self-government. To his judgment it seemed a grave problem whether it was not better for Texas, better for the cause of liberty and republican institutions, that there should be two great self-governing peoples instead of a single one.[2]

James Pinckney Henderson, who was sent to Washington to aid Isaac Van Zandt in making the annexation treaty in the spring of 1844, thought that Houston was an advocate of annexation and wrote to Rusk: "Houston I know is as strongly in favour of the measure as any person in Texas but those who doubted him would not believe it & therefore to quiet all I consented to go."[3]

As a result of his careful study of the annexation of Texas, Justin

---

[1] Lecture on January 28, 1851, *Writings*, V, 277.
[2] Ashbel Smith, *Reminiscences of the Texas Republic*, "Historical Society of Galveston Series," No. 1, December 16, 1875, pp. 69–70, 80.
[3] Henderson to Rusk, March 2, 1844, T. J. Rusk Papers.

Smith didn't say "yes" and he didn't say "no" but arrived at "maybe" as his answer to whether or not Houston was for annexation. As to Houston's real purpose, Smith wrote:

Mexican rule, then, he was fully determined of course never to accept. Annexation to the United States he regarded as tolerable if no better arrangement could be made, growing warmer or colder toward that plan according to circumstances. But his real desire was to obtain recognition from Mexico as the legal certificate of sovereignty, ensure an opportunity for growth by winning a guaranty—more or less formal—of Texas independence from the United States, England or both, lead his people forward then, unhindered, in the path of development, and gain a lofty place in history as the founder of a nation. To compass these ends, he designed to play off England and the United States against each other, exciting this country by dwelling publicly on the assistance received from across the ocean and letting it be felt that his relations yonder were dangerously intimate, and stimulating Great Britain at the same time by keeping the annexation issue alive and prominent. Finally the human element must not be overlooked. Though a patriot, Houston was no idealist. It was far from his intention to sacrifice his personal fortunes for the halo of martyrdom; and no doubt he proposed so to manage that, whatever wind should blow, the vessel bearing his pennant should reach a port.[4]

Here again, as in the matter of motive for going to Texas, it seems that the only approach to the Houston design must be an interpretation of Houston's own words on the subject of annexation with the on- and off-stage remarks of some of the other actors in the drama.

In May, 1836, a little over a month after San Jacinto, while Houston was still under medical treatment at New Orleans, William H. Wharton wrote Austin that he had intelligence from Nashville that Houston was opposed to the annexation of Texas to the United States. Wharton pondered and planned:

If this be so it is truly and deeply to be deplored. Like all triumphant conquerors he will be omnipotent for a time at least. I plainly see before me the turmoil and confusion and injustice and the demagoguism which must ensue in *Texas* after the war is over before we can establish an orderly and harmonious independent government. . . . Knowing therefore that I have some influence with Houston I shall be in misery until I see him before his opinions on this subject are generally known or firmly fixed.

•   •   •   •   •   •   •   •   •   •   •

P.S. Our friends say they will if possible keep congress together until August on account of this business. I trust in God that it is a mistake about Hous-

[4] From *Annexation of Texas* (98–99), by Justin H. Smith, published by Barnes and Noble, Inc., and reprinted by their permission.

ton's being opposed to annexation. If he is I will exert my little influence with him. We have always been and are the best of friends. Do hurry on home without a moment's delay.[5]

Knoxville, Tennesse, got a different report—this one from Houston himself, who, as he reached the Texas border, wrote to Richard Dunlap, "There is but one feeling in Texas, in my opinion, and that is to establish the independence of Texas, and to be attached to the United States."[6] True, he expressed Texas opinion and not necessarily his own.

In his inaugural address on October 22, 1836, Houston mentioned the unparalleled unanimity in which the people of Texas had declared their will to be joined to the United States, and voiced the doubt that the mother country would disregard the appeal. He encouraged his countrymen: "We are cheered by the hope that they will receive us to a participancy of their civil, political, and religious rights, and hail us welcome into the great family of freemen." To that end he accredited William H. Wharton as minister to the United States to make treaties of amity, commerce, and limits and to open negotiations on "all matters and things which are or may hereafter become desirable to this country." It seems that Wharton's "little influence" was effective. On November 16, two days before the date of Wharton's commission, Houston stated to the Senate, in reporting to that body that he was sending Santa Anna to Washington, that the Mexican general would then be in a position to facilitate the attainment of Texan objectives—whether independence or annexation. Houston took November 20, 1836, for letter writing, so that his missives could be taken to the United States by Hockley and Bee as they escorted Santa Anna. To his cousin John Houston he wrote:

By all means get Texas annexed to the U. States—I wish to retire, and spend the balance of my days in peace, and to review the past, as a Philosopher shou'd do—
See all *our* old friends, and tell them it is my soul's desire.—I never was ambitious, but *fortune* has given a semblance to my actions which my soul never *desired!*

And to Jackson, he wrote:

My great desire is that our country Texas shall be annexed to the United States and on a footing of justice and reciprocity to the parties. It is policy to hold out the idea (and few there are who know to the contrary) that we are very

[5] Wharton to Austin, May 28, 1836, *Austin Papers*, III, 360–61.
[6] Houston to Dunlap, July 2, 1836, *Writings*, I, 431.

118

able to sustain ourselves against any power who are not impotent, yet I am free to say to *you* that we cannot do it.[1]

Austin, as secretary of state, couched his instructions to Wharton in terms of annexation on a broad basis of equitable reciprocity. Securing recognition by the United States was the first problem, and Texans were greatly disappointed when, on December 21, 1836, President Jackson's message to the United States Congress advised delay. Jackson's action was based partially on reports made to him by his agent, Henry M. Morfit, who had been in Texas from August through September, 1836, and who reported to the American State Department on conditions in Texas, the threat of a new Mexican invasion, and the check which that threat had imposed upon continued immigration into Texas. While his report was generally favorable, Morfit advised against immediate recognition. Jackson's message gave his reasons for delaying recognition as doubt of Texas' ability to maintain her independence, unwillingness to offend Mexico, and the fact that recognition would be regarded by Mexico as a preliminary step toward annexation. He was also actuated by the fact that Martin Van Buren had been elected president in November, 1836, to take office in March, 1837; and Van Buren, for political reasons, opposed immediate action on the Texas question. Jackson, in a private interview with Wharton, said he was putting the responsibility on Congress and would approve recognition if Congress should recommend it.

On February 28, 1837, the House of Representatives passed an appropriation for payment of the salary of a diplomatic agent to Texas; on March 3, a year and a day after the declaration of Texas independence, the Senate passed a resolution that Texas ought to be recognized, and President Jackson appointed Alcée LaBranche to be chargé d'affaires to Texas. Houston exulted to Dr. Robert Irion, who two months later was to become his secretary of state:

You will have learned that we are Independent, and recognized by the U. States on the 4th inst., the last official act of Genl. Jackson's life. This alone is cause for joy, but annexation wou'd have rendered me truly happy, and secured all that we contended for. My only wish is to see the country happy—at peace and retire to the Red Lands, get a fair, sweet "wee Wifie," as Burns says, and pass the balance of my sinful life in ease and comfort, (if I can).

In the same strain he wrote to Albert Sidney Johnston: "We have heard *officially* of the 'recognition of our Independence,' and I hope our credit

[1] Houston to John Houston, November 20, 1836, *ibid.*, II, 27; Houston to Jackson, November 20, 1836, *ibid.*, I, 488.

will now rise. . . . The next thing to be *hoped* for is *annexation of Texas.*"

In his first message to the Texas Congress after it convened in the new Capitol at Houston, the President reported that the Texas attitude toward annexation had undergone no important change since Congress adjourned at Columbia on December 22, 1836. He commended the zealous and untiring efforts of the Texas representatives, said that the adjournment of the United States Congress in March, 1837, had prevented that government's action, and expressed the hope that the matter would receive early determination in the next session of that Congress.' On May 12, 1837, Memucan Hunt was accredited minister to the United States to succeed Wharton and on the following August 4 made the first and only proffer of Texas to the United States. He presented annexation in the light of a benefit to the United States, although at the moment Mexico was again threatening invasion of a Texas ill-prepared to maintain a national government and wage a war of defense. John Forsyth, Van Buren's secretary of state, declined the Texas offer on two grounds: the constitutional question of the legality of annexing a foreign independent territory, and the desire to avoid offending Mexico, since annexation would make the United States a party to the war still nominally being waged between Mexico and Texas. Considering the previous acquisition of Louisiana and Florida, even though not independent territories, the constitutional scruple seemed a little far fetched, but it was a point which John Quincy Adams used in his long speech presenting abolitionist opposition to annexation in the summer of 1838.¹⁰

By April, 1838, the Second Texas Congress was considering the unconditional withdrawal of the proposal of annexation, and Anson Jones, chairman of the House Committee on Foreign Relations, proposed a joint resolution authorizing the President to instruct the minister in Washington, D.C., to withdraw the proposition. The Jones resolution was defeated, but on June 25, 1838, Houston named Jones the minister to Washington. When Jones arrived in the United States capital, he found that on May 19 Houston had instructed the Texas minister to withdraw the annexation proposition. Fairfax Catlett, acting chargé after Hunt's resignation, had been puzzled over how to withdraw a proposition which the United States did not admit as pending. Jones, pleased with the situation, wrote in August, 1838: "Annexation is at an end & for

---

⁸ Houston to Irion, March 19, 1837, *ibid.,* II, 74; Houston to Johnston, March 21, 1837, Johnston Papers.

⁹ President's Message, May 5, 1837, *Writings,* II, 87.

¹⁰ Eugene C. Barker, "The Annexation of Texas," *Southwestern Historical Quarterly,* L (1946/47), 53–55.

120

the present Texas *can* if she *will* get on without it. *If the next administration pursues a proper course* not many in Texas will wish for it. How *glorious* will Texas be standing alone, and relying upon her own strength."[11]

If this quotation expresses Jones's true sentiments on annexation, then the Lamar administration pursued the proper course, for Lamar could see no advantage to Texas in annexation, which, according to him, "would produce a lasting regret and ultimately prove as disastrous to our liberty and hopes as the triumphant sword of the enemy." Envisioning a brilliant future for an independent republic stretching from the Sabine to the Pacific, he regarded Texas' union with the United States as "the grave of all her hopes of happiness and greatness."[12] Annexation was a dead issue until the end of Lamar's administration on December 13, 1841. During that administration, however, Texas was recognized by England, Holland, France, and Belgium. That recognition stimulated or revived United States interest in annexation and aroused some apprehension of European influence in Texas. As early as May, 1836, Daniel Webster was convinced that England was greatly interested in Texas and might take action to the detriment of the United States. During the Mexican invasions of Texas in 1842, American newspapers charged that those invasions were financed by British loans. Mass meetings held in the United States encouraged immigration into Texas to strengthen resistance to Mexico. With increased American interest in Texas there was also increased abolition sentiment against annexation, which the abolitionists insisted would be an infraction of the Constitution and identical with dissolution of the Union.[13]

With the beginning of his second administration, in December, 1841, Houston named Anson Jones his secretary of state, and James Reily replaced Barnard Bee as minister to the United States. On January 26, 1842, Jones gave Reily his instructions.

The new Texan representative near the government of the United States was to conclude without delay that trade agreement that Lamar's Chargé had failed for two years to negotiate, to exhort the United States to keep her Indians out of Texas, and—cautiously, noncommittally—to ascertain if the United States might be interested in inviting Texas into the Union. Reily would be discreet and suave; Jones counted on nothing immediately regarding annexation. Jones was unlatching the door that had been slammed in Texas' face—he

---

[11] Gambrell, *Anson Jones*, 128–29, 138.
[12] Barker, "Annexation of Texas," *Southwestern Historical Quarterly*, L, 55.
[13] *Ibid.*, 56–61.

did not open it, but Reily was to whisper to the United States that the door was no longer locked.[14]

Reily reported to his government that John Tyler, who became president on the death of William Henry Harrison, in April, 1841, was in favor of annexation, which was becoming increasingly popular with the Congress. To Reily, Tyler explained that he wished to conclude the matter at once but that he must have the consent of the Senate and that as matters stood it seemed best to mediate with Mexico in an attempt to bring about peace between that country and Texas.[15] Instead of peace in 1842 there came Mexican invasions in March and again in September. On July 20, 1842, upon Reily's resignation, Houston nominated Isaac Van Zandt as chargé to the United States. Van Zandt wrote on December 23, 1842, that Tyler and a majority of his cabinet were in favor of annexation but that they feared that they could not secure the necessary two-thirds vote in the Senate to ratify a treaty.

A month later Houston wrote to Charles Elliot, the British representative to Texas, asking his diplomatic assistance in saving the Mier prisoners in Mexico, and including in the letter a lengthy discussion of the matter of annexation, which the President of Texas said he thought would "appeal directly to Her Majesty's Government," since the probabilities of the measure's success were greater than they had been at any former period. Nine-tenths of the people of Texas favored the measure on the ground that it would give Texas peace. He thought that both the Whigs and the Democrats in the United States would favor the matter. To defeat the measure England need only demand of Santa Anna that he recognize the independence of Texas; and Santa Anna, to avoid war with England while there was probability of war with the United States and France, would use the threat of war to justify recognition and save face with the Mexican people. Houston concluded his argument: "In all these matters I may be mistaken, but I am honest in my convictions that Texas and England would both be beneficiaries by this course. Time will tell the tale."[16]

Late in January, 1843, Washington D. Miller, Houston's one-time private secretary and always a close adviser, wrote President Tyler a long letter on the subject of annexation. Miller described Captain Elliot as a most able and efficient representative, experienced in diplomacy—a man sent to Texas to turn the condition of that Republic to account for Eng-

[14] Gambrell, *Anson Jones*, 232.
[15] Reily to Jones, April 15 and July 11, 1842, quoted in Yoakum, *History of Texas*, II, 345–47.
[16] Houston to Elliot, January 24, 1843, *Writings*, III, 300–301.

land by counteracting French influence, by seeing that the interests and policy of the United States received as little attention as possible, and by planting British power in a prolific soil. Miller assured the President of the United States that the people of Texas, including Houston, were almost unanimous in wanting a treaty of annexation. He stressed the advantages to accrue to the United States from commerce with Texas. He pointed out British jealousy of the growing commercial power and sea power of the United States and was careful to mention British dictation of policy to Mexico, a policy which might first be directed against Mexican recognition of Texas independence but might ultimately lead to British acquisition of Texas and domination of trade in the Gulf of Mexico. His letter, Miller said, was prompted by a sincere regard for the permanent good of Texas and Tyler's lasting glory since he believed that perhaps destiny had placed Tyler in his exalted position just to accomplish the work of annexation. Miller concluded:

General Houston, *I am sure*, entertains for the measure the liveliest wishes; and for yourself the best good feelings. He has heard through various channels of your many partial inquiries & friendly expressions concerning him; and he reciprocates them freely. The time is favorable for the consummation of the work—none in the future can ever be more so. I pray you, therefore, let it be done. Let it be done before peace with Mexico is obtained. That is important. If you fail with the Senate, the fault will not be yours, and the loss [of] the country will be chargeable *alone* to that body.[17]

It is extremely unlikely that Miller would have written this letter without consultation with Houston, and more likely that it was written with Houston's consent, although much of the Miller correspondence leads one to wonder whether Houston gave Miller advice or Miller formulated the ideas which ostensibly were Houston's policy. To arouse fear of England and of Elliot was good tactical maneuvering. Elliot's key position in annexation proceedings is also indicated in a letter from William Henry Daingerfield to Anson Jones describing the diplomat:

He seems to entertain the greatest possible confidence in the President, and he swears by the usual English shibboleth, that in some manner or other, the question of recognition is to be solved by the Executive within the next six months. *Over our wine* he offered me to bet that it would; I of course declined. . . . I have written to the President to "hit him agen" on the subject of *annexation*. Since writing the letter I have dined with him, and think *that that is the spot* between wind and water with him.[18]

[17] Miller to Tyler, January 30, 1843, Miller Papers.
[18] Daingerfield to Jones, February 4, 1843, Jones, *Republic of Texas,* 208–209.

Elliot was not the only member of the diplomatic corps with whom Houston discussed annexation. To the American chargé, Joseph Eve, he wrote in February, 1843, that some of the oldest settlers of Texas, even some of the Old Three Hundred, were anxious for the event and that if annexation became a political lever in the United States, both parties would seize it.[19]

Houston was doubtless annoyed by American official indifference to Texas. Annoyed or not, it was not bad policy to seem so to Elliot, to whom Houston stressed the deep interest the United States was taking in Texas matters as indicated by editorial effusions. The political parties, he stated, had not decided what capital to make out of Texas, but the South at least hoped for annexation. The United States realized that Texas would have a sense of obligation to England if that country achieved peace between Texas and Mexico, and also that England would secure a friend and footing on the Gulf of Mexico too close for American comfort. Every act of kindness to Texas by a power of which the United States was jealous was regarded by the United States as unauthorized interference, for the older republic looked on Texas as an appendage—"nothing more than a pocket attached to their outer robe." In this letter, apparently for the first time on paper, Houston indicated a disposition adverse to annexation. Although the letter was marked "Private," he may well have thought that his remarks would not remain confidential but would become fuel to fire more annexation sentiment in the United States. He may have been sincere, or he may merely have been smarting under American affront to Texan dignity. In either case, he summarized the history of the annexation question for the British diplomat:

Texas once evinced a willingness, amounting to unexampled unanimity, to become annexed to the United States. We sought the boon with humble supplications. In this posture we remained in the outer porch of their Capitol for many months. Our solicitations were heard with apathy. Our urgency was responded to with politic indifference. Apprised of this, I directed our Minister to withdraw the proposition. This I did from a sense of national dignity. Since that time Texas has not renewed the proposition; and the United States now, in order to get it into an attitude before them that would be creditable to them, desire, no doubt, that Texas should again come forward soliciting the boon. They have not as yet received such indications as they desire. If it were the case, it would place the subject before the political parties of the U. States, in a position different from that in which it now rests. In that event there would be but one question to ask: Shall the Annexation of Texas to the U. States take

[19] Houston to Eve, February 17, 1843, *Writings*, III, 322.

place? As it is, there are two: First, Is Texas *willing* to be annexed? Second, in that case, shall it be annexed?[20]

Houston may have been speaking the literal truth when he said that Texas had not renewed the proposition for annexation. What he did not say was that Texas had indicated her willingness to be sued. In the same letter he went on to ridicule the rumors circulating about his being favorable to retrocession to Mexico, and to Texas' becoming a British colony with slavery abolished. He did declare that Texas was justly entitled, by her enterprise, daring, sufferings, and privations, to an independent position among the nations of the world and that he desired that independence, for "all that Texas requires, to make her healthy and vigorous is a respite from execution."[21]

By the time William S. Murphy arrived in Texas, on June 3, 1843, to replace Eve as chargé, Elliot's activities in Texas governmental affairs were common talk; and Murphy wrote on June 5 that it was general report that Houston was completely under British influence and opposed to annexation although the people were favorable to it.[22]

In July, 1843, the British and Foreign Anti-Slavery Society held its general convention in London. Among the delegates were Lewis Tappan, a New York philanthropist, and one Stephen Pearl Andrews of Massachusetts, who had spent some time in Galveston. Although Tappan had never been in Texas, both men represented themselves as accredited Texas agents, and Andrews reported that Houston and other leading men of the Republic were in sympathy with the abolition cause.[23] That same month the *Telegraph and Texas Register* ran editorials on Anglo-Texas relations. One, entitled "Price of British Mediation," gave credence to the report that Captain Elliot had been instructed to propose the abolition of slavery as the price of British intervention to compel Mexico to make peace with Texas, but pointed out that, fortunately, the Texas executive, even if he desired peace on those terms, could not accept it on his own responsibility. Another editorial, called "Secret Policy," commented that the people of Texas would view with suspicion any policy that was concealed from them and that the paper hoped that Texans would be alert to elect to the next Congress men who would repel any overtures made in secret.[24]

[20] Houston to Elliot, May 13, 1843, *ibid.*, 385–87.
[21] *Ibid.*, 388.
[22] George Lockhart Rives, *The United States and Mexico*, I, 559.
[23] Harriet Smither, "English Abolitionism and the Annexation of Texas," *Southwestern Historical Quarterly*, XXXII (1928/29), 194.
[24] *Telegraph and Texas Register*, July 12, 1843.

President Tyler, a former Democrat who had become vice-president on the Whig ticket and succeeded to the presidency a month after Harrison's inauguration, had made himself a man without a party by vetoing nearly all the Whig measures, and could not depend on support of either side in championing annexation. By September, 1843, however, Van Zandt wrote the Texas government that Secretary of State Abel P. Upshur was discussing annexation frequently and that Tyler was contemplating early action on the subject. Tyler received some more prompting from Miller, who on September 16 wrote him a three-page letter reinforcing the Texan's earlier observations on Elliot's shrewdness as a diplomat and the English advantage gained in the delay of annexation.[25]

A month later, when Upshur proposed opening negotiations for a treaty of annexation, Van Zandt replied that he had no instructions on the subject but would submit the matter to his government. Houston, on October 30, 1843, showed Van Zandt's dispatch to Elliot, whom he asked to assure Lord Aberdeen of the British Foreign Office that, "with the Independence of Texas recognized by Mexico, he would never consent to any treaty or other project of annexation to the United States, and he had a conviction that the people would sustain him in that determination." Elliot, in writing to Aberdeen the following day, stated that implicit reliance could be placed in Houston's sincerity and steadiness but that he perceived no such ground to depend upon the course of the people of Texas if the project of annexation were presented to them.[26]

Tyler's message to the United States Congress on December 5, 1843, declared that the United States was interested in seeing an end put to hostilities between Texas and Mexico, but it contained nothing on the subject of annexation; and the omission was approved by Andrew Jackson, who wrote William B. Lewis that the proper course was to enter on a treaty, with the first official action the presentation of that treaty to the Senate, for any other action would bring down the "abuse of J. Q. Adams and associates." Jackson told Lewis that he did not believe Houston would dare oppose annexation, and that if it were otherwise he was convinced that he could change Houston's mind in a day. The former United States president said that in order to prevent England's getting Texas the United States must secure it—peaceably if she could, forcibly if she must —for the dearest interest of the nation, "the safety of New Orleans, the

[25] Miller to Tyler, September 16, 1843, Miller Papers.
[26] Elliot to Aberdeen, October 31, 1843, Ephraim Douglass Adams, *British Diplomatic Correspondence concerning the Republic of Texas, 1836–1846,* 271–77.

prosperity of the great valley of the Mississippi and our whole union require the annexation of Texas."[27]

In January, 1844, the annexation movement and the comments upon it were greatly accelerated. Ashbel Smith, in Paris, got part of the European reverberation in a letter from Lachlan M. Rate, the Texas consul general in London, saying that he looked upon all the annexation talk as mere trash and hoped that Smith had no reason to think that there existed any desire or idea of such a measure on the part of either the people or the government of Texas.[28] That Rate guessed wrong about reaction in Texas is illustrated in a letter written on the same day from Christian F. Duerr on Clear Creek in Texas to a friend in the United States. Duerr gave reasons for his opinion:

You say you dread to hear from Texas for fear of getting some bad news. You may rest assured that things are greatly exaggerated in the U.S. papers & that Houston is *not* about giving this country up to England. Even if he were disposed to do so he could not do it of his own accord, & without the consent of Congress or the people & you may rely upon it that *they* would not consent. For myself I am very glad that the notion of Houston's wanting to sell Texas to England is gaining ground in the U.S., for it may possibly induce your Government to admit us into the Union & self interest may effect what sympathy could not. There is one thing very certain. England would be very glad to get us & will take us whenever we say so, but nothing will ever induce the Texan people to go under the British flag, but a *renewed* & *protracted* & *formidable* invasion of Texas by Mexico. This may & *very probably* would induce Texas to submit to England & to prevent this the U.S. Government ought to either admit us into the Union or coerce Mexico to acknowledge our Independence *at once*, for the longer we remain in our present state the more influence will the British Government gain in Texas. If Texas ever belongs to England, slavery will be abolished here & this will be the ruin of your southwestern country.[29]

Houston had no objection to, and probably a keen desire for, the wide circulation in the United States of such unofficial word as the Duerr letter. Interestingly enough, Duerr was reflecting opinion shown in Ashbel Smith's dispatches to his government: for instance, a Smith letter to Houston in November, 1843, to the effect that Great Britain would spare neither money nor effort to abolish slavery in Texas as a point of ap-

---

[27] Jackson to Lewis, December 15, 1843, *Correspondence of Andrew Jackson*, VI, 249.

[28] Rate to Smith, January 8, 1844, Ashbel Smith Papers.

[29] Duerr to Bennett M. Dell, January 8, 1844, Duerr Diary.

proach for attacking slavery in the United States, with the ultimate object of destroying the agricultural interests of the United States. Smith had also warned that his dispatches should not be printed while he was still at the court of St. James's.[30]

January 8, 1844, may have been a rainy day and good for letter writing. At any rate, Washington D. Miller wrote a long letter to his friend Daingerfield, then at The Hague. He reported on Texas finances and politics and presidential possibilities, reminded Daingerfield of a promise to buy him a suit of clothes for wedding attire, and went on to comment on annexation: "There is a great fuss about annexation both in the United States and Texas; but however much to be desired such an event might be, I must think its accomplishment highly improbable. If our independence as a Separate Nation is secured—annexation can never take place."[31]

This doubt concerning annexation was now expressed by the man who a year earlier had written Tyler the most urgent appeal for annexation. Was Houston's secretary reflecting the Texas President's opinion, or was he making sure that The Hague got the same type of propaganda that England got—independence secure and annexation would become a dead issue?

It was not a dead issue with Robert J. Walker, then United States senator from Mississippi, who wrote to Jackson that the former president's work for annexation would be the crowning act of his life. Because of the possibility that Texas would be lost forever if the annexation treaty were delayed, Walker requested that Jackson, if he thought there was any possibility of its success, urge Houston to instruct his Texas chargé to make the treaty. Jackson, accordingly, wrote a pressure letter to Houston and reported his action to the administration in a letter to William B. Lewis in which he said that if Houston opposed annexation, he would be placed in a perilous situation and destroy himself.[32]

Houston had not had time to receive Jackson's letter when he sent to the Texas Congress a secret message on foreign affairs, which he said were "becoming daily more and more interesting." He explained that during his current administration he had abstained from comment on annexation because he did not think it becoming for him to express any preference. If the Texas government made an effort for that object,

---

[30] Smith to Houston, November 29, 1843, *Houston Unpublished Correspondence*, IV.

[31] Miller to Daingerfield, January 8, 1844, *ibid.*

[32] Walker to Jackson, January 10, 1844, and Jackson to Lewis, January 18, 1844, *Correspondence of Andrew Jackson*, VI, 255, 257.

"which is so desirable," and the effort failed, the effect might be prejudicial upon the course England and France might take towards Texas. If annexation were not accomplished as a result of United States interest in Texas, that interest might still result in a treaty of alliance, defensive even if not offensive, which would be as important to Texas as recognition by Mexico. To that end, he requested that Congress appropriate five thousand dollars to send an additional agent to help Van Zandt in collecting information and representing Texas in Washington on the Potomac. Houston cautioned Congress not to allow his communication to be published until the measures sought were accomplished, since he wanted all initiative to be taken by the United States. "If we evince too much anxiety," he warned, "it will be regarded as importunity, and the voice of supplication seldom commands, in such cases, great respect."[33]

On January 29, 1844, Houston started a letter to Van Zandt to brief the chargé on what the Texas President and Secretary of State were about. They planned to revoke the instructions to suspend negotiations on annexation and give Van Zandt permission, if indications on the part of the United States Congress justified the course, to "open negotiations *and conduct them with the most profound secrecy*" lest failure of the United States to consummate the policy might prove detrimental to future negotiations with other nations. If annexation seemed impossible, then postpone it for future consideration and begin work on a defensive and offensive alliance with the United States against Mexico. If the alliance could not be secured, Van Zandt was to work for a defensive treaty. At least he could find out why the United States declined such a treaty, and Texas would know how far she could rely upon the United States in event of necessity. In his negotiations, Van Zandt was cautioned, the United States "must be satisfied that all the noise about British influence has had no foundation in truth—at the same time they must be convinced that England *has* rendered important service to Texas by her mediatorial influence with Mexico." Houston went on to say that if the United States was really in such dread of the interference of other powers in slavery in Texas, she might work some sort of antiabolition stipulation into the alliance.[34]

Before Houston could finish his letter, he was sidetracked and did not get it concluded until February 15, when he was able to report that J. P. Henderson was being sent to aid Van Zandt in negotiation of a treaty of annexation, that W. D. Miller (practically Houston's own voice and hand) had been appointed secretary for the legation, and that W. S.

[33] To the Texas Congress, January 20, 1844, *Writings*, III, 521–23; VII, 9–11.
[34] Houston to Van Zandt, January 29, 1844, *ibid.*, III, 538–41.

Murphy had just arrived from the United States with dispatches requiring immediate action. The dispatches, Houston told Van Zandt, were of such nature as to justify Texas' gambling on the annexation treaty. At the same time, Texas must use precautions to secure herself against accident, for the situation was such that she could not, without assurance of security from the United States, "hazard the consequences which might possibly result from rejection." That Houston was enthusiastic for annexation would appear from his statement: "It would be useless for me to attempt to portray to you, the magnitude of the consequences which are to grow out of these transactions. Millions will realize their benefits; but it is not within the compass of mortal expression to estimate the advantages to mankind."[35]

Murphy's dispatches were to the effect that the United States would protect Texas from Mexico during annexation proceedings, Van Zandt having requested a naval squadron on the Gulf and a military force on the Texas border to act as circumstances should require. On February 3, 1844, Houston wrote to Murphy that the avowals in Tyler's message and unofficial conversations with Murphy had convinced Houston that Tyler would comply with the request for identity of the two countries in the event of a hostile emergency. Texas requested that the United States order at least five vessels, subject to Murphy's command, to cruise off the Texas ports by early March. Houston insisted that the United States must take the initiative:

The United States must annex Texas—Texas cannot annex herself to the United States. A concurrent action is necessary. And yet, the U. States have adopted no course that could encourage a confident hope on the part of the friends of that measure in this country. What may be done at this session of our Congress, I do not pretend to know. I will not fail to look with intense interest to the subject; and I am sure I cannot be suspected of interposing any impediment to the ascertainment of our position in regard to the U. States.[36]

The *Telegraph*, on February 7, 1844, ran an editorial entitled "Crisis in the National Affairs of Texas," which stated that the Texas executive would abandon his policy of seeking British interference to obtain recognition from Mexico and would cheerfully accept American overtures, but went on to warn American statesmen that a prompt decision was necessary to determine whether European or American policy would prevail in Texas affairs. The same issue of the paper, in "Opposition to Annexation," reported that scarcely a voice in Texas was raised against

[35] *Ibid.*, 541.
[36] Houston to Murphy, February 3, 1844, *ibid.*, IV, 238.

130

annexation and that even the pro-Houston papers had given way to the irresistible current of popular feeling.

James Morgan, on February 9, 1844, wrote to Samuel Swartwout of the arrival of three letters from Andrew Jackson to Houston and commented:

The impression at W. City, is, that Genl. Houston is opposed to annexation, and old Hickory has been written to from that, to use his influence with Houston to bring him over it is surmised! "Old Sam" has managed his cards in this affair very well; but he is no more opposed to annexation than Genl. Jackson yet the English & French agents here think he is![37]

In his own graphic style, Houston addressed Henderson, newly appointed assistant in negotiation proceedings:

By all means come directly to Washington. You will then be on your way to Washington City, as the complexion of affairs will justify the movement. Matters are quite ripe, if we are to judge from developments making on the subject of annexation. The lions are all stirred up, and the menagerie is quite full, if the action of our small members in Congress has not spoiled the show. Matters appear about right, if they will only advance. You will be somewhat amused when you come to see all.[38]

Henderson traveled from Houston to Washington-on-the-Brazos with Murphy, saw the instructions indicating the strong American desire for annexation, and had Murphy's assurance that the United States would order a sufficient fleet to the coast and enough troops to the eastern frontier of Texas to protect Texas from any source. After his interview with the President, Henderson wrote to Thomas J. Rusk: "All things really prove now the *very great* desire of the U.S. to annex us. You would be amused to see their jealousy of England. Houston has played it off well & that is the secret of success if we do succeed."[39]

The demand for United States protection was an interesting aspect of "playing it off well." Both Houston and Jones had asked Murphy's assurance that his government would give either the certainty of protective forces or a guaranty of independence. Justin H. Smith analyzes the demand in the light of Houston's knowledge that the President of the United States could not legally employ armed forces against a nation with which she was at peace. Smith does not consider it entirely correct that Houston asked for the illegal pledge of protection in the expectation

[37] Morgan to Swartwout, February 9, 1844, Samuel Swartwout Papers.
[38] Houston to Henderson, February 10, 1844, *Writings*, IV, 253.
[39] Henderson to Rusk, February 14, 1844, T. J. Rusk Papers.

that it would be refused and that the Texas President would then have a plausible ground for rejecting the American effort; rather he holds that Houston calculated that if the demand were declined, he would have an adequate excuse for a pro-British policy and arousing resentment in Texas against the United States.[40]

Thomas Hart Benton condemned the United States for the pledge of protection, arguing that without it peaceful mediation would have succeeded and Texas and Mexico would have made peace in the spring of 1844. Texas would have come "into the union as naturally, and as easily, and with as little offence to anybody, as Eve went into Adam's bosom in the garden of Eden," without the resort to tricks of intriguing politicians to get her in. But, said Benton, Tyler sent detachments of the army and navy to Texas and made Houston the judge of the exigencies in which they were to fight.

This authority to the President of Texas was continued in full force until after the rejection of the treaty, and then only modified by placing the American diplomatic agent in Texas between President Houston and the naval and military commanders, and making him the medium of communication between a foreign President and our forces. . . . During all that time a foreign President was commander-in-chief of a large detachment of the army and navy of the United States. Without a law of Congress—without a nomination from the President and confirmation of the Senate—without citizenship—without the knowledge of the American people—he was president-general of our land and sea forces,—made so by the senator from South Carolina, with authority to fight them against Mexico with whom we were at peace—an office and authority rather above that of lieutenant-general!—and we are indebted to the forbearance and prudence of President Houston for not incurring the war in 1844, which fell upon us in 1846.[41]

In the summer and fall of 1847, after the fact of annexation, when Houston naturally would be quite willing to accept any and all credit for its accomplishment, he and Tyler got into a somewhat acrimonious newspaper debate over who should have the honors or the credit. Tyler had a letter in the *Weekly Union,* in which he stated that in 1844 he had been determined to scatter to the winds the web of intrigue with England by a direct proposal of annexation. Houston, on July 18, 1847, wrote to F. L. Hatch, editor of the *Texas Banner* at Huntsville, that there had been no web of intrigue to scatter and that the direct proposition for union had been brought about by his instructions to Van Zandt that an-

[40] Justin H. Smith, *Annexation of Texas,* 163–64.
[41] Thomas Hart Benton, *Thirty Years' View; or, a History of the Working of the American Government for Thirty Years, from 1820 to 1850,* II, 644.

nexation was no longer a subject for discussion and by the proclamation of the armistice between Texas and Mexico.[42]

But a discussion of political maneuverings and claims of honors in 1847 is anticipating the moves which were taking place on the diplomatic chessboard at Washington-on-the-Brazos as Houston coached Henderson and Miller on the objectives of their mission to the United States in the early spring of 1844. Miller was to proceed by way of the Hermitage to carry a letter to Jackson. That letter, tantamount to a state paper, seemed genial and open on the surface but was a shrewd document. In it Houston assured his old chief that the subject of annexation was commanding the most profound deliberation of which he was capable and that his situation in the midst of internal and external dangers had justified his hope of securing a respite from existing calamities, but that, so far as he was concerned or as his co-operation was required, he was determined upon immediate annexation. He pointed out that the measure was not so advantageous to Texas as it was indispensable to the United States, said that Texas would be unwise to entertain the proposition for a moment unless she had assurances of protection, and proclaimed that Texas, "a bride adorned for her espousal," must not be mortified by a rejection.[43]

Miller, described by Houston as an interesting acquaintance who would be able to answer all of Jackson's inquiries, reached Nashville on March 11; and Jackson, who had received letters from Washington, D.C., assuring him that all was ready to close the treaty, delayed Houston's envoy only long enough to write to R. J. Walker and W. B. Lewis, Tyler's special confidant, to urge the opportuneness of the moment for carrying annexation into effect lest delay force Texas to make arrangements with Great Britain. Houston was being reported accurately.[44]

Meantime, Houston gave Henderson private instructions in a letter conveyed to Washington by John G. Tod. Henderson was to find the precedents and principles for working out the treaty in the state papers on the cessions of Florida and Louisiana and in Austin's instructions to Wharton on annexation. Houston told Henderson to try to secure justice for Texas citizens whose land would, when the boundary line was run, fall within the area of the United States, and instructed him to urge the justice of retaining in the United States Navy or revenue service certain

[42] Houston to Hatch, July 18 and October 20, 1847, *Writings*, V, 14-27; *Niles' Register*, LXXIII (September 4, 1847), 11.
[43] Houston to Jackson, February 16, 1844, *Writings*, IV, 260–65.
[44] Houston to Jackson, February 17, 1844, and Jackson to Lewis, March 11, 1844, *Correspondence of Andrew Jackson*, VI, 264–65, 272.

men in the Texas Navy. The letter ended: "I hope you may be successful and will perfect a great work. If it is not done at once the situation of Texas will not allow her to remain with her arms folded, or as an ass between two cocks of hay. She will have to act promptly."[45]

On February 28, 1844, Secretary of State Abel P. Upshur, with whom Henderson and Van Zandt were to deal and whose whole soul, Jackson had said, was engaged in the accomplishment of annexation, was killed in an explosion on the sloop of war *Princeton*. For almost a month nothing further could be done on annexation. By that time, on March 16, 1844, John C. Calhoun, because of his interest in the Texas question, particularly his fear of English threats to slavery in Texas directly and in the United States indirectly, was persuaded to head the State Department. It must have seemed ironic to Jackson to have to write Houston that their ancient enemy was to be one of the instrumentalities of Texas annexation.

While the stalemate continued, the Texas government maintained its cordial relationship with European countries. Both the French and British governments presented to the United States protests against annexation. Elliot wrote Anson Jones his conviction that there was not a remote chance of getting the annexation treaty through the United States Senate. Besides, said Elliot, he was persuaded that, despite appearances that Houston was moving in the direction of annexation, Houston's real intention was to uphold the independence of the Texas Republic.[46] Sometime in March, Houston wrote Elliot describing how harassing and distressing his situation was, without assurance that a treaty with the United States would take place and with uncertainty about the desirability of the mediation of friendly powers with Mexico.[47] Elliot, who had been ill with dysentery in New Orleans and had been ordered to a different climate for his health, delayed his departure until he could have a personal interview with Houston. The interview, unofficial and private, took place on April 7. Immediately afterwards Elliot wrote Lord Aberdeen that he did not imagine that Houston had ever entertained much confidence in the success of annexation or any personal wish to postpone independence to such a solution, and that Houston hoped, if the project of annexation failed, that the French and English governments would prevent further complications by securing settlement of the question on the basis of Mexican recognition of Texas. Elliot also reported to his superior that Houston attached much importance to the stringent con-

[45] Houston to Henderson, February 20, 1844, *Writings*, IV, 268–70.
[46] Elliot to Jones, March 22, 1844, in Jones, *Republic of Texas*, 329–31.
[47] Houston to Elliot, March ?, 1844, *Writings*, IV, 288–92.

ditions Henderson would insist on before negotiations were opened.[48] Concerning those conditions, Houston had written to his secretary of state on April 6:

Rumor says the Government of the United States will not *avow* the acts of Gen. Murphy in relation to the pledges given antecedent to our Commissioners entering upon the negotiations with that Government. I presume when they see Henderson's orders, or learn their contents, they will readily see that the game is to be a two-handed one.

If the United States should interpose any difficulty at this time, you will find that my action will be prompt and my purposes resolved. We have done enough; and if they expect us to place ourselves out of the pale of all probable security to this nation, they are most woefully mistaken. So soon as they assume a ground adverse to what has been the understanding, and official notice to that effect is received, it will be an easy matter to say, "Gen. Henderson, your mission has terminated, because we cannot submit to *unreasonable* and *unjust sacrifices!*"

Already the subject of annexation has caused the failure of our negotiations with Mexico.[49]

Miller was exerting pressure from the other end of negotiations by urging Jackson to use his influence on the senators to whom the treaty would go in a few days. Miller said, à la Houston, that in event of the treaty's rejection the reaction in Texas would be mortification and that, "if she be spurned from the threshold of the mother, she may look to a better reception from the grandmother." Jackson was arguing along the same line when the next day he wrote to W. B. Lewis that delays were dangerous and that, although Houston and the people of Texas, at the moment, were united in favor of annexation, the next president of Texas might not be of the same mind. His plea was: "Altho I know my time is short here below, I love my country, and this subject involves its best interest—*The perpetuation of our republican system, and of our glorious union.*"[50]

The Texan commissioners were in constant negotiation with Calhoun from the time he took over his portfolio on March 30, but news was slow in reaching Texas, and Houston was impatient. On April 14, 1844, he wrote Jones that he had instructed the Texas agents that, if the treaty failed and the United States did not make a treaty of alliance, they were

[48] Elliot to Aberdeen, April 7, 1844, Ephraim Douglass Adams, *British Diplomatic Correspondence concerning Texas*, 304–308.

[49] Houston to Jones, April 6, 1844, *Writings*, IV, 295–96.

[50] Miller to Jackson, April 7, 1844, and Jackson to Lewis, April 8, 1844, *Correspondence of Andrew Jackson*, VI, 276–78.

to call upon the English and French ministers to ascertain the prospects of an indefinite truce and a guarantee against further molestation from Mexico. He had, he said, so arranged matters with Elliot that Texas should suffer no serious detriment but had not committed himself or Texas. Two days later Houston wrote to Henderson and Van Zandt describing the Texas situation as the most interesting that it had been since April 21, 1836, and declaring to them that if the United States did not consummate annexation immediately Texas was forever lost to them. "Texas," he asserted, "has *done all* that *she could do* to obtain annexation, and you may rely upon this fact, in the event of a failure, that Texas will *do all* that it *should do*." He told the agents that the news of annexation prospects had brought about the anticipated rupture with Mexico, so that he had to be particularly careful to require pledges that would secure Texas against all possible contingencies. This letter was not designed to cancel former instructions but to anticipate possible emergencies. In it he gave his envoys a short course in diplomacy:

A Diplomatic agent may eat and sleep enough for health, and may drink generously with the Diplomatic agents of other countries, provided, he can induce them to take two glasses to his one. Men are fond to be thought knowing, as well as wise, and when listened to with attention, frequently impart knowledge, at a wine table, which they would not dream of in the forenoon of the day. You can instruct yourselves much by the course intimated.[51]

The required pledges had been secured, constitutionally or unconstitutionally; for Calhoun, on April 11, 1844, told the Texas agents that the matter had been put before the President, who had directed him to say that the navy would have a force in the Gulf of Mexico strong enough to meet any emergency and that the Secretary of War would move disposable forces to the southwestern frontier, the President deeming it his duty to protect Texas during the pendency of the treaty.[52] The next day the treaty was signed.

The treaty provided that Texas was to be annexed to the United States as a territory, subject to the constitutional provisions for the government of territories. Texas ceded its public land and public property, and the United States assumed the obligation to pay the debt of the Republic, up to ten million dollars. The United States was to make adjustments of the boundary between Texas and Mexico.

Tyler's message transmitting the treaty to the United States Senate on

[51] Houston to Jones, April 14, 1844, and to Henderson and Van Zandt, April 16, 1844, *Writings*, IV, 297–301.
[52] Calhoun to Van Zandt and Henderson, April 11, 1844, Houston Unpublished Correspondence, IV.

April 12, 1844, emphasized the benefits of annexation to the United States and the danger of British interference if annexation failed. Apparently he expected no failure, but the timing on the eve of national nominating conventions was bad. As Miller summarized the situation for Ashbel Smith, the Democrats, both North and South, were favorable to the measure but were powerless without strong co-operation from the Whigs. Clay, the strongest Whig candidate for the presidency, feared that agitation on the subject would affect his chances. Van Buren, Miller said, had not declared himself but would probably follow his friends among the Democrats. Miller felt that a protest or remonstrance from the British would help the Texas cause and even awake the Whigs "from the embrace of blue light federalism to the preservation of their national security." He suggested that Smith tell the British that the application for annexation originated with the United States and that should it fail Texas would be as free as ever to form such a connection with some powerful friend as would afford her permanent peace and independence. Miller thought that a British guarantee of independence would serve Texas a very valuable purpose in Washington and in event of failure of annexation would serve Texas in the future.[53]

In much the same strain as Houston had written to the Texas agents and Miller had written to Smith, Houston, increasingly restive, wrote to Miller on April 16, 1844, that it was "now or never" with the United States, for "if Texas is not fully met, it places annexation forever out of the question." He would never consent to annexation at a future date, provided that England and France would "secure us from further molestation." Continuing, perhaps disingenuously, he said that sentiment in Texas was less unified on the subject of annexation, which was losing "many of its charms."[54]

Four days later Houston was fuming impatiently in Galveston, expecting the arrival of the *Neptune,* and writing Jones that he was weary of waiting upon good news from Washington and was curious to know the next move they would have to make upon the chessboard. He enclosed for Jones's perusal a copy of his instructions to Henderson and Van Zandt, which the Secretary of State endorsed as an "officious interference with my department (with a view of ultimately defeating annexation)."[55]

Other Texans were also writing of the Houston policy. Judge Andrew

[53] Miller to Smith, April 19, 1844, Ashbel Smith Papers.
[54] Houston to Miller, April 16, 1844, *Writings,* IV, 301–303.
[55] Houston to Jones, April 20, 1844, *ibid.,* 303–304.

Hutchinson confided to Miller that Houston's course from July of 1842 until early in 1844 had seemed so dark and inscrutable that he had entertained doubts of the President's sanity but that now the issue was unraveled: a general jealousy of England had been aroused from the St. Lawrence to the Gulf, and "if, in the sequel, the lone star shall be gathered into the constellation, President Houston will have no cause to resent the suspicions & criminations that have been so liberally indulged concerning him."[56]

A copy of the treaty which went to the United States Senate on April 22 reached Houston by express on April 28. He read the document and wrote Jones that he presumed it would do very well, although on the portended demise of the Republic he commented a little bitterly: "All we had to do was to dispose of ourselves decently, and in order." Because of omission of any allusions to guarantees of Texas security, Houston observed to Jones that he saw that "Mr. Calhoun has jockeyed; and if our commissioners have ever presented the matter, he has clearly outwitted them," but added: "The United States will have to sustain us in future, if not annexed, or take water most shamefully." To Van Zandt and Henderson he complained that the security guarantees were made only for the period during which the treaty was pending and did not provide for contingencies which might arise should the treaty fail: when "our file is uncovered, the enemy may charge through our ranks and we have no reserve to march up to our rescue." Houston agreed that Texas could not go backward and had to march forward decisively, but he maintained that although the crisis was everything to Texas it was also worth the Union to the United States. Should the treaty fail, the commissioners were to fix their eyes steadily upon the salvation of their country and pursue the course which he had indicated.[57]

While the treaty was hanging fire in the Senate and the United States politicians were jockeying for position, Houston took occasion to write Murphy a letter meant for circulation in the United States and crammed with Houston "quotables" on annexation. He was solicitous for a speedy consummation of the union of the countries, a union not based on sentiment but on practical considerations. In closing he threatened: "If the Treaty is not ratified I will require all future negotiations to be transferred to Texas."[58] This letter to Murphy contained something of a blueprint of Houston's dream of a greater Texas, a Texas peopled with in-

[56] A. Hutchinson to Miller, April 20, 1844, Miller Papers.

[57] Houston to Jones, April 29, 1844, and Houston to Van Zandt and Henderson, April 29, 1844, Writings, IV, 308–11.

[58] Houston to Murphy, May 6, 1844, ibid., 320–25.

dustrious European immigrants, joined with Oregon in a natural union, and controlling all of northern Mexico—the result of an inevitable destiny. The President put a copy of the Murphy letter in a dispatch he sent to Henderson and Van Zandt, saying that, upon reflection, Murphy might forward it to his government since it contained "some speculations which might have more or less influence on the subject of annexation." To the envoys he intimated that as he had had more time to reflect upon the treaty he had begun to wonder whether or not it would be ratified by the Texas Senate since the terms were not quite liberal to Texas. He had no objection to the territorial status, but the debt to be assumed by the United States was really trifling and actually the United States would realize everything from the treaty and Texas very little. The commissioners were to "always sleep with one eye open" and "do the best you can."[59] Maybe he was not particularly worried about their best, for, should annexation negotiations be transferred to Texas, he knew that he and Anson Jones could "manage them tolerably well!!!"[60]

With the news that the United States was prone to delay the annexation plan, Houston wrote that it seemed useless for Henderson to remain longer in Washington but that, before he left, he and Van Zandt were to visit Tyler to tell him that Texas relied on his pledges that no molestation by Mexico would be permitted. As to Texas, "We must therefore regard ourselves as a nation *to remain forever separate*." In the same pouch with the official letter to the diplomats, Houston sent a private letter to Henderson instructing him to profit from presidential hints and assuring him: "Matters in Texas are wearing on in their accustomed mode. There is some little talk about the Presidential election, but our people are not quite so loud as they were in 1841. I hope we will not have to inaugurate another."[61]

Houston's fears of failure of the treaty were well founded. Despite Tyler's efforts and a message to the Senate on May 16, 1844, in which he urged that "the present golden moment must not be lost," the Senate, on June 8, defeated the treaty by a vote of 35 to 16. Fifteen of the 35 negative votes were by Whig senators from slave states. On June 10, on the eve of the adjournment of Congress, Tyler sent all the documents concerning Texas to the House of Representatives and asked for annexation by act of Congress. He knew that such action was not immediately

---

[59] Houston to Van Zandt and Henderson, May 10, 1844, *ibid.*, 317–19.
[60] Houston to Jones, May 8, 1844, *ibid.*, 317.
[61] Houston to Van Zandt and Henderson and Houston to Henderson, May 17, 1844, *ibid.*, 325–28.

possible, but his move left the question pending before the country to become an issue in the presidential campaign.[62]

Murphy, in Texas, announced the failure of the negotiations in a laconic message to Houston on July 3, 1844: "The treaty is rejected, and so is my nomination: the tail went with the hide." Simultaneously, Houston received assurances that annexation at some time not too remote was inevitable. As Henderson wrote to Miller when he announced the failure of the treaty:

I think if he could be here & see how very sanguine & determined our friends are he would await the outcome of the pending contest. . . . If Genl. Houston could be here to see all & hear all I think he would not despair. I hope still he will agree to wait until after this election before he attempts to carry out any other plan. If the question of annexation is kept a pending question it will aid the Democrats very much in the Presidential contest.[63]

Houston's answer to the news of the treaty failure was a statement that Texas was free from all involvements and pledges, that he hoped she would act only upon considerations of her own nationality, and that when the United States opened the doors and removed all impediment, "it might be well for Texas to accept the invitation." That statement was not a complete closing of the door. On July 6, he called a general election for September 2, 1844, to choose a president and vice-president for the Republic of Texas. Anson Jones and Edward Burleson were the announced candidates for the presidency.

Texas opinion was reflected in letters from Edward Hall in New Orleans to Ashbel Smith in London. On June 4, 1844, Hall wrote that hopes of annexation were on the wane and that Clay's "inevitable" election might destroy all chance of annexation in the future, especially since the influx of foreigners, the flourishing state of business in Texas, and the flow of money had produced a reaction among Galvestonians, who had decided that they could get along without union with the United States. As to the Texas President, Hall wrote: "Old Sam visited Galveston a few days since and made a speech in his usual eloquent manner, but as he is soon to abdicate in favor of *Burleson* [actually Jones] it passed with little interest." That Hall was a remarkably poor prophet was further shown in a letter of three days' later date informing Smith that the nomination of James K. Polk indicated disunion in

[62] Tyler to the Senate of the United States, May 16, 1844, James D. Richardson (comp.), *Messages and Papers of the Presidents*, V, 2172; Barker, "Annexation of Texas," *Southwestern Historical Quarterly*, L (1946/47), 65.
[63] Henderson to Miller, June 7, 1844, Miller Papers.

the Democratic party and predicting that the disunion would prove fatal to annexation, so that Texas would have to paddle her own canoe and make the best arrangements she could with foreign powers to sustain her in the difficulties with Mexico. In Hall's opinion the current speculations on annexation were that a modification in the treaty stipulations and a pacification of Mexico might induce Clay, when elected, to consent to annexation, but by that time Texas' pride would be so affronted that she would reject all overtures.[64]

Not all of the reports that Smith received on Texas' economic conditions were so sanguine as Hall's. He heard from Dr. John H. Bauer in mid-July:

> Times are very hard in Texas. . . . In politics Annexation has been the hobby for the last six months but since it was lost in the U.S. Senate there is very little said about it although it is the general hope of the people that it will take place yet. Genl. Houston is very unpopular—more so than he has ever been before and in my opinion deservedly. You may form an opinion of his standing amongst the people when I tell you that a few weeks ago he was literally hissed out of a large & respectable meeting in Galveston & had to leave town from fear of further personal insults. There are two candidates for the presidency. . . . As it looks at present Burleson's election seems to be certain. The anti-Houston party say that by electing Dr. Jones they would have a Houston administration under another name. It is thought that whatever candidate may be elected . . . you will not be recalled. Jones is a personal friend of yours and entirely under the management of old Sam and Burleson it is said has the highest respect for your talents.[65]

The LaGrange *Intelligencer* declared that the people of Texas would have to choose between becoming "hewers of wood and drawers of water" for England and deciding, annexed or alone, to maintain the freedom bequeathed them by their ancestors, and challenged the Texans to vote for "Jones, England, and Abolition or Burleson, Texas, and Liberty."[66]

As soon as the treaty was rejected, England proposed the passage of a "Diplomatic Act," in which Great Britain, France, Texas, the United

---

[64] Hall to Smith, June 4 and 7, 1844, Ashbel Smith Papers.

[65] Bauer to Smith, July 11, 1844, *ibid.*

Houston was especially unpopular in Galveston, where a secret society for impeachment of the President was formed sometime before January 6, 1844. A letter signed "Argus" described the announced object of the society as opposition to Houston, both personal and political, "during his life and for no other purpose." The group appointed a committee of five to lobby in the Congress for Houston's impeachment. See Argus letter, January 6, 1844, in Miller Papers.

[66] LaGrange *Intelligencer*, July 18, 1844.

States, and Mexico should work out peace with Mexico, recognition by that country of Texas independence, and the establishment of a boundary line, excluding all idea of annexation in the future. Should Mexico or the United States decline to unite in the proposed act, the remaining parties were to accomplish it among themselves. Lord Aberdeen, originator of the plan, said that of course the British government could not afford to enforce peace with Mexico as a preliminary and so remove the only real obstacle to annexation—in effect "beating the bush for the United States to catch the bird." Houston directed Anson Jones to accept the Diplomatic Act without delay, but as soon as the President rode off to an Indian conference, Jones refused to carry out the instructions and instead called Ashbel Smith home from Europe for a conference.[67]

In the United States, the Whigs, on May 1, 1844, had nominated as their candidate for the presidency Henry Clay, who called the annexation proposal "idle and ridiculous, if not dishonorable." Van Buren, the leading Democratic candidate, also published a letter against annexation and was discarded chiefly on that score. On May 27, 1844, the Democrats nominated Houston's old Tennessee friend James K. Polk, who entertained "no doubts as to the power or the expediency of the re-annexation of Texas." Polk wrote another Tennessean, Andrew J. Donelson, on July 22, 1844, that perhaps he should help Jackson compose a letter to Houston, using a disguised handwriting and sending the missive without his frank lest it be arrested in passing through the mail.[68]

In July, Jackson confided to Francis P. Blair of the Washington *Globe* that he had written to Houston but that candor compelled him to say that he feared Texas was lost. He urged the publisher to support Polk and Dallas, let Tyler alone, and leave Calhoun to himself, for "we in the south and west will attend to the Federal union, it must be preserved."[69] Blair responded with an article in the *Globe* of August 4, 1844, pointing out that Houston, coming into the Union with Texas, might hope to be "president of a confederacy stretching from the Canadas to the Del Norte instead of a dependency of European farms cramped in between the U. States and Mexico."[70] There was dangled another inducement for annexation.

[67] Ashbel Smith to J. E. B. DeBow, September 18, 1857, Ashbel Smith Papers; Gambrell, *Anson Jones*, 357–60.

[68] "Letters of James K. Polk to Andrew J. Donelson, 1843–1848," *Tennessee Historical Magazine*, III (March, 1917), 58.

[69] Jackson to Blair, July 26, 1844, *Correspondence of Andrew Jackson*, VI, 305.

[70] Blair to Jackson, August 3, 1844, *ibid.*, 312.

Jackson's next letter to Blair said that Houston had been cruelly treated in being deceived in the promise of the number of senators who would ratify the treaty. According to the old General, Mexico's currently threatened invasion was timed to force Texas to accept English and French propositions and might turn into a formidable invasion to drive the Texas government beyond the Sabine and then sell the area of Texas to England to pay off the Mexican debt to that country. Whether he really feared England or was just playing Houston's game of putting such fears into words in the American newspapers, Jackson stated that he was afraid Texas was lost to the United States unless regained from England "at the point of the bayonet."[71]

On June 19, 1844, General Adrian Woll gave Houston notice that Mexican hostilities were to be renewed. Trouble in Mexico prevented the General's carrying his threats into execution, but the Texas government asked Tyler if American forces were to be withdrawn from the Texas borders. The answer was that the forces were to remain, under orders of the American chargé instead of the Texas President.[72] Houston wrote Zachary Taylor for confirmation of those orders and expressed regret that, in case of emergency, Taylor's command would have to delay for orders from Washington. Taylor replied from Fort Jessup, Louisiana, on August 13, 1844, that he could not believe the meditated Mexican invasion was serious and that, even if it should be, the story of San Jacinto would be repeated. Under his existing instructions, Taylor said, he could not cross the Sabine, but he had no doubt he would receive early notification were any changes in instruction to be made.[73] Houston, in his correspondence with United States officials, seemed to be displaying considerably more fear of Mexico than his actions in Texas indicate that he possessed.

Dr. Anson Jones and K. L. Anderson were elected president and vice-president of Texas on September 2, 1844. James Hamilton wrote John C. Calhoun on September 12 that he would go to Texas in November and that the moment he got there he would

give such a direction to public affairs as may be in conformity to President Tyler's views and your own. I can carry the country in the direction we desire against Houston. But my friends will be in power and he will be out of power on the 1st Dec. and we will carry matters with a rush. Houston goes out of

---

[71] Jackson to Blair, August 15, 1844, *ibid.*, 313.

[72] Yoakum, *History of Texas*, II, 434.

[73] Houston to Taylor, August 6, 1844, *Writings*, IV, 357–58; Taylor to Houston, August 18, 1844, Houston Unpublished Correspondence, VI.

office on the 1st Dec. and I will aid Genl. Howard in getting a new treaty through which before President Tyler goes out of office will checkmate the Whigs and yet give his administration I hope the renown of annexation."

Tilghman A. Howard, who had succeeded Murphy as chargé on June 11, 1844, died in Washington-on-the-Brazos on August 16. President Tyler received the news exactly a month later and immediately appointed A. J. Donelson, of Jackson's own family, to the Texas post. Tyler wanted strong influence applied to Houston. A few days later Francis Blair wrote Jackson that he blamed Tyler and Calhoun for persisting in a course that they knew would end in defeat—that is, insisting on annexation by treaty (requiring a two-thirds vote in the Senate) instead of by bill, and so laying Houston and Texas open to their enemies."

Christian F. Duerr copied into his diary a letter to Florida which gave the current Texas reaction:

As regards the annexation of Texas to the United States, it is a subject which *amongst us* is scarcely thought, much less spoken of *now*, for everybody seems to have given up all hopes of it, & I much question whether our Government will again listen to overtures from the United States, not indeed that we would not at present be very willing to belong to the Union, but, being satisfied that the measure cannot be carried through in the U.S. Senate, the Government as well as the people of Texas are not disposed again to hazard our relations with foreign Governments by negotiations with the United States."

In November the Democrats and Polk won the United States presidency. Donelson, "lively" in his solicitude for annexation, arrived in Galveston on November 10 and spent his first evening in Texas discussing the subject with G. W. Terrell, who was preparing to leave for Europe. When Terrell reached New Orleans, he reported to the President-elect of Texas the political chatter in New Orleans, where Whig politicians described Houston as a traitor, his cabinet as no better, and Jones as bought in advance by British gold." Terrell, for one, had no cheer for annexation, "that *ignis fatuus* of the distempered imagination of some of our reckless speculators," and he knew, after interviews with

---

[14] Chauncey S. Boucher and Robert P. Brooks (eds.), *Correspondence Addressed to John C. Calhoun, 1837–1849,* in American Historical Association *Annual Report, 1929,* 250.

[15] Tyler to Jackson, September 17, 1844, and Blair to Jackson, September 28, 1844, *Correspondence of Andrew Jackson,* VI, 319–20, 323.

[16] Duerr to Bennett M. Dell, September 27, 1844, Duerr Diary, 155–56.

[17] Terrell to Jones, November 22, 1844, Jones, *Republic of Texas,* 405.

Alphonse de Saligny, that France was willing to guarantee the independence of Texas on condition that Texas pledge herself neither to make nor to receive further propositions of annexation. Terrell thought the French advice should be accepted.[78]

Donelson hurried from Galveston to Washington-on-the-Brazos, where Jones received his credentials with the remark that if the hope of a common destiny of the two countries had failed, he trusted that friendly relations would continue to exist between them. Houston, soon to retire from office, answered Donelson's expressed hope that nothing could ever weaken the chain that held the interests of the two republics together with the comment that Texas had done all that she could do and that the failure of annexation to that point could not be attributed to any lack on the Texans' part of a disposition to see the union speedily accomplished. Houston had greeted Donelson as the "intimate friend and pupil of the illustrious patriot and sage of the Hermitage."[79] That pupil the master had coached in a letter warning of British ascendancy but ending: "My friend Genl. Houston has too much patriotism not to see the great benefit of being united with us as one great state of our confederacy."[80]

With the convening of the Texas Congress, His Excellency the President laid before the body a survey of the principal events of the past year. Relations with the United States, he said, remained *in statu quo* since all attempts at treaty stipulations had been negatived by the United States Senate. In his valedictory as president, Houston took the position that the United States had spurned Texas twice and that the younger republic must proceed upon the supposition that she was to remain independent. She would degrade herself should she beg again for admission. If, now under a new conductor, she found the door of invitation opened by the United States, her people should go in "united in one phalanx, and sustained by the opinion of the world." If left alone, she had her destiny in her own hands and might become a nation of power and wealth.[81]

Retired from office, Houston finally broke his silence to Jackson, writing his "venerated friend" that Texas was free from all involvements and pledges and that it was becoming for her to remain as she was, acting only from considerations of her own nationality. He promised that,

[78] Terrell to Miller, November 26, 1844, Miller Papers.
[79] Address upon Being Presented to A. J. Donelson, *Writings*, IV, 389–91.
[80] Jackson to Donelson, December 2, 1844, *Correspondence of Andrew Jackson*, VI, 335–36.
[81] Valedictory to the Texas Congress, December 9, 1844, *Writings*, IV, 401–405.

since Polk's election seemed to indicate that the people of the United States favored annexation, he would not interpose any obstacle to achievement of the union.[62] On the same day that he wrote Jackson, Houston set down a confidential memorandum of what he considered satisfactory terms for annexation. Those terms included full community of interests, admission of Texas as a territory, retention by Texas of her public lands if the United States did not assume the Texas debt, division of Texas into as many states as the United States considered proper, reimbursement of Texas citizens for loss of land resulting from running the boundary line, and redemption of public liabilities *"at the price at which they were issued."* Evidently Houston talked his "terms" over with Donelson, who sent a copy of the memorandum to President Jones with the comment that the only use he had made of it was to suggest to Calhoun that the terms ought to be made provisions in the annexation bill.[63]

While Houston and Donelson and Jones and Miller exchanged confidential memoranda, other Texans also exchanged comments on annexation. William Beck Ochiltree, newly appointed secretary of the treasury, writing to O. M. Roberts to describe the opening sessions of the Ninth Congress, declared, "Annexation is for the present a dead cock in a pit."[64] Memucan Hunt complained to George W. Smyth, a member of that Congress, that Houston's diplomacy had damaged the Polk cause by producing the belief in the United States that Texans were opposed to annexation. The former president's "secrecy relative to any steps we may take to annex Texas to the U.S. is all humbuggery," declared Hunt. "The question is an open one and ought to be treated as such."[65] Christian Duerr's diary recorded that Texans were much rejoiced at Polk's election, although the matter of annexation was not much spoken of and not desired by many if they could have peace with Mexico—and peace seemed not too far off since England had offered to coerce Mexico into an acknowledgment of Texas independence as soon as Texas should withdraw the treaty of annexation. Duerr listed England's motives as a desire to divert Texas trade to England, to promote free trade, and to place a barrier to slavery in the South, the abolition of slavery in Texas to come gradually as immigration from the United States dwindled and that from Europe increased. Mexico would be willing to

[62] Houston to Jackson, December 13, 1844, *ibid.*, 406–407.

[63] Memorandum Setting Forth Terms for Annexation, December 13, 1844, *ibid.*, 407–408.

[64] Ochiltree to Roberts, December 17, 1844, Letters to Oran M. Roberts, Roberts Papers, III.

[65] Hunt to Smyth, December 15, 1844, George W. Smyth Papers.

acknowledge independence as soon as the government could find a pretext to satisfy the people, for the government knew that the incorporation of Texas into the United States would mean the ruin of Mexico, with a re-enactment of the Texas Revolution south of the Rio Grande within twenty years.[86] John G. Tod, late of the Texas Navy, made an interesting observation, epitomizing the difficulty of pinning down the hero of San Jacinto on his actual attitude towards annexation: *"When sober* he was for annexation but when *drunk* . . . he would express himself strongly against the measure!"[87]

In December, 1844, President Tyler sent to the second session of the Twenty-eighth United States Congress a message reviewing the treaty of annexation and its failure, stating that the election in November had shown a majority of the people in favor of the measure, and recommending annexation by a joint resolution in accordance with the terms of the proposed treaty. Between December 10, 1844, and February 13, 1845, seven annexation bills or resolutions were introduced in the Senate and ten in the House. The first bill, introduced by George McDuffie, Calhoun's friend from South Carolina, provided for annexation according to the terms of the treaty. Thomas Hart Benton's bill, introduced on December 11, would authorize the President of the United States to open negotiations with Texas and Mexico for annexation and adjustment of boundaries. The bill stipulated that the boundary should be on the desert prairie west of the Nueces River, that the state to be admitted as Texas should be no larger than the largest state in the Union, and that the remainder of the area should be called the Southwest Territory. Slavery was to be prohibited west of the one-hundredth degree of longitude. Finally, Mexican consent for annexation was to be obtained by treaty if possible.[88]

Donelson wrote Jackson that Texas would not come into the Union on Benton's terms and that she had no idea of receiving her rights by permission of Mexico. On the contrary, he said, "Houston could march into the Territory and compel her to give independence to his country. He is only restrained by the wish to spare the further effusion of blood, and to maintain a position favorable to the measure of reannexation." Houston, Donelson said, liked to dwell upon the capacity of Texas to extend her territory to the Pacific and even detach Oregon from the

[86] Duerr to Dell, December 12, 1844, Duerr Diary.

[87] Tod to Walker, December 18, 1844, Robert J. Walker Papers.

[88] Sarah Elizabeth Lewis, "Digest of Congressional Action on the Annexation of Texas, December, 1844, to March, 1845," *Southwestern Historical Quarterly*, L (1946/47), 251–54.

United States. "But this may be treated as a fancy originating in the belief that the United States served his country unkindly. His mind is now fixed upon the hope of reannexation, and neither he nor the present Government will favor an opposing movement while there is a prospect of success."[89]

With Jackson directing from the side lines, the annexation plays continued in Congress. C. J. Ingersoll, on December 12, 1844, proposed the joint resolution by which, as later amended, Texas was annexed. It was not until the first week in January that the two branches settled down to discuss the various measures before them and to debate the constitutionality of annexing a foreign state, the extension of slave territory, the amount and disposition of the Texas debt, whether Texas should be annexed as a state or as a territory, and the possibility of a war with Mexico in the event of annexation. As finally adopted, after a long debate in a night session of the Senate on February 27, 1845, the resolution for annexation gave the consent of Congress to the union of the two republics either by terms of the joint resolution or through new treaty arrangements. The territory of the Republic of Texas was to be erected into a state. That state should be admitted into the Union with several conditions and guarantees: boundary disputes with other powers were to be settled by the United States; Texas was to surrender all public means of defense and retain her funds, debts, dues, and liabilities; four new states might be created out of the area with Texas' consent, slavery to be prohibited in states north of the Missouri Compromise line; and the ratification of the people of Texas was to be transmitted to the President and laid before Congress before January 1, 1846.[90]

So the ball went over to Texas. There, according to Jackson, Houston was "still the leading star" and proved enigmatic as ever. Duff Green,

[89] Donelson to Jackson, December 28, 1844, *Correspondence of Andrew Jackson,* VI, 349–50.

Donelson also said to Jackson that there need be no difficulty on the subject of the boundary, and Polk had given assurance that he would maintain the Texas title "to the extent which she claims it to be." In December, 1836, Texas had included in the definition of her boundary the phrase "beginning at the mouth of the Sabine River and running west along the Gulf of Mexico three leagues from land, to the mouth of the Rio Grande." It was not until June, 1950, in the case of *United States* v. *Texas,* one of the so-called "tidelands cases," that the Supreme Court, by a 3 to 4 decision, annulled the annexation boundary provision, deciding apparently that the acceptance of the Texas boundary unwittingly violated the United States Constitution. See *United States* v. *Texas,* Brief for the State of Texas in Opposition to Motion for Judgment, 22, 24, 82–88.

[90] Lewis, "Digest of Congressional Action on the Annexation of Texas," *Southwestern Historical Quarterly,* L (1946/47), 263–68.

Calhoun's agent to watch Texas developments, reported to the Secretary of State that "the only serious impediment to annexation is to be found in the ulterior aspirations of Genl. Houston." J. S. Mayfield of the Texas State Department wrote Calhoun that Green's position in Texas as a functionary of the United States government placed him in a false attitude and subjected him to the charge of intermeddling in Texas domestic affairs.[91] The fact that Duff Green represented Calhoun was sufficient cause for Houston to accuse him of meddling, regardless of any "ulterior aspirations" on the part of the President. Thomas H. Benton, not seeing any ulterior objectives, wrote Donelson that he was glad to learn that Houston, instead of being "indisposed to" or "spurning" annexation, was in favor of it.[92]

England and France began their last efforts to maintain the independence of Texas, realizing at the same time the jealousy with which the partisans of annexation in the United States would regard any manifestation of interference—"or even interest"—expressed in the matter by a foreign state. Lord Aberdeen wrote Elliot that excitement in the United States might force that government into a course of action from which "the National Pride, if once engaged in it, would not easily allow of a retreat." In his letter he included a dispatch from the British agent in Mexico to the effect that Santa Anna was willing to recognize, on certain conditions, the independence of Texas. Elliot was ordered to confer unreservedly with the French chargé, who would have similar instructions, and to ask a full and frank explanation of the views of the Texas government, avoiding all unnecessary mention of the government of the United States.[93]

Terrell, who had gone on to Europe, even though his appointment as chargé to France had not been confirmed by the Texas Senate, wrote President Jones that England was prepared to go to any length to prevent annexation and that, from his own personal viewpoint, "if Texas is not blind to her own interest she may, within the next three years, . . . become one of the most prosperous little communities on the face of the globe. I pray Heaven in its mercy, and our rulers in their wisdom, to avert the evil of annexation, with all its concomitant dire calami-

---

[91] Jackson to F. P. Blair, January 1, 1845, *Correspondence of Andrew Jackson*, VI, 351; Duff Green to Calhoun, December 8, 1844, J. Franklin Jameson (ed.), *Correspondence of John C. Calhoun*, Vol. II of American Historical Association *Annual Report, 1899*, 1006–1007; J. S. Mayfield to Calhoun, February 19, 1845, Boucher and Brooks, *Correspondence Addressed to John C. Calhoun*, 282–83.
[92] Benton to Donelson, January 10, 1845, Donelson Papers.
[93] Aberdeen to Elliot, January 23, 1845, Ephraim Douglass Adams, *British Diplomatic Correspondence concerning Texas*, 428–33.

ties, insignificance, degradation, oblivion and annihilation, which must follow in its train."[54] In February, 1845, Terrell reported to Jones that he had assured Lord Aberdeen that the object of both Houston and Jones had been to allay excitement in Texas, to lead the people to rely upon themselves, and to keep the Texas Congress from being hurried into action upon annexation. For further assurance he had added that "if our people saw a certain prospect of the recognition of our independence by Mexico without further molestation, there was a strong probability they might declare in favor of a strong national Government. That my opinion was that both Gen. Houston and the present President would contribute all in their power to produce this result." Jones endorsed the letter with the note that Terrell reflected Houston's sentiments, not Jones's, when he told Aberdeen that after the rejection of the treaty Texas had abandoned all hopes of annexation. According to Jones, it was Houston who had "changed his front," while Jones had been willing to await the result of the issue before the American people, and the issue had not been determined when Terrell left for Europe.[55]

On March 3, 1845, eight years to the day since Jackson had sent Alcée LaBranche as the first United States chargé to Texas, John Tyler wrote A. J. Donelson to return to Texas to secure the prompt acceptance of annexation. Jackson's nephew was in Nashville on March 7, when he received his instructions from Tyler, and, anticipating a Texan interest in federal patronage, wrote his uncle to recommend a federal position for Washington D. Miller, "a meritorious" friend of General Houston, whose "prudence and patriotism" had saved the annexation measure.[56] Jackson promptly forwarded the recommendation to Polk, who had been inaugurated on March 4.

Donelson's arrival in Texas was eagerly awaited by friends of annexation and dreaded by Elliot and Saligny. The diplomats received their instructions from Europe on March 24 and were in Washington-on-the-Brazos, ahead of Donelson, on March 27, determined "to use every effort consistent with the object of our instructions to induce this Government neither to assemble Congress, nor to entertain any negotiation for Annexation, at all events for such a length of time as might enable our Governments to determine the Government of Mexico to acknowledge the independence of this Country." With Ashbel Smith, the new Texas secretary of state, and with President Jones, they finally worked out on March 29, 1845, a memorandum that was in effect a Texas ulti-

[54] Terrell to Jones, January 21, 1845, Jones, *Republic of Texas*, 416.
[55] Terrell to Jones, February 13, 1845, *ibid.*, 425, 430.
[56] Donelson to Jackson, March 7, 1945, James K. Polk Papers.

matum to Mexico. Mexico was to acknowledge the independence of Texas; Texas would agree, for ninety days, not to annex herself to, or become subject to, any country; limits and other conditions were to be arranged in a treaty, and disputed points would be submitted to arbitration.

Before leaving the Texas capital, Elliot and Saligny secured a promise from Jones to send Smith back to Europe to explain to their governments the situation in Texas. Then Elliot proceeded to Galveston, ostensibly to sail to Charleston to meet his wife. As soon as he was at sea, in order to keep his destination secret—a secrecy later regretted by Aberdeen lest it cast any shadow upon British intentions—he was to have the *Electra* change her course towards Mexico and to send him ashore there in an English or French warship. En route to Galveston, Saligny and Elliot met Donelson, who reported them most uncommunicative. Donelson found the Texas government reticent also, for Smith was quietly preparing to leave for Europe, and Jones had to contrive the ninety-day delay to give the Texans the alternatives of annexation or independence. The European diplomats rested their hopes on a "portion of the intelligence and respectability" of Texas, who would rally for independence when they knew what was within their reach, despite the fact that Donelson's influence, operating directly upon Houston, was powerful. As Elliot assured Aberdeen: "General Houston however has other friends in this country who will endeavour to keep him in the way of his abiding honour and duty and we have certainly heard nothing which leads us to dismiss the hope of their success."[97]

Hope of the diplomats' own success ebbed as they worked in Mexico with Luis Cuevas, Mexican minister of foreign affairs, and were put off with *mañana* until May 19, 1845, when Cuevas signed the preliminary conditions for a definitive treaty granting independence on condition that Texas agree not to be annexed to any country. Elliot was back in Galveston by May 30, when he reported to his government that he feared that the Mexican concessions had come too late to act successfully upon the people of Texas.[98]

In Texas, in fact, proannexation and anti-Jones sentiment had been mounting. The President had to make his delay seem reasonable; he had to keep his pledge of secrecy. Finally he called Congress to meet on June 16 and called a convention to assemble in Austin on July 4 to

[97] Elliot to Aberdeen, April 2, 1845, Ephraim Douglass Adams, *British Diplomatic Correspondence concerning Texas*, 462–72.

[98] Charles Bankhead to Elliot, May 20, 1845, and Elliot to Aberdeen, May 30, 1845, *ibid.*, 487–93.

consider propositions concerning the "nationality of the Republic." Meantime official delegates such as Donelson and unofficial propagandists such as Archibald Yell of Arkansas had applied pressure. Donelson concentrated on Houston. As he had written Polk from New Orleans on March 18, 1845: "I will lose no time in repairing to Washington in Texas, and shall request Houston to meet me there. It is upon him that I mainly rely to bring the question to the earliest practicable settlement."[99] Donelson reached Galveston on March 26, and Yell wrote the President of the United States a letter marked "private and confidential":

Houston is looked upon as occupying a doubtful position, tho Donelson has a letter from the chief that he thinks will settle that matter. If Houston is out & open for it so will the President be. . . . If H. doubts, Jones will be against it and may possibly refuse to call an extra session of Congress with the hope that it may be ultimately defeated by the management of the opponents of the measure![100]

Yell told Polk that he had spent twenty-five dollars towards publishing two thousand extra copies of an address to the citizens on annexation. The United States agents pledged their government to grant numerous benefits to Texas: to clear out rivers, to deepen harbors, to build lighthouses, to erect fortifications, to make internal improvements, and to attract capital to develop the natural resources of Texas.[101]

Houston was in East Texas when he received Donelson's letter from Washington, Texas. In his reply he did not commit himself as to when he would be in the Texas capital—maybe during the court term. As to annexation, he thought the United States President had "assumed a wrong *basis*" for its accomplishment, since no means could succeed except negotiation of commissioners. It was possible that Texas prosperity might be advanced by an equitable arrangement, but the salvation and safety of the United States depended upon annexation, and United States officials did not seem sufficiently impressed with the importance of Texas.[102] In reply to another letter from Donelson, Houston wrote that he would have tried to get to Washington had it not been for high water, but the spring rains would delay him some three weeks more. He refused to discuss annexation officially but again expressed

[99] Donelson to Polk, March 18, 1845, *Correspondence of Andrew Jackson*, VI, 384.

[100] Yell to Polk, March 26, 1845, Polk Papers.

[101] Barker, "Annexation of Texas," *Southwestern Historical Quarterly*, L (1946/47), 72.

[102] Houston to Donelson, April 3, 1845, *Writings*, VII, 11–12.

his private opinion that it could be effected only by negotiation and with a boundary defined. That same day, April 6, 1845, the *Telegraph and Texas Register* carried an editorial on Jackson's letter congratulating Houston upon the success of annexation:

We are happy to learn that Genl. Houston's intimate friends who have conversed with him within a few days, state that he is not opposed to annexation; that he is willing to accept the conditions offered in Mr. Brown's resolutions [admission as a state, retention of lands and debts, and creation of new states with slavery abolished north of the Missouri Compromise line], trusting to the honor and justice of the American Congress to rectify hereafter all their objectionable features.

While the editorial was being read in the city of Houston, Houston himself was at home at Huntsville penning a long letter on annexation to Donelson: "I am in favor of annexation, if it can take place on terms mutually beneficial to both countries. I have, on all occasions, evinced the most anxious solicitude touching the matter, and have withheld no means in my power, towards its completion."[103]

Houston was writing every third day, but he was not giving satisfactory answers to the restive Donelson, who wrote his wife that he began to see a safe end to the Texas question, even though he had to say: "Tell Uncle, Houston has disappointed me and has not given the question the support I expected. But I will write Uncle in a day or two, and give him a narrative of my troubles."[104]

Donelson confided his troubles to Calhoun also, reporting a long correspondence with Houston in which the General represented the willingness of Texas to retain her public domain and pay her own debts, and giving that as his reason for having urged Calhoun to change the terms of annexation to conform to the Houston demand.[105] Almost three years later, when reviewing the events leading to the Mexican War, Donelson gave Calhoun a few more details of his encounters with Houston, emphasizing that he commended Houston for self-denial in agreeing to annexation rather than taking part of Mexico and adding Oregon to a potential Texas empire.[106]

By early May, 1845, Donelson and Yell were in Galveston, and Yell wrote President Polk that Donelson had accomplished more in the

---

[103] Houston to Donelson, April 9, 1845, *ibid.*, IV, 410–17.

[104] A. J. Donelson to Elizabeth Donelson, April 16, 1845, Donelson Papers.

[105] Donelson to Calhoun, April 24, 1845, Jameson, *Correspondence of John C. Calhoun*, 1030–31.

[106] Donelson to Calhoun, January 8, 1848, Boucher and Brooks, *Correspondence Addressed to John C. Calhoun*, 421.

peculiar state of Texas affairs than any other individual could possibly have done:

When the Executive and his cabinet was *disinclined* to say the least of it, it required more than ordinary address to bring the Executive to terms—secret as he desired them—and to place *others* in a *position* from which they willingly retreat. Since the issuance of the Proclamation convening Congress everything goes on well, the people are full of enthusiasm and there will be but one voice either in Congress or with the people! Even unconditional independence recognized by Mexico will not . . . change the result. . . . You may now rest assured that nothing but a Providential interference can prevent annexation—so far at least as Texas is concerned.

Yesterday President Houston reached this place on his way to the Hermitage. . . . He now seems willing to have the matter succeed; at least he will not oppose it, nor is he disposed to be considered in opposition. *He is now safe* and no apprehensions need be feared from that quarter—and he is "the Power behind the Throne greater than the Throne itself." All dissensions and opposition in Texas will now cease and nothing can make a change but a proposition more favorable from some foreign government.[107]

On the afternoon of May 16 the retired president addressed the local citizenry of Houston at the Methodist church and that evening was guest of honor at a banquet at the old Capitol. Six official toasts were followed by thirty-eight volunteer toasts. The official offerings honored "Our Country," President Jones, "the Tree of Liberty," "the heroes of the Texian Revolution," San Jacinto, and Houston—"Our city, like the Roman matron, displays the jewel of which she is most proud, and wears it next her heart." After the sixth toast, Houston spoke "in his happiest vein," and his allusions to Jackson were described by the official reporter as "the most chaste and elegant that an audience ever listened to." Of the volunteer toasts ten were to Houston; Houston's own toast was to Jackson. T. M. Bagby, local cotton dealer, contrived to toast the two "old chieftains" in combination: "To the trio in the heart of the hero of the Hermitage: Democracy, Houston, Annexation! May they fill his entire wishes."[108]

And his wishes were fulfilled, if one judges by Jackson's letters. He wrote Donelson that he rejoiced in Houston's course as one worthy of a "true patriot and friend to the rights of man." To Polk, the dying man at the Hermitage also commended his old friend: "Texas comes into the Union with a united voice, and Genl. Houston, as I knew, puts his

[107] Yell to Polk, May 5, 1845, Polk Papers.
[108] *Telegraph and Texas Register*, May 28, 1845.

shoulder to the wheels to roll it in speedily. I knew British gold could not buy Sam Houston."[109]

Houston and his family went from Houston to Galveston to catch a boat for New Orleans. From Louisiana Houston wrote to Polk and at Nashville received Polk's reply congratulating him for his assurances that Texas might virtually be regarded as a part of the Union. Polk promised Houston that with the prospect of a Congressional majority favorable to annexation he felt sure that the full measure of justice would be given to any desires of Texas citizens. The President urged that Texas accept the terms of annexation unconditionally so that the "reunion" might be placed beyond danger and regarded as accomplished, for "the next Congress as a matter of course will redeem the National faith and admit her into the Union." He promised a liberal policy for Texas and the guarding of her boundary interests with "vigilance and care."[110]

While Houston was writing to Polk, Donelson was prompting Thomas Ritchie, editor of the Washington *Union,* the organ of the administration. Donelson enumerated Houston's services to Texas, justified (for print at least) his seeking better terms of annexation than those incorporated in the joint resolution, and in summation said: "During the whole of his administration he kept at bay all foreign influence: and though always tempted never once swerved from the road which led to the restoration of Texas to the Republican family."[111]

During his stay in New Orleans, Houston made a temperance speech, declined a public dinner tendered him, and delivered a lecture to explain his course on the annexation question. His oration before an overflow audience at the Arcade rejected as false imputations on the American name the charge that emigrants had gone to Texas to rob Mexico of that dominion, and described the advantages, beauties, and attractions of Texas. But one sentiment existed in Texas, he stated: the people favored annexation, and when the Texas Congress met, it would assent to the measure, as the Texas President had already done. As to whether he himself was opposed to or in favor of annexation, it was true, he said, "that he had coquetted a little with Great Britain and made the United States as jealous of that power as he possibly could."[112]

---

[109] Jackson to Donelson, May 24, 1845, and to Polk, May 26, 1845, *Correspondence of Andrew Jackson,* VI, 408, 412.

[110] Polk to Houston, June 6, 1845, Polk Papers.

[111] Donelson to Ritchie, May 28, 1845, "Selected Letters, 1844–1845, from the Donelson Papers," *Tennessee Historical Magazine,* III (June, 1917), 157–58.

[112] *Telegraph and Texas Register,* June 4, 1845, copied from New Orleans *Bulletin,* May 29, 1845.

Some two weeks later, in a Nashville speech, Houston again used the term "coquetted." The New Orleans papers had interpreted the Arcade speech as a jibe at England. That interpretation was promptly branded as false by W. D. Miller in a letter to Hamilton Stuart of the Galveston *Civilian* the day after the speech was made. Miller wrote that it might be inferred from the New Orleans journals that Houston had stated that during his presidency he had dealt unfairly in his diplomatic intercourse with the European governments, but, according to Miller, that interpretation was not correct.[113]

Evidently the Miller interpretation of the New Orleans speech was not widespread or was not accepted, for the British diplomats took offense, doubtless as Houston's enemies had intended. Anson Jones later endorsed a letter from Charles Elliot with the comment that Elliot was perfectly satisfied with Jones's fulfillment of all his promises but uttered the bitterest complaints against Houston.[114] William Kennedy, British consul at Galveston, wrote Aberdeen that he was obliged to decline an invitation to a dinner in Houston's honor so long as Houston's statement that he had "coquetted" with Great Britain remained uncontradicted. Kennedy knew of the authoritative denial that Houston had made the remark but thought it unfortunate that a public dinner was not made a suitable occasion for a public denial.[115]

Houston had a larger theater and a wider audience when he finally did make a public denial—in his Oregon speech in the United States Senate on April 15, 1846. Then he proclaimed that if the term "coquetry" had been employed "it was in reference to the United States, but not to England. It was not applicable to the relations of Texas and England, and would apply to our relations with the United States."[116]

In 1848, in a debate with Calhoun over United States policy with regard to Yucatán, the old charge of coquetry was resurrected, and Houston described it as "absolutely unfounded." In the Senate debate he said:

What I said was, that if Texas had been guilty of coquetry with England, she would be perfectly justifiable, in consequence of the indifference with which she had been treated by the United States. It was true, that after the United

---

[113] Miller to Stuart, Ephraim Douglass Adams, *British Diplomatic Correspondence concerning Texas*, 486. Adams misspells Stuart's name as "Stewart" and incorrectly dates the letter May 9 instead of May 29, 1845.

[114] Jones, *Republic of Texas*, 508.

[115] Kennedy to Aberdeen, December 8, 1845, Ephraim Douglass Adams, *British Diplomatic Correspondence concerning Texas*, 564.

[116] *Writings*, IV, 467–68.

States had treated Texas with indifference and even repulsion, some influence was brought to bear upon the public mind to dispose it more favorably towards Texas.[117]

Jackson was dying at the Hermitage as Houston traveled from New Orleans to Nashville. In his last hours the old General talked of his farm, his business, his country, and of the annexation of Texas and "the stand taken by his old & early friend & companion in arms Genl. Houston on the Subject—all of which convinced him that it would soon take place."[118] Shortly after six in the evening on Sunday, June 8, 1845, Houston met the Jackson family physician on the road between Nashville and the Hermitage and learned that by only a few hours he was too late to receive the blessings of his old friend. At midnight, from the Hermitage, the former president of Texas wrote the President of the United States of the death of that other president from Tennessee.[119]

The Houstons were guests at the Donelson plantation while Tennessee feted the prodigal son, who, "instead of the large and fleshy man he was six years ago," was in 1845 "a spare, tall, and thoughtful looking person, rather pale and more reserved than formerly in his intercourse with the masses."[120] Even the Whigs co-operated in having a barbecue for the visitor, who there spoke of annexation as a "fixed fact."[121] While he lingered in Tennessee, he was elected a delegate from Montgomery County to the convention called to meet at Austin on July 4, 1845, to vote on annexation and prepare a state constitution. But Houston continued with his family on a long vacation. After several weeks with his friends and relatives in Tennessee, he took his wife to see her family in Alabama. In September he made speeches at Marion and at Greensboro, wherein, according to the local press, he acquitted himself of all suspicion of having been opposed to annexation.[122] He did not return to Texas until October. Newspapers and letters in Texas, during the sessions of Congress and the convention, continued to comment on Houston and annexation. From Galveston, Donelson advised Miller, then editing the *Texas National Register* at Washington-on-the-Brazos:

[117] Speech in the Senate, May 8, 1848, *ibid.*, V, 52.
[118] Andrew Jackson, Jr., to A. O. P. Nicholson, June 17, 1845, James H. Parks (ed.), "Letter Describes Andrew Jackson's Last Hours," *Tennessee Historical Quarterly*, VI (1947), 177.
[119] Houston to Polk, June 8, 1845, *Writings*, IV, 424–25; Culver H. Smith, "Andrew Jackson, Post Obitum," *Tennessee Historical Quarterly*, IV (1945), 196.
[120] J. George Harris to Polk, June 12, 1845, Polk Papers.
[121] *Niles' Register*, LXVII (July 12, 1845), 294.
[122] *Alabama State Review*, September 17, 1845, quoted in *Writings*, VI, 14–15.

You should take care to connect Houston with annexation, and see that his enemies do him no injury. There is no harm in his wishing better terms for Texas, provided you show that he has been in favor of the measure in the abstract, in its previous stages. You may rely on my doing him justice, and not forgetting the testimony borne by Genl. Jackson to his motives and agency.[122]

David S. Kaufman rejoiced, while United States troops passed at Nacogdoches, that everything was as "quiet as a summer morning," that everyone admitted that affairs had been managed successfully, and that if the convention did not delay matters, annexation would be "several months ahead of the prescribed time." His letter to Jones ended: "I cannot learn where the old General is." Jones sourly endorsed the letter: " 'I cannot learn where Old Sam is.' He don't know 'where he is' himself on the annexation question; so he is NOWHERE, unless he has 'holded himself' or 'taken a tree.' "[124]

There was no doubt about where the Texas Congress and the Texas people stood. Elliot returned from Mexico with the agreement for the recognition of Texas the last of May, 1845. On June 4, he presented the Cuevas agreement to President Jones, who made an immediate proclamation of peace with Mexico. Jones was able to offer to Texas "the alternatives of peace with the world and Independence, or annexation and its contingencies." The called session of the Ninth Congress, which met from June 16 to June 28, 1845, was rabidly antiadministration and accordingly refused to acquiesce with Jones's wish that the entire Congress consider the American offer of annexation while the Senate advised with him on the Mexican treaty. He hoped to propose that the United States and Texas negotiate a treaty, as provided in the third section of the joint resolution, so that Texas, in that treaty, could stipulate the arrangements she wanted rather than have to accept what the United States offered. In this his hopes were in conformity with Houston's proposals. The Texas Senate, however, unanimously rejected the Mexican treaty, and both houses unanimously approved the annexation resolution.[125]

The convention called to meet on July 4 also knew where it stood. An informal committee of delegates drafted an ordinance assenting to annexation on the night of July 3, before the formal opening of the session. With Thomas J. Rusk presiding and with Richard Bache of Galveston casting the only dissenting vote, the ordinance was adopted

[122] Donelson to Miller, July 27, 1845, Miller Papers.
[124] Kaufman to Jones, August 14, 1845, Jones, *Republic of Texas*, 484.
[125] Gambrell, *Anson Jones*, 403–404.

without debate. Before adjournment on August 28, the convention framed a state constitution. Ratified by popular vote, the constitution was submitted to the Congress of the United States, by which it was approved on December 29, 1845. From that day, Texas was a state in the Union, although the transition ceremony to end the government of the Republic did not take place until February 19, 1846.

In the interim, before the last steps were taken in the process of annexation, Houston returned to Texas—a proponent of annexation, as he had been in his speeches made in Tennessee and Alabama. His old enemies and political opponents of his election to the United States Senate accused him of being a twelfth-hour friend of annexation, now determined to ride the wave of popularity of the measure. An anonymous newspaper clipping sent to Lamar stated that "the Milliner Queen [Victoria] cannot boast of three more willing servants than Elliot, Houston, and Jones." Houston was, even at that late date, accused of having wanted to annex Texas to Mexico—"a bloody betrayal of the people of Texas."[126]

Home-folk accusations apparently caused Houston no concern, but he was beginning to be concerned about what was said of him in the United States. George W. Terrell wrote Polk that Houston was much annoyed when he learned that men who had slandered him in Texas and had succeeded in creating the impression in the national capital that he opposed annexation were received with courtesy and attention by Polk and his cabinet. According to Terrell, Houston was busy preparing the documents "to prove that he set the measure of annexation on foot, and that he gave it his aid throughout."[127]

Houston refused a public dinner proffered him after a mass meeting of citizens in the city of Houston, but used his letter declining the dinner to state his case on annexation. He said that those who were acquainted with the circumstances surrounding his actions knew his integrity of motive, and then continued:

> To vindicate myself against charges that have been made, that I was ever opposed to annexation, has not been my course of life. If the accusations have resulted either from ignorance or malignity, I can pity their authors.—My conduct is a refutation to all such charges. I am no new convert to the policy of annexation, therefore, I have deemed it unnecessary either to become clamorous, or troublesome, in support of a measure which originated under my ad-

[126] *Telegraph and Texas Register*, October 22, 1845; *Lamar Papers*, IV, Part I, 111–12; VI, 9–10.
[127] Terrell to Polk, October 23, 1845, Polk Papers.

ministration, and was conducted under my directions, until my term as Executive expired in December last.[128]

When this letter was published in the *Telegraph and Texas Register*, November 5, 1845, the anti-Houston faction derided him for claiming paternity of annexation, saying that the honor really belonged to the "spontaneous patriotism of the people."[129]

Whatever Elliot, in chagrin at the failure of his diplomacy, may have said to Anson Jones in private, he reported to his chief that he appreciated Houston's difficulties and was not ignorant of the influence brought to bear on him and the prospects held out to him of the senatorship and even of the presidency. Elliot was satisfied in his own mind that Houston was acted upon more by his attachment to Jackson than by less excusable motives and said that Houston's election as senator showed that the people knew he considered the true welfare of the country, his leaning to the preservation of its independence not being the worst of his recommendations. To discountenance a possible charge of double-dealing against Houston, the British chargé reasoned that directness, in a republican government, might be hazardous to prominent persons whose "power to avert mischief is quite incommensurate with their political risks," and he ended his report with an interesting generalization on American politics: "It is rather a matter of surprise that there should be so many public men in America constant to common sense and justice, than that there should be many more skilful in catching the turn of events, and unscrupulous in tergiversation; or still greater numbers, drifting with the popular tide, let it run which way it will."[130]

Before Houston was ever in Texas, he had, at different times, envisioned three different futures for Texas: a separate Mexican state, a part of the United States, an independent republic. He was an opportunist, but his force was such that control of the tide was more characteristic of him than drift with the current. His annexation technique, in the long view, seems to have been masterful and shrewd. Whatever his deepest personal convictions, he commended Donelson's conduct in the matter and announced to that friend that he had consented to run for the Senate. Urging Donelson to return to Texas for a visit, Houston assured him that the true friends of Texas and annexation, nine-tenths of the

---

[128] Houston to J. L. Farquhar and others, October 27, 1845, *Writings*, IV, 425.

[129] T. P. Anderson to Lamar, *Lamar Papers*, VI, 12.

[130] Elliot to Aberdeen, January 20 and 26, 1846, Ephraim Douglass Adams, *British Diplomatic Correspondence concerning Texas*, 586, 591–92.

"solid" people, rendered him thanks. Then he inserted a Houstonesque paragraph:

I suppose you have felt for me! Just think of the books and letters written against me!! Well, it is true, I have—never read one of them, nor do I think, I ever will, so long as I have my senses. Occasionally to pester these rascals, I will let something be published, or about the time that they are ready to enjoy a triumph, I write a letter, or make a speech, or publish some letter, or "secret message," to throw them all back!!! In this way I amuse myself and harass those who love me not![131]

Houston was less ironic and equally honest when, in the Senate in later years, he had occasion to mention annexation. In 1850 he said that Texas had to purchase the boon of annexation by giving up her arms, her ammunition, her property, her stores, and her nationality, when "drawn by the cords of affection and fraternity, and great, not humiliated, but firm, she entered this Union for the purpose of benefiting and not of disturbing it."[132] And again in January, 1859, only weeks before his term as senator ended, while the bitterness of disunion mounted and after John Quincy Adams and many others who had accused him of deliberately stealing Texas from Mexico were dead, Houston declared that, even when a citizen of Texas, he had engaged in struggles for the perpetuation of the United States: "We gave national existence to Texas, that she might become a part of this great Confederacy."[133]

[131] Houston to Donelson, December 9, 1845, *Writings*, VII, 15–17.
[132] Speech on the Public Domain, January 30, 1850, *ibid.*, V, 118–19.
[133] Speech of January 12 and 13, 1859, concerning the Pacific Railroad and Other Matters, *ibid.*, VII, 204.

Senator Houston of Texas

Back in April, 1829, when Sam Houston and William Carroll were competing candidates for the governorship of Tennessee, Robert L. Caruthers, one of Houston's cousins, wrote A. J. Donelson that should Houston be defeated in the gubernatorial contest, the people would probably "lift a fallen favorite from the ground" and make him United States senator from Tennessee.[1] The former congressman from Tennessee might well have had dreams of following in the footsteps of his hero, Jackson, from the House to the Senate and even to higher position; but Caruthers' surmise was voiced only one day before Houston wrote his father-in-law that "Eliza was cold to me" and only eight days before Houston's

[1] Caruthers to Donelson, April 8, 1829, Donelson Papers.

162

resignation as governor. Whether or not there was a recurrence of the dream during the Indian exile and the early years in Texas, there is nothing in his words to indicate, although there is a somewhat apocryphal story of his meeting Jefferson Davis at a sutler's store somewhere in the Indian Territory in the 1830's and saying to him: "The future United States Senator salutes the future President."[2]

It took seventeen years for the senatorial prophecy to be realized; then it was not as a fallen favorite, but as the hero of San Jacinto and the illustrious president of the Republic of Texas, that Houston entered the Senate. That the office was his if he wanted it seemed to be taken for granted in Texas and the United States. John G. Tod wrote from Maryland to Anson Jones in 1843 that Baltimore talk was that Houston would be elected senator from Texas and that ultimately his "military fame and name" would unite the scattered elements of the Democratic party, which would make him president of the United States.[3] Milford P. Norton, postmaster at Houston while the annexation treaty was being discussed early in 1844, pondered the problem of potential state officials and wrote Jones that he saw no reason why Houston should not be elected the first governor of Texas and still be able to go into the Senate when the national Congress met in December, 1844.[4]

The Senate seat seems to have been part of the bait which Elliot thought constituted the pressure on Houston to persuade him to come out for annexation. Certainly President Polk did not fail to dangle the prospect. In 1845, as in 1829, Donelson was receiving letters concerning Houston; one was from Polk expressing hope of Houston's election to the Senate. Polk declared his pleasure in the prospect to Houston: "I shall be rejoiced to see you as one of her Senators bearing the constitution in your hands ready to introduce the young Republic."[5]

Although the session of the Ninth Texas Congress called to consider the joint resolution of annexation did not meet until June 16, 1845, its acceptance of annexation was such a foregone conclusion that the *Telegraph*, on May 21, 1845, ran an editorial entitled "Make Room for Texas," with the note that seats for the new senators were to be placed in the area fronting the chair of the president.

Party organization in Texas had been a matter of Houston and anti-

[2] Davis, *Jefferson Davis*, I, 282.
[3] Tod to Anson Jones, October 25, 1843, Jones, *Republic of Texas*, 261–62.
[4] Norton to Jones, February 26, 1844, *ibid.*, 322–23.
[5] "Letters of James K. Polk to Andrew J. Donelson," *Tennessee Historical Magazine*, III (March, 1917), 65–66; Polk to Houston, June 6, 1845, Polk Papers.

Houston factions, but now that Texas was soon to come into the Union, it became important to know how the Texans would align themselves in relation to the national political parties. The Democratic party had declared for annexation, and it seemed impossible to conceive of Jackson's protégé as anything but a Democrat, but nothing was to be taken for granted where Houston was concerned. J. George Harris, keeping Polk informed of the state of political fences in Tennessee while Houston visited in Nashville in the summer of 1845, wrote that Donelson was exceedingly anxious that Houston should not fall into the hands of the Whigs, who, on second thought, had joined in inviting Houston to a Nashville barbecue and so deprived the affair "of an exclusive democratic character."[6]

Senator Thomas H. Benton, also, was eager to see that the Houston footsteps followed the proper path and wrote to his old friend, who was visiting in Alabama: "I hope our next meeting will be like our first, citizens of the same country, and serving together in the same field, the Senate being substituted for the camp."[7]

Polk got some promptings from G. W. Terrell of Texas on Houston's annoyance at the kind treatment by the administration of some of the Houston foes and on the treatment due a potential senator:

His predilections are of course to go back to the bosom of his old friends, the democrats—and nothing but some personal insult could drive him from them, but I know him well and know that he will fly off sooner on such account than any other in the world. He has received invitations to visit both New York and Philadelphia—whether he will do so or not he has not yet determined.[8]

Houston arrived at his Grand Cane place on the Trinity River in mid-October of 1845. He declined public dinners at Washington-on-the-Brazos and Houston and had a long and satisfactory reunion and visit with Ashbel Smith in Galveston.[9] Houston was still in Galveston awaiting his family early in December, when he accepted a gift of fine Durham cattle and wrote the editor of the *American Agriculturist* of his plans to cross Durhams and Texas Longhorns and at long last do what he had originally gone to Texas to do—raise cattle.[10] He broke his Galveston sojourn with a trip to Houston to make a speech in which he defended his administration and made a bitter attack on Burnet. Much of

[6] Harris to Polk, June 17 and 21, 1845, *ibid.*
[7] Benton to Houston, October 1, 1845, Houston Unpublished Correspondence, V.
[8] Terrell to Polk, October 23, 1845, Polk Papers.
[9] Smith to Radcliff Hudson, November 8, 1845, Ashbel Smith Papers.
[10] Houston to A. B. Allen, December 1, 1845, *Writings*, IV, 430–32.

the same material he put into a letter to Editor Hamilton Stuart. The letter was widely copied in Texas newspapers in January of 1846 and served as a good campaign document with its ending: "I will not envy any man, who may have it in his power to render more numerous and important services to my country, and to mankind than I have done."[11]

The potential senator spent the Christmas holidays in the city of Houston. Inured as he was to criticism, he may not have felt that the spirit of the season was greatly marred by an especially abusive letter which he received from Anthony Butler. Butler, seething with accumulated bitterness, threatened to check Houston's career by revealing information, long in his possession, that Jackson was not a Houston supporter and admirer.[12] The timing would indicate that Butler meant to use his information to defeat Houston's ambitions for the Senate. Houston's Christmas Day reply, after a "leisurely perusal" of his "gift of the season," was a classic in sarcasm addressed to one whose name was "synonymous with infamy" but who was "one of the most intelligent, amusing, and agreeable scoundrels" he had ever known. Houston had D. D. Culp copy Butler's letter and returned the original to the sender with the recommendation that he drop the correspondence.[13]

By October, 1845, the Texas newspapers were announcing their choices for the senatorial seats. The LaGrange *Intelligencer* and the Galveston *News* came out for Rusk and Lamar. The *Red-Lander* and the *Harrison Times* were for Rusk and Houston. The *Telegraph and Texas Register* deplored the ill feeling between East and West Texas and withheld an opinion, saying that it would await the decision of the people.[14] Jesse Grimes was of the opinion that the Lamar-Rusk combination would tend to unite the east and west but would not suit a large portion of the people because Texas had suffered under the profligate administration of the one, and the other had recently kept bad company. The Texas legislator felt that Houston was the one man upon whom opinion could be united but was worried about who should be paired with Houston "lest he be clogged," for "if he has to carry weight, he may be beaten."[15] Ashbel Smith had no fears of his friend's defeat: "Gen. Houston's popularity in this country is undiminished; indeed it appears to me more solidly established than ever. You may rely on his being elected one of the Senators

[11] Houston to Stuart, December 21, 1845, *ibid.*, 437–41.
[12] Butler to Houston, December 14, 1845, *Correspondence between Col. Anthony Butler and Gen. Sam Houston.*
[13] Houston to Butler, December 25, 1845, *Writings*, IV, 444–48.
[14] *Telegraph and Texas Register*, November 5, 1845.
[15] Grimes to Anson Jones, October 1, 1845, Jones, *Republic of Texas*, 496–97.

of Texas in the next Congress. Who the other senator will be cannot be yet safely conjectured."[16] Washington D. Miller's *Texas National Register* naturally agreed with Smith.[17]

Houston had announced his intentions on December 9, when he wrote Donelson: "My friends have urged me to permit my name to run for the Senate, and I have consented on certain conditions, and they are, that should my friends and the true friends of the country be satisfied that my services are of paramount importance in the Senate to all others, and really necessary, I have agreed to serve, if elected."[18] In the same letter, which listed James Love of Galveston as the leading Whig candidate, Houston also indicated a little of his political philosophy in what may have been a simple statement of his belief or may have been a desire to give wider dissemination to his political thoughts:

I hope such men as you are, will, on all occasions, and always, be as you have been, the sturdy friends of the people, not to amuse them with baubles, but, secure, to the industrious classes, a recompense for their toil, and a reward for their thrift—I am more impressed of late with the dangers arising to free governments, from monopolies, than, I have been at any former period of my life. . . . The Federal powers as defined, are worth the union, but the moment that they cease to be limited to the objects to which they were designed, it will require a great political, if not a civil Revolution, to restore matters to a healthy Democratic State again.

The people of Texas were less interested in political philosophy than in personalities. F. W. Johnson was not numbered among those who thought Houston's services in the Senate would be paramount to those of all others. In stressing to Rusk the necessity for selecting as senators the men of best moral character and intelligence, Johnson said that it was with pain and regret that he saw Houston's name among the nominees, for he considered Houston a plague spot upon Texas and begged Rusk to use his influence against one who had "studiously sought his own elevation and the ruin of the country."[19] T. W. Ward reported to Rusk on the political scene as viewed from Austin, where opinion favored James Pinckney Henderson although a few persons "too contemptible to have any influence" were eager to make a breach between Houston and Henderson. Ward discounted the rumor that Henderson had said he could

[16] Smith to ——, November 12, 1845, Ashbel Smith Papers.
[17] *Texas National Register*, January 10, 1846.
[18] Houston to Donelson, December 9, 1845, *Writings*, VII, 15–16.
[19] Johnson to Rusk, September 26, 1845, T. J. Rusk Papers.

beat Houston, on the grounds that "whatever his faults may be it is not supposed that he partakes of the braggart."[20]

Houston seemed noncommittal as to preference for a running mate, although, according to Terrell, "the old dragon" would have liked Anson Jones's name to be associated with his own. Terrell reported to Jones a "long and confidential" interview with Houston on the senatorship and said that Houston intimated that the Georgia (Lamar) faction had some sort of hold over Rusk by which they could control his action so that Rusk would not permit his name to be submitted.[21]

Henderson, elected first governor of the new state of Texas, commented briefly to Ashbel Smith that "Houston will surely be elected to the U. S. Senate if he will take the place and so it is with Genl. Rusk."[22] Two weeks later, as he arranged his court docket and private business in San Augustine and left his wife and month-old daughter to depart for Austin, Henderson forecast the certain election of Rusk and Houston and approved the selection of Rusk as "Houston's friend & a good *Democrat*."[23]

Peter W. Gray, "wholly unpledged to anyone," declared his personal intention to vote for Houston. While he was an intimate friend of Colonel Love, he felt it a duty to vote against Love: "I look upon it as an essential . . . that whoever may be chosen as Houston's colleague should be one who will amicably co-operate with him; that there should be no variance either personal or political between them. It is altogether desirable that the first delegation from Texas should be composed of men who entertain mutual feelings of respect and esteem."[24]

In Austin the news was scant, and the general impression among the "thought to be knowing ones" was that Houston and Jones would be elected.[25] In Houston the *Telegraph* mentioned possible pairing of Lamar and Rusk, Houston and Rusk, and Houston and Jones—with the pointed remark that the matter rested with the Legislature and that the speculations of journalists would have little influence.[26] The Legislature met on February 16. On February 20, 1846, C. G. Keenan wrote a hurried letter to Henderson Yoakum in Huntsville to describe the "funeral of the Republic" and to fulfill the promise to keep his and Houston's fel-

[20] Ward to Rusk, November 27, 1845, *ibid.*
[21] G. W. Terrell to Jones, December 30, 1845, Jones, *Republic of Texas,* 507.
[22] Henderson to Smith, January 10, 1846, Ashbel Smith Papers.
[23] Henderson to Miller, January 26, 1846, Miller Papers.
[24] Gray to Albert Sidney Johnston, February 6, 1846, Johnston Papers.
[25] Joseph C. Eldridge to Smith, January 28, 1846, Ashbel Smith Papers.
[26] *Telegraph and Texas Register,* February 18, 1846.

low townsman informed of the Austin "doings," and added a postscript: "P.S. Feb. 21st 4 o'clock P.M. The election for Senators came off today— Rusk & Houston received 69 & 70 votes, a few scattering."[27] Memucan Hunt received 1 vote, Dr. J. B. Miller 1, and Colonel Love 2 of the scattered votes.[28]

Dr. John Salmon Ford had worked valiantly for the election of the two East Texas senators. In his memoirs he recalled the personal friendship between Houston and candid, intellectual Rusk and commented on their place in Texas history:

It might be justly said that, the infant republic of Texas, like a beautiful and innocent girl, had two friends on whom she could lean with equal trust and confidence. The impression of a large majority of the people of Texas was that, these two great men placed country before self. . . . These noble co-laborers in the cause of liberty and constitutional government deserve a warm place in the hearts of Texians for all time to come.[29]

Rusk preceded his colleague to Washington, D.C., going via the so-called "eastern route." While Houston waited for the March 12 boat for Galveston and New Orleans, he accepted an invitation of Houston citizens to give his views on "Oregon and other questions" and on the afternoon of March 11 spoke at the Methodist church, avowing his "determination to sustain the policy of President Polk relative to the great questions at issue between the Whig and Democratic parties of the union."[30] From New Orleans, Houston probably went up the Mississippi to St. Louis to catch his stage for the East. The *Chronicle* at Cincinnati described the prospective senator as he passed through that city: "The person of the civilian and quondam savage was distinguished from his *suite* by being enveloped in a huge Mexican blanket."[31] The New York *Tribune*'s Washington correspondent reported his arrival by train from Pittsburgh and his registration at the familiar Brown's Hotel.[32]

If Houston wore his serape for his first official call in Washington, Polk did not record the fact in his diary entry for Sunday, March 29, 1846: "At 6 o'clock this evening Gen'l Samuel Houston, late President of Texas and now a Senator in Congress, called. I was much pleased to see him, having been with him in Congress twenty years ago and always his

[27] Keenan to Yoakum, February 20, 1846, Domestic Correspondence, Texas State Archives.
[28] *Telegraph and Texas Register*, March 4, 1846.
[29] Memoirs of John Salmon Ford, II, 216–17.
[30] *Telegraph and Texas Register*, March 18, 1846.
[31] *Niles' Register*, LXX (April 4, 1846), 65.
[32] New York *Tribune*, March 31, 1846.

friend. I found him thoroughly Democratic and fully determined to support my administration."[33]

Rusk had arrived in Washington on March 25; the next day he took his seat in the Senate and was "very cordially received by all parties."[34] On Monday morning, March 30, he presented the credentials of his colleague, who took the oath of office and was escorted to his seat. Because a classification was necessary to conform to the ruling that one-third of the Senate retire every two years, three ballots were placed in a box from which the Texas senators were to draw. Houston's ballot determined his term to expire in 1847; Rusk drew the six-year term.

Not dressed in the height of fashion as he appeared at his trial in the Stanbery case, nor clothed in the Indian attire that had so offended Calhoun, the fifty-three-year-old hero of San Jacinto with his panther-skin waistcoat was an interesting contrast to most of his fifty-five fellow senators in the first session of the Twenty-ninth Congress. "Dressed usually in sombre, long-skirted coats, with tall silk hats, carrying watches in fobs with dangling seals, and using eyeglasses suspended on long ribbons, many of the Senators were gravity incarnate. . . . They wrote with quill pens, sanded their ink, and frequently resorted to the two great snuffboxes standing on the Vice-President's desk."[35] Some of the faces in Congress were familiar to Houston. Clay was there; so were Webster and Calhoun and Van Buren and Benton. Over in the House, John Quincy Adams represented the "conscience Whigs" of the North.

The senators were busy during their first weeks in Washington. Houston worked until after midnight each night answering letters that averaged twenty or thirty a day. He expressed thanks for advice and information from Texas and urged his correspondents to write frequently, even though he promised but infrequent answers. As for anything unpleasant that had happened before he and Rusk left Texas, he shrugged it off as a "spree" and advised Memucan Hunt to think no more about it, for "Rusk is a clever man, and you may rely upon it will act cleverly and patriotically."[36] Rusk, too, was swamped with correspondence, no less than thirty applications for the position of United States marshal awaiting him when he got to Washington. He wrote his brother: "We have done nothing here since I came but debate the Oregon question. Houston professes great friendship and I have been so far treated with kind-

[33] M. M. Quaife (ed.), *The Diary of James K. Polk during His Presidency, 1845–1849*, I, 309.

[34] Rusk to David Rusk, March 27, 1846, David Rusk Papers.

[35] Reprinted from *Ordeal of the Union* (I, 269), by Allan Nevins, and used by permission of the publishers, Charles Scribner's Sons.

[36] Houston to Hunt, April 6, 1846, *Writings*, VI, 15.

ness by all parties. I am far from being content with my position. I am surrounded by men of talent vastly my superiors and it greatly embarrasses me."[37]

When Texas changed its status from republic to state, W. D. Lee sealed up all the books and papers of the Texas legation and left them in the care of Lewis R. Hammersley, a clerk in the adjutant general's office. Governor Henderson authorized Houston, in behalf of the Texas delegation, to break the seal and take over the legation archives so that they and other documents could be used by the congressmen in presenting Texas matters to the national government. Matters of immediate concern included claims for the payment of ranger companies called into service for Zachary Taylor's army of occupation in Texas, claims for the expenses of the convention which voted for annexation and framed the state constitution ($20,543.52), the expenses of the special session of the Ninth Congress ($6,741.88), claims for indemnity for seizure of goods in the Red River customs district, and the claims arising out of the Snively Expedition.[38]

Houston used the archives for another purpose, or had C. Edwards Lester use them. The former United States consular agent, just home from Italy, became acquainted with Houston in 1846 and was commissioned to write a record of the General's career in Texas. For three months, in Houston's "private room" Lester examined the archives and met the stream of other actors in the Texas drama who came to call at the senatorial headquarters at the National Hotel. His record, published as *Sam Houston and His Republic*, had a mixed reception in Texas. Lester subsequently expanded the book under the title of *Life of Sam Houston*.[39]

The bulk of senatorial mail is always concerned with applications for patronage. With all of the federal positions in the new state to be filled, the requests for appointments began even before the senators were chosen, and long before they could reach the presidential ear in Washington. Henderson sent on to Rusk the request of former State Treasurer Moses Johnson for appointment as head of an Indian agency in Texas. Memucan Hunt had asked Houston for the same post and had been told that his wishes could probably be gratified as soon as the place was cre-

[37] Rusk to David Rusk, April 18, 1846, David Rusk Papers.
[38] Charles Mariner to Houston, March 7, 1846, to Hammersley, March 7, 1846, and to Houston, March 9, 1846, Domestic Correspondence; Henderson to Rusk, March 9, 1846, T. J. Rusk Papers.
[39] C. Edwards Lester, *Life and Achievements of Sam Houston, Hero and Statesman*, 6–7.

ated.⁴⁰ Among the applicants for the position of United States marshal were William Cazneau and David Rusk. Mrs. Cazneau assumed that Rusk's brother would get the place, but Senator Rusk wrote his brother: "Houston said he would have went for you but was committed to another. I felt some delicacy in saying anything much upon the subject."⁴¹

The plum of appointments was the federal judgeship, and there the competition was particularly keen. As early as November 19, 1845, "in anticipation of the admission of Texas into the confederacy of the U. States," Houston wrote James Buchanan that Judge A. B. Shelby of the First Texas Judicial District would be an applicant for the federal judgeship and would present "testimonials of the very highest character" when the time arrived for such application.⁴² On February 1, 1846, Samuel M. Williams wrote to John C. Calhoun on behalf of John C. Watrous for judge as opposed to James Webb and David G. Burnet. Disclaiming any personal preference, Williams said that Webb was rated as a good lawyer but Burnet was not so esteemed and that in Galveston Watrous was considered "the most able lawyer of Texas." Williams continued:

You are no doubt fully aware of the local party spirit which has prevailed in Texas, and it has been the misfortune of both Judge Webb & Judge Burnet to have figured largely on the weakest side—whereas Mr. Watrous has had no connection with either party and cannot be objected to by either. It is a fact Sir that every day develops that Genl. Houston is the most important figure in Texas in spite of every thing that his opponents may urge against him, and although I have not had any communication with him on this subject, and do not know his opinions, I do not hesitate to say that he would never aid either of the first two gentlemen named for they have both been bitter opponents of his.—Besides which I am fully satisfied that the appointment of Mr. Watrous as District Judge would prove universally satisfactory in Texas.⁴³

Webb, Watrous, and Shelby all went to Washington to present their petitions in person. Shelby, according to Webb, urged "his poverty, & inability to live without the office as a reason why he should receive it." Calhoun thought that he and Rusk would be able to swing the appointment to Webb, but Webb opined that Calhoun was hardly aware of the extent of Houston's influence and to what degree it would be exerted against him. Webb went to see Polk, who was "courteous and

⁴⁰ Henderson to Rusk, March 9, 1846, T. J. Rusk Papers; Houston to Hunt, April 6, 1846, *Writings*, VI, 15.

⁴¹ J. M. Storms to Lamar, March 27, 1846, *Lamar Papers*, IV, Part I, 130–31; Rusk to David Rusk, April 18, 1846, David Rusk Papers.

⁴² Houston to Buchanan, November 19, 1845, *Writings*, IV, 430.

⁴³ Williams to Calhoun, February 1, 1846, T. J. Rusk Papers.

polite" but gave him to understand that "Genl. Houston's opinion will have much weight with him in making appointments for Texas."[44] Then Webb began to hope that Texas might be divided into two federal judicial districts and that he might be removed from competition with Watrous by being appointed to the Western District. By May 20, 1846, he was en route to Texas and, stopping in Baltimore, wrote Rusk a letter that was a lecture on the proper position of senators in regard to appointments. It was but one among many letters to Rusk urging him not to allow himself to be overshadowed by his colorful colleague and not to fail to exercise his due control of appointments.[45]

Watrous was appointed to the judgeship on May 29, 1846; so one pressure point was lessened; but there were sufficient others. The competition for rival mail routes and requests for new routes occasioned many letters. Personal friendship was invoked to make requests. Adrian R. Terry, in Michigan, solicited Ashbel Smith to speak a word for him with Houston regarding a captaincy in a new rifle corps to be ordered to the Southwest. Another acquaintance of Smith's European days asked the Doctor to recommend that he be appointed consul to Antwerp to replace one F. J. Grund; the incumbent, he said, had made charges against Houston in the Augsburg *Journal*.[46] And always there were the endless requests for autographs and the answers to be made to the questions propounded a public man. One wonders if Houston had his secretary do his research for him or if he was so conscious of every matter concerning Texas that he had the information at his finger tips, so that he could tell an inquirer in Connecticut that Texas had no motto on her coat of arms and that "the great seal consists simply of a Star with five points encircled with a wreath of live oak and olive branches with the words 'The State of Texas.' "[47]

There were other responsibilities too. In view of tension in Mexican relations, President Polk called Senator Houston into conference on April 10, 1846.[48] It was natural also that Texas' creditors should interrogate her senator as to when they could expect some payment. Houston wrote one such creditor that although Texas had means they were not

[44] Webb to Lamar, March 23, 1846, *Lamar Papers,* IV, Part I, 128.

[45] Webb to Rusk, May 20, 1846, T. J. Rusk Papers. The enmity between Webb and Houston dated back at least to Webb's opposition to removal of the archives from Austin.

[46] M. P. Norton to Rusk, June 11, 1846, T. J. Rusk Papers; Terry to Smith, February 2, 1846, and Sam Naight to Smith, April 25, 1846, Ashbel Smith Papers.

[47] Houston to W. G. Webster, April 9, 1846, *Writings,* IV, 450.

[48] Quaife, *Diary of James K. Polk,* I, 327.

available and he could offer only sympathy, knowing that "that affords no relief to those who need money."[49]

When the Texas delegation was seated, Congress was debating the Oregon question. The Democratic platform of 1844 had called for the "reoccupation of Oregon and the reannexation of Texas." Texas was in the fold, but what of Oregon? Polk was inclined to favor taking the entire territory to "fifty-four forty" but had authorized Secretary of State Buchanan to renew the offer of the forty-ninth parallel as a boundary between Canada and the United States. When the British minister refused to negotiate on that basis, Polk asked Congress to allow him to give the required one-year notice of termination of the agreement for joint occupation. Texans were anxious to learn what course Houston and Rusk would take, especially since there was a report that the vote would be delayed until they reached Washington and that the result would depend upon their vote. Governor Henderson felt that most thinking men in Texas were against giving the notice, for it would lead to war with England, and with England and Mexico "both upon us we would be in a worse condition in Texas than we have ever been." Henderson wrote Rusk that an attempt in the Texas Legislature to formulate instructions for the senators to vote for the notice had failed, so that they were free to act as they chose.[50]

On Monday, April 13, 1846, Houston announced that he planned to speak on Wednesday on the subject of Oregon. He wrote Smith that the speech was unexpected and told Judge John Hemphill that he was quite unwell when he spoke. Obviously he was no slave to the tradition that a senator was supposed to be silent during his first term. His motivation may have been a request from the President for support, or a desire to advocate a measure opposed by Calhoun, or a plan to place himself in the national spotlight. According to one biographer his speech was "long, rambling and discursive" and, though forcible in language, "indicated that he was not likely to take his place among the leaders of the Senate in logical and legal argument."[51] Houston said that he saw no detriment to the interests of the country in giving the notice, no advantage to be gained by delay, and no cause for war. He felt that the President had been left no alternative to opening the question and that he

[49] Houston to Leslie Combs, April 11, 1846, *Writings*, IV, 450–51.
[50] Henderson to Rusk, March 9, 1846, T. J. Rusk Papers.
[51] Houston to Smith, April 25, 1846, and to Hemphill, April 28, 1846, *Writings*, IV, 473–75; Alfred M. Williams, *Sam Houston and the War of Independence in Texas*, 297.

should not be trammeled by any legislative qualifications attached to the notice. Houston's affirmative vote would be an earnest that he had not "sought to embarrass the Executive, or failed to strengthen his hands while toiling for the honor, the interests, and the glory of his country."[52] The Senator may have been recalling days when he, as a president, would fain have secured like support from members of the Texas Senate. Discursive as the speech was—embracing executive authority in the American system, English territorial avarice, the history of the annexation of Texas, and American opposition to taxation for defense in time of peace—one portion of the address proved Houston a better prophet than he was ever to realize. In discussing the fact that no preparations were being made for war, even while the Mexican situation was acute, he questioned:

Will we ever be prepared until it comes upon us? Never. It is not in the genius of this people. They are bold, daring, and confident; and until the shock of danger comes, every American is proud of the national character; and, glorying in his individual liberty, each feels that he is indeed a freeman, and therefore cannot be conquered. They cannot realize the necessity of concert and preparation.[53]

That particular motion concerning Oregon was finally passed by a vote of 40 to 14, and a treaty with England ultimately set the boundary at the forty-ninth parallel. It was his vote on the bill for the organization of Oregon as a free territory that was later to win Houston bitter condemnation from his Texas constituents. In 1846 there was no quarrel with his vote in support of the motion to abrogate the joint occupation. His wife approved his stand and told him she was delighted with his speech; but by the time she received a copy—it took a month for letters to travel from Washington to Raven Hill—she was worrying over his stand on the Mexican War and the possible effect of that war on their family life.

Houston's age, his responsibilities, and the change from bachelorhood to a happy married life meant that his environment and his habits in the national capital were quite in contrast to his earlier life there as a dashing young representative. Soon after his arrival in Washington he wrote a friend: "I did not bring Madam and Sam with me. I left them well, and am crazy to get home." Complaining of his heavy load of work, he wrote to another: "The truth is, I can only get time to write to my wife, which I usually do, once, a day. So you see my dear Sir, I am a home man, and

[52] Speech on the Oregon Question, April 15, 1846, *Writings*, IV, 451–71.
[53] *Ibid.*, 457.

one that longs to be there, and to stay there."⁵⁴ Because Margaret was, in her own words, impatient and restless without him and because he was so lonely without his family, he proposed that she join him in Washington; but she was expecting another child in September and was persuaded by Houston's sister, Eliza Moore, that for her health's sake she must not make the long journey. For diversion, she helped design a flag for a Texas company to carry to Mexico.⁵⁵

The war which Mexico had threatened in case Texas was annexed had materialized. Zachary Taylor's "army of observation" had landed at Corpus Christi on the Texas coast in August, 1845; and after Mexico broke off diplomatic relations and John Slidell's effort to negotiate and to purchase territory west of Texas had failed, Taylor advanced towards the Rio Grande in March, 1846. On April 23, General Mariano Paredes y Arrillaga, at the head of the Mexican government, declared war on the grounds that Mexican territory had been invaded. Taylor's troops had a skirmish with Mexican soldiers on April 24, and on May 8 and 9 engagements were fought at Palo Alto and Resaca de la Palma in the vicinity of Brownsville.

Washington was filled with anxiety about the happenings on the southern frontier, and Houston wanted decided action from the President. He called twice, on May 9 and May 10, at the White House and, according to the President, approved administration policy and thought that the war should be prosecuted with vigor.⁵⁶ Cabinet meetings on those same days recommended a declaration of war in case of any hostile moves against Taylor's men and worked out details of the President's message which requested that Congress recognize that a state of war existed. The Military Affairs Committee, of which Houston was a member, agreed to support a war bill that would provide ten million dollars and authorize the creation of an army of fifty thousand men.⁵⁷ Houston spoke twice in support of the President's message—briefly because he said the occasion required action, not words. Calhoun, John M. Clayton of Delaware, and Willie Mangum of North Carolina opposed the bill, maintaining that there was not sufficient evidence that war existed by act of Mexico. In his speech of May 12, Houston ridiculed such objection; he said that war between Mexico and Texas had existed for ten years and that annexation had placed the United States in the position

⁵⁴ Houston to W. V. Cobbs, April 8, 1846, *ibid.*, 449; Houston to Samuel Swartwout, April 29, 1846, *ibid.*, VI, 16.
⁵⁵ Margaret Lea Houston to Houston, May 16, 1846, Archives Collection, University of Texas Library.
⁵⁶ Allan Nevins (ed.), *Polk: The Diary of a President, 1845–1849*, 84–85.
⁵⁷ Alfred Hoyt Bill, *Rehearsal for Conflict: The War with Mexico, 1846–1848*, 102.

formerly occupied by Texas in relation to Mexico.[58] The war bill passed by a vote of 40 to 2.

Letters from Texas informed Houston of war activities at home. Smith wrote from Galveston on May 13 that Mexican relations absorbed public attention and that Henderson had ordered out troops in conformity with Taylor's requisition. If a Texas company was to be taken into Mexico, said Smith, Texans looked to the Old Chief to lead them to victory. Public opinion would not be "preoccupied or balked," even if a legislative resolution had given the command of Texas troops to the governor.[59] Houston's wife, desperately hoping that her husband would come home early in the summer, was melancholy when his letters told of a prolonged session because of the war situation and asked her to decide whether or not he should "go out with the army." Her answer may be indicative of her success as a wife.

Alas, what has always been my decision when my own happiness or the good of the country was to be sacrificed? Have I not invariably ascertained your views and then coincided with them, let my own sacrifices be what they might? And even now, though your personal danger will be far greater than it has been on any previous occasion, since our marriage, I will not express one word of opposition, but I cannot look around upon my widowed hearth and hear my poor boy's plaintive cry, "What makes pa stay so long?" and then tell you that I am willing for you to go. . . . I wish you to be governed entirely by your own judgment, and though the decision may bring misery upon me beyond description, I will try to bear it without a murmur.[60]

Houston's activities for the remainder of his first "tour of duty" in the Senate were chiefly concerned with the war. He spoke in behalf of giving the President freedom in the appointment of officers for newly organized regiments. On May 28, 1846, he submitted a resolution suggesting a vote of thanks to General Taylor and his command and the presentation of a sword to Taylor. As finally passed, the resolution was amended to provide for a gold medal rather than a sword as a tribute to the General's "good conduct, valor, and generosity."[61] This was before Taylor made some disparaging remarks about the Texas Rangers which drew down the wrath of the Texas delegation. Military preparation included strengthening of the navy, and a bill was introduced to augment

[58] Remarks in the Senate, May 11 and 12, 1846, *Writings*, IV, 475–80.

[59] Smith to Houston, May 13, 1846, Ashbel Smith Papers.

[60] Margaret Lea Houston to Houston, June 20, 1846, Archives Collection, University of Texas Library.

[61] *Writings*, IV, 480–83.

the United States naval establishment by adding to it the Texas Navy. As early as February, 1844, Houston had urged the justice of retaining in the United States service certain officers of the Texas Navy.[62] He listed certain *"gentlemen who will obey orders"* for such retention, not naming E. W. Moore. Maybe it was knowledge of that omission that caused Jane Cazneau, in conjuring up any method to embarrass Houston, to propose to Lamar in 1846: "Now for instance it would be easy, one would think, to call up a strong public sentiment in favor of the admission of the Texian officers into the U.S. Navy. Public meetings and perhaps legislative instructions may be obtained urging your Senators to press the matter. Houston must take the pill and either way it will taste bad."[63]

The measure, if pill it was, had no bad taste for Houston when the war precipitated the issue. When a motion was made that the bill be postponed indefinitely, Houston made a long speech in support of the measure, saying that Donelson's pledges in urging annexation had virtually covered admission of the navy. Complimenting the officers of the United States fleet, the Texas Senator contended that Texas officers had also displayed skill and courage. In reply to the argument that no injustice would be done them and that the cession of ships did not include officers, Rusk entered the debate to insist on providing for the officers, and Calhoun argued that the inclusion of personnel was implied. The vote was 31 to 18 for postponing the bill and against the Texas contention.[64] It was not the last time that the subject of the Texas Navy was to bring Houston to his feet in the Senate. Twelve years later he was still arguing for compensation for the Texas naval personnel.

The speech and the failure of the bill had newspaper repercussions in Texas. Houston had intimated that Texas might have been less eager to be annexed had she been able to predict such treatment; he had also made some sarcastic comments on the exclusion of Texas officers because they had not had the same opportunities as others for possessing "all the adornments and embellishments which put the last finish on a military man." The *Telegraph and Texas Register* regretted that the Texas senators found themselves in "so meagre a minority" and regarded "as the mere tools of the dominant party."[65]

Also in the line of national defense, Houston proposed that the Com-

[62] Houston to Henderson, February 20, 1844, *ibid.,* 269.
[63] J. M. Storms to Lamar, March 27, 1846, *Lamar Papers,* IV, Part I, 130–31.
[64] Speech on Texas Navy, July 31, 1846, *Writings,* IV, 486–98; *Telegraph and Texas Register,* August 19, 1846.
[65] *Telegraph and Texas Register,* August 19, 1846.

177

mittee on Commerce consider lighthouses for the Texas coast and that the Committee on Military Affairs consider surveying, improving, and fortifying the Texas harbors. As chairman of the Committee on Military Affairs, Houston particularly urged making Galveston a deep-water port and the construction of an intercoastal canal to connect the Sabine River and the Rio Grande. The immediate problem was appropriations for making the surveys, and Houston's report on the resolutions included a letter from W. L. Marcy, secretary of war, and another from J. J. Abert of the Topographical Engineers.[66] Houston had urged the printing of two thousand copies of the report of the survey made by United States engineers of the Texas coast. Finally two thousand extra copies of Abert's report on Texas and his expedition among the Comanches were ordered printed.[67]

Houston probably sent some of those Abert reports to friends in Texas as one of the usual prerogatives of a congressman while he is striving for patronage and "pork" for his constituents. After all, he received public documents free and mailed them at public expense. M. P. Norton chided Rusk: "I have not heard from you or Gen. Houston in any shape since you left Texas and would be glad to see your frank on something, even an old Almanac if nothing more interesting offers."[68] Something more interesting went to the Telegraph, which acknowledged its indebtedness to General Houston for "a beautiful copy of the excellent report of the exploring expedition to the Rocky Mountains, by Brevet Captain Fremont."[69] A book by the son-in-law of his old friend Benton would interest Houston. The Telegraph, during the early period of his senatorship, seemed willing to bury its grudge against Houston and found much to commend in his policy. Save for a few die-hards who were unsuccessful in pursuit of patronage, his constituents seemed generally satisfied. That he was not infallible in "knowing the ropes," Houston himself admitted. He and Rusk had recommended James Auchinclose to the President, but Houston gave the applicant no encouragement, for he had not learned "the 'hang of things' in the Treasury patronage."[70]

The Texas senators, at least on the surface, collaborated perfectly. Houston wrote Hemphill early in their Washington career that Rusk

[66] Concerning Lighthouses and Defense Measures, June 15 and 29, 1846, Writings, VII, 18–22.
[67] Congressional Globe, 29 Cong., 1 sess. (June 25, 1846), 1026.
[68] Norton to Rusk, June 11, 1846, T. J. Rusk Papers.
[69] Telegraph and Texas Register, May 6, 13, 1846.
[70] Houston to Auchinclose, August 10, 1846, Writings, IV, 499.

had acquitted himself admirably in his first speech and would continue to sustain himself fully and added: "You will see by the papers, that we are not considered Savages, but decent men!"[71] Some divergent reports, however, went back home; and Hiram George Runnels, hearing that Rusk was not happy in his position, assured Rusk that he was "the first man in Texas," where the only fear was that he would not exert enough influence in securing a proper distribution of the offices to be filled.[72] Rusk, discouraged to the point of considering resignation, wrote his brother: "I have got along here very well with the Senate. Everyone who talks to me upon the subject says I have sustained myself so far better than Houston but with the President it is different. I think I was set down at first as being friendly with Calhoun and the consequence is that I have not been able to procure from him a single appointment."[73]

The first session of the Twenty-ninth Congress finally closed on August 10, 1846. Houston was still writing letters at two o'clock the next morning before he caught the train at six o'clock for the three-thousand-mile trip to Texas. He too was weary of Washington, where there had been "little else than commotion, and at times, nearly amounting to uproar." Besides, he wrote, "I am most painfully anxious to see my dear Wife, and my young Pioneer. I was always fond of home but I now place something like a true estimate, upon the source of true happiness —Home."[74]

Rusk thought that with good luck they could get home by September 1. If that luck held, Houston may have reached Raven Hill before his first daughter, Nancy Elizabeth, named for her grandmothers, was born on September 6, 1846. He attended a public barbecue in his honor at Huntsville on September 26. On October 8 he was at his old capital, Washington, Texas, but declined a public dinner there. The next week, in the Presbyterian church in Houston, he made a speech in which he vindicated his course and that of his colleagues in Congress, a Congress so absorbed in the Oregon question and the tariff that little could be effected for Texas. He described the perfect harmony within the Texas delegation, and the *Telegraph* commented: "It was gratifying to the friends of our worthy representative of this district [David S. Kaufman] that he spoke of him and his colleagues with the utmost kindness and

---

[71] Houston to Hemphill, April 28, 1846, *ibid.*, 475.
[72] Runnels to Rusk, June 21, 1846, T. J. Rusk Papers.
[73] Rusk to David Rusk, July 8 and 11, 1846, David Rusk Papers.
[74] Houston to Nathaniel Levin, August 11, 1846, San Jacinto Museum (typescript copy in Biographical File, Barker Texas History Center, University of Texas Library).

regard. It is evident from his remarks that the whole delegation acted like a band of brothers, so perfect was their unanimity and mutual confidence."[75]

Houston was in Texas about a month longer, but just how he used his time is not certain. Sometime during the fall of 1846 receipts signed by Sam Houston or witnessed by Sam Houston were given Indians to acknowledge bundles of deerskins received at Torrey's Trading Post at New Braunfels.[76] The General had an interest in the Torrey trading enterprises and probably visited the Torrey post on the Brazos. One of his first acts after his return to Congress was to propose that the Committee on Indian Affairs look into the necessity of establishing a superintendency, agencies, and subagencies for the various Texas tribes.[77] In January, 1847, he transmitted to Indian Commissioner William Medill papers concerning Indian affairs in Texas and including a dispatch from R. S. Neighbors from Torrey's Trading Post.[78] It would seem that some of the Senator's constituents had jogged his elbow in the matter of securing an Indian agency and its necessary staff in Texas.

A public dinner honored the General in Houston on November 20, 1846. He and Rusk took their seats in the Senate on December 21, three weeks after Congress had convened. By December 27 the entire Texas delegation was in Baltimore en route to New York for a week's visit. The Texas reporter noted with pride: "Our Senators, Messrs. Houston and Rusk, and our Representatives, Messrs. Pillsbury and Kaufman, visited New York on the 30th ult., and received calls at the Governor's room from a large number of gentlemen of the city."[79]

The visitors in New York had probably discussed the course of the Mexican War. It had been a topic of absorbing interest when they were at home, and many of their friends were away in the service. Governor Henderson had given up his office to take command of the Texas troops; Lamar was in uniform, as was Albert Sidney Johnston. East Texas, by June, 1846, had exceeded its requisition by turning out nineteen companies. Joseph L. Hogg was a private with the East Texans—"in fine spir-

[75] *Democratic Telegraph and Texas Register,* October 14, 21, 1846. This change in the name of the newspaper indicates the effort made in 1846 to organize the Democratic party in the state.

[76] John K. Strecker, *Chronicles of George Barnard,* Baylor University *Bulletin,* September, 1928, p. 24.

[77] *Congressional Globe,* 29 Cong., 2 sess. (January 7, 1847), 128.

[78] Library of Congress, U.S. Miscellany, Box 4, Item 17.

[79] *Telegraph and Texas Register,* November 23, 1846, and January 25, 1847; Rusk to David Rusk, December 27, 1846, David Rusk Papers.

its"—and Bill Scurry was along.[80] Houston must have been mentally balancing Margaret's wishes and his own political future against his military reputation. He would have been interested in an entry in Polk's diary dated November 11, 1846, in which the President wrote that he had told Benton that he was committed to Houston if another major general was to be appointed.[81]

A bill for creating the office of lieutenant general was indefinitely postponed in the Senate on January 15, 1847, Houston and Rusk voting nay. On January 22 and February 1, 1847, Houston debated on the Senate floor amendments he had proposed to a bill to organize a new army corps. Because of the differences among the states in choosing officials of the state militia, he advocated a sort of federalization of the volunteer corps with the officers to be chosen by the volunteers and commissioned by the President. Contrary to his declarations of 1835 discounting volunteers, his speech was a strong advocacy of volunteer as opposed to regular forces, pronouncing a regular army inconsistent "with the genius of our institutions." The amendments were ultimately rejected.[82] While the Senator was debating on February 1, David S. Kaufman was calling on the President to discuss appointments in Texas and to tell the executive that Houston was dissatisfied with the administration. Polk recorded in his diary:

I told him that I had received an intimation of the kind before, but that he had no cause to be so. The truth is that Senator Houston desires to be a candidate for the Presidency and probably thinks that I do not throw my official influence into the scale to promote his views. He probably thinks, also that he should have been looked to instead of Col. Benton for Lieutenant-General.[83]

On returning home, Houston assured Ashbel Smith that he and Rusk had both declined army appointments for reasons "unanswerable in their character." He declined a commission as major general because he differed in opinion with the officers who would outrank him and he would not assist in carrying out measures "directly antagonistic" to his judgment. Specifically, he objected to marching to Mexico with a cumbrous train of wagons and did not wish to be "encumbered with all the splendor and pomp" attending General Winfield Scott. On the contrary,

[80] M. P. Norton to Rusk, June 11, 1846, David Rusk Papers.
[81] Nevins, *Polk: The Diary of a President,* 165.
[82] Speech in favor of Volunteer Forces, *Writings,* IV, 504–22; *Telegraph and Texas Register,* February 15, 1847.
[83] Nevins, *Polk: The Diary of a President,* 194–95.

he preferred invading Mexico with Texans, who required but one mule to a mess and could lay all night with but one blanket around them, and with their rifles hugged close to their bosoms ready to fight at a moment's warning. Whenever his country called him and he was allowed an independent command of any, who, like Texans, were inured to toil, and could feed their horses on grass, and themselves on jerked beef, if necessary, he was then ready to take his life in one hand and his sword in the other, and go as far as his country's good required.[84]

In the closing weeks of the second session of the Twenty-ninth Congress, the Texas delegation had recommended John C. Howard for a commission in the army and E. L. R. Wheelock for a federal position and had continued to work for the establishment of a customs district at Paso Cavallo and at the mouth of the Sabine. Rusk's correspondence contained notes recommending future Swedish consul Swante Palm for postmaster at LaGrange and Reuben R. Brown for collector at Velasco. Often in the letters to Rusk there was the undercurrent of insistence that he demand proper consideration in conferring patronage.[85] Houston himself went by the Treasury Building and left a note for Robert J. Walker asking for a position during the remainder of the session for Rusk's seventeen-year-old son and noting: "This application is made *without the knowledge* of Genl. Rusk. I will be gratified if you can find a place for the Youth."[86]

In the House, Kaufman again introduced a bill for incorporating the Texas Navy with that of the United States, and the Texas papers hoped that party hatred had subsided sufficiently in Washington that both Democrats and Whigs might view Texas interests with more kindly regards.[87] This feeling that Texas was not properly appreciated is reflected in a letter from Washington D. Miller to Anson Jones: "And the fact is, our State stands so low (certainly not above Arkansas) that it requires extraordinary influences to elicit the attention of the powers that be. She has but little weight now, and God only knows how much less it will be when the *prestige* of annexation dies entirely away."[88]

There was divided opinion as to the degree of Houston's influence on Polk. True, the Senator was a member of the committee of congressmen

[84] Houston to Smith, April 17, 1847, *Writings*, V, 10; *Niles' Register*, LXXII (May 1, 1847), 132.
[85] J. S. Mayfield to Rusk, January 5, 1847, and H. G. Runnels to Rusk, January 7, 1847, T. J. Rusk Papers.
[86] Houston to Walker, January 14, 1847, *Writings*, IV, 501–502.
[87] *Telegraph and Texas Register*, February 8, 1847.
[88] Miller to Jones, June 19, 1847, Jones, *Republic of Texas*, 514–15.

who, on Washington's Birthday, conducted the President to the ball at Carusi's Saloon and another larger ball at Jackson Hall,[89] but that was an official function. Miller, however low he felt Texas' prestige might be, continued to give the President advice, even to suggesting inclusion in the treaty with Mexico of a provision for compensation for, or the return of, fugitive slaves who had escaped from Texas to Mexico. One of Miller's slaves had been taken to Mexico by American troops and had been captured and, according to Miller, "General Houston has also two valuable slaves in Mexico which doubtless he would be much pleased to have restored to him. One of them has been for some years an *officer in the Mexican army*, and the other a barber in Matamoros."[90] That Lamar considered Houston's influence with the President too potent is indicated in a letter to Burnet: "The post I occupy in this war is certainly a very petty and unsuitable one, but the President is determined to gratify his favorite, your *'demented monster'*—in all his resentments. Polk is but a poor tool to the malice of that bloated mass of iniquity."[91]

No coolness between Houston and Polk is indicated in Houston's letter to the President requesting a captaincy for one of the Senator's fellow residents at the hotel, Charles F. Vernon of Kentucky, or in Houston's speech on the bill to appropriate three million dollars to enable the President to negotiate a treaty with Mexico. In the speech he justified Polk's course in the war and advocated conquering Mexico and producing a peace as soon as possible. Houston's opening remarks had concerned the extent to which topics unconnected with the bill had been dragged into the discussion. These were a fitting introduction to what he described as his own duty of "noticing matters somewhat irrelevant to the question." In pursuit of those irrelevant matters he gave a history of Texas colonization—partly to refute old charges that the early settlers went as vagabonds to despoil Mexico of territory—and a detailed history of the process of annexation, with a vindication of the British position in the affair. To all this was added another irrelevant discourse on the expulsion of Thomas Ritchie, editor of the *Union* and Congressional printer, from the floor of the Senate because he had published a correspondent's note containing remarks disparaging several senators. In 1847, as in the Stanbery case in 1832, Houston questioned the sanctity of Congressional privilege. As usual he was voting against Calhoun. The Texas press ignored its senator as a Texas historian but extolled his remarks on in-

[89] Nevins, *Polk: The Diary of a President*, 199.
[90] Miller to Polk, April 12, 1847, Miller Papers.
[91] Lamar to Burnet, March ?, 1847, *Lamar Papers*, IV, Part I, 165.

fringement of the rights of the press: "Senator Houston sustained with becoming dignity, the principles of republican freedom that are embodied in our own Constitution."[92]

Earlier in the session the *Telegraph* had described the acrimony which characterized many of the Congressional debates, with members "giving each other the lie" and "reverting to language more befitting the grogshop, or gambling table, than the legislative halls of an enlightened nation." The day before the end of the regular session Houston and Maryland's James A. Pearce engaged in debate marked more by good-humored banter than by bitterness. When Pearce said he wanted no more annexation and no more partnership with "the outside barbarians," the Senate laughed, and Pearce hastened to explain that he meant nothing offensive to Houston or his state. Houston declared that Pearce's remarks were entirely inapplicable to Texas but that he didn't know how they would operate on the world and "therefore, he intended that the 'band and antidote' should go together."[93]

A special session of the Senate lasted until March 20, 1847, but Houston left Washington early because of his wife's serious illness at Grand Cane, the home of her brother, Vernal Lea. Her brother-in-law, Charles Power, had written Dr. Smith, on February 3, of her need of an operation to remove a breast tumor. Three weeks later, Lea urged Dr. Smith to come to Grand Cane immediately to perform the operation. By the day the Senate adjourned, the operation had been successfully performed, and Power wrote the Doctor that he hoped that when the Old Chief got home he would be satisfied that all "has been done well."[94] Houston indicated his satisfaction in a letter to Smith expressing his "deep, and abiding sense of obligation" for the Doctor's medical skill and kindness to Mrs. Houston.[95]

Houston spoke at San Augustine on April 19 and spent San Jacinto Day of 1847 at home in Huntsville, where he made a speech that was "mostly on local interests."[96] A week later he was back at Liberty and wrote the Doctor that Mrs. Houston was not recovering as rapidly as could be wished. The family was at home at Raven Hill by June 3, and the Senator wrote to New York to refute an article in the *Evening*

[92] *Telegraph and Texas Register*, March 8, 1847; Speech on the Three Million Bill, *Writings*, IV, 523–47.

[93] *Telegraph and Texas Register*, January 18, 1847; *Congressional Globe*, 29 Cong., 2 sess., 545.

[94] Power to Smith, February 3 and March 27, 1847, and Lea to Smith, February 24, 1847, Ashbel Smith Papers.

[95] Houston to Smith, April 12, 1847, *Writings*, V, 11.

[96] *Telegraph and Texas Register*, May 3, 1847.

Mirror which quoted him as making disrespectful remarks about Zachary Taylor. Houston had his newspaper duel with former President Tyler concerning annexation during the summer and fall of 1847. He gave directions for cutting his timber at Cedar Point, looked after various legal interests, and visited East Texas points generally. His correspondence does not indicate that he was making any particular campaign for re-election to the Senate, but those visits to Houston and Crockett, Nacogdoches and San Augustine, were good political fence-building.

The question of his re-election had come up only a few weeks after he drew the short senatorial term. A joint resolution introduced in the Texas Legislature on May 11, 1846, to fill the vacancy to occur in 1847 had failed to pass. Opponents of Houston's re-election claimed that the Legislature had not been officially notified that a vacancy would occur and that the Governor, therefore, had the right to appoint a senator. When John Salmon Ford heard that Henderson contemplated appointing a *"western man,"* the doctor-editor called on the Governor, who denied any such intent, reiterated his gratitude and obligations to the Senator, and expressed his conviction that "should he dream of making any man but Sam Houston the appointee to the U.S.S. the world would justly regard him as 'a brute.'" Ford reported to Houston the efforts of the Lamar party to organize and the attempts of John Chalmers to unite them with the Democrats in bringing up the old issue of Houston's opposition to annexation and friendship with France—a stratagem to "row Houston up Salt River."[97] Ashbel Smith also reported that the appointees under the state administration were of Lamar's old league and that a party was being organized in an effort to exclude Houston from the Senate. But, according to the Doctor, "Their hopes are more than idle. The people of Texas have seen with great pride their Senator take his place with the very foremost of the powerful men of the American Senate. The accounts of your influence and estimation everywhere have come to Texas and strengthened the hands of your old friends here."[98]

One of Governor Henderson's possibly anti-Houston moves was the request that Albert Sidney Johnston command the Texas troops. The request was made, Henderson said, in consequence of "the great injustice done you by Houston during his whole administration as well as that of Jones, both personally and politically."[99] So the old order in Texas continued—Houston and anti-Houston alignment. In January,

[97] Ford to Houston, May 19, 1846, Houston Unpublished Correspondence, V.
[98] Smith to Houston, May 26, 1846, Ashbel Smith Papers.
[99] Fragment dated May 1, 1846, and endorsed, "The executive requesting Genl.

185

1847, David G. Burnet was writing long letters to Rusk and George W. Smyth to repudiate the material in *Sam Houston and His Republic* and to "throw the book" at Houston in reviving the old charges of intoxication, of cowardice at San Jacinto, and of partiality to the Indians.[100]

When his first term ended on March 4, 1847, Houston had not been re-elected. Miller wrote Anson Jones that Houston had told Polk that were he himself not returned to the Senate he and Rusk would support the appointment of Jones. Ashbel Smith, however, wrote that Houston's course in the Senate had commanded so much attention and given such universal satisfaction that he would be sent back to Washington regardless of his private wishes. Houston had "but one desire, and that is for home & peaceful retirement, with competency, and social quiet!"[101]

Political quiet of any kind was not the pattern in Texas. James W. Robinson said in July, 1847, that the press at Victoria was anti-Democratic and anti-Houston, but the next month Hamilton Stuart of the *Civilian* of Galveston wrote that Houston would be returned to the Senate without difficulty, although there were a half-dozen other persons who would aspire to the place were there the slightest chance of their success.[102] From the Texas capital, John D. McLeod reported in November that no person was spoken of for senator as yet but "the man in the *blanket coat*."[103] In the same mail with the McLeod letter, Rusk received another letter concerning his colleague. Thomas F. McKinney wrote, not to press his own claim for appointment as United States marshal, but to condemn the incumbent, chiefly because he was a Houston appointee. Of Houston appointees McKinney made a blanket indictment:

If anyone were to take the trouble to collect the evidence there would be abundance of evidence to convict them of the basest conduct possessing no merit except blind subserviency to old Houston and a disposition to do any dirty work he would bid them and you know he would not himself scruple at swindling in open day and in a low degree. My good friend the country will look

---

Johnston to command the army because of his ill treatment by Sam Houston," Miller Papers; Zachary Taylor to George Hancock, February 8, 1846, Johnston Papers.

[100] Burnet to Rusk, January 10, 1847, T. J. Rusk Papers; Burnet to Smyth, January 12, 1847, Houston Unpublished Correspondence, V.

[101] Miller to Jones, March 8, 1847, Jones, *Republic of Texas*, 514; Smith to Houston, April 4, 1847, Ashbel Smith Papers; Houston to Smith, April 12, 1847, *Writings*, V, 10.

[102] Robinson to Miller, July 5, 1847, and Stuart to Miller, August 12, 1847, Miller Papers.

[103] McLeod to Rusk, November 14, 1847, T. J. Rusk Papers.

to you to prevent his doing so much harm and I do hope you will counteract his influence to some extent.[104]

After the first session of the Thirtieth Congress had already assembled in Washington, the issue was still not settled. H. G. Runnels wrote Lamar on December 11, 1847:

I hope you will be able to make at least a formidable show of opposition to Houston's election to the Senate. If there are but ten members of the Legislature against him that opposition should by all means be made to appear in the election—I know not who you can make the most available, but that individual be he who he may should be run: From all that I can learn there will be in the Legislature a respectable opposition if not formidable. It is humiliating to [have] so large and respectable a minority of the State succumb to so great a tyrant, without putting to test his real strength.[105]

The opposition shown was not formidable. On December 18, the Legislature re-elected Houston senator. He received 69 votes; the other votes were scattered. Houston wrote Ebenezer Allen that the only negative votes he regretted were those of Thomas Hardeman and Samuel G. Haynie of Bastrop and Travis counties. In the same letter to Allen, Houston for the first time indicated a rift in his relations with J. P. Henderson. In discussing a lawsuit in which he had presented a petition at Henderson's request, Houston said that he had signed the petition as he "would for any friend, whom I loved, as I *then* did Genl. Henderson. Now, I know him wide!!!"[106]

On January 24, 1848, Rusk submitted the credentials of Sam Houston, "elected a senator from the state of Texas for six years," and General Houston "then took the customary oath and his seat."[107] On the evening of January 24, Houston presided over the Democratic caucus held in the Senate Chamber to discuss the time and place for the Democratic National Convention, the decision being to meet in Baltimore on the fourth Monday in May. Back in Texas renewed efforts were being made for stronger state organization of the Democratic party. The Democratic State Convention, which met in Austin on February 21, 1848, named as delegates to the national convention the Texas delegation in Washington plus E. M. Pease, J. L. Allen, L. D. Evans, James Davis, and John A.

[104] McKinney to Rusk, November 15, 1847, *ibid.*
[105] Runnels to Lamar, December 11, 1847, *Lamar Papers,* IV, Part I, 188.
[106] Houston to Allen, December 21, 1847, *Writings,* V, 27.
[107] *Niles' Register,* January 29, 1848.

Greer. On motion of J. W. Henderson, the names of Thomas Jefferson Chambers and Phillip Cuney were added to the list of delegates. Judge R. M. ("Three-Legged") Williamson had proposed a resolution that the state convention endorse such candidates as would support the federal compromise on slavery and the establishment of the Texas boundary line as defined by the laws of the Republic of Texas.[108]

In the midst of politics the senators coped with the perennial problems of patronage. John T. Mason applied to both Rusk and Houston for financial assistance, and Thomas F. McKinney kept up his barrage against Houston's appointments and demanded of Rusk at least an answer to his letters. Wrote McKinney: "If it be as many here say that Sam Houston does everything he wishes to do in relation to Texas affairs (and circumstances seem to justify the opinion) then truly should we feel mortified and humiliated and truly may we be called Sam Houston's state as we have been his Republic heretofore." Finally even Rusk's patience wore thin enough for him to reply to McKinney: "I had nothing to do with the recommendation of Maj. [James H.] Cocke to the President: with his confirmation, however, I had. That took place before Genl. Houston arrived here, and met my approbation, after a careful examination of all the testimony submitted for and against him."[109]

There was criticism of Houston from another quarter. The Senator made several speeches in New York in the winter of 1848. He talked to the New York Democrats on the Texas boundary, stressing the good bargain of annexation and proclaiming a manifest destiny that would lead the United States to pervade the continent. In one of the New York addresses he recalled an ancient enemy, James Hazard Perry, who had lectured on the Texas Revolution in New York in 1843 and 1844 and of whom Houston had written a scathing opinion in 1844. Now, four years later, Houston resurrected the quarrel with Perry which Robert M. Coleman had related in his pamphlet called *Houston Displayed, or Who Won the Battle of San Jacinto.* Perry complained to Rusk that Houston had forgot his dignity as senator and had descended so low as to "injure the character and reputation of an humble preacher of the gospel." Because Perry had been befriended by Rusk back in 1836, he now asked that Rusk write a private letter for the sake of clearing him in the eyes of his family and the Methodist church.[110] The quarrel did not end in

---

[108] *Telegraph and Texas Register,* February 24, March 2, 1848.

[109] Mason to Rusk, December 18, 1847; McKinney to Rusk, March 23, 1848; Rusk to McKinney, April 30, 1848, T. J. Rusk Papers.

[110] Houston's Opinion of Perry, *Writings,* IV, 272–76; Perry to Rusk, February 12, 1848, T. J. Rusk Papers.

1848. In Febuary, 1859, eleven years later, Perry again lectured in New York on the Battle of San Jacinto, proclaiming that that victory was achieved in spite of Houston and that "the wreath that now encircles his brow as the hero of that battle has not in it one green leaf." Houston's last long speech in the United States Senate gave his rebuttal to the Perry charges.[111]

More pleasant reading for Houston than a letter from Perry was one from Ashbel Smith—also on San Jacinto and in a somewhat prophetic vein. Smith wrote that San Antonio was being considered as the location of an army arsenal and that Galveston ought to become the site of a federal marine hospital. In his opinion San Jacinto should have some proper memorial because "if something of this nature be not done, the great battlefield of Texas will in a few years be a sugar plantation or maybe a cow ranch. The appropriation of San Jacinto to some public use is due to the State—it is due to yourself."[112]

Marine hospitals and San Jacinto monuments took a back place with an administration busy with the Mexican War and a senator busy making speeches in Boston, at Norwich and Hartford in Connecticut, and in New York, all in March, 1848. Houston may have been back in Washington when he received news of the birth of his second daughter, Margaret Lea, at Huntsville on April 13, 1848. On May 8 he spoke on the bill to empower the President to send United States troops to Yucatán for a diversionary attack against Mexico should their services be required. As a Texas congressman, he had been faced with similar questions of sending the Texas Navy to Yucatán for use against Mexico. In 1848 he used the occasion to introduce extraneous material on the Monroe Doctrine, love of France, sympathy for Ireland, Calhoun's stand on annexation, coquetry with England, and the proper boundary of Texas. After all, it was an election year, although the Senator insisted that elections belonged to the people and that he "should be sorry to participate in the legislation of this Hall, if honorable Senators were to so far forget themselves as to huckster in a Presidential canvass, or render aid to the aspirations of any candidate for that high office."[113]

[111] A Refutation of Calumnies Produced and Circulated against His Character as Commander in Chief of the Army of Texas, February 28, 1859, *Writings*, VII, 327–30.

Of interest to Texas historians is the inscription on the monument at Perry's grave at Cypress Hills Cemetery in New York, which reads in part: "To the memory of a brave soldier; an eminent minister; the hero of San Jacinto." Quoted in letter of Paul North Rice, reference librarian, New York Public Library, to Llerena Friend, February 18, 1949.

[112] Smith to Houston, March 25, 1848, Ashbel Smith Papers.

[113] Speech on Yucatán Bill, May 8, 1848, *Writings*, V, 37–52.

Later in May, Houston's Texas constituents heard that he was lecturing and "making an impression" in North Carolina. On May 26 the Texas delegation was in Baltimore, and Houston's speech to the Democratic Convention was reported by the *Telegraph* as "excellent" in its justification of the Mexican War. In that speech he said that the Wilmot Proviso was "very much like anti-masonry, which would wear itself out if let alone." The Texas delegates voted for the nomination of Lewis Cass for president. For vice-president they supported John A. Quitman of Mississippi until the last ballot, when their vote was divided between Quitman and William O. Butler.[114] The Whig Convention at Philadelphia nominated Zachary Taylor; Free-Soilers, meeting at Buffalo, New York, chose Martin Van Buren. Houston electioneered earnestly for Cass, making speeches in New York and in Pennsylvania although he was ill during much of the summer.

His old friend George W. Hockley was in Washington soliciting favors; so was Andrew B. Gray. On June 23, Houston went with Gray to Secretary of State Buchanan to present the Texas claim to control appointments of the officials to run the boundary line of the territory ceded by Mexico in the Treaty of Guadalupe Hidalgo, which had ended the Mexican War on February 2, 1848. Buchanan countered that the Topographical Corps would work on the line, but Houston said Texas wanted civil appointments and expected to get them. "Old Sam" wanted Texas to have the surveyorship and a secretary, and Gray wrote Miller: "The Old General . . . will leave no stone unturned to procure for us those berths."[115]

As tempers flared over the problem of slavery in the territory acquired from Mexico, it was evident that the current session of Congress would take no action upon the organization of California and New Mexico but would leave those areas under military rule. Oregon, where all idea of slavery was preposterous, was a different matter, but the slavery issue was forced into its organization by the warring factions. On June 2, Houston offered an amendment which he hoped would terminate the "unprofitable if not injurious discussion." When Calhoun questioned whether or not the people of the South emigrating to Oregon would be permitted the enjoyment of their "property," Houston replied that he did not think Congress had anything to do with the subject of slavery,

---

[114] F. L. Hatch to W. D. Miller, May 20, 1848, Miller Papers; *Telegraph and Texas Register*, June 8, 1848; E. W. Winkler (ed.), *Platforms of Political Parties in Texas*, University of Texas *Bulletin No. 53*, 20.

[115] Hockley to Smith, July 13 and August 1, 1848, Ashbel Smith Papers; Gray to Miller, June 24, 1848, Miller Papers.

which was a matter to be determined by the Supreme Court. He thought no person from south of the Missouri Compromise line would ever go to the area, and he would stand on that compromise. In the closing days of the session he spoke again on the Oregon Bill, again upholding the compromise line and proclaiming that he had no fears of disunion. He declared himself as of the South and ready to defend the South but said "he was for the Union" because "the Union was his guiding star, and he would fix his eyes on that star to direct his course."[116] When the Oregon Bill finally passed on August 13, 1848, it had attached to it the slavery prohibition of 1787. Calhoun went angrily home to declare that the South's defeat on the measure was the more lamentable since it had been accomplished by the vote of two Southern senators, Benton of Missouri and Houston of Texas, or, as the Charleston *Mercury* put it: "The South has been beaten by the South."[117] Again and again in the next ten years, as Houston's position in Texas was assailed, his vote on the Oregon Bill was to be charged against him.

Congress adjourned on August 14. Houston was at home in Huntsville in mid-September, and the *Telegraph* was carrying a notice that the report in the *Civilian* and other Texas newspapers that the General had been offered the post of secretary of war was contradicted in the Eastern exchanges.[118]

Senators Rusk and Houston, by mid-November, started back to Washington, where they arrived on December 2, "after a hard journey." Houston wrote his wife that he had been up for seven days, had been exposed to cold, and had had a headache for two days.[119] Part of his headache may have been caused by his new annoyance with Anson Jones, who had become increasingly tired of Houston's appropriating to himself the credit for what in Jones's opinion were Jones's achievements, particularly the achievement of annexation. As Jones, in semiretirement on his Barrington plantation, had reread his correspondence and diaries and memorandum books, he had become convinced that he could demonstrate that not Calhoun nor Tyler nor Jackson nor Houston but Jones was the indispensable man in annexation.[120] While Houston was warring verbally with Tyler on the subject, he asked Jones to reply also to Tyler's claims and to "draw your strokes fine," for he knew no man

---

[116] Remarks on Oregon, June 2 and August 12 and 14, 1848, *Writings*, V, 53–56, 58–61.

[117] Nevins, *Ordeal of the Union*, I, 25 n.

[118] *Telegraph and Texas Register*, September 21, 1848.

[119] *Ibid.*, November 23, 1848; Houston to Margaret Lea Houston, December 3, 1848, *Writings*, V, 62.

[120] Gambrell, *Anson Jones*, 424.

better able to "render him a requital than Ex-President Jones." But Jones's "requital" was unexpected. He wrote the editor of the *Western Texian* at San Antonio a communication on "misrepresentations in relation to the relative courses of Jones and Houston on the subject of annexation," claiming for himself the credit for its accomplishment and accusing Houston of conniving with England and France to the prejudice of Texan interests.[121] Washington D. Miller sent the *Western Texian* for November 17, 1848, posthaste to Houston, and the General, so Rusk wrote his brother, "flourished about" much annoyed by the Jones letter. Anthony Butler was not annoyed but most pleased at any attack on Houston, who, he wrote, was beginning to be "pretty well understood not only in Washington but in the U. States. The lies which he was compelled to tell . . . has made him quite notorious if not distinguished." Butler continued his letter: "And I can assure you that on the termination of Mr. Polk's presidential term it would be injurious to an applicant to have Houston's recommendation. Gen. Taylor knows him thoroughly."[122]

The hero of Buena Vista had been elected president in November, 1848; on March 4, 1849, the Whigs would take over the administration. The election had intensified sectional animosities; many Northerners were more firmly committed than ever against any expansion of slavery into the new territories; many Southerners were more resolved than ever to maintain their rights in those territories and defend slavery at home. As soon as Congress met in December, agitation of the slavery question recommenced, and the question was entangled with the governmental organization of the territories and the boundary of Texas. Texas had come into the Union with a "statute asserting that the Rio Grande line plus a long panhandle extension northward to the forty-second parallel was her western boundary." With New Mexico ceded to the United States, the adjustment of that boundary was an internal question, reserved by the annexation resolution to Congress. The free-soilers wanted to reduce the area of slaveholding Texas; Texans and other Southerners demanded for Texas the Rio Grande limits or the Santa Fe area.

Early in Texas statehood, the *Telegraph* had carried a long editorial to show the historical background of the Texas claim to Santa Fe and had expressed the hope that the Texas delegation would soon ascertain whether the general government was disposed to maintain the Texas

[121] Houston to Jones, October 18, 1847, *Writings*, V, 19–20; Miller to Houston, November 28, 1848, Miller Papers; *Telegraph and Texas Register*, December 28, 1848.
[122] Butler to ———, January ?, 1849, Ashbel Smith Papers.

192

claim, for "if it does not, it will be necessary for our State government to adopt such measures as will secure our title, provided this can be done without violating our compact with the General Government."[123] Even earlier a committee in the Texas Legislature had reported a resolution asking the Texas delegation to open negotiations with the United States for the cession of the public lands in return for "adequate consideration to enable Texas to pay her public debt." The land, particularly in the area along the unsettled boundary line, seemed Texas' best asset for liquidating that debt, and Texans were disturbed when, as a part of war strategy, United States troops seized the Santa Fe country and established a territorial government. Theoretically that government was temporary, and the *Telegraph* wishfully thought that it was no evidence of administrative desire to infringe on Texas rights. When the war emergency was over and the government was dissolved, Texas jurisdiction would extend west to the Rio Grande.[124] Texas papers in March, 1848, reported that Senator Houston had presented a memorial protesting against the relinquishment without an indemnity of territory conquered from Mexico and also against the application of the Wilmot Proviso to any territory that might be acquired. Just before the Texas senators went to the Baltimore Convention, Rusk had written back to Texas that there would be no difficulty in establishing the lower Rio Grande as the Texas boundary but that enforcing the Santa Fe claim would give trouble. Securing title to that area was of incalculable importance to Texas, however, as a means of caring for its public debt. With that debt gone and a railroad connecting the Gulf of Mexico and the Pacific, Texas would be "in a proud and commanding attitude."[125] Back in Congress a half-year later, Rusk assured his brother that he faced a busy session "as the question of Santa Fe will become a subject matter of investigation."[126]

For the most part, Texans were more interested in boundary, debt, and railroads than in the slavery issue per se; but a few militant Southerners such as Louis T. Wigfall were ready to follow Calhoun in protesting any exclusion of slaveholders from the newly acquired territory. In August, 1848, speaking at Charleston to justify his opposition to the Oregon Bill, Calhoun had advocated that South Carolina not participate in the 1848 election but take the lead in organizing a Southern party

[123] *Telegraph and Texas Register*, April 29, 1846.
[124] *Ibid.*, May 13, 1846, and January 4, 1847.
[125] Rusk to George W. Smyth, May 14, 1848, Houston Unpublished Correspondence, V.
[126] Rusk to David Rusk, December 16, 1848, David Rusk Papers.

to deliver an ultimatum to the North and follow that action, if necessary, by secession. Calhoun's opportunity to further his plans came in January, 1849, when Joshua Giddings and Abraham Lincoln brought up in the House a proposal to restrict and gradually abolish slavery in the District of Columbia. Calhoun called a caucus of Southerners from which a committee of fifteen were appointed to draw up a Southern Address. Houston, Benton, and Polk all opposed the caucus, and Rusk, one of the committee of fifteen, objected to Calhoun's wording of the address as too threatening to be politic. Rusk's opposition brought him into collision with Calhoun, and when Rusk's substitute resolution was refused, Kaufman was appointed to replace him on the committee. Rusk wrote of the circumstances involving the Southern Address: "I yield to none in my devotion to the just and constitutional rights of the southern states but I doubt much if they are to be benefited by the formation of a new party, by using threats which are not to be executed, by bringing into disrepute the bonds of our Union, or by an appeal to the fears of any section of the union."[127]

Calhoun's Southern Address, adopted after bitter debate in the caucus of slave-state members, was signed by forty-eight congressmen, but not by Houston or Rusk. Then Calhoun and his followers persuaded Isaac P. Walker of Wisconsin to propose an amendment to the civil appropriation bill which would extend the Constitution and laws of the United States over the Mexican cession, thus abrogating the old Mexican statutes against slavery. Calhoun and Webster collided bitterly over the measure, which passed the Senate but was blocked in the House and so held up all appropriations. Congress met all night on March 3/4, 1849. "Epithets were exchanged, threats uttered, and even blows struck. . . . In the Senate several members were grossly intoxicated, and the disorderliness became so shocking that Sam Houston rose to say that though he was familiar with the license and turbulence of the frontier, the present spectacle filled him with shame."[128] Congress adjourned about six o'clock on Sunday morning of March 4 without providing any civil government for California or New Mexico. Houston's letters do not reveal whether or not he stayed to see Taylor inaugurated before he left Washington for Texas.

In part, Houston's actions in the short second session of the Thirtieth Congress had conformed to the wishes of the majority of his constituents. He had introduced, on January 8, 1849, resolutions recommending the appointment of a committee to report upon the feasibility of a rail-

[127] Rusk to ———, January 30, 1849, T. J. Rusk Papers.
[128] Nevins, *Ordeal of the Union*, I, 227.

road to the Pacific and the establishment of a military road dotted with sufficient army posts for the protection of the frontier. His proposal that the Senate procure five hundred copies of Jacob de Cordova's map of Texas had brought on a debate with Jefferson Davis of Mississippi, who said that an accurate map was being prepared by the Topographical Bureau. With Timothy Pilsbury and Rusk, Houston had asked the Committee on Commerce to provide for a lightboat off the bar at Galveston Harbor.

Because of Calhoun's criticism of his vote on Oregon, Houston, on Texas Independence Day, prepared an address to his constituents to explain his action on that measure and to give his opposition to the Southern Address. He questioned Calhoun's position as "guardian of the whole South" and traced the history of the Calhoun-Jackson relationship to unmask what he termed Calhoun's "long cherished and ill-concealed designs against the Union." After attacking both the "mad fanaticism" of the North and the "mad ambition" of the South, Houston proclaimed his willingness to lay down his life to defend any one of the states from aggression and ended with Jackson's words: "The Federal Union, it must be preserved." The next day, in the heated debate over California's government, he averred that he would vote for no measure which seemed "even to menace the rights of the State which I have the honor, in part, to represent." Later in the debate he tried to restore some calm in the Senate and there, as in his address to his constituents, proclaimed his love of the Union.[129]

Houston had used no oratory, but equal candor, to express himself concerning Calhoun and the Union in a letter to Huntsville to his neighbor Henderson Yoakum.

Ah! we have a Southron Convention here—a second act (or so intended by Mr. Calhoun) of nullification. Rusk and myself smoked Johnny and would not indorse for him. We are not done with him yet—but I think he has *nearly done with himself.* Less than half the South will not be a sweet morsel for him. Whiggery has nothing to do with the question. It is "the Union," or "disunion." You know I am as unionfier as General Jackson was, and cannot look with one grain of allowance upon any fanatical project while selfish and unholy ambition is to be gratified at the expense of the Republic. We were among the last to come into it, and being in, we will be the last to get out of it.[130]

Calhoun's followers, such as F. W. Byrdsall, were equally vehement in their attacks on Houston, denouncing his "demagoguism" and ambi-

[129] *Writings,* V, 65–68, 78–91.
[130] Houston to Yoakum, January 3, 1849, *ibid.,* 70–72.

tion and classing him among "certain fools and traitors from the Slave States."[131]

At home in the summer of 1849, Houston devoted considerable time to his private business but managed to swing some weight in local and national politics. A state gubernatorial contest was under way, with George T. Wood, who had succeeded Henderson as governor in December, 1847, opposed by Peter Hansborough Bell. Although Wood charged his defeat to his indifferent support by Houston, the anti-Houston forces led by J. P. Henderson and W. B. Ochiltree had fought the incumbent. Miller was informed that the anti-Houston men would "move heaven and earth to defeat Wood, if for no other cause simply to cripple Houston in this state."[132] Houston spoke in support of Wood at Henderson on May 21. In his speech at Marshall, a strong Democratic center, on June 24, he paid less attention to Texas than to national politics as exemplified in the Mississippi movement to implement Calhoun's proposal for a Southern Convention by summoning representatives of the slave states to a grand sectional convention, which was finally called to meet at Nashville in June of 1850. Houston's encounter at Marshall with future Senator Wigfall, usually described by Houston as "Mr. Wiggletail," was but a curtain-raiser to debates between the two men in 1857 and 1859, when Wigfall was to be the foremost oratorical opponent as Houston battled for the governorship. Texas newspapers were inevitably drawn into the fray, publishing such parts of the speeches as suited their purposes. Henderson wrote Rusk of the threats which he had to use to make one editor publish an editorial to clear up the authorship of his report on the Houston-Wigfall debate. "I then told him, in a way that made him convinced there *might* be some danger to refuse, that he *should* publish it. He is a vile puppy or perhaps a fool & I will make him stand strait."[133]

Bell's victory over Wood in 1849 may have resulted partially from his advocacy of a more aggressive policy in asserting Texas' claim to the Santa Fe area. Even before the ratification of the Treaty of Guadalupe Hidalgo, the Texas Legislature had created Santa Fe County, had asked the United States to sustain state officials sent there, and had dispatched Spruce M. Baird to organize the new county and serve as its judge. Although Polk had ordered no interference with any government

[131] Byrdsall to Calhoun, March 16 and May 7, 1849, Boucher and Brooks, *Correspondence Addressed to John C. Calhoun*, 500, 503.
[132] F. L. Hatch to Miller, May 20, 1849, Miller Papers.
[133] Henderson to Rusk, August 30, 1849, T. J. Rusk Papers.

the Texans might establish at Santa Fe, the army officers in control there refused to let Baird set up a government. When Taylor became president, he refused any support to the Texans and favored granting statehood to both California and New Mexico. The Texans' dislike for the Whig President was intensified by General Taylor's ill regard for Texas troop activities in the Mexican War. Houston did not spare crudity in his comment on the new occupant of the White House: "I have no doubt that old Zackery will carry out all his notions of the 'inefficiency' of the Texians, and slap them whenever he can. If he cou'd keep quiet he would be decent, but if he undertakes to climb, his exposure, I apprehend, will be like a certain *animal* whose exposure is said to arise from climbing."[134]

Houston, however, was still more interested in attacking Calhoun than in local politics. Those matters, he assumed, would be well taken care of by other sufficiently assertive Texans. Early in September, 1849, he came out with a letter stating that he had always opposed the Wilmot Proviso and would continue to vote against it. He explained that he was for the Missouri Compromise, since Calhoun had used it to "fleece Texas of a large portion of her territory and gave it to free soil." The vote on Oregon, he said, "was for the Missouri Compromise, but had no relation to the Wilmot proviso."[135] He took the same stand in a long letter to James Gadsden, replying to a Gadsden letter which berated him for opposing Calhoun in March, 1849. The bitterly sarcastic letter to Gadsden was again strong in its condemnation of Calhoun as a "moonstruck seer" with the "air-built theories of the abstractionist."

In my humble judgment, the course pursued by Mr. Calhoun, and the *Abolitionists*, tend to the same end. So far they are co-workers and confederates. Could their designs be accomplished, the end would be the destruction of the Union, and the degraduation of the country from its present elevated position, to the control of reckless demagogues; from the enjoyment of liberal institutions, and the government of the free people to a condition of anarchy, weakness, and civil commotion.[136]

Houston never deviated from his stand against the Wilmot Proviso, for the Missouri Compromise line, and in opposition to advocates of disunion, North or South. The Senator made a political speech in Houston on October 23 and declared his determination to maintain the boun-

[134] Houston to T. M. Bagby, May 7, 1849, *Writings*, V, 92–93.
[135] *Texas State Gazette*, September 15, 1849.
[136] Houston to Gadsden, September 20, 1849, *Writings*, V. 95-107.

daries of Texas as defined by the Republic. By November 4 he was back in Huntsville packing to leave for Washington by way of Alabama to visit relatives. As he made ready for his departure, his enemies planned a surprise for him that was to develop into a seriocomic imbroglio. The surprise was in the form of a letter by Memucan Hunt to be published in the Galveston *News* at such a time that its appearance would "utterly *annihilate*" Houston as he passed through the Southern states. Hunt used as his excuse for the attack a verbal greeting brought him from Houston by Robert S. Neighbors. As Neighbors took leave of the General at Huntsville, Houston remarked that he supposed Neighbors would see his friend General Hunt in Austin, and said in effect: "Well, tell the General he has my highest respects but damn his Whiggery." When Hunt took offense at the message, delivered in the presence of Peter H. Bell, Neighbors said that really he did not think his quotation of Houston was correct as he did not recall that Houston had actually used the word *damn*. Whatever Houston's choice of words, Hunt had an excuse for an attack. Ably assisted by Anson Jones, he wrote a thirty-page letter which, when printed, filled five columns in the *Texas State Gazette*. In the letter Hunt gave his own personal history as a Democrat but said that Houston, by his Oregon vote, had become a "free-soil" Democrat, deserting the rights and interests of his constituents. He accused Houston of neglecting the affairs of Texas while he made northern electioneering tours, and assured the Senator that he would need Northern "society" the next time he stood for election. Rusk came in for condemnation for his part in suspending the rules of the Senate so that the Oregon Bill might become law and for his refusal to sign the Southern Address. The climax of the attack was Hunt's description of Houston's technique as a "boss" of Texas politics.[137]

Neighbors was so startled when he saw the *Gazette* that he demanded that the editor publish a letter to the effect that Hunt had "drawn upon his own brilliant imagination for the 'political' and 'insidious' portions of the message" delivered by Neighbors to Hunt and had "perverted a simple message of compliments between gentlemen, into a political hobby." Bell, asked for his version of the Neighbors-Hunt exchange, recalled that it was certainly nothing to cause any difficulty.

The *Gazette* must have had a jump in circulation as it published a blow-by-blow and letter-by-letter version of the affair, including a poem signed by "Jim Crack" and titled "Farewell Ode to Senator Sam Hous-

---

[137] *Texas State Gazette*, November 10, 1849.

ton."[138] "Jim Crack" is not identified. Were the ode better poetry, it might be attributed to Washington D. Miller, who had written confidential letters to both Houston and Rusk describing the content and purpose of the Hunt letter. Houston, as was so often the case, followed Miller's advice to ignore the letter.

Miller had been correct in his predictions of anti-Houston activities in the Legislature. W. G. W. Jowers wrote Rusk that as soon as he got to Austin he urged the propriety of the immediate election of a senator and was amazed to find that some who claimed to be Rusk's political and personal friends opposed the move. Jowers told of the circulation in Austin of the proceedings of a public meeting at Marshall, "giving Old Sam & yourself particular H." The notice of proceedings was referred in the Texas Senate to the Committee on Federal Relations. Jowers then questioned: "*Ain't* you & old Sam badly scared? I am expecting every day something of the same character will be introduced into the House, which will be referred to a similar committee of which I am chairman; then I know you will both cry out, 'Political murder.' "[139] Jowers may have been a little too facetious. The Texas Senate was following pretty much the Southern pattern and passed unanimously and verbatim, according to John G. Tod, the same resolutions in relation to the powers of the general government that Calhoun had introduced into the United States Senate on the Oregon question; and the Calhoun restrictions, said Tod, "Houston would not touch with a ten foot pole."[140] W. J. Mills of Liberty County, writing to Rusk, who was chairman of the Senate Post Office Committee, to suggest an alteration in mail routes up Lynchburg way, diverted from his subject to mention Rusk's refusal to sign the Southern Address and to say that he thought that Rusk must surely see that Calhoun's doctrines were the only safety for the South. Mills protested that he had always been Houston's friend but was dead against his stand on Oregon and the Southern Address.[141]

As party differences in Texas were accentuated, there was a strong effort, led by Henderson, to differentiate the stands taken by Houston and Rusk, with Rusk representing the Southern-rights Democrats.[142]

[138] *Ibid.*, December 8, 1849; Note of November 21, 1850, Houston Unpublished Correspondence, V.

[139] Jowers to Rusk, November 24, 1849, T. J. Rusk Papers.

[140] Tod to John T. Mason, January 15, 1850, quoted in Kate Mason Rowland, "General John Thomson Mason," *Quarterly of the Texas State Historical Association,* XI (1907/1908), 197.

[141] Mills to Rusk, January 19, 1850, T. J. Rusk Papers.

[142] Henderson to Rusk, February 24, 1850, *ibid.*

There was urgent need of co-operation and compatibility as the senators went back to Washington to face the problems before Congress in the winter of 1849/50 and all of the turbulent summer following. The members of Congress had begun to arrive in Washington by the last of November. Calhoun was there, defiant as ever. Henry Clay, aged seventy-three, was sent back to the Senate by a unanimous vote of the Kentucky Legislature after an absence of seven years. Jefferson Davis represented Mississippi; Lewis Cass was there, as was Daniel Webster. It took nineteen days and sixty ballots for the Democrats to elect Howell Cobb as speaker of the House by a majority of two votes. Meantime the Senate adjourned from day to day, and the President delayed his message on the state of the nation. After Christmas, sectional antipathies broke out again over election of the clerk of the House. While Washington was so fevered, the press and legislatures over the nation were delivering manifestoes and pronunciamentos on slavery.

When President Taylor finally sent his message and recommended that California be admitted as a state as soon as it applied for admission to the Union and that Congress leave territorial questions to the spontaneous movement of the people in the areas, his unrealistic proposal was dubbed the "no-action plan." Immediately proposals flooded Congress to organize the territories on the basis of the Wilmot Proviso; others called for organization without any mention of slavery. Benton wanted to create a new state within the Texas boundaries and pay Texas fifteen million dollars for her consent. Henry S. Foote suggested a new state called Jacinto to be created from the Texas area east of the Brazos River. After debate started on James M. Mason's bill for rendition of fugitive slaves, there were talk of secession and hints that Southern members might block all legislation in the House. Senator Clay decided once more to play the part of the pacificator. On January 29, 1850, he presented an eight-point program combining solutions of the issues of California statehood, the government of the territories, the boundary of Texas, slave trade in the District of Columbia, and a more effective Fugitive Slave Law. The administration and the Whig newspapers would not support Clay. On February 13, Taylor sent the California constitution to the House, and the Southerners organized a filibuster. Jefferson Davis presented the Southern position, as did Calhoun, who, too ill to speak, had Senator Mason read his speech for him. Calhoun declared that the South faced the choice of abolition or secession. The Northern rejoinder came from Webster, who, four days after Calhoun's speech, made his famous Seventh of March oration with its historical

review of the slavery struggle, an examination of the sources of recrimination between the sections, and an exposition of the futility of
a rupture and the criminality of a fratricidal conflict. The speech marked
the turning point in the struggle; by the end of March, opinion of the
nation began to crystallize in favor of compromise.[143]

What of Houston during those dramatic days? He was not ingratiat-
ing himself with the Henderson-Wigfall faction at home. *The Texas
State Gazette* published an unsigned letter from a "distinguished" source
in Washington complaining that

if Texas were not so unrepresented and so far behind the times with her elder
sisters in stating and advocating her claims [in New Mexico], there could be
no failure in Congress. . . . At present the whole subject is in abeyance. No one
but a few sleepless statesmen and the Texans are giving it much attention; but
in this long pause, Texas is losing the vantage ground. Whatever is done, is
done to her disfavor, for every act is a new impediment, or a new rival.[144]

In the midst of the charges and countercharges of the abolitionists
and the fire-eaters, every person was suspect, particularly every foreigner. When a resolution was introuuced that one Rev. Theobald
Mathew, a temperance leader from Ireland, be admitted within the bar
of the Senate, Southerners objected on the score that Mathew's descriptions of poverty in Ireland were aimed at comparison with slave areas
in the South. Houston ridiculed any political connotation in the question
of the courtesy to be extended to the foreign visitor and refused to be
guilty of making a "patriot and philanthropist" a victim of party bickering. "My reasons may be imperfect," he declared, "but I know that my
impulses are all right."[145] Henderson did not consider them all right and
wrote Rusk that Texans were rejoiced to see Rusk's vote recorded with
the South on the issue.[146]

A week after the "Father Mathew" affair, Houston presented a resolution that the President submit to the Senate all the correspondence concerning the government at Santa Fe, the boundary of Texas, and the
reasons why Texas judicial authority had not been recognized at Santa
Fe. On January 14, 1850, he introduced a resolution to the effect that
as Congress had no power over slavery in the states, either to establish
it or abolish it, the establishment or prohibition of slavery in the states
formed by the people of a territory should be deemed no objection to

[143] Nevins, *Ordeal of the Union*, I, 250–302.
[144] *Texas State Gazette*, January 12, 1850.
[145] Speech on Privilege of the Floor, December 20, 1849, *Writings*, V, 109–12.
[146] Henderson to Rusk, January 28, 1850, T. J. Rusk Papers.

the territory's admission to statehood. In both cases his action received editorial approval in Texas.[147]

On January 30, 1850, the day after the introduction of Clay's compromise bill, Houston proposed that the Committee on Public Lands inquire into the expediency of granting from the public domain a homestead of 160 acres to each family not owning land worth fifteen hundred dollars. The resolution brought sparks from the Virginia, Mississippi, and Georgia senators and bitterness from Henderson, who questioned Rusk: "Why did he present his bill proposing to give foreigners and abolitionists lands to induce them to settle in the Territories? (He knew that every slaveholder was worth more than $1500.)"[148]

More interest was aroused by Houston's long speech of February 8, 1850, on the subject of the compromise. Houston criticized the Southern Address, denounced the proposed Southern Convention, condemned the Wilmot Proviso, and, above all, pleaded for compromise to save the Union. He anticipated Lincoln in scriptural quotation on disunion when he ended his speech:

I beseech those whose piety will permit them reverently to petition, that they will pray for this Union, and ask that He who buildeth up and pulleth down nations will, in mercy, preserve and unite us. For a nation divided against itself cannot stand. I wish, if this Union must be dissolved, that its ruins may be the monument of my grave, and the graves of my family. I wish no epitaph to be written to tell that I survive the ruins of this glorious Union.

He had worked carefully to prepare his speech on the compromise and had copies ready for reporters before he appeared on the Senate floor. The correspondent of the Boston *Post* wrote:

General Sam Houston speaks tomorrow. He too, will make a Union speech, calm, patriotic, and becoming the brave and heroic senator who represents the youngest child of the American Union. It has been said that "Sam" means to attack Calhoun. He will not do so. He will merely defend himself from the aspersions thrown upon his views in regard to the slavery question. Sam is no fanatic either way; and seeks no remedy for the evils under which the South are now laboring in disunion and anarchy. He will insist on the constitutional rights of the South; and he will ask nothing more. Texas is for the Union *and* the constitution now and forever.[149]

The speech won high commendation in New England and New

[147] Resolution on Submission of Certain Correspondence, December 27, 1849, *Writings*, V, 112; *Telegraph and Texas Register*, January 26, February 7, 1850.

[148] Henderson to Rusk, April 14, 1850, T. J. Rusk Papers.

[149] On the Compromise of 1850, February 8, 1850, *Writings*, V, 119–44; Boston *Post*, quoted in *Texas State Gazette*, March 9, 1850.

York. Radcliff Hudson had written from Hartford, Connecticut, even before the speech: "Genl. Houston has won the highest esteem of *all* the North by his conduct in the Senate. It was as I think the right ground to take & for him it will tell most strongly." From Providence, Rhode Island, one A. Woods wrote Rusk to thank him for Houston's "noble speech on the preservation of our glorious Union"; and R. W. Judson of St. Lawrence County, New York, commended the "able and eloquent speeches of Hon. Sam Houston."[150] The opposite reaction came from the Texas extremists as expressed by Henderson: "And now Mr. Clay has the *impudent effrontery* to propose to us that we shall yield *all* the North now claim of us on this subject and calls it '*compromise*.' Houston too must outrage his state and the feelings of the whole South by his resolutions of *submission* to the dictates of abolitionists. This is the *damnedest* outrage yet committed upon Texas."[151]

Rusk was having to handle both his and Houston's correspondence, for the week after Houston had made his February 8 speech, he had started for Texas. The Texas press broke into a lather of speculation about why the Senator had left Washington when the situation was so explosive and no Southern vote was expendable. A letter in the *Texas State Gazette* of March 16, 1850, said that reasons for such a strange and unexpected step must be imperative but that the people of Texas had a right to know those reasons. Two weeks later the *Gazette* quoted a Huntsville citizen as saying that the situation of Houston's family had not demanded his presence in Texas and that his intimates were as much surprised at seeing him as at seeing a ghost. In true Houston fashion, the Senator had answered one interrogation with, "Oh Major, they won't do anything at Washington until I get back."[152] Henderson was writing Rusk that in Harrison County "they gave *Sam* h——l, well that's just," and asking, "Why did he run off just as the California constitution was about to come before you?" By April 18, Rusk was writing to San Augustine: "Genl. Houston has not yet returned and it is exciting some remarks here as I see it has done in Texas."[153]

True to his habit of being taciturn when he pleased and telling his constituents only what he chose, Houston never gave any public explanation of his trip home. He had, in declining an invitation to make an address before the National Reform Association in New York City,

[150] Hudson to Smith, February 7, 1850, Ashbel Smith Papers; Woods to Rusk, March 8, 1850, and Judson to Rusk, March 11, 1850, T. J. Rusk Papers.

[151] Henderson to Smith, February 25, 1850, Ashbel Smith Papers.

[152] *Texas State Gazette*, March 16, March 23, April 6, 1850.

[153] Henderson to Rusk, April 14, 1850, T. J. Rusk Papers; Rusk to David Rusk, April 18, 1850, David Rusk Papers.

written the secretary of the association that the serious illness of a member of his family compelled his presence at home.[154] His private correspondence reveals that he had serious domestic problems. Mrs. Houston was pregnant and had sprained her ankle. There were complications at the farm; the manager, according to Mrs. Houston, was a "good soul" who did the best he could, but the "farms and the pigs and the cattle do not prosper as they should." Furthermore, in October, 1849, Mrs. Houston's ward, a girl named Virginia Thorne, had eloped with Thomas Gott, the overseer, who had had himself appointed her guardian. Later in the year, after the Senator had returned to Washington, Mrs. Houston was indicted for assault and battery against Virginia Thorne. The case resulted in a mistrial, and a Baptist church investigation acquitted Mrs. Houston. Henderson Yoakum, the Houstons' attorney in the case, made a memorandum in his papers that it was generally understood that the matter had been brought to court at the instance of some of Houston's enemies to do him harm.[155]

Surely the combination of circumstances was enough to take Houston the three thousand miles home and also to entitle him to silence. That he hastened back to Washington as soon as possible is indicated by the fact that he was as far east as Vicksburg on April 6, three days before his third daughter, Mary Willie, was born at Huntsville on April 9, 1850. He resumed his seat in the Senate on April 23 and a week later wrote his wife: "Since my return I have had the pleasure of reading several letters from you, which arrived in my absence. They all give me great pleasure, for by my visit home, I was able to remedy some things, and leave you in a more comfortable situation. . . . I hope now, you will have peace & more happiness than you otherwise could have enjoyed." The same letter expressed his grief over the death of his sister Eliza, gave instructions on how to bathe little Nannie to cure a cough, and praised young Sam's good reports. As for the newest member of the family, a lock of whose hair had been sent her father, he wrote: "Well, I am very happy to hear that it was a little daughter, tho' I would have been equally gratified if it had been a son. Poor Sam, he will feel the apparent injustice, I fear, and think he is not treated with justice, or fairness! . . . This looks but little like giving him the six little brothers, tho' it appears something like the 'six little sisters.' "[156]

---

[154] Houston to John H. Keyser, February 13, 1850, New York *Daily Tribune*, March 2, 1850.

[155] Margaret Lea Houston to Houston, January 28, 1850, Archives Collection, University of Texas Library; Memorandum and Notes, November 8, 1850, Henderson Yoakum Papers.

[156] Houston to Margaret Lea Houston, April 30, 1850, *Writings*, V, 145–47.

Houston had been partially correct when he had said that nothing would be done in Washington until he got back. Much wrangling had taken place; many threats had been exchanged; a committee of thirteen, mostly moderates, had been appointed in the Senate to consider the Clay compromise proposals. On March 31, 1850, John C. Calhoun had died, and the next day Rusk delivered one of the Calhoun memorial discourses in the Senate. It was the middle of May before the big battle over the omnibus bill began again. Taylor threw his influence against the compromise and broke openly with Clay, and Houston wrote Yoakum that "the President and Cabinet have been prodding at Clay and he knowing it, has determined to oust the Cabinet and make poor old Zac come to his feet or disgrace him." Yoakum's reply combined observations that Houston's family was well, his corn was looking good, Huntsville was growing and the penitentiary (with ten convicts) growing, and Texas politics were "perfectly quiet." "Public opinion is getting right here, nobody voted for the Convention."[157]

The South had begun to lose its enthusiasm for the Nashville Convention by the first of April. Only nine states sent delegates to the meeting, which opened June 3, 1850, and some of those delegates had dubious credentials. Henderson attended from Texas and at the meeting secured promises from the states represented that they would stand by Texas in the boundary dispute with New Mexico. The tone of the meeting was fairly moderate, and all extremist schemes were dropped.[158] After the convention, Henderson and Wigfall made fiery speeches at several public meetings, but to little avail. Ashbel Smith, in writing to Houston concerning Texas medicine, sugar refining, crops, and politics in general, had reported:

Everything is going on well here—*the people will not respond* to the course suggested by Gov. Henderson and Mr. Wigfall in their published letters. I have received several letters from the North and West, in which your course is highly lauded and approved. I was rejoiced to see it announced you would sustain the proposed compromise—though I am apprehensive it will not receive the sanction of Congress.[159]

New Orleans opinion on Houston's stand was divided. The *Crescent* wrote that although Houston's action had brought him denunciation, the editors were not surprised that he supported a measure which gave assurance of a satisfactory adjustment, for he had "shown himself emi-

[157] Houston to Yoakum, May 14, 1850, *ibid.*, 153; Yoakum to Houston, May 31, 1850, Houston Unpublished Correspondence, V.
[158] Nevins, *Ordeal of the Union*, I, 315–16.
[159] Smith to Houston, June 7, 1850, Houston Unpublished Correspondence, V.

nently conservative in his views, a patriot and a devoted lover of the Union." On the other hand, a New Orleans letter signed "Independent" berated the Texas representation in Washington and threatened a day of reckoning when Texas frontiersmen would refuse to vote for those who had "been afraid to open their mouths on the Compromise subject, the partition of our State, and the payment of our debts."[100]

"Independent's" criticism was hardly fair to Rusk, who wrote his brother on June 9: "We are in great excitement upon the compromise. The Texas part of it has been up for two days past and I have had to battle it for two days. Houston did not take part. I got on extremely well with the exception of losing my temper a little yesterday."[161]

Houston soon began to participate in the fray. On June 11 he introduced a resolution that the President inform the Senate concerning the United States orders to hold Santa Fe to the embarrassment of Texas jurisdiction. On the next two days he spoke on the Texas–New Mexico boundary, including comments on the deficiency of the national policy on the frontier, a realistic presentation of the Indian problem on that frontier, and a strong defense of the Rio Grande boundary. He admitted the right of the United States to settle the boundary with Mexico, but not to adjust, without consulting Texas, the boundary between Texas and the United States. When the senator from Florida, in line with promises made at Nashville, spoke of the forfeiture of Texas' claims to New Mexico as prostitution of the state, Houston implied that Texas could well handle her own affairs: "I will . . . assure him that all Texas will return him thanks, and in the name of Texas I return him my thanks, for becoming the special guardian of her purity and her honor; and I hope it will suffer no danger from his friendly interposition." At the same time Houston vigorously denied the right of the United States government to coerce Texas:

I have been accustomed to resistance to central governments. . . . Let a Central Government lay a rude hand upon her banner, and that Star will never be eclipsed, though gentlemen by treading on stars here, may not seem to think much of it. Our banner floats on the wind, and I would let gentlemen remember that from the darkest clouds of the revolution, it has led us to association with this Union, which we are ready to contribute the last drop of our blood to maintain—faithful to the Union, faithful to the Constitution, and faithful to Texas.[162]

[100] *Texas State Gazette*, June 8, 22, 1850.
[161] Rusk to David Rusk, June 9, 1850, David Rusk Papers.
[162] *Writings*, V, 155–64.

The last words of the speech sounded like a well-chosen ending for a Fourth of July celebration on the Texas prairies. They were an exact statement of the position that Houston was maneuvering to maintain: Texas' rights based on a states'-rights interpretation of the Constitution without any threat of secession.

President Taylor enhanced his unpopularity with Texas and the South when, on June 17, he sent a special message to Congress declaring that the federal government should maintain possession of Santa Fe until the boundary quarrel was adjudicated. Southerners would flock to the aid of the Lone Star if a shooting war started. The Southern Whigs were agreed on that, and Alexander H. Stephens was their spokesman to present their ultimatum to Taylor: that he cease insisting on the admission of California and New Mexico and agree to compromise. After Stephens' visit to the President on July 3, Stephens wrote the editor of the *National Intelligencer* that "the first federal gun that shall be fired against the people of Texas without the authority of law, will be the signal for the freemen from the Delaware to the Rio Grande to rally to the rescue. . . . You should recollect that the cause of Texas, in such a conflict, will be the cause of the entire South."[163]

Even as Stephens and Toombs talked to the President, Houston was also firing at the administration as he continued on July 3 a speech that he had begun on June 29 on the Texas–New Mexico boundary. In his remarks condemning Taylor and his cabinet for illegally convoking a convention within the boundary of an area claimed by Texas, he cited all the examples of Taylor's disparaging and abusive comments on Texas troops during the Mexican War, defended Texas' historical claims to the territory, and castigated the Nashville Convention. In one instance he said that the President was presuming on the potency of his authority when he claimed that Texas would not "*practically interfere* with the *possession of the United States*," for it was arrogance to suppose that Texas would "submit to the usurpations of the military authorities in Santa Fé." At the same time, Houston denied any idea of secession in Texas when he concluded:

Think you, sir, that after the difficulties they have encountered to get into the Union, that you can whip them out of it? No, sir. New Mexico can not whip them out of it, even with the aid of United States troops. No, sir!—no, sir! We shed our blood to get into it, and we have now no arms to turn against it. But we have not looked for aggression upon us from the Union.[164]

[163] Quoted in *Texas State Gazette*, August 3, 1850.
[164] Speech on Boundary, June 29, July 3, 1850, *Writings*, V, 167–92.

On July 8, Houston again gibed at Taylor in a speech introducing resolutions that the Senate be informed about plans to evacuate Fort Isabel. The next day Taylor was dead from typhoid fever, and Millard Fillmore was the president of the United States. Two days later the Texas Senator wrote to that new president a long and earnest letter, advising him to use his own judgment, and not the pressure of cliques, in the choice of his cabinet, and promising "no factious opposition." In a spirit of true patriotism and high statesmanship, Houston said to Fillmore:

My object in writing to you, is to let you know, that I feel, as I believe you do & as every citizen, ought at this moment to feel. Duties of high moment have by a marked dispensation of Providence, been devolved upon you. . . . You now have it in your power, I verily believe to render your country more important benefits than have been rendered for the last quarter of a century by any one individual. With your capacity and intelligence, you will, I have no doubt, [have] perceived, that there is but one course to pursue for the attainment of the vast object—peace to the country. . . . To do this you have only to compass the whole and not feel that you are of or belong to any *one* section or another. . . . To accomplish this end it will only be necessary to compromise matters in such sort as will give quiet to the people by either consummating some plan which has now been suggested or by devising a better and procuring its adoption.

You were elected as a Whig, and I presume no rational man will expect you in party matters to deviate from party principles. Nevertheless, you are elected by the American people and are their President. The present agitations can not be settled by either of the political parties of the country, but it must be done by both parties acting for the Union as a great Union Party. . . . For my part, as a Senator & a citizen, I feel, that the object of restoring peace, and tranquillity to the people of the country, rides high above all party considerations and would be worthy of the fame of Washington if he were now on earth. I doubt not, but what you will believe me sincere when I assure you that the first, and most ardent, as well as the most sincere wish of my heart, is to see our country at rest. Nor do I care by whom the great work is accomplished. Party and party influences never enter into my estimate of the value of the Union, or my country's happiness or prosperity.[165]

Fillmore had once told Taylor that in the event of a tie on the compromise he, as vice-president, would vote in its favor. Webster rejoiced that Fillmore favored compromise; and the orator from Massachusetts, who, as Houston told Fillmore, would be a "tower of strength to your administration, South as well as North," became secretary of state. Not

[165] Houston to Fillmore, July 11, 1850, Millard Fillmore Papers.

all observers were so sure of Fillmore's policy. Francis P. Blair wrote Van Buren that he went in to Washington "to witness Clay's oration over his dead Bills, but instead I found the Senate in conclave—giving life to a new cabinet." James A. Pearce of Maryland was to go into that cabinet as secretary of the interior, and Blair remarked to Van Buren:

Pearce made his finale in the Senate by the defense of the late President from the attack of Houston. I infer from it, that the kind of policy adopted by Taylor in regard to the present ruling in Texas requires New Mexico still be upheld by the new administration.

It is certain now that the omnibus goes to the bottom of the Hill much faster than it climbed up. . . . Benton says, he strangled the Bill on his last grapple with it. The truth is, I believe, nobody was at heart in favor of it but Clay & Foote.[166]

The bill was not dead. Instead it became an administration measure. Webster spoke again for compromise on July 17. Houston warned the Senate of mass meetings in Texas and on July 22 again demanded justice for his state. Both Webster and Fillmore thought the boundary of Texas too pressing a problem to be left unsettled, but the compromise was stronger in its parts than as a whole. It was in parts that the bill finally passed the Senate: the Utah Bill on August 1; the Texas Boundary Bill on August 9; the California Statehood Bill on August 13; the New Mexico Bill on August 14; and the Fugitive Slave Bill on August 19. Each measure met stiff opposition; each passed by a decisive majority, the Texas Boundary Bill by a vote of 30 to 20. Then the scene shifted to the House of Representatives. It was to be mid-September before the contest was over and a wild celebration was begun in Washington. Secession and war were averted, at least for a time.

Houston had fought every step of the way. Because the boundary bill provided that Texas should be paid ten million dollars for the area north of the thirty-second parallel and west of the one hundred and third meridian, it was charged that Texas was being bribed to give up her territorial claims. Houston's speech of July 30, 1850, denied that Texas asked for any money or any new boundary: "It is her boundary she asks—not your millions."[167] When the vote on the admission of California as a free state came up, he announced that he would vote for the bill, as he had for the Oregon Bill, and received censure as being unfriendly to the South. On that score he declared that his feelings were purely Southern and that, although his concept of what was beneficial

---

[166] Blair to Van Buren, July 20, 1850, Martin Van Buren Papers.
[167] Speech on Boundary Bill, July 30, 1850, *Writings*, V, 204–208.

to the South might not be right, his motives were pure. He spoke, he said, not to vindicate himself, but to vindicate his discharge of the trust delegated to him. He denied that the "surreptitious" meeting at Nashville was a true indication of Southern sentiment and held that California's right to prohibit slavery was inherent in the rights of American citizens to govern themselves. Jefferson Davis of Mississippi broke into the speech with a defense of his state's position in implementing the Nashville Convention, and in the ensuing exchange Houston insinuated that it was Calhoun who had been the influence behind Mississippi's action. Daniel Wallace, a representative from South Carolina, demanded a copy of the speech. Houston complied. Then on August 23, 1850, Wallace had a bitter attack on Houston printed in the Washington *Southern Press*. Describing the difference between Calhoun and Houston as the difference between the "eagle and the owl," Wallace held that the quarter-of-a-century enmity between the two men dated back to Houston's malfeasance in his office as an Indian agent in 1817. Houston answered the newspaper attack in a speech in the Senate on September 9, 1850, and denied he had intended any reflection on Calhoun.[168] There might be general rejoicing that the compromise had brought tranquillity, but the ghosts of old hatreds continued to stalk in Congress.

In Texas during the late summer and early fall of 1850 the excitement was equally as great as that in Washington. Rusk was told that the people of Texas probably would not listen to any proposition for compromise, and that if he and Houston voted for such a measure, the special session of the Legislature which was to meet in August would select someone to succeed Rusk at the end of his term and would request Houston to retire. The writer, R. D. Johnson, himself believed that Rusk could not be beaten and that no instructions on Houston's resignation could be secured.[169] Certain Texas papers accused the senators of conniving at outrages on the rights of Texas, but the *State Gazette* said that those editorial effusions were just expressions of partisan spleen to help defeat Rusk, whose term would expire in March, 1851. As for Houston, his term "does not expire for some years, and very little is to be gained by his enemies by assailing him. We will only remark, so far as he is concerned, that his ability, enlarged patriotism, and devotion to his duties, have won for him a high place among the distinguished men of the Senate."[170]

---

[168] *Texas Monument*, September 25, 1850; Reply to Reflections upon Record as Subagent, September 9, 1850, *Writings*, V, 238–52.
[169] Johnson to Rusk, July 28, 1850, T. J. Rusk Papers.
[170] *Texas State Gazette*, August 24, 1850.

The local situation in Texas was aggravated by the ultra press in the South, which kept insisting that Texas would be dishonored should she give up any territory or agree to compromise. John A. Quitman of Mississippi took his stand on the indisputable title of Texas to the Rio Grande and declared that in the event of collision, it would be his duty to call the Legislature of Mississippi and recommend aid for Texas. A student at Princeton University wrote the editor of the *Red Land Herald* that he and fellow students were so moved with sympathy for Texas that they were almost induced to leave college and rush to her assistance. Alabama citizens assured Texas of the cordial support of the people of the slaveholding states but warned that the people of the South also had a right to expect that Texas would not be so false to herself or to them as to "accept a sum of money for admitting an enemy within her gates, and establishing therein a stronghold for abolitionists and a harbor for fugitive slaves."[171]

It was no wonder that the minute the boundary bill had passed both houses, a wire was sent to Governor Bell of Texas. Signed by Daniel Webster and J. J. Crittenden and endorsed by Rusk and Houston, the telegram read in part:

Pearce's Bill, Texas bill, has passed, all the Texas delegates voting for it, and as soon as signed by the President it will be sent to Texas by Express. This dispatch is intended for Governer Bell of Texas & is sent to you [collector of the port at New Orleans] to be forwarded to him with the least possible delay by Special Express. . . .

P.S. The Legislature ought to continue in session till the Bill reaches them.[172]

The next day, September 10, 1850, David S. Kaufman prepared an address for his district, assuring his constituents that the Texas delegation in voting for the bill had not committed Texas to its support but had, by their vote, submitted the decision to the people of Texas themselves. He sent a map showing the territory ceded and prayed that the popular decision would redound to the interests and honor of Texas.[173] George T. Wood, a visitor in Washington during the debates, thought the Texas senators were correct in "pursuing the bill as far as it was reasonable to do" and then voting for it. The measure, Wood felt, was too vast to be settled by the vote of two men, even senators. Submitted in its present shape, the matter would be settled if sanctioned by Texas. Its rejec-

[171] *Ibid.*, September 7, 14, 1850.
[172] Telegraphic Dispatch, September 9, 1850, Governors' Letters.
[173] *Texas State Gazette*, October 12, 1850.

tion would "place our senators in a position to insist on better and different terms."[174]

In the two months preceding the final decision in Texas, the press indulged in a heated battle over whether Texas by acceptance of the measure would "seal the bond of dependence and subjection to Northern men." South Carolina died hard, and her governor, Whitemarsh B. Seabrook, wrote confidentially to Governor Bell that she would heartily support any measure adopted by Texas to preserve the integrity of her territory, even to lending her the South Carolina portion of the surplus revenue in the United States Treasury and sending men to the aid of Texas.[175] The *Nueces Valley*, the Matagorda *Tribune*, the *Lone Star*, the *Star State Patriot*, and the Galveston *News* beat the war drums against a measure which made "Congress our guardian to pay our debts as if Texas could not be trusted with her own business," and declared that any Texan would spurn the bill as an "unclean thing—disgraceful in its requirements and robbery in its consequences." "Gold might buy the votes of members of Congress," ran one editorial, but "we rely upon the uncorrupted and incorruptible people of the Lone Star State for a glorious triumph over abolition artifice and the intrigues of speculators."[176] Marshall, the hotbed of ultra Texas Democracy as usual, held a demonstration that J. K. Holland described as "Anti-Everything" and as "condemning the United States Congress, cursing our Senators & Representatives, swearing that they were bribed—and that the Legislature had practiced a fraud upon the people in electing Rusk—condemning the Legislature for non action and for not sustaining Gov. Bell *et al.*"[177]

By contrast, at a meeting at San Augustine, Colonel S. W. Blount proposed a resolution to approve the action of the Texas senators on the boundary question. The *Gazette* copied an editorial from "Pennsylvanian" to the effect that Texas might congratulate herself on the vigilance and ability of her two eminent sons "so constantly exercised to protect and preserve her cherished interests."[178]

Gradually the Texans decided that more years of trading would not give Texas a better bargain than did the compromise. At a special election the vote was two to one in favor of the proposition; Governor Bell signed the act of acceptance on November 25, 1850. The northern and western boundary of Texas was fixed to begin at the intersection of the

[174] Wood to Miller, September ?, 1850, Miller Papers.
[175] Seabrook to Bell, September 11, 1850, Governor's Letters.
[176] *Texas State Gazette*, September 15, 21, 1850.
[177] Holland to Miller, October 3, 1850, Miller Papers.
[178] *Texas State Gazette*, September 28, October 12, 1850.

one-hundredth meridian and the parallel of thirty-six degrees and thirty minutes and to extend west along that parallel to the one hundred and third meridian, thence south to the thirty-second parallel, from that point west to the Rio Grande, and then down the river to its mouth. For renouncing all claim to territory beyond that boundary, Texas was to receive ten million dollars, one-half to remain in the United States Treasury to pay the revenue debt, the other five million to be turned over to Texas in bonds. The payment of the revenue debt, scaled and prorated among the creditors, continued to be an issue for some six years longer and caused more ill will against the general government.

Rusk arrived at San Augustine on his way home from Washington on September 26, 1850, and Houston reached there on October 30. Both made speeches in favor of the "ten million proposition." David Kaufman also spoke at San Augustine on the Pearce bill, assuring Rusk later that he answered everything in advance that Henderson said in opposition to the bill and that "Old Sam is on rapidly rising ground."[179]

On November 26, Henderson Yoakum recorded in his journal that the news had just reached Huntsville that the third session of the Third Legislature had accepted the Congressional compromise with one dissenting vote in the Senate and five in the House. As Houston rode into town in the late afternoon, Yoakum relayed the news, and Houston received it with the words: "I may now retire then, for it is consummation of what I have struggled to attain for eighteen years past."

The senators had only a few short weeks at home before they returned to Washington for the opening of Congress in early December. They discussed the Texas governor's race to take place in 1851 and were inclined to support George W. Smyth against pro-Southern Bell. They considered the attitudes of Texas newspapers and the advisability of supporting an organ which would advance their views. As always they had many requests for roads and for appointments. Guy M. Bryan was convinced that they would approve his nephew Henry's appointment to West Point.[180] It is doubtful that Houston had time to answer Gail Borden's plea, sent via Ashbel Smith, that he visit the Borden meat biscuit factory to see its machinery and apparatus so that he could influence Congress to adopt the biscuit for army rations.[181]

In the short session of Congress, the popularity of the compromise in saving the Union caused conservative Whigs and Democrats to manifest general good feeling towards each other. Although radical elements

[179] Kaufman to Rusk, November 6, 1850, T. J. Rusk Papers.
[180] Bryan to his sister Eliza, November 21, 1850, Guy M. Bryan Papers.
[181] Borden to Smith, October 30, 1850, Ashbel Smith Papers.

in the North flatly rejected the Fugitive Slave Law, Southern extremists had little encouragement save in South Carolina and Mississippi. Back in the Senate, Houston again took up the cudgel with South Carolina, this time in the person of his old antagonist, James Hamilton. Writing from Retrieve Plantation in Brazoria County, Texas, in November, 1850, Hamilton had suggested to Langdon Cheeves that Virginia take the lead in summoning a meeting of the slave states at Richmond as a preliminary to a convention of all the states to consider a constitutional amendment to secure new guarantees of Southern rights. Houston, strongly opposed to the reopening of a question supposedly solved by the compromise, countered with a letter to his kinsman John Letcher, newly elected congressman from Virginia, objecting that any such move on Virginia's part was unnecessary and could serve no good end but instead would "protract agitation, and furnish a sort of safety-valve for the over-charged patriots of South Carolina and Mississippi to let off their *extra gas*." Houston thought Virginia would spurn the "proffered ensign of treason" offered by South Carolina but submitted his ideas to Letcher to stimulate him and others to rescue Virginia from the least shade of suspicion.[182]

Having warned Virginia, the Senator took off to Philadelphia to lecture on "The Trials and Dangers of Frontier Life" as a benefit to raise money for rebuilding Southwark Church. His rambling lecture got in much Texas history and a plea for Union with a quotation of a toast offered in Texas on July 4, 1850: "Our friends, from Maine to the Rio Grande, from the Atlantic to the Pacific; our hearts embrace them with paternal affection."[183]

Kaufman died in Washington on January 31, 1851. Houston was probably back from Philadelphia in time to attend the funeral services in the National Cemetery. By February 11, he was planning to speak for the ladies of the Episcopal church at Harrisburg, Pennsylvania, on Washington's Birthday and to speak on February 24 for the Sons of Temperance in New York, where he had been elected a member of the Tammany Society. He took time between lecture tours to appear in the Senate on February 12 to oppose the creation of the rank of lieutenant general in the army and on March 3 to oppose a river and harbor bill, which he described to Yoakum as "an Internal Improvement Bill of the most extravagant character ever seen." On March 1 and again on March 3, 1851, he cautioned Yoakum as the attorney in the assault trial against Mrs. Houston to get a continuance of the case so that he could get home

[182] Houston to Letcher, January 24, 1851, *Writings*, V, 261–67.
[183] Lecture of January 28, 1851, *ibid.*, 267–81.

in time for the trial, for he "would not fail to be present for *millions*."[184] He wrote his wife that he had asked for continuance of the trial lest business detain him in the East longer than he expected and told her that the next day, March 6, he planned to take communion at the L Street Baptist Church in Washington and asked for her prayers that he might enjoy full evidence of his regeneration.[185]

The summer of 1851 Houston spent as a father and a farmer and a gracious host. He wrote a New York friend to thank him for sending a nurse for the children and described himself as raising fodder for his dairy cattle and as "planting peas, corn, rice and millet—all in a small way." A disagreement with his renter, Samuel McKinney, over when the fodder should be pulled was settled by Yoakum. On June 13, Yoakum was invited to come over for a "family dinner" at noon when E. M. Pease, the candidate for governor, would be a guest. The family visited in Houston and Galveston, and Houston made two speeches, one at the laying of the cornerstone of the Masonic Lodge and Academy in Houston. In late August he planned to go as far north as Dallas and proposed that John R. Burke accompany him, promising no liquor but a full share of "good spirits" for the trip, with the explanation that for years past he had been a teetotaler and intended so to be as long as he lived. In mid-October he attended court at the Falls of the Brazos. His letters reveal little interest in politics. He saw no good to come from filibustering in Cuba. As for Texas, he was glad that the members of the Supreme Court had been re-elected, but "the Governor might have been mended much." As to his own political future, he was thinking in terms of retirement when he wrote:

I assure you, when I am at home, in my woodland residence, with my wife and brats, I feel no disposition to return again to scenes of official conflict and disputation. Nevertheless, I have yielded so far to my friends [as] to agree to a return if spared, and serve a part of next session of Congress, but not for the entire session. I would have to be absent for at least eight, but probably ten months! This is too long an absence for a man who loves his home and family!

Two months later he was still of the same opinion and wrote: "I am anxious to get out of public life, and remain in quiet the residue of my days."[186]

He broke away from pastoral pursuits in September to make a speech for the home folks in the Presbyterian church at Huntsville. After a

[184] Houston to Yoakum, March 1 and 3, 1851, *ibid.*, 287, 292.
[185] Houston to Margaret Lea Houston, March 5, 1851, Domestic Correspondence.
[186] Various letters, May 8–September 10, 1851, *Writings*, V, 297–309.

compliment to Rusk, he devoted his remarks to a defense of his record in state and national affairs, with what the reporter called a "clear elucidation" of the boundary controversy. The *Texas Ranger,* in covering the discourse, stated that Houston was never more firmly seated in the affections of the people of Texas, who had "unlimited confidence in his fidelity—in his patriotism and in his ardent devotion to the Union of the States."[187]

Political habit reasserted itself on October 7, also, when the Senator wrote President Fillmore to suggest that should John Watrous resign as United States judge, it might be well to defer a new appointment until after the meeting of Congress, when the Texas delegation could inform the President of the character of the men whose names would be presented. Houston assured Fillmore that he was induced to write the letter because of a "real desire to see the public interest promoted and confidence restored to the Federal Judiciary of Texas." Of Watrous his only comment was: "If we are to rely upon the charges against Mr. Watrous, no country or community ever labored under a greater cause [curse?] than Texas has."[188] Watrous did not resign, and Houston's blast against the Judge was not to be made in full force until 1859.

In the same mail with the letter to Fillmore went one to John Woods Harris to report "mission accomplished": "I did as you wished me. . . . It was a task. I wish it [could be] held in *abeyance,* until we could reach there, and tell him who are clever fellows. Spoke of his own Party and told him *some* were *cleverer* than *others.*"[189]

Houston went east by way of Alabama and was in Washington to take his seat in the Senate on December 9, 1851. He made only one long speech before the Christmas holidays; but that one got him into what John H. Moffitt described to Rusk as a "terrible stew or broil" with Henry S. Foote, who had introduced a resolution that the compromise measures were "a final settlement of the dangerous and exciting subjects which they embrace, and ought to be adhered to." Houston's position was that affairs were so harmonious generally that the good sense of the American people would take care of matters without legislative interposition. By innuendo, according to Whig Senator Foote of Mississippi, Houston intimated that the resolution was introduced for "illicit party purpose." In answer, Foote, who had announced his intention to "give a Roland for an Oliver," declared that Houston delivered a "regular party harangue" as a demonstration of his "demagoguism and

[187] Defense of Record, *ibid.,* 310–14. The date should be September 22, 1851.
[188] Houston to Fillmore, October 7, 1851, Fillmore Papers.
[189] Houston to Harris, October 7, 1851, *Writings,* V, 314.

wire pulling for the Presidency." Houston's elephantine memory doubtless made him relish the opportunity to be caustic at the expense of one who had written, in 1841, with the assistance of Mirabeau B. Lamar, a *History of Texas and Texans,* a book in which Houston had said he found "very little orthodox," and which he had called the "Foot history because it will be more footed than eyed."[190] It was now ten years since Houston had given that book review, and he and Foote had both worked valiantly in support of the compromise; but 1852 would be a presidential election year, and the Texas Senator did not let the opportunity slip to give a somewhat detailed history of his own course in the Senate, disclaim ironically any fishing for political influence in South Carolina, present a realistic picture of political maneuvering of the times, and portray himself as a national instead of a strictly Democratic senator. Admitting that on occasion he had been at variance with his party, he proclaimed himself a "conservative" Democrat as he said: "I know that I have been arraigned for having been too latitudinous in my feelings; but I must confess that my country seems not too large to love, to cherish, and support. Then, sir, if the object of the party is conservatism, and to preserve what we believe the true constitutional principles of the Government, whoever loves and supports that Constitution strictly, is my fellow."[191]

En route to Hartford, Connecticut, to speak on a favorite topic, "The North American Indians," Houston was in New York on December 29, 1851, and was initiated into Tammany Hall as member No. 3322.[192] Early in January, 1852, he was back in Washington and was introduced to Louis Kossuth when the Hungarian patriot was being lionized in the capital. The *Congressional Globe* noted that as "the martial figure of General Houston approached Kossuth, there appeared to be a special attraction in the person of the hero of San Jacinto." Judging from the comment of a Washington correspondent in this instance, it was not the Senator's dress, but his bearing and renown, that attracted the distinguished visitor. Describing the scene in the Senate, the correspondent wrote:

Sam Houston sat dressed in dark pantaloons, a single breasted blue military coat, with bright buttons, and a vest made out of the skin of a panther, with the hair outside. It is, I presume, a relic of Sam's old Indian days, when he

[190] Houston Address, November 25, 1841, *ibid.,* II, 395.
[191] Speech Opposing Reaffirmation of the Compromise, December 22, 1851, *ibid.,* V, 317–36.
[192] Society of Tammany of the Columbian Order, Constitution and Roll of Members, 1789–1916.

was chief of a tribe. He always comes on in some singular dress, of half savage, half civilized character, which, however, he soon lays aside and puts on what used to be called in Kentucky, his "store clothes."[193]

In late February, 1852, Houston made a visit home. He had no political worries in Texas at the moment, for the Democratic State Convention, meeting in Austin on January 8, had adopted a resolution presenting his name to the national party as "a patriot, chieftain, and statesman eminently worthy to be the standard bearer of the party in the approaching canvass for the Presidency."[194] It was a visit to see his family, particularly the newest member of that family, Sam Jr.'s fourth little sister, Antoinette Power, born on January 20, 1852. Houston started back from Huntsville to Washington on April 6, traveling part of the way to San Augustine in company with Jane Kaufman, widow of the late congressman, and conversing with her on petitions then in Washington to have the stages cross the Trinity at Strothers instead of Sabinetown, a change which Mrs. Kaufman wrote Rusk would ruin her and the town.[195]

It was well that Houston made the spring trip to Texas, for the long session of Congress was too absorbed in the presidential election to accomplish much business and sat all through the summer of 1852, so that it was not until September that he started west again, stopping for speaking engagements in Pennsylvania, Ohio, and Tennessee. While in Washington he took part in a debate on the Deficiency Bill to explain the inadequacy of federal protection of the frontier, with emphasis on the resulting deterioration in Indian relations. He took a moment off in the Senate Chamber to write a letter of introduction for his friend Congressman Andrew Johnson of Tennessee, with the request to his correspondent that he "make my friend cheerful while he is with you."[196] Houston was supposed to talk at New Hope, Pennsylvania, and Lambertville, New Jersey, on July 5, but Henry Clay died on June 29, and Houston was selected as one of the members of the Senate committee to accompany the body of the "Great Compromiser" back to Lexington.[197]

Speeches for the party, introductions, official senatorial delegations, and the usual patronage requests were all a part of the routine of a pub-

---

[193] Quoted in *Texas Republican* (Marshall), January 24, 1852. For the Connecticut and New York trips see Houston to John H. Houston, October 11, 1851, and Lecture at Hartford, January 5, 1852, *Writings*, V, 316, 337.

[194] Winkler, *Platforms of Political Parties in Texas*, 51.

[195] Houston to Smith, April 5, 1852, *Writings*, V, 338; Jane R. Kaufman to Rusk, April 13, 1852, T. J. Rusk Papers.

[196] Houston to A. H. Mickle, May 25, 1852, Andrew Johnson Papers.

[197] Houston to Lewis S. Coryell, June 30, 1852, *Writings*, V, 346–47.

lic servant, as were requests for information. Wherever possible Houston exploited his bibliophile friend Peter Force and the Force library in securing his answers. Once he asked Force to lend him a pamphlet translated from the Spanish and containing a report by Luis de Onís on the Florida treaty. Again, he asked Force for citations on Jean Lafitte.[198]

In debating on the appropriations to be made for the Indians in California, Houston drew on his own experiences to defend his long-time friends—in California or Arkansas or Texas—and urged: "Let not the sin lie at our door any longer that they are starving and famishing by the connivance of this Government or its officers; but provide the means, and trust to Heaven, if not to the officers, for their application to the good design."[199]

For once, a Houston defense of the Indians seemed to draw no fire from Texas newspapers. Texas did not mind how much the Senator criticized the Fillmore administration or the federal government in general. Disgusted at indications from Washington that nothing would be done for protection of the frontier, the *Texas State Gazette* mixed complaint of Texas' low position in administration esteem with praise for the "activity, ability, and industry" of the Texas delegation.[200] The *Gazette* approved Houston's stand on the payment of the Texas debt and doubtless approved also his action in refusing to let the river and harbor bill "be forced down our throats" without Senate investigation at a time when the regular appropriation bill was pending, his defense of Thomas Ritchie's financial claims against the government after the editor was forced to transfer control of the Washington *Union*, his insistence that public building in Washington be strictly according to contracts given on competitive bids, his urging of regular promotion of navy officers, and his refusal to vote for the lighthouse bill because it was recommended by a government board and had not passed a Senate committee. As a legislator he distrusted bureaucracy and insisted on economy in government, just as he had when he was president of the Republic of Texas. When Congress finally adjourned, he was "harnessed" as a political war horse and battled for party principles on his way home to his "young Barbarians," and at home continued in political harness to speak for King and Pierce at a barbecue in Washington County on October 12, 1852.[201]

[198] Houston to Force, August 8, 1850, Houston Papers; Houston to Force, July 23, 1852, *Writings*, V, 349.
[199] On Indian Appropriations, August 11, 1852, *ibid.*, 349–54.
[200] *Texas State Gazette*, August 21, 1852.
[201] Houston to Lewis S. Coryell, August 28, 1852, *Writings*, V, 361.

The first week in November, Franklin Pierce and William R. King were elected president and vice-president of the United States, "a glorious result for the Democrats," as M. B. Menard wrote Rusk, asking appointment as collector at Galveston. Charles Power, Houston's brother-in-law, also wanted the place, wrote Menard, but would not apply for it, "through motive of delicacy." Evidently Houston had no taste for nepotism. Because of that aversion to relatives' asking appointments, Charles Power made his own appeal for appointment as consul to Le Havre, not to Houston, but to Rusk.[202]

Houston's chief activity in the second session of the Thirty-second Congress was service as chairman of the special Senate committee for the investigation of frauds, especially frauds involving private claims, government contracts, and Indian claims. The day before the close of the session he moved the continuance of the committee during the Senate's executive session, which began on March 4, 1853, the day of Pierce's inauguration and the day that Houston, for the third time, took his oath of office as United States senator. He had been re-elected on January 15, 1853, in a joint session of the Texas Legislature. The vote in the Senate was 19 to 3; in the House it was 45 to 12. His term would expire on March 4, 1859.[203]

At a little past the halfway mark of his senatorial career, Houston was still on "rising ground." He had experienced opposition in a negligible degree, but Texas had thrice elected him senator and had nominated him for the presidency.

[202] Menard to Rusk, November 10, 1852, and Power to Rusk, January 4, 1853, T. J. Rusk Papers.
[203] *Texas State Gazette*, January 20, 1853.

Alone in the Senate

His re-election as senator and his work for the party during the 1852 campaign made Houston feel entitled to write President-elect Pierce a letter of advice on cabinet-making early in 1853. Houston's opinion was that the President was responsible for the action of his counselors and therefore had the right to select them "independent of all extraneous influences." "A cabinet of irreproachable and unapproachable integrity, if intelligent and industrious, is all you want," he wrote Pierce; "the rest depends upon yourself." Houston assured Pierce that he was able to submit his reflections freely "because no consideration would induce me, if spared, to remain in *official position* in Washington."[1] Between the writing of that letter and the time of the inauguration, Houston

---

[1] Houston to Pierce, January 28, 1853, *Writings,* V, 370–73.

was busy in Senate debate. He recommended a reorganization of the Marine Corps, questioned a salary raise for the head of the Census Bureau, defended the constitutionality of federal construction of a railroad to the Pacific, spoke in defense of the Florida Indians, advocated civil instead of military superintendents for the national armories, urged the passage of the appropriation bill to avoid the expense of an extra session, discounted any necessity for reaffirming the principles of the Monroe Doctrine, and made two long speeches on the bill providing for payment of the Texas debt.[2] The creditors who insisted on being paid face value of their Texas promissory notes he represented as speculators who had invested ten cents or less and wanted a dollar in return. He wanted justice done in payment for every dollar Texas had actually realized, not the nominal amount of her liabilities. Of the creditors he declared:

Let them not talk of Texas' honor, Texas' renown, and Texas' escutcheon cleared. She cleared them herself, sir. It was not a speculation; it was a real transaction; and she will keep it clear. It is her best guardian under the aegis of the Constitution. I desire justice and liberality to all who aided Texas; and no matter how they have acquired their demands, give them an earnest for everything they have, and upon that earnest give them interest, and, if you please, be liberal, but let Texas have the credit of doing justice to her creditors, and let not the United States intervene to save her soiled honor, as it is called. She will take care of that article herself, and she will take care of her money, too, I trust, and make a useful application of it in paying all just demands, but not the demands of Shylocks.[3]

The *Gazette* described the speech as able and convincing and was satisfied that it "placed the matter in its true light."[4] Texans had more involved in the speech than the mere academic interest expressed by one young visitor to Washington who inspected both houses of Congress and reported that he was "not particularly edified by the wise men of the nation." "In the Senate," he said, "I heard Genl. Houston ranting about the debt of Texas. He was making what the Politicians call a Buncombe speech. I soon got tired of him."[5] A young New York lawyer, according to the stories he told his son, received a different impression of Houston. The son, Franklin D. Roosevelt, wrote many years later:

Soon after my father was admitted to the Bar he went into the office of the famous Benjamin D. Silliman in New York City as a law clerk. Very shortly

[2] *Ibid.*, 374–440.
[3] Speech on Texas Debt, February 11, 1853, *ibid.*, 375–88.
[4] *Texas State Gazette*, April 9, 23, 1853.
[5] Robert L. Brown to S. C. Wade, February 15, 1853, S. C. Wade Papers.

thereafter, in 1853, I think, he was sent by Mr. Silliman to Washington to deliver some legal papers to Senator Sam Houston. Senator Houston was living at one of the old hotels on Pennsylvania Avenue and in the middle of the day my father went to his room to deliver the papers. On entering the high ceiling room he saw the Senator propped up in a huge bed and a row of chairs extending from the door to the bed. As the Senator completed transacting his business with the caller next to the bed, the line moved up one chair. My father talked to him for several minutes and was always impressed by the Senator's splendid head and face and by his personality and force.[6]

Willing to be individual in his manner of holding conferences, Houston was also willing to welcome changes wrought by invention. He was a century before his time in advocating that the Senate have an inventor named Henry Johnson install a new mechanical method of counting votes, provided that the cost not exceed fifteen hundred dollars. He set no limit on cost, however, when he recommended that ten thousand additional copies of the report of the Committee on Frauds and Abuses be printed for the use of the Senate.[7] A lot of constituents were going to receive franked copies of the report of the committee headed by Houston.

The Texas Senator also denied that expense weighed with dissemination of scientific information as a consideration in the passage of his resolution that the Senate have printed one thousand copies of Bartlett and Gray's *Exploration of the Mexican Boundary.* The resulting debate exhibited Houston in a nonoratorical give-and-take in which he combined insistence, humor, and a keen appreciation of the scientific information in the report. Even as in his days in Texas politics, he feigned a lack of interest in reading and in books, but his general knowledge belied his words.

About the middle of April or early in May, 1853, Houston returned to Texas. A delegation of ministers at Nacogdoches, knowing of his membership in the Sons of Temperance, asked him to use his influence in securing the enactment of a Sunday prohibition law. While agreeing that disturbance of the Sabbath was censurable, he replied that it was "far better to endure and suffer from the ills of even a great evil than to violate, in the least, a vital principle of civil and religious liberty." His contention was:

When a government like ours undertakes to declare certain acts of individuals unlawful, that a considerable portion thereof honestly believe in, it is an

[6] Roosevelt to Adolph S. Schwars, March 18, 1935, Roosevelt Papers.
[7] Resolution Proposing Construction of a Voting Machine in the Senate Chamber, April 6, 1853, *Senate Journal,* 32 Cong., 2 sess. (Serial No. 657), 360-62.

abridgment of their inalienable rights, it cannot be enforced, and is calculated to lessen the respect for the laws of their country.

. . . .

To undertake to prescribe rules for conduct for others . . . by legislative enactments, is a species of legislation that will not be tolerated in a free land.[8]

Retirement from fighting and politics was hardly in Houston's mind when he sent Washington D. Miller secret instructions to organize a meeting in Austin and invite Houston and Rusk to attend. The Senator planned to take Sam Jr. to Independence the last of June and suggested that Miller meet them there to further plans for a visit to Austin, where interesting old battles might be renewed, including a lawsuit against Thomas W. Ward and hostilities with Edwin Ward Moore. Houston was also planning a fight with President Pierce. Texas was getting none of the national spoils, and the cabinet (according to Houston there was no president) even hesitated to comply with Rusk's and Houston's recommendations for local officers. "I did too much for Pierce," Houston said, "and he is jealous of me. *If God wills, I will make him more so!* . . . The wish and effort will be to crush me between Disunionists & Freetraders. Well, let him try the game. . . . The war will begin at the commencement of next session, if I live."[9]

While Houston was at Independence, he bought the Hines place and a tract of timbered land for a new location for his family, moving them from Raven Hill on October 25, 1853. The older children were in school, Sam and Nannie both studying Latin, and their father thought that Independence had the best educational advantages in the state. On October 31, the trustees of Baylor University wrote into their minutes resolutions of thanks to General Sam Houston for a contribution of $330 for the education of young ministers.[10]

As soon as the family was settled in the new home, Houston made his long-projected trip to Austin, and on Saturday, November 12, made a speech in front of the Capitol because the hall of the House of Representatives was too small for the crowd that had assembled to hear him combine "wit, eloquence, and argument." As always, he possessed the magic touch with a Texas audience. Said the *Gazette:*

The thick-coming memories of the past thronging upon him, his voice at one time faltered, and tears almost choked his utterance, while the moistened eyes

[8] Opposing Legislation Concerning Religion and Prohibition, 1853, *Writings,* VI, 21–25.
[9] Houston to Miller, June 10 and 30, 1853, *ibid.,* V, 447–52.
[10] Houston to Miller, September 13, 1853, *ibid.,* 457; *Texas State Gazette.* November 8, 1853; Worth S. Ray, *Austin Colony Pioneers,* 41.

224

of many of his hearers told how deeply they were affected by the evident emotion of the orator. Referring to ancient differences, in a vein of racy humor, which produced shouts of laughter, he rubbed out old scores, struck the balance, and opened a new book of accounts.[11]

In the audience were James G. Swisher and Thomas W. Ward, both of whom had threatened to attack Houston if he dared appear in Austin. Under surveillance because of their threats, they listened to Old Sam as he summarized his career, spoke of the beauties of Austin and of his identification with Texas, and prophesied the magnificent destiny within the reach of Texas. They cried too, as the tears streamed down the cheeks of Houston, who "looked like a prophet inspired by a vision unfolding the events of a thousand years to come." At the end of the speech, as Houston started down the hill, Swisher had one of his arms and Thomas Ward the other.[12]

The primary interest in Texas legislative circles at the moment was railroad construction in Texas and to the Pacific. Both Houston and Rusk had spoken in the Senate on the subject, and Houston, at Nacogdoches, had urged that it was expedient for Texas to concentrate her energies on the transcontinental railroad because feeder roads would follow as a natural consequence. He regretted the Legislature's granting of too many charters to fly-by-night companies who were more interested in peddling their shares in New York than in actually building the lines in Texas.[13] In his Austin speech, Houston had expressed his opposition to state loans for railroad construction, saying he would "sooner see every dollar in the treasury sunk in the deepest hole in the Colorado than so loaned."[14] Texas had neither freight nor passenger travel sufficient to persuade capitalists to build her roads, but she did have land, and alternate sections of land along the right of way could be given as a bonus for railroad construction. According to Rufus C. Burleson, Houston, while in Austin, was further persuaded in favor of land grants to railroad companies and, when he returned to Independence, solicited Burleson's assistance in the matter which was to decide whether Texas "was to be a mere cow pen and sheep ranch, or a great Empire State." With no mountains to tunnel, and possessed of almost a natural grade which could be readied for ties and railroad irons at comparatively little cost, she was "best adapted for a grand system of cheap railroads of any State on the continent." Opposition could be expected from Dr.

[11] *Texas State Gazette,* November 15, 1853.
[12] Memoirs of John Salmon Ford, IV, 650–51.
[13] Extract from Speech at Nacogdoches, *Writings,* V, 453.
[14] Jones, *Republic of Texas,* 618.

Francis Moore of the *Telegraph* and from the city of Houston, which was south of the logical route of the transcontinental road. "To overcome this vast array of opposition," Houston urged Burleson, "we must have the vigorous aid of every man who thinks, whether he wears a black cravat, a white cravat, or no cravat at all. And our committee wants you to spike the big cannon at Houston and silence its thunders against railroads and use all your influence for railroads."[15]

Among other developments of the summer and fall of 1853 was an exchange of letters between Houston and Guy M. Bryan, a correspondence which went back into early political rivalries in Texas and was ultimately to develop into bitter political differences between the Senator and Stephen F. Austin's nephew, when Bryan went to the House of Representatives as an ardent Democrat and opponent of Houston's nationalist views. Back in November, 1852, in answer to Bryan's question whether or not Houston had been unfriendly to Austin's memory or fame, Houston had written a letter summarizing his relationship with Austin from the time of Houston's arrival in Texas until Austin's death in December, 1836, and declaring: "Indeed, it would be useless to attempt to vindicate myself, against any charge of unkindness, or disrespect, either to the person or the memory of Genl. Austin, *for no one, can truthfully charge me with either*."[16] Bryan kept the matter open in the spring of 1853. Houston lost some of the letters and asked Bryan for copies, promising an answer: "As it is a matter of some interest to both of us, and not without some connection with the truth of history, when it may be written, I wish to attend to it soon." Bryan's suspicions that the correspondence had not been lost, but instead was retained as "a trap" by a "cunning and insincere man," elicited an impatient letter from Houston stating that he had been sincere in presenting his facts and that Bryan must state the charges against him and name the authors of those charges or the correspondence would have to close. The correspondence closed, but the breach widened into a bitter struggle in the succeeding six years.[17]

There were soon developments in Washington that gave renewed cause for Texas Democrats of the ultra stamp to attack Houston. When the first session of the Thirty-third Congress met in December, 1853, Clay and Calhoun and Webster were all dead; old party lines were breaking. The slavery quarrel, temporarily and uneasily stilled by the

[15] Georgia J. Burleson, *Life and Writings of Rufus C. Burleson*, 575–76.

[16] Houston to Bryan, November 15, 1852, *Writings*, V, 364–69.

[17] Houston to Bryan, May 1, August 3, and November 1, 1853, *Writings*, V, 447, 454–55, 459–63.

Compromise of 1850, was likely to burst out any moment. Pierce, trying to woo all factions, had scattered his patronage and possessed an inharmonious cabinet resulting from "shoving, hauling, and bargaining."[18] Administration prestige was low by the time Congress met, but the country was prosperous and foreign relations were calm.

Railroads were the absorbing interest, especially since the purchase of the Gila River area from Mexico had implemented the choice of a southern route for a road. Rusk was advocating that the line run from El Paso to San Diego as an extension of a projected Atlantic and Pacific Railroad, the promoters of which hoped to receive from Texas sixteen sections of land for every mile of road constructed across the state. Chicago, Memphis, New Orleans, and St. Louis were all alert. Four expeditions had surveyed four possible routes in 1853.

Among the senators most interested was Stephen A. Douglas of Illinois, who was fast assuming leadership in Democratic circles. While seemingly trying to avoid sectional views by proposing northern, central, and southern routes, each with connecting branches to the east, he was also considering, as chairman of the Senate Committee on Territories, the question of the organization of the Nebraska country west of Iowa and Missouri. His early efforts to organize the area had been obstructed, and had failed again in the spring of 1853. Houston had spoken briefly on territorial organization in 1853, saying that he was determined to discuss it and "prevent its passage if every bill in this body should be lost." His opposition grew from the violation of treaty stipulations with the Indians in the area.[19] At that time every Southern senator except the two from Missouri had voted for tabling the bill. The situation was to be quite different exactly one year later.

During the summer of 1853 a presidential commission bargained with the Indians until they ceded to the United States over thirteen million acres of land north and south of the Kansas River, to be subject to pre-emption and settlement as soon as the treaties were ratified and the Indian Office had created reservations for its wards.[20] Settlers were eager to enter the region. By June 11, 1853, Senator David R. Atchison of Missouri declared for immediate organization of Nebraska Territory on condition that "all citizens of all States, slave or free, might settle on equal terms." With the opening of Congress in December, Senator A. C. Dodge of Iowa introduced a bill for territorial organization. The measure went to the Douglas Committee on Territories and was re-

[18] Nevins, *Ordeal of the Union,* II, 45.
[19] Remarks Concerning Territory of Nebraska, March 2, 1853, *Writings,* V, 411.
[20] Nevins, *Ordeal of the Union,* II, 91.

ported on January 4, 1854, as the Nebraska Bill. Originally the bill provided for organization of the territory with no statement regarding
slavery. A section added on January 10 transferred the power to decide
for or against slavery from Congress to the people of the territory, im-
plying that the Missouri Compromise restriction was dead. As finally
modified, the bill called for division of the area into two territories and
the repeal of the Missouri Compromise.[21] Whenever Douglas had hesitated, the Southern Democrats, demanding the right to take their property north of the compromise line and denying the right of Congress
to legislate slavery out of the territories, had pushed him forward. Jefferson Davis, most influential member of the cabinet, helped to put
pressure on Pierce to bring the administration behind the measure,
which went to the Senate in its final form on January 23, 1854. The bill
became the "touchstone of true Democracy," and indignation of free-
dom-loving Northerners mounted to fury. A battle began to rage in
Congress and in the country. Because of Democratic majorities in both
houses and strong party discipline, the free-soilers were sure to lose
the Congressional struggle, though in the nation at large they might
win a moral victory. One of their chief fears was that the bill would be
pushed through before public opinion could be aroused. Douglas
opened the formal debate in the Senate on January 30.

Houston was probably back in Washington in time to hear the Douglas speech, but the Texas Senator had been in Philadelphia on January
28, delivering a speech at Spring Garden Institute on the history of
Texas.[22] Although a Democrat and from the South, Houston had early
indicated his intention to vote against the bill, and the rumor of his
alienation from the "true cause" prompted the Washington correspondent of the Richmond *Enquirer* to write to his paper on February 6:
"What objects Mr. Houston has in view, and what excuses he may have
to gratify them, I know not. Nothing can justify this treachery; nor can
anything save the traitor from the deep damnation which such treason
may merit. It will, however, effect no injury; and its impotency will
but add to its infamy."[23]

Houston knew what would appear in the *Enquirer* when he rose in
the Senate the next day to demand a time for speaking on the bill, saying that he was already prepared to vote but that the minority should
be heard "with some degree of patience and indulgence, if necessary."[24]

[21] *Ibid.*, 93–99.   [22] *Texas State Gazette*, February 28, 1854.
[23] Quoted in *Telegraph and Texas Register*, May 13, 1857.
[24] Remarks Concerning a Speech to be Made on the Kansas-Nebraska Bill,
February 7, 1854, *Writings*, V, 467–68.

He appeared to make his speech on February 13, but was so sick that he had to postpone the address. Still indisposed, he made a long speech on February 14 and 15, 1854. The first day he devoted to advocacy of the Indians and their rights, bolstering his remarks with a formidable stack of books containing references to the failure of the government to live up to its promises to the Indians. The Kansas-Nebraska Bill proposed, he said, to form a territory in advance of extinguishment of Indian title; and, as he never expected "to have an opportunity, probably, of addressing the Senate again . . . in relation to the Indians," he hoped he would be excused if he evinced "an unusual degree of anxiety and zeal."

Resuming his speech on the second day, he made one more plea for justice to the red men and gave their plight as sufficient cause for his opposition to the bill. Then he defended the consistency of his stand on the Missouri Compromise, which he said formed a part of the Constitution of Texas. He had defended the compromise in 1848 and 1849 because "the word of one section of the Union should be kept with the other." Houston asserted that in resisting the attempt to repeal the compromise, he was discharging an obligation and that as a Democrat he was bound to vote against a proposition to disturb the Compromise of 1850. He did not wish to be regarded as sectional and for the South alone, but his identity was with the South, which had prospered under the Missouri Compromise and for which its repeal would be no benefit. He argued with cogence and foresight that "the preponderance in favor of northern influence and northern votes is every day in progress of increase, and must continue so in after times. It is not to cease. The vast northwestern portion of our continent, unadapted to slave labor, will not be filled up by southern men with slaves, and northern people will increase that preponderance until the North is connected with California." He ended his speech: "Our children have two alternatives here presented. They are either to live in after times in the enjoyment of peace, of harmony, and prosperity, or the alternative remains for them of anarchy, discord, and civil broil. We can avert the last. I trust we shall."[25]

Two days after Houston's speech, William H. Seward of New York made such a forceful denunciation of the bill that Houston had the Seward address reprinted in German for the benefit of the German settlers in Texas.[26] Douglas finally secured agreement that the Senate vote

[25] Speech Opposing the Kansas-Nebraska Bill, February 14-15, 1854, *ibid.*, 469-502.

[26] William Ernest Smith, *The Francis Preston Blair Family in Politics*, I, 311.

should be taken on March 3. It was a half-hour before midnight when he finally gained the floor and forced the vote. Houston moved adjournment; there was a shout of "No!" Then Houston gave notice that he would speak after Douglas had finished. Douglas, turning to Houston's objection to Indian mistreatment, insisted that but one tribe was affected, some two hundred Ottawa Indians, "owning less than two townships of land."[27] Houston finally secured the floor in the small hours of the morning. He warned that the Republic would be shaken by the measure and pointed out the fallacy of the popular-sovereignty theory since sovereignty implied a power of organization and a self-acting principle which the territories would acquire only when they achieved statehood. The repeal of the compromise, he implored, "holds a promise to the ear, but breaks it to the hope." Texas, if calamities fell upon the South, would be in the most unfortunate position in the South. If the measure was a boon to propitiate the South, he as a Southern man would have none of it. Charges that he was going with the abolitionists and free-soilers, he minded not. He had considered the abolitionists fanatical, but by 1853 the abolitionists and the ultra-secessionists to him had become Siamese twins. At the end of three hours,

as dawn peered into the chamber, Houston was uttering his words of warning and protest. . . . His final plea for the sake of the Union, *"Maintain the Missouri Compromise! Stir not up agitation! Give us peace!"* was still echoing when at a few minutes before five o'clock, the Senate proceeded to vote. "Aye!" called Adams, Atchison, Badger, and Bayard: "No!" said Bell—and the bill passed by thirty-seven ayes to fourteen nays.[28]

The Senate vote was finished; the tumult and shouting continued until the House passed the bill on May 22 by a vote of 113 to 100. But the end of the voting in the Senate was not the end of the fireworks there. The clergy in the North had become articulate politically for almost the first time. Motivated and admonished by religious periodicals and by resolutions passed by religious bodies, they began to petition Congress, and on March 14, a memorial signed by 3,050 New England ministers protesting the Kansas-Nebraska Bill was laid before the Senate by Edward Everett. Senators James M. Mason of Virginia and Andrew P. Butler of South Carolina "upbraided the remonstrants for usurping spiritual functions for the purpose of agitation." Douglas pro-

[27] George Fort Milton, *The Eve of Conflict: Stephen A. Douglas and the Needless War*, 133.
[28] Nevins, *Ordeal of the Union*, II, 144; Speech Opposing the Kansas-Nebraska Bill, March 3, 1854, *Writings*, V, 504–23.

tested that the memorial was an attempt to coerce Congress and "sneered at ministers who posed as spokesmen for the Almighty."

When Douglas commenced his attack, Houston cried out to Charles Sumner, "Don't speak! don't speak! leave him to me."

"Will you take care of him?" asked Sumner.

"Yes," was Houston's response, "if you will leave him to me."[29]

Houston intervened in order that Douglas might not be able to sustain his charge that the memorial was the work of abolitionist confederates such as Chase, Sumner, and Seward. He was also able to say "I told you so" about the excitement he had predicted for the country. Defending the right of ministers to petition and to express themselves concerning a breach of faith on the part of the government, he said that while he himself might hold the contents of the protest heretical, he still could not deny the right of the signers to memorialize. Here again he was consistent in his stand, as in the Father Mathew case and in his defense of Thomas Ritchie. In calling the ministers the vicegerents of God, Houston said he meant to describe them as "harbingers of peace to their fellowmen." In conclusion he solicited: "I pray Heaven that we may never have another such protest in this body. But for the necessity or cause, which originated in this body, this memorial would never have been laid upon your table. This is but the effect; the cause was anterior to it. If we wish to avert calamitous effects, we should prevent pernicious causes."[30]

The day before his speech on the ministerial memorial Houston had spent in proposing a series of resolutions for Texas. The Texas Legislature wanted Brownsville instead of Point Isabel to be the port of entry for the Brazos de Santiago collection district. That resolution went to the Committee on Commerce. Legislative resolutions for paying Messrs. Cooke and Lockwood for damages done their property by United States troops in 1851 went to the Committee on Claims. Resolutions in favor of more pay for the mail contractor between Austin and Waco and the establishment of triweekly mail service between Huntsville and the mouth of Red River went to the Committee on Post Offices and Post Roads. The Committee on Agriculture got a memorial from one Denton Offutt, who offered to make public his system of treating domestic animals and his "mode of improving their breeds, for the general good."[31]

[29] Edward L. Pierce, *Memoir and Letters of Charles Summer*, III, 367; Nevins, *Ordeal of the Union*, II, 129.

[30] Defending the Right of Petition, March 14, 1854, *Writings*, V, 523–30.

[31] *Congressional Globe*, 33 Cong., 1 sess. (1853/54), Part I, 607.

Having taken care of both Mr. Douglas and his own Texas constituents, Houston hurried home. The *Texas State Gazette* carried a notice on April 4, 1854:

We see it intimated that General Houston is returning home and intends resigning his seat in the Senate of the United States.—Notwithstanding our objections to his course on the Nebraska bill, we should regret to see him leave the Senate at this time. Texas has large interests in many questions likely to arise in Congress during the present session, and his great abilities and enlarged experience would materially aid in securing them. We hope that he intends only a short visit to his family, and does not design permanently vacating his seat in the Senate.

Not all of the Texas papers were so generous in their comments. As he stood before the Baptist church at Independence, the Senator told his wife's pastor, Rufus C. Burleson, that some of the editors and politicians of Texas were denouncing him and that some old friends had refused to speak to him, saying he was a traitor to the South. Only he and John Bell among the Southern men had voted against the repeal of the Missouri Compromise, but, said Houston, "while that is the most unpopular vote I ever gave, it was the wisest and most patriotic." Then he prophesied:

The result of all this will be, in 1856, the Free Soil party will run a candidate for president, and the whole vote will be astounding. In 1860 the Free Soil party, uniting with the Abolitionists, will elect the president of the United States. Then will come the tocsin of war and clamor for secession. . . . But, alas! I see my beloved South go down in the unequal contest, in a sea of blood and smoking ruin.[32]

Burleson was among the Washington County citizens who asked Houston to make a talk at Brenham on matters of national politics. He spoke there in the Baptist church on April 15 to a crowded and noisy house, and the Brenham *Inquirer* reporter was unable to hear him distinctly but wrote that many of his supporters were dissatisfied and that he "failed to meet the expectations of his friends."[33] Rusk got a report from Henderson, Texas: "The people here are down on old *Sam* for his Nebraska vote and say go it *Tom*. But yet you know how they will cry out against and then turn right round and vote for him."[34]

On his way east, the Senator stopped at Houston, where he spoke at the courthouse to defend his vote on the Kansas-Nebraska Bill. De-

[32] Georgia J. Burleson, *Life and Writings of Rufus C. Burleson*, 579.
[33] Quoted in *Texas State Gazette*, May 6, 1854.
[34] S. P. Hollingsworth to Rusk, April 30, 1854, T. J. Rusk Papers.

spite the humor in his talk, which was able and ingenious, according to the reporter for the *Telegraph,* the applause indicated little sympathy in the minds of his hearers, who thought his position indefensible. The *Telegraph,* however, was resigned to the fact that no one who ever attacked Houston managed to prevail, and said that even the unpopularity of his Nebraska stand would not hurt him in Texas. The *Gazette,* copying the *Telegraph* account, doubted that the people of Texas would surrender their right of thought, even at Houston's bidding.[35]

By June 13, 1854, Houston was back in his chair proposing that the Senate meet an hour earlier each day. When a fellow member joked that he had been absent so much that he needed to improve his attendance record, Houston replied that while he was in attendance nothing of importance was discussed except one "great principle" which he did not understand and that he left in self-defense lest he be surfeited. Now that he renewed his associations with pleasure, he wanted to see his colleagues longer each day.[36]

Houston's mail from home was coming from his oldest daughter, Nancy. Sam Jr. finally had a little brother; Andrew Jackson Houston was born at Huntsville on June 21, 1854. On Independence Day, the Senator was off to make a patriotic address at Reading, Pennsylvania. His mail from Texas revealed that his name was much in the state press. The Marshall *Meridian* used verse to indicate its feelings toward Houston:

> Wires in and wires out
> And leave the people all in doubt
> Whether the Snake that made the track
> Was going South or coming back.

Ben Vansickle of the Gilmer *Star* replied in kind:

> There is sugar in the gourd
> And he can't get it out
> The way to get it out
> Is to roll the gourd about.

The Texas papers were trying to "roll the gourd" to find where their senator stood. The *Gazette* said that it attached no blame to Houston, presuming that he acted honestly, and had no desire to "start runners out on his trail to publish his faults and conceal his virtues."[37]

[35] *Texas State Gazette,* May 13, 1854.
[36] On a Resolution to Advance the Hour of the Senate's Meeting, June 14, 1854, *Writings,* VI, 26–28.
[37] *Texas State Gazette,* June 17, 24, 1854.

A familiar political device of Houston's was to divert attention from himself by directing it to someone else. He may have been, as his detractors claimed, working desperately for the presidential nomination. If so, he lacked political astuteness in speaking concerning matters of interest to Texas only and not to the nation. In the summer session of 1854 his two longest speeches were directed at enemies of his Texas career, E. W. Moore of the Texas Navy and Thomas Jefferson Green, author of *Journal of the Texian Expedition against Mier.* The speech on Moore grew out of the long-protracted effort to get relief for officers of the Texas Navy. In it, Houston had occasion to mention Texas bickerings of a decade before. Ancient animosities came to light also in the speech against the former Texas soldier and author whose sobriquet in Texas, Houston said, was T. Jefferson "Dog" Green. Houston asked the Senate to meet early in a special session to give him the time for a speech, which, on its face, seems to have been prompted by his discovering a copy of what he called Green's "History of Texas, Mexico, and the United States" in the Library of Congress. The library had been opened in the spring of 1853 in its new hall in the western extension of the Capitol. Although Houston disclaimed any idea of asking that the book be removed from the library, he left no doubt that the work of "this general loafer and follower of the army," which mentioned Houston 117 times in 484 pages, belonged more properly in the Washington sewers. Green had taken digs at Houston through Butler of South Carolina in the summer of 1850. A new element may have entered the picture by 1854. Green, a member of the California Senate, was also interested in a transcontinental railroad and may have been a promoter in the New York Pacific Railroad Company. Houston wrote Governor E. M. Pease to reveal the secret operations of the New York company, which professed to have bought many railroad charters in Texas. Houston's own opinion was that the Gadsden Purchase "secures the best route to the Pacific. That and the Texas Charter open it better for us than a thousand contracts with Robt. J. Walker, T. Jefferson Green & such men to whom no one would loan a dollar and no capitalist would risk his reputation in the money market by having any connection with men of such standing."[38]

Incidental speeches in the summer of 1854 included remarks opposed to discharging an auxiliary guard for the city of Washington, support of Rusk in advocating that government clerks of equal rank should receive equal pay, approval of a proposed homestead bill, an-

---

[38] Houston to Pease, June 22, 1854, T. J. Rusk Papers.

other plea to put the armories under civil rather than military super-intendents, approval of including in the naval appropriation bill the men of the Texas Navy who were in service at the time of annexation, and a resolution that the Attorney General examine records of the boards appointed to adjudicate claims under the Cherokee treaties of 1835 and 1836.[39]

On October 11, 1854, a meeting in New Hampshire nominated Houston for president of the United States. The Senator returned from Washington to Texas by way of Chicago and by October 28 was at Waco to make a speech. On November 7 and 15 he was advising and commending the Texas governor for his stand on railroad contracts.[40] The commendation struck a sour note with old Eph Daggett, who was concentrating on developing the Fort Worth area and was "down on old Sam" because his "hart . . . has long since gone to the north."[41]

Rufus Burleson was working on directing Houston's heart in still another direction. On November 19, 1854, during a revival meeting, he had baptized Houston into the Baptist church at Rocky Creek near Independence. When Houston remarked, "Dr. Burleson, you have baptized my pocketbook," the minister replied, "Thank God! I wish the pocketbook of every Baptist in the world had been baptized."[42]

In his *Ordeal of the Union*, Allan Nevins characterizes the year 1855, with its establishment of rival governments in Kansas, the development of the Republican party, filibustering in Nicaragua, and the split in the Democratic party, as "the year of violence." Certainly it was a year of conflict and violent language for Houston, but the battles he waged were more on the Texas than on the national field. Indians were always a favorite topic with the General, and he used debates on the bill to increase the size of the army and on the Indian Appropriation Bill to make long pleas for his red brethren. The first speech provided a chance to criticize the inadequacy of federal protection of the Texas frontier, but his remarks on Indians were by no means restricted to the tribes of the Southwest. The speech also gave his debate opponents an entree for interpolating a question about his attitude on the Know-Nothing party. Houston's laughing reply was that he knew nothing of the party but that he could say that he concurred

[39] *Writings*, VI, 29–103; VII, 25–26.

[40] Houston to Pease, November 7, 1854, *Writings*, VI, 103–105; Houston to Pease, November 15, 1854, *Texas State Gazette*, December 16, 1854.

[41] E. M. Daggett to O. M. Roberts, January 10, 1855, Letters to Oran M. Roberts, Roberts Papers.

[42] J. B. Cranfill, *From Memory: Reminiscences, Recitals, and Gleanings from a Bustling and Busy Life*, 252.

in many of its principles, particularly resisting the encroachments of one religious sect upon another.[43]

Texas newspapers had been carrying editorials in opposition to the Know-Nothing, or American, party since June, 1854. On December 5, 1854, Gail Borden, Jr., had written Ashbel Smith that he understood Houston was a member of the party. The Washington correspondent of the *Texas State Gazette* wrote on January 24 that the rumor that W. C. Dawson would be the Know-Nothing candidate for governor of Georgia was pretty generally believed, since "Sam says he will, and his say so is apt to be official."[44]

February saw the resumption of an old fight. Thomas Jefferson Green had a printed card placed on the desk of each United States senator, refuting the Houston speech of the last session and giving what Green considered new proof of Houston's duplicity: Green charged that Houston, despite his ancient enmity for Clay, had knelt to kiss Clay's coffin when a member of the official entourage at Clay's funeral. Houston's answer was that the Senate's time was too valuable to be consumed in remarks on Green's character and that the charge was "a reflection upon the memory of the dead, and a calumny of the living." Regarding the Great Compromiser, Houston's comment was: "In his life he had my respect, and our relations were as intimate as could be expected between one so humble as myself, and one so illustrious as Henry Clay."[45]

As soon as he had answered Green, Houston boarded a train to go by way of New York to Boston to make a speech on slavery at Tremont Temple on Washington's Birthday. None other than William Lloyd Garrison delivered the reply. The *Gazette*, in reporting the speech made to a crowded audience, said:

In treating the subject of slavery he did not advocate slavery in the abstract, nor would he discuss it as an abstract question. He dealt with it as an existing fact, much apprehended and the cause of too much agitation and discord. The people of the South did not create slavery. The South did not love it; but it exists there, and, as a necessity in the present condition of the South, it must be used, but guarded from abuse; the South should not encroach upon the rights and institutions of the North, nor the North upon the rights and

---

[43] Speech on Indians, January 29–31 and February 14, 1855, *Writings*, VI, 111–54, 159–64.

[44] *Texas State Gazette*, February 10, 1855.

[45] Thomas J. Green, card (copy), February 17, 1855, Governors' Letters; Remarks Concerning the Pamphlet of Thomas Jefferson Green, February 15, 1855, *Writings*, VI, 165–66.

institutions of the South. Union is what is needed, and freedom for every man to hold and express his own opinion.

Houston ended his speech with a plea for union:

Our country is too glorious, too magnificent, too sublime in its future prospects, to permit domestic jars or political opinions to produce a wreck of this mighty vessel of State. Let us hold on to it, and guide it; let us give it in charge to men who will care for the whole people, who will love the country for the country's sake, and will endeavor to build up and sustain it, and reconcile conflicting interests for the sake of prosperity. This can be done, and let us not despair and break up the Union.[46]

On his New England trip Houston stopped at Hartford to pay his respects to Lydia Howard Huntley Sigourney and received a book of her poems to take home to Texas to read with Margaret, who also wrote poetry. On March 3, 1855, he made a brief speech in favor of Rusk's amendment to the Civil and Diplomatic Bill to provide a payment to Mexico from funds reserved for completing the survey of the boundary between Texas and Mexico. Then he went home to his "Dear Wife and bairns."[47]

He could not have been with the family much during the entire summer, for he spoke in every part of the state. He was at Huntsville on April 14 and attended the Democratic State Convention there on April 21, when no nominations were made but E. M. Pease and D. C. Dickson were recommended for re-election. Prior to the meeting of the convention he spoke in opposition to the state, or "Sherwood," plan for railroad construction. The reporter of that speech ended his news story: "Gen. Houston is now an old man in years, yet he still wears a fine appearance and promises to live many years yet."[48] Houston had changed his opinion of Pease because of the Governor's advocacy of amending the Texas Constitution to provide for a state-constructed system of railroads, and Rusk planned to write Pease of their joint opposition.[49] On May 11, Houston was at Nacogdoches, and he and Rusk met in a friendly debate in which each senator spoke more than two hours discussing the debt, the railroad proposals, and their actions in Congress. Houston opined that he did not expect to ride on a railroad in Texas anyway; instead, "if I do not get rode on a rail, I shall

[46] Extracts from a Speech on Slavery, February 22, 1855, *Writings*, VI, 167–77; *Texas State Gazette*, March 31, 1855.
[47] Houston to Lydia H. H. Sigourney, March 6, 1855, *Writings*, VI, 179.
[48] *Texas State Gazette*, April 28, 1855.
[49] Rusk to Houston, May 2, 1855, T. J. Rusk Papers.

come off well." He went on to disclaim any catering to the presidency and insisted, "I am about to leave the service ot the State, and retire to private life, and shall most certainly resign my commission as Senator."[50] No mention of resigning was included in a delayed San Jacinto speech made at the battlefield on June 9, 1855, when Houston intimated that some conspiracy had prevented his receiving the invitation to speak on April 21. After reviewing the Battle of San Jacinto, he paid his respects to that "low, dirty sheet" the Galveston *News* and its editor, Willard Richardson, who was "too mean to steal," and declared that he was willing for his enemies to "fester in the putrescence of their own malignity."[51]

Among those enemies he probably included the *Leon Pioneer* (Centerville), which carried a note that Dr. W. G. W. Jowers was on his way to the Brazos (Independence was not too far from the Brazos) to try to make the acquaintance of "Sam," that gentleman, who in imitation of Minerva's favorite bird—the owl—stays housed in holes, hollows, and shady places during the light of day, coming out and stalking round only under the covers of mystery and darkness." And the *Gazette* quoted the *Pioneer* concerning Jowers, the Know-Nothing candidate for lieutenant governor, and added: "Sam has taken him to his embraces, and in some dark abode, in Washington on the shady side of Whiggery, he has at last got a bid for a passage up Salt River in August next."[52]

Practically positive passage up the river was assured by Houston's so-called "Independence Letter" of July 24, 1855, in which he answered the charges as to the "secrecy" of the Know-Nothing order, defended it, not as an organization to put down Catholics, but to prevent Catholics' putting down Protestants, and stated: *"I believe the salvation of my country is only to be secured by adherence to the principles of the American Order."*[53] The *Gazette* said that the Houston principles were the principles of the order more honestly expressed than by "the milk and cider candidates who state principles contrary to the secret oaths," and prophesied that Houston would soon meet Benton's fate because "the people of Texas cannot be allied to the abolitionists and free soilers upon the Nebraska or any other question."[54]

The state election was scheduled for August 2. The Grand Council

[50] Synopsis of a Speech at Nacogdoches, May 11, 1855, *Writings*, VI, 180–84.
[51] Review of San Jacinto Campaign, June 9, 1855, *ibid.*, 184–91.
[52] *Texas State Gazette*, June 30, 1855.
[53] Houston's Opinion Concerning the American Order, July 24, 1855, *Writings*, VI, 192–99.
[54] *Texas State Gazette*, August 11, 1855.

of the American party held at Washington-on-the-Brazos on June 11, ostensibly as a "river improvement convention," had nominated David C. Dickson for governor, Jowers for lieutenant governor, Stephen Crosby for commissioner of the General Land Office, and L. D. Evans and John Hancock for Congress. When Dickson's nomination was known to the Democrats, they had to hold a "Bomb Shell" Democratic Convention in Austin on June 16 to drop Dickson's name from their ballot. On June 30, Hardin Richard Runnels was named as the Democratic candidate for lieutenant governor.[55]

W. S. Oldham and L. T. Wigfall sustained the attack on Houston in 1855, but there were other opponents of long standing eager to get in one more blow against him, even though the instruments they used must long since have been blunted. Anson Jones again broke into print with the claim that Houston opposed annexation, and asked for space in the Galveston *News* to present that measure in its true light. And Burnet and Lamar compared notes as they prepared pamphlets describing Houston's character and cowardice. Burnet warned that they should avoid unprofitable repetition, although he could not think of a suitable subject for Lamar, who was "to think of something that will excite your scribbling humors and overcome your laziness." Hugh McLeod had his quota of advice: "Don't think of any personal attack upon Houston—he will make capital out of it. Wait till you have published the pamphlet, & then if you think there is any thing left of him, I will stand by you, while you thrash him."[56] A fight with Houston seemed to take the place of hormones or whatever was required for rejuvenation of aging Texas politicians.

Dickson and most of the other Know-Nothing candidates were defeated in the August election. The Clarksville *Standard*, describing Houston as a man of expedients, governed by policy instead of principle, predicted that thereafter the General would find his influence in Texas on the wane, for "that anti-Nebraska vote was the last feather that broke the camel's back."[57] From election day to the meeting of the Legislature in November there was no cessation of the newspaper attacks on Houston. The *Gazette*, as the leading Democratic organ, and the Galveston *News*, as his ancient enemy, had no intention of desisting before they had made certain that he was not re-elected to the

[55] Winkler, *Platforms of Political Parties in Texas*, 63–64.

[56] Jones, *Republic of Texas*, 586; Burnet to Lamar, August 6 and October 6, 1855, and McLeod to Lamar, September 15, 1855, *Lamar Papers*, IV, Part II, 24, 26, 28.

[57] Quoted in *Texas State Gazette*, September 16, 1855.

Senate. The *Gazette* quoted the *Prairie Blade* (Corsicana) to the effect that "Houston yet goes unwhipped of political justice, yet holds his place in the Senate from a State whose interest he has twice betrayed, on a subject paramount in vital importance to any that ever came before that body." As if to point out what a "true" Democrat should do, the *Gazette* published Stephen A. Douglas' refusal to speak on slavery in Boston "to the same abolitionists, whose invitation to Sam Houston to address them was accepted."[58]

On October 20, Houston made a speech at Brenham in which he disclaimed following after strange gods and said that he had always been consistent—at least in politics—and had always been a Democrat of the Jefferson-Jackson school. Pierce he accused of securing election on a Democratic platform and then forming a cabinet representing "Disunion, secession, Freesoilism, Abolitionism, and Popery," to create a bogus democracy which endangered the Union. The Washington *American* report of the speech said that it had a "telling effect at Brenham, the hot bed of Houston-anti-ism," and ranked among the Senator's best efforts. But the *Gazette* quoted A. V. Brown of Tennessee in answering Houston's complaint of abuse from the press: if he had not "thrown down his gauntlet to Democracy, the democratic press would not have mentioned his name."[59]

For the first time in almost twenty years there was a political difference between Houston and Ashbel Smith, a strong Democrat and member of the Texas Legislature. As Houston was on his way to Austin just before the meeting of the Legislature, he wrote Smith to arrange a meeting at Hall's House in the capital city and to assure him "that whatever our political [differences] may be, they will not with me disturb our personal regards."[60] Friends accompanied Houston from Washington to Austin, where, despite lowering weather, a Know-Nothing procession paraded around the city. Headed by the San Antonio delegation, it included a group of young ladies dressed in tricolor, "each bearing a shield representing the several States of the Union." At the end of the parade, Hugh McLeod, himself a Know-Nothing despite his enmity with Houston, harangued the gathering and, alluding to the weather, said:

I hope it is not an omen of the failure of your cause, but if it is, fellow citizens, propitiate it by a timely sacrifice, throw Jonah [Houston] overboard. The prophet has failed to deliver the true message to the people—his excuses

[58] *Ibid.*, October 6, 20, 1855.
[59] Synopsis of Speech at Brenham, October 20, 1855, *Writings*, VI, 204–207; *Texas State Gazette*, November 5, 1855.
[60] Houston to Smith, November 20, 1855, *Writings*, VI, 207–208.

are ingenious, but deceptive, and the ship will labor as the storm increases. The sacrifice is due to Nineveh, and the ship to Democracy and America. Jonah should be thrown overboard.[61]

McLeod may have been trying to pick the fight he had promised Lamar, but Houston was being baited in a different fashion by an unruly House of Representatives. When he appeared at the Capitol, Representative Isaac Parker of Tarrant introduced a resolution that the Speaker invite the Senator to a seat within the bar of the House. Mathew Ector then proposed as an amendment that the Speaker invite Commodore E. W. Moore to sit within the bar—no veiled insult to the former president of Texas. John W. Dancy and William Stedman finally carried their point that the invitation to Houston was a mere matter of courtesy, not to be construed as an endorsement of his Kansas-Nebraska vote. The original resolution was ultimately adopted by a vote of 48 to 32, but the various motions had consumed three hours, "during which time the great shanghai of Know-Nothingism was kept waiting on the porch of the capitol. He was finally admitted, and left, no doubt, with heightened ideas of the stiffneckedness of a Texas Legislature."[62]

That night the big barbecue in his honor was held in a grove of live oak trees on the University Hill and featured the presentation of a banner and an ode of welcome sung by a company of young ladies.[63] Houston's remarks included his favorite story of the goat which butted itself all away except the tail—to illustrate that his determined enemies were "wonderful, and *game* to the last." After giving the history of his senatorial career, he proclaimed his platform as the "Constitution and the Union," described the ruins of the Democratic party, stated that he adopted and admired the principles of the American party, and predicted the ultimate triumph of true democracy.[64]

Three days after the speech was made, the Texas Legislature considered a resolution "that the Legislature approves the course of Thomas J. Rusk in voting for the Kansas-Nebraska Act and disapproves the

[61] Lubbock, *Six Decades in Texas*, 198–99.
[62] Dallas *Herald*, December 5, 1855; *Texas State Gazette*, December 22, 1855. The *Herald* embroidered this story with a fanciful "good 'un" which related that Houston and Moore had gone to Austin in the same stagecoach, riding, alternately, one on the inside and one on the box with the driver, each telling the driver of the villainy of the other. It was probably just a good story, for Moore was in Austin several days before Houston's arrival.
[63] Brown, "Annals of Travis County," XVII, 28.
[64] Speech at Know-Nothing Mass Barbecue at Austin, November 23, 1855, *Writings*, VI, 209–34.

course of Sam Houston, in voting against it." The vote for engrossing the resolution was 77 to 3, and the only defense of Houston was made by Charles Cleveland of Liberty, who questioned the sincerity of some of the members, saying that the reason for the resolution was Houston's work for the Know-Nothings and that the Legislature was not the proper place to quarrel with him for his political leanings.[65] Texas had written finis to Houston's senatorial career, even though his term would run to March 4, 1859.

Houston started back to the national capital soon after December 13, 1855, stopping at Crockett and Nacogdoches to speak again against the Kansas-Nebraska Act and to declare his intention to stand astride the line of thirty-six degrees and thirty minutes and there "perish in defense of the rights of the South."[66] While at home he had received a request from the Young Men's Mercantile Library Association of Cincinnati to stop for a talk to them as he went back to Congress. He had hoped to be with them by the middle of December, but he was delayed in Texas and had a slow journey east during exceptionally bad weather. When he finally got to Covington, Kentucky, the Ohio River was blocked with acres of ice and the temperature was twenty degrees below zero. He wrote from Covington on January 10 that he would cross the river to Cincinnati as soon as a ferry could operate. The same paper that recorded his registration at the Burnet House in Cincinnati on January 11 carried a Texas item: "The weather on Christmas day was the coldest ever known in Texas and great damage had been done to fruit trees by ice."[67]

In contrast to the temperature, politics in Texas were hot. Houston's opponents in the Legislature "allowed no occasion to pass without thrusts at the old gentleman," and the Dallas *Herald* asked why he did not go ahead and carry out his announced intention to resign and thus no longer outrage the sentiments of nine-tenths of his fellow citizens by "retaining a position he has forfeited by misrepresenting them."

His day has passed, his course is run, and therefore let the old man

> "Wrap the drapery of his couch around him,
> And lay down to gentle dreams"

Let him heed for once the voice of an outraged, misrepresented, and betrayed

[65] *Texas State Gazette*, December 1, 22, 1855.
[66] Extract from Address at Nacogdoches, December 21, 1855, *Writings*, VI, 236–38.
[67] Houston to A. B. Merriam, September 12, 1855, and January 10, 1856 (copied from originals in Miscellaneous Houston Manuscripts, New York Historical Society); Cincinnati *Daily Commercial*, January 12, 1856.

constituency, so that Texas may for once have a united voice and present an undivided front in the Senate of the United States.[68]

The *Texas Republican* of Marshall on January 5, 1856, carried a ten-verse bit of doggerel entitled "Up Salt River Sammy Must Go," to be sung to the tune of "Old Rosin the Bow."

Another stage of the "up the river" trip was reached at the Democratic State Convention held in Austin from January 15 to 18. One of the resolutions adopted by the convention endorsed the votes of Rusk, Smyth, and Bell upon the Kansas-Nebraska Act and disapproved the vote of Houston "as not in accordance with the sentiments of the Democracy of Texas."[69]

The Know-Nothing State Convention met in Austin a week later. However much Houston may have been present in spirit, his name was not mentioned in the resolutions adopted, although one was a measure apparently advocated by Houston in his December speech at Nacogdoches, favoring extension of the time required for naturalization of foreigners to twenty-one years. By 1856 the Know-Nothing party had already lost national influence. Its seeming importance in Texas politics in that year came partly from the fact that its membership included many strong Union men such as Ben Epperson, J. W. Flanagan, John S. Ford, J. A. Wilcox, and John Hancock, but chiefly from Houston's support. Because of anti-Houston sentiment and also because of Know-Nothing attacks on Germans and Mexicans, which drove those elements in Texas into the Democratic party, that party for the first time became a strong organization in Texas and a staunch support of the states'-rights wing of the national party. It had a few obstacles to overcome, as exemplified by a mass meeting, supposedly of Democrats, at Marshall on February 26, when the Know-Nothings voted down the Democratic nominees in "a perfect storm of voices—Sam was there in all his strong."[70]

"Sam"—the official Texas name for the Know-Nothings—was making no great show of strength in the Thirty-fourth Congress, where it had taken two months to elect a speaker, and where attention was divided between the warring factions in Kansas and the approaching presidential election. Houston took no part in the debates on Kansas and delivered his only long speeches in connection with action of the Naval Retiring Board, which had recommended dropping, furlough-

[68] Dallas *Herald*, December 8, 1855.
[69] Winkler, *Platforms of Political Parties in Texas*, 68.
[70] J. N. Clough to O. M. Roberts, February 26 [1856], Roberts Papers, I.

243

ing, and giving indefinite leave to a number of naval officers. He opposed the board's action as "the greatest outrage on record," speaking especially on behalf of Matthew Fontaine Maury, who a few years later was to remember his help. Texans were not especially concerned with the navy, with the possible exception of Peter W. Gray, whose brother Lieutenant E. F. Gray had sought Houston's assistance in keeping his place.[71] The *Texas Republican* did quote the Philadelphia *Ledger* on Houston's preparation for his speech. "General Houston surprised the Senate today by introducing into that body a large bowl of coffee, standing upon a huge saucer from which, as he spoke against the action of the Naval Board, he would take a sup now and then. It looked more like a breakfast scene in a play than anything else."[72]

The problems of naval officers were but a slight ripple in the waves of angry Congressional debate over Kansas which occupied most of the time of both houses in April, May, and June of 1856. Houston was away from Washington during much of the period and so did not hear Sumner's speech called the "Crime against Kansas" or witness the resulting attack on Sumner by Preston Brooks. Plans to visit "my Dear Wife Maggie and the addendas" were temporarily postponed; but the hero of San Jacinto knew that he would be represented at home on San Jacinto Day, for Sam Jr. had been asked to make a speech that day at Independence, and the proud father agreed, "It might be well to do so!"[73]

While one Texas senator planned a happy family reunion, the other was prostrated with a grief from which he never fully recovered. Mrs. Rusk died on April 23, 1856. Unlike the presidential year of 1852, when both senators were delegates to the National Democratic Convention, now both were absent and ill in Texas when the Democrats met in Cincinnati and nominated James Buchanan and John C. Breckinridge. By the middle of June there were rumors that neither senator from Texas would return to Washington, and L. L. Lewis was pleading with Rusk to throw off his depression, bring his children, Tom and Helena, with him, and return with General Houston.[74]

On July 10, his health restored, Houston passed through Louisville,

[71] Houston to Peter W. Gray, March 22, 1856, *Writings*, VI, 298–99.

[72] *Texas Republican*, May 31, 1856. Houston was not one to miss the opportunity to figure in a drama, but he had begun his speech by pleading his hoarseness and indisposition. See Speech of April 23, 1856, *Writings*, VI, 306. The bronchial difficulty continued and Houston was quite ill when at Independence in May. See Charles Power to Ashbel Smith, May 26, 1856, Ashbel Smith Papers.

[73] Houston to Margaret Lea Houston, April 18, 1856, *Writings*, VI, 306.

[74] Lewis to Rusk, June 14 and 17, 1856, T. J. Rusk Papers.

Kentucky, on his way back to Washington, where on July 15 he was once more talking on the action of the Navy Board, demanding that the *esprit de corps* of the navy be preserved and the naval arm maintained in "a world in commotion."[75] On July 17 he was busy making resolutions concerning post roads in Texas and had on hand an extensive correspondence on patronage and politics. Radcliff Hudson wanted a job as paymaster in the army, and John Hancock asked for an opinion on politics. Houston's answer was that he could not accept the Democratic platform, that Republican principles were sectional, and that, under the circumstances, he would support the American party nominees, Millard Fillmore and A. J. Donelson, who had been chosen at Philadelphia in February. Texas, he hoped, would make a "united rally" for the ticket and "take the course best calculated to restore harmony to our distracted country, and promote the general good."[76] The Senator was convinced of his own promotion of the general good when he voted against a bill to make increases in the pay of senators retroactive. The increase itself was just because the salary was not a living wage; he objected to the retroactive feature.

On August 15, Houston was writing his son of his plans to start home within a few days. As the Senate session was protracted, he had to delay his trip to Texas, and on August 30 asked permission to speak in order that he might in some degree allay excitement in a crisis portending "such imminent evils to the country." He asked no sympathy for his own situation, taking it for granted that he was exactly where his "inclinations and opinions" had placed him. He explained why he could not vote for the Democratic ticket, defended the American party against the charge of being proscriptive, and, as always, pleaded for the quieting of sectional strife.[77]

Houston continued to make much the same appeal as he went "politicking" in Texas in the last weeks before the election. On September 16, he and Rusk debated at Nacogdoches, paying each other high compliment while each defended his political position. Houston was milder in his handling of Buchanan than was Rusk in his treatment of Fillmore. Houston spoke in Polk County on September 29 and at Huntsville on October 2, at Brenham on October 6 and at Anderson on October 12. What the pro-Houston papers may have said about his speeches is difficult to find. The "anti" papers were numerous and

---

[75] Dallas *Herald*, August 2, 1856; *Writings*, VI, 357.
[76] Houston to Hancock, July 21, 1856, *ibid.*, 358–62.
[77] Remarks on Antagonism among Members of the Thirty-fourth Congress, August 30, 1856, *ibid.*, 377–93.

vocal; their descriptions of his speeches ranged from "weak" and "flat" through "bitter doses" to "complete failure." At Brenham, according to the *Gazette*, "the old man reiterated the same budget of stories and slanders against the Democratic party which he has told on past occasions, and being a twice told tale, it must have been an exceedingly dry one." The Galveston *News* quoted the Liberty *Gazette* on Houston speeches: "As regards the abuse bestowed upon this and so many other occasions, we have only to reply by reminding General Houston that he appears to be verifying his own favorite and oft repeated anecdote about the 'butting ram.' 'There is now little of him left besides the tail.'" The meeting at Anderson was a "formidable set-to" between Houston and J. W. ("Smokey") Henderson, a set-to which was evidently protracted beyond the time of the formal debate, for the report was that Smokey and General Houston "as usual slept together; but they quarrelled so tempestuously as to disturb the household."[78] Truly it was an era of personal politics.

Texas voted overwhelmingly for Buchanan and the Democrats. Within a month after the election John Marshall, the leading Democratic organizer of the state, accepted the fact that Houston would run for governor in 1857, and the editor wrote Rusk that he was to have no uneasiness over that prospect because Texas wanted Rusk in the Senate until it could put him in the White House. Marshall also advised Rusk that if he were offered a cabinet position under Buchanan he should take nothing less than that of secretary of war or secretary of state.[79]

Rusk went on back to Washington for the opening of Congress, taking his daughter Helena with him. For a time Houston was undecided about returning to the Senate. Mrs. Houston was ill, and he was lame from his old San Jacinto wound, but on November 8 he wrote Rusk to advise a proper school for Helena and promised to try to get off to Washington. He was there by Sunday, December 7, when he wrote Sam Jr. that he had not yet had time to look around.[80]

Houston's senatorial duties before Christmas seem to have been slight. He did introduce a resolution that the Committee on Finance look into the expediency of suspending duties on sugar and molasses for two years. While there was gloating in Texas that Walker County, once the

---

[78] For reports on political speeches see *Texas State Gazette*, October 4, 11, 18, 25, 1856, and Galveston *News*, October 14, 1856.

[79] Marshall to Rusk, December 6, 1856, T. J. Rusk Papers.

[80] Houston to Rusk, November 8, 1856, *Writings*, VI, 394–95; Houston to Sam Houston, Jr., December 7, 1856, *ibid.*, VII, 27.

stronghold of Sam, had "abandoned the hero of San Jacinto like rats abandoning a sinking ship," the hero himself was spending the Christmas holidays at the Metropolitan Hotel in New York, taking a respite from politics.[81]

In the spring he was still working for his constituents in advocating a mail route from Huntsville to the mouth of Red River in Louisiana, but he took little part in Senate debate, confining himself chiefly to speeches on navy discipline and the best methods of controlling Indians. When an increase in the pay of army officers was being debated, he again condemned the "West Point system," insisting that the country was made for all and that every man who fought in its defense was entitled to an equal share in its favors and honors. On one occasion he seemed to show his age—he would soon be sixty-four—when he complained of the noise and informality in the Senate and of the change in that body from the decorum of twenty years before.[82] On his birthday he spoke in opposition to the federal government's accepting Jackson's Hermitage as the site of a national cavalry training school. The next day, arguing in behalf of Washington property owners who were about to be evicted as part of a program of enlarging the Capitol grounds, he shot a barb at the depleted condition of the national treasury and advised postponing the expansion program for a year. He was not so economy conscious when it came to expenses for printing Patent Office reports and distributing free seeds and fruit-tree cuttings for farmers; he described the appropriation for seeds as "the most beneficially expended money that is expended by this Government."[83]

The lame-duck session of the Thirty-fourth Congress ended on March 4, 1857. The Senator spent one day answering requests for autographs before he started home. En route to Huntsville, he stopped to talk at Crockett; he displayed no interest in state office, said he intended to resign his senatorship, and expressed satisfaction with Buchanan's cabinet appointments. The *Gazette*, even granting its bias, had listened to the resignation threat before and could be excused for saying, "But we are far from expecting to see any resignation from Sam unless it is to his permission to stay at home which he will receive from the next Legislature."[84]

Potential Democratic candidates would have appreciated a Houston

[81] W. W. Leland to Smith, January 13, 1857, Ashbel Smith Papers.

[82] Remarks Concerning the Counting of the Presidential Votes, February 11, 1857, *Writings*, VI, 425—28.

[83] Speeches on March 2 and 3, 1857, *Writings*, VI, 435–43.

[84] *Texas State Gazette*, April 4, 1857.

247

declaration of intention. They were convinced that he would run, but he had proved unpredictable before. John H. Reagan wrote O. M. Roberts that he had no present desire for the governorship, but if Houston should be a candidate, no one called on by the Waco Convention would be at liberty to decline. Henderson, Reagan thought, was the logical man to oppose Houston, but perhaps a preconvention trial of strength between Middleton T. Johnson and Hardin R. Runnels should determine the nomination.[85] On April 29, Hiram G. Runnels, uncle of the probable candidate, wrote Ashbel Smith, a member of the central committee, in behalf of his nephew, "a pure and good Democrat," and warned that the convention would be unwise to create new issues as the enemy was on the lookout for action on which to base hope of a successful opposition.[86]

The convention met at Waco on May 4, 1857, and for the first time nominated candidates for the three top state positions: Hardin R. Runnels for governor, F. R. Lubbock for lieutenant governor, and Francis M. White for land commissioner. Candidates for treasurer, comptroller, and attorney general would be nominated at a convention in Austin on January 8, 1858. The body declared for the national Democratic platform adopted at Cincinnati in June, 1856, and the platform of the State Democratic Convention adopted at Austin in January, 1856.

On May 12, Houston announced his candidacy for the governorship. To Rusk he explained that he had decided to run because at Waco the issues had been declared as "Houston and anti-Houston," adding what was probably true: "The people want excitement, and I had as well give it as any one." Although he had but recently assured Smith that he would not run, Houston now wrote: "I must try and if spared, I hope to regenerate the politics of the State & save the public money & the land, for public purposes and uses."[87]

He did give Texas an exciting summer. For a man of his years it must have been strenuous. There is an interesting story of how he secured free transportation for his electioneering trip and how a plow salesman named Ed Sharp attracted attention to his wares by furnishing the vehicle for the General, whom everyone turned out so see. Sharp rode in a bright crimson buggy with the words "Warwick's Patent Plow" painted in huge gilt letters on either side. He was in Huntsville the

[85] Reagan to Roberts, April 15, 1857, Roberts Papers.

[86] H. G. Runnels to Smith, April 29, 1857, Ashbel Smith Papers.

[87] Houston to Rusk, May 12, 1857, and to Smith, July 6, 1857, *Writings*, VI, 444, 446.

morning after Houston's decision to make the race, and when he learned that the Senator could not get a seat on the stage or hire a conveyance at the livery stable, Sharp volunteered to furnish his buggy. Houston accepted and in the midsummer jaunt across Texas took interest in calling attention to his conveyance as he met some sixty-seven speaking appointments from Montgomery to San Antonio. According to Sharp, the salesman and the Senator carried coffeepot, frying pan, and gridiron and spread their blankets at night under the Texas stars. His most vivid recollection was of the stop at Nacogdoches and the meeting between Houston and Rusk. "Both senators approached the Speaker's stand, met each other, embraced, and sobbed like women. Without uttering a word, Rusk took Houston by the hand, led him to his carriage and to his home. Neither was seen again that day."[88]

A detailed study of the campaign would reveal no punches pulled in a free-for-all battle of words exhibiting Texas politics in their most "rambunctious" form. E. H. Cushing of the *Telegraph and Texas Register* sent letters and telegrams to Ashbel Smith beseeching him to meet Houston in debate, and his paper ran a series of articles entitled "Sam Houston's Record." Cushing did not choose the details to make the record a pretty one. John Marshall of the *Gazette* declared "War to the Hilt" and waged it. James Reily belittled the Houston speeches as all being identical and creating little impression. Denying the contention that the issue was Houston and anti-Houston, Reily said: "We know it is a struggle for political existence & if elected governor in the present crisis, the Northern party must take him up for President."[89] As the voice of Texas organized Democracy, the *Gazette* also tied the Texas gubernatorial contest up with the national political scene. In describing Houston's protest against "Democratic conventions, Democratic platforms, and Democratic nominees," the paper predicted:

The fight of 1860 will find the Democracy where it is now, and trusting alone to those men, tried and true, nominated in their conventions.

On the other hand, Bell and Ethridge of Tennessee, Houston of Texas, and countless others who harmonize in political feelings, will be on the one side, whatever it be, but we predict it,—they *will not be with the Democracy, yet in that fight will be decided forever the existence of a constitutional Union.*

"Old Texas Democrat," writing from Galveston to the *Gazette,* contended: "Sam Houston will not be able to carry one vote in four for

[88] Dallas *News,* April 4, 5, 1892.
[89] Reily to Rusk, May 14 and 21, 1857, T. J. Rusk Papers.

249

re-election to the Senate, for which he is seeking. Every sensible man knows he desires to be elected Governor in order to get back to Washington still further to commit Texas to freesoilism."[90]

According to M. D. Ector, "Our most effective way to beat Gen. Houston is to draw the party lines—and to do this our leaders must take the field, present the true issues, and arouse the party." One of the leaders whom they implored to take the field was Rusk. Although Henderson knew that Rusk was not disposed to interfere in state elections, he wrote his friend that if the Know-Nothings kept circulating rumors that Rusk was in favor of Houston, the other senator might be called upon to "respond fully." Ector sent Rusk a letter from Wigfall saying that, at Carthage, Houston had intimated that Rusk regretted his own Kansas-Nebraska vote and was satisfied that Houston's position was correct. Tyler citizens wrote Rusk that Houston, in his Smith County speech, had said that his enemies meant first to get Houston out of the Senate and then treat Rusk in the same way.[91]

His enemies had cause to fear the potency of the Houston name in Texas; a letter to John Marshall reported that the General was creating a furor in the east and that Nacogdoches was almost unanimously for him. By June 3, W. D. Ward at Marshall was writing to John H. Reagan: "But to tell you the truth old Sam and Lem [L. D. Evans] have a stronger hold upon the people of this country than did Fillmore in the last election, and if we succeed in beating them we yet have to manufacture the strength to do it with for you know that this is a Lem county and old Sam is the strongest man in the state in the opposition."[92] It was no wonder that Marshall wrote Rusk on June 11 of Richard Hubbard's report that Rusk and Houston had reached agreement when Houston visited Rusk on May 30. Marshall demanded that Rusk "place himself right," for the rumors were swelling the Houston vote. "For God's sake, Rusk," he implored, "take a bold & decided course." The next week Marshall sent Rusk two letters. One he wrote as chairman of the State Democratic Central Committee asking that the Senator's voice "be heard in the canvass as one of the faithful supporters of the Democratic party & the rights of the South"; the other was a private letter lamenting Rusk's admission that there was "little or no difference politically" between himself and Houston.[93]

[90] *Texas State Gazette,* May 30, July 4, 1857.
[91] Ector to Rusk, June 3 and 6, 1857, Henderson to Rusk, June 5, 1857, Citizens of Tyler to Rusk, June 10, 1857, T. J. Rusk Papers.
[92] Ward to Reagan, June 3, 1857, John H. Reagan Papers, 1857–80, I.
[93] Marshall to Rusk, June 11 and 17, 1857, T. J. Rusk Papers.

While Rusk continued to take no part in the campaign except to state that he would vote for the Democratic candidates, Houston covered Texas: the Nacogdoches and Redlands area in late May and early June, Henderson's bailiwick in Rusk and Smith counties on June 6 and 8, and Wigfall's domain in Harrison and Cass counties the middle of June. Between June 19 and June 25 he spoke in the North Texas area in Hunt, Denton, and Tarrant counties and then moved south across Central Texas from Waxahachie to Palestine and reached Cameron and Waco by July 13. Wigfall, Henderson, Oldham, and F. R. Lubbock met him in face-to-face debate or followed his trail. Scurry was denouncing him, as was R. M. Williamson. Whether Eph Daggett heard him speak or not, he was converted from his 1854 opinion of Houston and wrote to Roberts: "The Governor election is all the go out here. Old Sam I think will git the vote quite easy. He is certain to cary Parker Co. I go it for old Father Sam Houston—altho I expect you and me differ this time—altho I have not heard."[94]

Roberts received a report in a different vein when Marcus de LaFayette Herring wrote of Houston's Waco speech:

Old Sam spoke here on last Monday. . . . He spoke nearly three hours. His speech was a compound of abuse and egotism—abusive without the merit of wit or sarcasm and egotistical without the sanction of historical truth, or the relish of his most ultra adherents. (His spleen seemed to be morbid)—It was vented without stint, without point, without reason and without decent and refined language, indiscriminately and generally upon the Waco Convention and especially upon Gov. Henderson, Col. Wigfall, and Judge Oldham. It was characterized throughout from beginning to the end, by such epithets as fellow thieves, rascals and assassins—these he hurled against the Waco Convention and the above named trio. The dish he served up for his large and intelligent audience, being composed of such ingredients without any condiment save the spice of low-flung bawdy-house vulgarity, *turned the stomachs* of some and caused other to *disgorge* the last predilection for Sam Houston.[95]

Herring was prejudiced, though not so biased as the *Gazette*, and his letter may be a fairly accurate description of many of the Houston campaign speeches of 1857—accurate enough, in any event, to suit Henderson, who said every speech was the same, and to suit contributors to the *Gazette*, who described each utterance as guaranteed to lose votes.

[94] Daggett to Roberts, July 19, 1857, Roberts Papers.
[95] Herring to Roberts, July 15, 1857, *ibid.*

Houston was at Belton on July 20 and at Austin on July 22. For a full month the *Gazette* had been issuing extra editions called the *Gazette for the Campaign;* now it gave ample coverage to the Austin speech, not a verbatim account, but its own version of what Houston said, describing the speaker as "a melancholy picture of imbecility, vindictiveness and hate in old age." According to the *Gazette:* Houston said that Rusk had written Marshall that he would support the standard-bearers of the party only because he had been dogged by the Democrats, and they would find, Houston prophesied, "that there was a cat in the meal bag about Rusk's voting for the Waco nominees"; for it was Houston's time now, but "it was to be Tom's after a while, and . . . the man to fill his place was already staked out."[96] The paper called Houston's attempt to claim Rusk's support—while all the Rusk sons and David Rusk were working for the Democrats—"a low down trick disgusting to all honorable men."[97]

Election day was August 3, and Houston closed his campaign at San Antonio on July 28. Neither he nor Marshall was to know how Rusk would have voted on that election day, for Rusk committed suicide on July 29. Houston was as far east as Columbus on his return home when he heard the sad news from Nacogdoches. According to the *Colorado Citizen,* his first words were: "It was the Waco Convention that killed him." In quoting the *Citizen,* the *Gazette* added: "Houston has looked with horror upon the Waco Convention during the whole canvass. He used to say that Tom's turn would come next, significantly admitting that his turn had already come. The Waco Rooster had politically killed Houston.—He never again will crow on this side of Mason and Dixon's line."[98]

That prophecy looked better in 1857 than it was to look in 1859. The vote in 1857 was 32,552 for Runnels and 28,678 for Houston. The Democrats did not win overwhelmingly, but they won. Houston was at home in Huntsville by August 8 or 10 and from there wrote Ashbel Smith:

The fuss is over, and the sun yet shines as ever. What next? Will the spoils be equal to the wants of the spoil seekers? I fear not. Will the late victory be equivalent to the State, & the country, for the murder of Genl. Rusk? I should say not. . . .

In the result of the election I am cheered, and were it not for my friends, I assure you, I wou'd rejoice at the result. If I am spared to take my seat in the

[96] Speech at Austin, July 22, 1857, *Writings,* VII, 28–32.
[97] *State Gazette for the Campaign,* July 25, 1857.
[98] *Ibid.,* August 22, 1857.

Senate, I will, as the Frenchman said, "Have some fish to fry." Had I been elected, I would have had "other fish to fry."[99]

When he did take his seat in the Senate and Clement C. Clay of Alabama derided him for his Nebraska vote and declared that it had cost him the confidence of his constituency, Houston provoked the Senate to laughter with his version of the election.

I grant him [Clay], very truthfully, that I have received an earnest and gratifying assurance from my constituents that they intend to relieve me of further service here. I say gratifying, for in the recent election, they beat me; and it is gratifying because I had every disposition to retire on the fourth of March next from public life. How it was brought about, I cannot exactly tell. I know that I had a chevalier and ex-President mounted with boots, spurs, and whip, and a hind rider from Illinois, both after me ever since I voted against the Kansas-Nebraska bill; and that was enough to break down any old gray horse. Besides all the Federal influence was marshalled, drilled, and prepared for the combat; and so I was defeated. But I am very much obliged to my State, because they have not disowned me in beating me—they have only preferred another. I have this further assurance, that I made the State of Texas, but I did not make the people; and if they do wrong, the State still remains in all its beauty, with all its splendid and inviting prospects, with nothing on earth to surpass it in its climate, soil, and productions—all varied and delightful. It remains the same beautiful Texas.[100]

Texas preferred another—both for governor and for senator. If there had been any last die-hard hope in Houston's mind that his old attraction could shake the 1856 resolutions of the Legislature and the Democratic Convention censuring his Senate votes, it was effectively dispelled by the gubernatorial campaign. As the Legislature prepared to meet in November, 1857, the political talk in Texas was all of the choice of two senators—successors for both Rusk and Houston. The Dred Scott decision, handed down by the Supreme Court on March 6, 1857, just as Congress adjourned and Buchanan began his term, had declared the Missouri Compromise unconstitutional and guaranteed Southern slave-owners their property rights in federal territory, but it had roused a fury of indignation in the North. Southern sympathizers were moving on Kansas in an effort to set up a constitution recognizing slavery. The country as a whole had experienced a business panic in the summer of 1857. Texas Democracy wanted proper representation of its interests in the national capital. A few lone voices in the Texas wilderness de-

[99] Houston to Smith, August 22, 1857, *Writings*, VI, 447.
[100] Remarks on the Admission of Kansas, March 19, 1858. *ibid.*, VII, 41.

nounced the Dred Scott decision; Joseph L. Hogg called it a mere party trick, but the *Gazette* described Hogg as a "Whig—Know-Nothing—Jackson–Houston Democrat" and said that he expressed the opinion of all of Houston's friends north of Mason and Dixon's line and a few of those south of it.[101] One new member of the Texas delegation in Washington would be certain to express the wishes of organized Texas Democracy. Guy M. Bryan, who during the campaign had been congratulated on his "hard licks" at Houston, had been elected to the House of Representatives. The other successful candidate for the House was John H. Reagan; he too would be a regular.

The Legislature would choose the senators, and that choice was the center of interest. One logical candidate was Rusk's close friend and partner, former Governor James P. Henderson. Henderson had been the chief reason for Ashbel Smith's coming to Texas, and Smith, as a member of the Democratic Central Committee, began promoting the Henderson cause soon after Rusk's death. When the Legislature acted on November 10, "J. Pinckney Henderson had a walkover as the successor of Rusk, his single opponent, G. W. Smyth getting only three votes." The struggle over Houston's seat was mainly between Scurry and Hemphill, and when, after the twenty-second ballot in the Democratic caucus, Wigfall withdrew Scurry's name, Hemphill received the nomination. In the Legislature his election was unanimous. Lubbock reminisced of the scene: "I was present as an onlooker when the elections occurred, and in noting the unanimous way in which Houston was shelved in this contest, a feeling of sadness came over me, from personal regards for the man. After this, it could not be said that any man's personality could count against principles with the Democracy in Texas."[102]

O. M. Roberts called the election "a splendid thing." To Richard S. Walker it was "an occasion for pious rejoicing—the sunbeam after a polar night."[103] Ashbel Smith regretted not seeing Houston before his departure for Washington to tell him things "not easily expressed in writing" and gave his own view of the election: "The new Senators do not displease me. Gen. Henderson was my choice from the East; and if there was to be a change in the West, Judge Hemphill is greatly preferable to most of the persons spoken of from this district. I should have been deeply mortified, had one of the itinerant pedlars of politics been chosen."[104]

[101] *Texas State Gazette*, August 15, 1857.
[102] Lubbock, *Six Decades in Texas*, 224.
[103] Walker to Roberts, November 14, 1857, Roberts Papers.
[104] Smith to Houston, November 20, 1857, Ashbel Smith Papers.

Houston was a delegate to the Baptist Convention which held a four-day session at Huntsville beginning on October 24, 1857. As chairman of the Committee on Indian Missions, he presented the committee's report to the convention, recommending a government appropriation to erect buildings and schools to be under the supervision of a missionary appointed by the convention. As he prepared to leave for Washington, Houston renewed a note for the Baptist minister at Huntsville and "knocked off the interest" because he knew the congregation thought Brother Baines could "afford to preach to them gratis." Said the prominent parishioner: "They ought to know that money currency will not pass in Heaven. . . . Cotton fields, and Cotton Bales will find no market in Paradise!"[105]

The Senator's return to the national capital came in for editorial condemnation. The Dallas *Herald* was sarcastic: "Wonderful man! What a tremendous influence he will exercise at Washington; how his words will be received as oracles with a popular majority of 10,000 of the freemen of his own State freshly recorded against him! Gen. Houston, don't!" And the ever dependable *Gazette* declared:

It must indeed be a sad spectacle to witness Gen. Houston again in his seat at the present session of Congress. . . . He stands there deserted and alone—his own party denying him and scrambling into all corners for shade and obscurity. Look, then, at him, and ask ourselves, what must be the sadness of this spectacle, when with this picture of evident distrust and dissatisfaction—this unyielding determination of the people of Texas to condemn him—he still holds on to the barren office and sits in his place among fellow Senators merely to receive his *per diem allowance*.[106]

Such editorials were not enough. There was talk in Austin of asking Houston to resign. P. W. Kittrell wrote that although he opposed Houston, he regretted such moves, for he saw "no necessity for kicking the *dead lion* or for dragging the dead body of Hector around the walls of Troy." Failure of the move may have resulted from what H. P. Bee called the "squirming" in the Legislature over Governor Runnels' taking the initiative in the Southern rights question and his veto of the Houston Central Railroad project. Bee described the Governor as "morose, bitter, and malevolent."[107]

[105] Georgia J. Burleson, *Life and Writings of Rufus C. Burleson*, 284–86; Houston to G. W. Baines, November 3, 1857, *Writings*, VII, 32.

[106] Dallas *Herald*, August 29, 1857; *Texas State Gazette*, November 14, 1857.

[107] Kittrell to Smith, December 3, 1857, and January 8, 1858, and Bee to Smith, December 29, 1857, Ashbel Smith Papers.

In Washington, Houston again greeted old friends, among them F. P. Blair, who wrote to Martin Van Buren:

My friend Genl. Houston met me to day in the Senate with his usual hearty greeting. . . . I promised to see him and have a talk on Saturday. I shall tell him to stand out fearlessly against all dough faces. . . . He has a beautiful leopard skin turned into a waistcoat—Laying hold of it, I inquired whether it was a wildcat's, a panther's, or a tiger's coat. He said neither—but a leopard— which I have chosen to wear next my bosom because the scripture says "a leopard cannot change his spots"!![108]

One of Houston's first moves in Congress, according to repercussions in Texas, was pressure for a change of postmasters at Huntsville. His friend William Randolph had been put out of the office as a Know-Nothing and replaced by E. J. Addicks, "a sound and reliable" Democrat. Early in December, 1857, Addicks was removed to make room for Robert Bristol, "a particular friend of Houston." A. P. Wiley, related by marriage but not by politics to Houston, wrote Bryan to lament that Henderson had not yet arrived in Washington to aid Bryan and Reagan in preventing Addicks' removal and urged Bryan not to allow "this movement of Gen. Houston to succeed." Wiley revealed the political instability in Texas by saying: "As equally divided as we are in this county, the control of the post office would turn the scale in favor of our opponents." Not satisfied with writing to Bryan, Wiley took the issue to the Legislature to protest the ancient custom of senatorial courtesy under which Houston had demanded the change as a personal favor.[109]

Houston was delaying other matters until Henderson reached Washington, but when the new senator had not yet arrived on January 19, Houston proceeded to his remarks on the death of Thomas J. Rusk and his resolutions that the Senate adopt proper measures of respect. Stating that it was the duty of the historian, and not the eulogist, to go into the minutiae of private life and character, Houston gave but a brief sketch of Rusk's career and paid tribute to his conservative principles as a senator with a national, not a sectional, fame. Closing his description of a "wise, considerative, and patriotic" statesman, Houston declared: "He will be remembered here; he will be remembered throughout the nation; he will be unforgotten in Texas whilst either history or tradition lives. Texas has lost one of the bright and staunch pillars of her edifice; and she has no material to replace him in this body."[110]

[108] Blair to Van Buren, December 11, 1857, Van Buren Papers.
[109] Wiley to Bryan, January 4, 1858, Bryan Papers; *Southern Intelligencer*, February 3, 1858.
[110] Remarks on the Death of Thomas J. Rusk, January 19, 1858, *Writings*, VI,

On five different occasions in February, 1858, Houston spoke against increasing the size of the regular army and altering the rules of promotion of army officers. His opposition to a large standing army in time of peace was nothing new; neither was his insistence that Texas needed not regular army troops but rangers to protect her frontier. Into his speeches he brought his antipathy to West Point training, his theory of the proper method of dealing with the Indians, his confidence in a volunteer army—even if just to "take wives from amongst the Mormons, and that will break up the whole establishment"—and always his love of the Union. The debate brought him into hot conflict with former Secretary of War Jefferson Davis.[111] There was nothing new either in Houston's recommending the appropriation of five years' pay for officers of the Texas Navy or their heirs and his urging of the organization of a regiment of Texas Rangers.[112] He did present something novel and startling, however, when on February 16, 1858, he introduced a resolution proposing the establishment of a United States protectorate over Mexico and Central America. On April 20 he moved that the resolution be taken up so that it could be referred to a special committee of seven for consideration. Ten days later he changed the resolution to have the committee of seven inquire into the expediency of a protectorate over the "so-called Republic of Mexico." He could not get any Senate action when he moved on May 31, and again on June 6, to take up his resolution in order to get a vote upon it. The senators were to recall his efforts and speculate upon his resolutions after he became governor of Texas in 1859. In 1858 they could not have their interest diverted from Kansas to Mexico.

Houston was leaving Kansas alone. The troubles there were the aftermath of the repeal of the Missouri Compromise and vindicated his course in opposition to that repeal, he wrote his wife, and he was more concerned over her and the children and some calico, chintz, and dress hoops he was sending to Texas than over bleeding Kansas.[113] When he announced his intention of voting for the Lecompton proslavery constitution for Kansas, he denied that he was either the enemy of or propagandist for slavery and explained that he was acting to execute the will

---

463–66. In a retrenchment move, the Committee on Printing had discontinued printing obituary addresses; in March and April, 1858, Houston made several speeches urging printing the addresses made on Rusk and other recently deceased members of Congress. See *ibid.*, VII, 43, 67–70.

[111] *Ibid.*, VI, 466–68, 487–507, 512–15, 517–29.

[112] *Congressional Globe*, 35 Cong., 1 sess. (1857/58), Part I, 919; *Writings*, VII, 33, 103, 132.

[113] Houston to Margaret Lea Houston, February 10, 1858, *Writings*, VI, 486.

of his constituents because three-fourths of the Texas Legislature favored the measure.[114] While debating the civil appropriations bill, he provided amusement for himself and the Senate by an oration on the statues which were to be used in the redecoration of the Capitol. Admitting that he was no competent critic, he ridiculed alike choice of subject and poses, drawing from Jefferson Davis scathingly sarcastic retorts that Houston was ignorant of art and was misplacing his wit to reflect on an eminent artist.[115] At that point Houston had nothing political to lose, and baiting Davis came under his category of diversion. While he could, even if indirectly, criticize government expenditures on sculpture whose symbolism he did not choose to understand, he could also speak fearlessly in behalf of property owners whose holdings were included in the Capitol expansion program, and again in behalf of underpaid civil service workers who made up the bulk of Washington population and who were to be taxed for maintenance of an adequate police force in the federal district. In that case he thought the federal treasury should bear the expense.[116]

Aside from his vote on the Lecompton constitution, Houston's position as a lame-duck senator seems to have inhibited him not at all. He complained at times of the noise in the Senate, particularly when he was trying to talk with a hoarse voice, and he kept up a perennially futile effort to save time by abolishing the habit of adjourning from Thursday to Monday, urging also an earlier time of meeting in the morning in order to eliminate night sessions. He never ate supper, and he went to sleep in at least one of the night debates.

When the internal improvement bill contained an appropriation for the improvement of transportation on Red River by removal of the raft, Houston became an economy advocate, saying there would be less waste of the money if it were just thrown on the raft; then the people would remove the obstacle in process of getting the money. On the other hand, he spoke in favor of a number of relief bills; approved fishing bounties to build up a merchant marine, which would be an auxiliary to the navy; urged extra compensation for the work of John C. Hays as a surveyor in California; spoke vehemently in opposition to eliminating the appropriation for the distribution of seeds and cuttings and Patent Office reports; and again crossed swords with Jefferson Davis in opposing the

[114] Remarks on the Kansas Lecompton Constitution, March 23, 1858, *ibid.*, VII, 42.
[115] *Congressional Globe*, 35 Cong., 1 sess. (1857/58), Part III, 2463.
[116] Concerning the Washington City Police Bill, April 5, 1858, *Writings*, VII, 61–67.

abolition of the franking privilege, insisting that elimination of free use of the mails would not save money because more clerks would have to be employed in mailing necessary government documents.[117]

On May 22, 1858, Houston made a logical and intelligent speech advocating the Homestead Law in principle and opposing the proposed amendment of Senator T. L. Clingman of North Carolina which would not have restricted the homestead grants to actual settlers but would have issued warrants for the land to all heads of families in the United States. Houston pointed out that the amendment would lead to depreciation of land values and to speculation, while disposing of the public domain to settlers who made improvements would be a grant "in consideration of service rendered to the Government fully equivalent to its value."[118]

Various Houston speeches in the spring and summer of 1858 were directly concerned with Texas matters. On April 17 a Pacific railroad was again under consideration, and Houston continued to advocate the southern route. He wished the railroad issue divested of all appearance of sectionalism and pointed out the superior natural advantages of the southern route, the only one, he asserted, that was feasible and practicable as demonstrated by the mail routes then in operation to San Diego. On another occasion he advocated the consummation of the boundary survey between Texas and New Mexico so that land titles on the border could be settled. While urging that the agents of the Texas Indian reservation on the Brazos River be made permanent, not special, officials and that the Indian reserve in Oklahoma be attached to the Texas rather than the Fort Smith superintendency, he again took a shot at the regular troops—"very regular; regular in doing us no good, giving us no protection, pursuing no Indians, and preventing the incursions of none." He was also insisting on an appropriation to pay Texas for her expenditures for rangers on the frontier.[119] When there was objection that the amendment for paying Texas for ranger service was out of order, Houston complained that it was strange that he was not permitted to explain a matter of importance to his state when he was in the Senate "alone, wearied out with watching."

He was alone again, for Henderson died on June 4, 1858. The next day the senior Texas senator delivered his eulogy and recommended official senatorial signs of mourning. The speech was a brief obituary of a man who "made his mark upon the history of Texas . . . a bold, enterprising

[117] *Ibid.*, 100, 113, 118, 120, 154.
[118] Remarks on Bill Concerning Homesteads, *ibid.*, 114–16.
[119] *Ibid.*, 79–83, 110, 159–65, 180.

spirit; a man of indomitable will, of daring enterprise, and firm of purpose." Houston's remarks were well chosen, not maudlin or sentimental; they did not deserve the treatment they received in the *Texas State Gazette*, which attacked Houston as a hypocrite, calumniator, and slanderer who had no right to speak in praise of a man whom he had denounced and vilified in the 1857 campaign.[120]

The Texas press made little effort to be either fair or accurate in reporting on Houston. Both the Dallas *Herald* and George W. Paschal's *Southern Intelligencer* at Austin made malicious comments on the Senator's purchase of the patent rights for Calvert's Bee Gums, with the observation that Houston would find cultivating bees more lucrative than mileage and per diem.[121] The *Intelligencer* reported that those in the know in Washington said that Buchanan would put Houston in charge of the government of Arizona, and sarcastically opined: "Judging, however, from the open, kindly feeling expressed by the President towards Gen. Houston for his cordial support of the administration, such a result in these days of tergiveration, would not have surprised us."

Paschal wrote from Washington back to Texas that the Senator had confidential meetings with the President and was instrumental in having W. F. Wilson of Galveston appointed Indian agent in Nebraska, achieving the appointment by "threatening the President with the constant presence of Wilson's wife." Paschal grumbled that Houston practiced a kind of *ruse de guerre* upon the Democratic party, not openly confessing his sins as had other Know-Nothing backsliders like John S. Ford, J. M. Steiner, and T. J. Chambers, but working his way in at the back door by making himself intimate with Buchanan and supporting administration measures from "the admission of Kansas through the deficiency bill, and appropriation to put down Brigham Young and his wives."[122]

Houston's reported intimacy with Buchanan does not coincide perfectly with what he wrote his wife. He complained to her that Buchanan exercised no common sense as an executive, depending too much upon the advice of his cabinet rather than directing it, and so could not ascend the mountain for stumbling over the molehill. The cabinet, said the Senator, had not a wise man in it. Incredulous over reports that Buchanan was a candidate for re-election, he was moved to comment in

[120] On the Death of James Pinckney Henderson, June 5, 1858, *ibid.*, 140–43; *Texas State Gazette*, August 21, 1858.

[121] *Southern Intelligencer*, June 30, 1858; Dallas *Herald*, July 24, 1858.

[122] *Southern Intelligencer*, May 5, June 9, 16, 30, August 11, 1858.

the same vein that "an old fool is the worst of fools."[123] Such confidences, however, were for the family only; for Houston was still cajoling the President, working for appointments for his friends, including a commercial agency in Portugal for Washington D. Miller, which Miller declined.[124] Despite Houston's grumblings about Buchanan and his opposition to Buchanan's election, the two men, who had been friends so many years before, had worked out a sort of rapport during Houston's last months in the Senate.

To his old friend Nat Young in Delaware, Houston wrote:

I am truly glad that I will soon retire from all the cares of public life. The grapes are not sour! Though I have no doubt from events in Texas many will think the grapes are sour. I assure you that I have not since the halcyon days we spent in Nashville, felt so much delighted with my prospects as I am with the prospect of retirement. God has granted us six fine children, two boys and four girls, and there is another in the shuck for June, and for these I wish to be at home and render them all aid in my power.[125]

His daily letters to Margaret expressed his anxiety concerning her and his wish to be home "in time." The third Houston son, William Rogers, was born at Huntsville on May 25, 1858. His father did not make his acquaintance before the last of June.

For a man of sixty-five who was rejoicing at the opportunity to retire, Houston spent a remarkably active summer. Henderson's death had left a vacancy in the Senate to be filled by the Texas Legislature, and that was sufficient explanation to the Dallas *Herald* for Houston's making a speaking tour in a by-election year. He spoke at Washington, Texas, on August 12, at Independence on August 14, at Hempstead on August 17, made two more speeches before August 31, and talked at Danville on September 11. At the barbecue at Washington he was supposed to define his position on the Democratic administration, the "Southern League," and his protectorate. As to the protectorate, he said, accurately or not, that it was a policy of the country. On the subject of states' rights he was silent, but he remarked to a friend that the time for the South to act was past because the South was helpless and the only reliance left was on the magnanimity of the North.[126] The *Intelligencer* said that secession advocate James Willie had invited Houston to make the Washington talk in the belief that the Senator could be made the head of the

---

[123] Houston to Margaret Lea Houston, May 19, 1858, *Writings*, VII, 112.
[124] John S. Williams to Miller, June 19, 1858, Miller Papers.
[125] Houston to Young, April 17, 1858, Houston Papers.
[126] *Southern Intelligencer*, August 11, 18, 25, 1858.

Southern League. The paper ridiculed the effort: "This was a worse *sell* than sending for the Hon. Guy M. Bryan to come here and curse Bell and the Independent Democracy, who supported him. Houston truly *cursed* the Union with Balaam's curse. For whatever may be Houston's sins, disunion sentiments are not among them."[127]

By late August and early September, the Dallas *Herald* was copying from the Waco *Democrat* an editorial on "The Program for 1859," which declared that if Houston's course in the next session of Congress was as satisfactory as in the last, his strength would be greatly augmented. The *Herald* accused the Waco paper of trying "to resurrect the dead fortunes of Sam Houston, to dig up the fossil remains of the decayed Lion, and galvanize him with a little spasmodic life."[128] At Hempstead, Houston had mentioned the weakness of the South and the ease with which the North and West could win a war in case of Southern resistance. At Danville, he denounced a Southern League and opening of the slave trade and contended that nothing had been done to justify a dissolution of the Union. That his 1858 speeches had a telling effect is indicated in the comment of the reporter of the Danville speech: "I think there is no doubt about the fact that sober second thought is slightly mollifying the bitterness of his bitterest enemies."[129]

Houston also used his few weeks at home to investigate the possibility that residence in the Redlands would benefit his wife's asthma, to buy a new home at Cedar Point in Chambers County, and to make plans to breed fine sheep. By December 8, he and Reagan had left for Washington. Matthias Ward had been appointed to fill the vacancy in the Senate. Bryan was back in the national capital also, but his relatives were giving him accurate predictions of things to come in Texas affairs. Thomas M. Jack wrote from Galveston on December 23, 1858: "It seems to be understood that Genl. Houston will 'fight his battle o'er again' next summer—and that he will give the Democracy some trouble. 'Nous verrons.' "[130]

On that day in Washington, Houston was urging that the Senate move into its new hall on January 4 instead of waiting for the opening of the new Congress. Of course he would not be there for the new session, but he pointed out the cold-inducing drafts in the old room and the more spacious galleries to seat visitors in the new quarters. With almost a

[127] *Ibid.*, September 1, 1858.
[128] Dallas *Herald*, August 21, September 1, 1858.
[129] Synopsis of Danville Speech, September 11, 1858, *Writings*, VII, 183–86.
[130] Jack to Bryan, December 23, 1858, Bryan Papers.

touch of pathos, he assured his fellow members that if he chanced to draw a desirable seat, an exchange could be arranged.[131]

Houston probably went to New York for the New Year. At any rate he was there on January 4 and declined the hospitalities of the city as offered him by the city council.[132] The next day he was back in his seat in time to add to the eulogies for General John A. Quitman. On January 12 and 13, 1859, he made yet another speech on the advisability of the southern route for the Pacific railroad. On the surface it would seem that his advocacy of the southern route would have meant that his debate adversaries would be those senators favoring a more northern route. Actually, his remarks on the distinction between North and South gave him an opportunity to discant on the madness of the talk about disunion and to define secession as rebellion. At the same time, he warned men of the North to cease to agitate the subject of Southern institutions. His insistence that all states had equal rights and that there was no such thing as "Southern rights" per se brought on a debate with Senator Alfred Iverson and incidental remarks from his new colleague from Texas, Matthias Ward. On the second day of the debate the galleries were crowded with visitors, members of the foreign diplomatic corps, and many members of the House. The correspondent of the *True Delta* described Houston's technique in the debate:

Gen. Houston rose quietly from his seat—as quietly as if to reply to some trifling inquiry. Thousands of eyes were upon him, and all were anticipating a violent and excited retort upon the Senator from Georgia. But expectation in this respect was sorely disappointed. . . . The General's countenance was all the while beaming with amiability. And his expressions of kind feeling toward the Georgia Senator were altogether overpowering. Those who have known him intimately in Texas and seen him prepare for the annihilation of an opponent, can readily appreciate his peculiar mood. There is such a thing as killing a man with kindness—but Houston's great forte is the adroit mixture of flattery with the most consummate ridicule and sarcasm. Today he opened with all his power upon Mr. Iverson, and it was with difficulty the presiding officer could keep the galleries in order—Several times applause was heard, but it was promptly checked.[133]

To Iverson, Houston said: "As a Union man, I have ever maintained my position, and I ever shall. I wish no prouder epitaph to mark the

[131] *Congressional Globe,* 35 Cong., 2 sess. (1858), 192.
[132] Dallas *Herald,* February 2, 1859.
[133] Quoted *ibid.,* February 9, 1859.

263

board or slab that may lie on my tomb than this: 'He loved his country, he was a patriot; he was devoted to the Union.' If it is for this that I have suffered martyrdom, it is sufficient that I stand at quits with those who have wielded the sacrificial knife." When Ward interposed that he preferred disunion to the violation of constitutional rights, Houston answered: "I hope that my honorable colleague does not suppose I would submit to any infraction of our rights. Our rights are rights common to the whole Union. I would not see wrong inflicted on the North, or on the South, but I am for the Union, without any 'if' in the case; and my motto is, 'it shall be preserved.' "[134]

On January 27, Houston talked again on the constitutionality of constructing a transcontinental railroad as a national, not a sectional, project, stressing the generosity of Texas in granting land and money for the building of eight hundred miles of the road and the resulting right to insist that she have a fair competition with other sections of the Union. Other Houston speeches during his last session included arguments for a customhouse at Galveston, and for an Indian reservation west of the Pecos River, and another declaration against abolition of the franking privilege, arguing that it was a means of disseminating intelligence throughout the country and giving the people information on subjects connected with the well-being of the government.

On January 22, 1859, John H. Reagan wrote the editor of the Dallas *Herald* that in a few days Houston would move in the Senate to abolish the Eastern Judicial District of Texas, the district presided over by Judge John Charles Watrous, and attach it to the Western District under Judge Thomas H. Duval. Efforts made since 1851 to impeach Judge Watrous had failed, partly because there was not sufficient evidence of corrupt acts, and partly because of indefinite methods of impeachment procedure. In February, 1858, the Texas Legislature requested the Congressional delegation to investigate and secure final action.[135] Houston presented the legislative resolutions and on February 19, 1858, made a personal explanation of his action, which had been challenged on the grounds that as a potential judge, if the Senate sat as a court of impeachment, his presentation of the measure had disqualified him.[136] On December 15, 1858, the House again refused to impeach the Judge.

---

[134] Concerning the Pacific Railroad and Other Matters, January 12 and 13, 1850, *Writings*, VII, 194–216.
[135] Walace Hawkins, *The Case of John C. Watrous, United States Judge for Texas*, 35.
[136] A Personal Explanation, February 19, 1858, *Writings*, VI, 515–17.

Simon Mussina, spokesman of opposition to the jurist, began writing a speech to summarize all of his charges and called on Houston to present them in the Senate. The abolition of the district would be a short cut to the Judge's removal, and even the anti-Houston *Herald* declared: "We wish Gen. Houston success in the move. If he can carry it he will have earned the thanks of an outraged people." After several unsuccessful attempts to get the floor, Houston finally spoke on February 3, 1859, using Mussina's findings as the basis of his speech, entitled "A Vindication of Texas from Charges Made by Judge John C. Watrous before the Congressional Committee Investigating His Conduct." Mussina's research plus Houston's sarcasm unraveled a conspiracy to take advantage of land controversies and hard-to-prove land titles in Texas to defraud title holders for the advantage of the conspirators, one of whom was Watrous, who used his official position to benefit himself and his partners.

The Washington *Evening Star,* in reporting the speech, was careful to use legal qualifiers such as "allegedly" and "purports" in the description of "one of the most gigantic schemes of fraud ever attempted to be fastened upon any community" by men who hesitated at nothing and were bold, unscrupulous, and defiant, "pressing into their service men of talent and apparent position."[137] The correspondent of the New Orleans *Delta,* mayhap in true Southern spirit, was less judicial but more eloquent in his report of the Watrous exposé and said of Houston's effort:

The speech of the Honorable Senator is as admirable for its boldness, as it is convincing in its conclusions. In protecting the interests of his State against the grasping and defiant spirit of judicial misrule, the fearless and eloquent Senator has given indications of patriotism, which his people must gratefully appreciate, and which the country will number among its best examples of true moral heroism.[138]

Not only did the Dallas *Herald* quote favorable comments on the speech; its own editorials used the descriptions "powerful," "lucid demonstration," "indignant denunciation of robbers," and "doesn't leave a grease spot of Watrous & Co." Explaining its apparent about-face, the paper called the speech "the crowning glory of Gen. Houston's eventful life," which "entitles its author to the thanks of every Texian, and of every lover of justice and enemy of corruption." The *Herald* admitted that it had always opposed Houston and had no proclivity for praising

---

[137] Dallas *Herald,* February 9, 23, 1859. The speech is given in *Writings,* VII, 232–97.

[138] Quoted in Dallas *Herald,* March 9, 1859.

him, but added: "We would not do him deliberate injustice, and if the gratulations of one so humble as ourself, could be of any consequence to him, we give them most gladly and cordially, and thrice thank him for dragging this Watrous enormity, in all its hideous deformity, before the gaze of an outraged people."[139]

The length of the speech prevented the *Herald* from printing it in full, but the *Intelligencer* ran it in installments and accompanied the series with complimentary excerpts from other papers, such as the following from the *Texas New Era*:

We have no choice but to admire the energy with which this task was undertaken, and the manliness with which it was carried to completion. Now upon the eve of closing his long senatorial career, when about to retire from the wearisome duties of a public servant, he makes this *expose* of a fraud which is equalled in its baseness by its stupidity only; striking right and left—fearing nothing, daring everything—unmasking all, and screening none—he leaves this, another act of virtue among the many which stand as proofs of his unwavering devotion to his country, and adds it as another testimonial of the guardian care with which he has ever watched over the interests of the people of his own loved Texas.[140]

The *Intelligencer* also had to face charges of inconsistency when it found anything commendable in Houston, but it insisted that it had always accorded the Senator due credit for any redeeming act and asserted that assuredly, in the Watrous case, "the country will be under obligations to Genl. Houston for his manly defense of Texas." When the Galveston *News*, not to be convinced against its will, came out with a "smashing card" against Houston and intimations of further developments in the case, the *Intelligencer* retaliated that "such epithets as 'infamously false' applied to Gen. Houston, unaccompanied by any denial of the authorship of the letters, or of the record facts, only evince a weakness in their cause." When friends of Watrous said that they would show that the Senator had "drawn stronger inferences from the party than they warrant," the *Intelligencer* answered: "We hope the judge will publish the residue of the rich correspondence. The specimens published by Houston indicate that the residue is too spicy to be lost."[141]

The end-of-the-session action of an expiring senatorship elicited no Congressional action, but who can say that the Great Designer had not

---

[139] *Ibid.*, March 2, 1859.

[140] *Southern Intelligencer*, March 16, 1859. According to Hawkins (*The Case of John C. Watrous*, 53), every newspaper in Texas except one, the *Nueces Valley*, was against the Judge.

[141] *Southern Intelligencer*, March 2, 9, 1859.

again made an adroit move. The speech was noted in the national press; at home it was a factor in a change of attitude to reverse the gubernatorial defeat of 1857 into victory in 1859.

Perhaps the Watrous speech was also an opportunity to end a Senate term in some semblance of a blaze of glory. To Houston all criticism was intensely personal; and he had determined, at least as early as the publication of the *Texas Almanac* of 1857, that before he left Washington he would make one more defense against his enemies' attacks, a defense that would guarantee the capital's last impression of him as the hero of San Jacinto. Willard Richardson, in that first issue of his *Almanac,* had published a biography of General Rusk, probably written by Sidney Sherman, which gave Rusk credit for the victory at San Jacinto: "It was the mission of Rusk to win laurels on that day and for other men to wear them." The 1858 issue of the *Almanac* had continued a running account of the history of Texas begun in the first issue and had given a narrative of the battle written by Dr. N. D. Labadie, which asserted that San Jacinto was won "almost against the will of the Commander."[142]

When Houston learned of the Labadie article, he wrote Stuart of the Galveston *Civilian and Gazette* that the account was utterly unfounded in truth and that he would ignore it but for its attack on the conduct of John Forbes at San Jacinto. Forbes sued Labadie for libel and involved the Galveston *News* as publisher of the *Almanac;* Houston was later to work on the brief in the case. On February 28, 1859, four days before the "termination of his political life," Houston declared that he deemed it due to himself, to the truth of history, and to his posterity to vindicate himself "against uncalled-for charges and unjustifiable defamation." Beginning with the declaration of Texas independence, he recounted his version of his Fabian retreat across Texas, documenting it with letters from Rusk, Joseph L. Bennett, Philip Martin, and Ben McCulloch. Houston's final remarks indicated that he meant his "Refutation" speech to be his valedictory. He closed it with a statement of his confidence in the ability of the Senate to harmonize on national subjects and so cement the Union, and concluded: "My prayers will remain with them, that light, knowledge, wisdom, and patriotism may guide them, and that their efforts will be perpetually employed for blessings to our country; that under their influence and their exertions the nation will be blessed, the people happy, and the perpetuity of the Union secured to the latest posterity."[143]

[142] Sam Acheson, *35,000 Days in Texas: A History of the Dallas News and Its Forbears,* 40–43.

[143] Refutation of Calumnies, February 28, 1859, *Writings,* VII, 306–35.

Alas for intention, habit was strong. On March 1 he defended Texas once more in demanding that the El Paso–San Diego mail route not be abandoned. As he wrote his wife, his longing to throw off the harness and submit himself to "petticoat rule" was increased by the fact that, despite his resolve to get to bed by ten o'clock, he was immersed in business at midnight and often until two in the morning.[144] It was on this note of weariness that he spoke his last words as senator the day after his sixty-sixth birthday: "My opinion is, that if we leave the Senate Chamber, we shall not meet again. Members are exhausted, and have been for several nights; and if they once retire to repose, they will not wake up again."[145]

On March 11, 1859, the Washington *Evening Star* carried a note:

This distinguished man left Washington yesterday afternoon for his home in Texas. Up to the hour of his departure, his rooms were crowded by his friends calling to take leave of him. No other public man ever made more, or more sincere friends here, nor was severance of a gentleman's connection with American public affairs ever more seriously regretted than in his case.[146]

To say that Sam Houston was a colorful figure as a United States senator is as trite as it is true. Measured against Clay and Webster and Calhoun, with whom he served his first years in the Senate, he perhaps did not prove their equal in statesmanship. He was always personal, he was vindictive, he dramatized himself, he used sarcasm and ridicule and even vulgarity to make his point. He could be small in small things, but he was always right on fundamental issues, and he was, regardless of what his enemies said, entirely consistent. Too frequently in his speeches, he dragged in extraneous material with slight provocation, never forgetting the Indians, but who can say that the Indians had no need of a friend at court?

In the tedious details of weighty correspondence and the pleas for patronage, it was characteristic of Houston to leave much of the burden to Rusk, but he secured patronage fairly effectively and he labored unceasingly to benefit his friends. On the big issues to benefit Texas he spoke long and frequently and eloquently—on the railroad, on the debt, on the boundary, for proper recognition—and he made the nation Texas-conscious. The unfairest charge against him was that he pandered to Northern interests to seek Northern votes and so sacrificed Southern rights. He always identified himself as a Southern man—but a Southern

[144] Houston to Margaret Lea Houston, January 20, 1859, *ibid.*, 219.
[145] *Congressional Globe*, 35 Cong., 2 sess. (1858/59), 1651.
[146] Quoted in *Southern Intelligencer*, April 6, 1859.

man in the Union. It took courage and fearlessness to condemn the Southern conventions, to speak for the right of Northern ministers to petition, and to vote alone against the Kansas-Nebraska Bill, when he knew that it would ruin him politically in Texas. For, if anything, Houston was politically astute and could measure political reaction in Texas.

His last years as senator, the veritable symbol of love of the Union, were years of true statesmanship, when he measured well above most of his colleagues. It was his tragedy to achieve his time of greatness when the Union was so torn with conflict that vision was too distorted to measure his true worth. Perhaps also his own vision of his greatest possibility was always clouded by a dream of achieving a position even higher than that of a great United States senator.

Aspirations to the Presidency

THE HIGH DIGNITY of the office of President of the United States may once have made it unseemly for a man to declare himself openly and avowedly a candidate for that office. Houston was not a modest man; he wanted to be president, and he sincerely thought that he might be an improvement over the men who did achieve the position between 1848 and 1860. He was once advanced by the Texas Democracy as a candidate to put before the National Democratic Convention; for a few months in 1860 he was an independent candidate. Surely it was a part of his "great design," and yet he never admitted in actual words, preserved in his writings, that he truly wanted the position. It may have been that the very strength of his desire precluded his putting it into words, for he was not one to bear defeat with equanimity; so that by never openly admitting that he wanted to be president, he would never, whether he achieved it or not, have to bear the onus of defeat. Yet, ironically enough, he was for twelve years taunted by his enemies for his failure to secure the office, and his every political move was viewed by them in the light of whether or not it furthered his plans.

Finally, once defeated as a candidate for governor and facing the end of his Senate term, he evolved one more "grand plan"—one more vast design whereby he might, by diverting national attention from secession to his own success as a conqueror in Mexico, win national recognition and the presidency and so save the Union. His failure lay perhaps in his personality, perhaps in the fact that he represented a Democratic state not geographically so located or possessed of enough votes to make its candidate politically powerful. By 1860 he was too old and too burdened with family to take the ultimate risk, and the forces of disunion were too strong for him to battle. He was never a logical or a powerful candidate, but the story of his aspiration is an interesting saga of a high dream and the steps, circuitous, not direct, made to attempt its realization.

Early in 1829, when Houston was the popular governor of Tennessee and Jackson was about to be inaugurated as president, Judge J. C. Guild thought that Houston's re-election as governor would guarantee a bright political future, culminating perhaps in the White House.[1] Later events of 1829 brought an eclipse to such a potentiality. It was not until 1843 that Houston's name was again mentioned for chief executive. Then, as the San Jacinto hero and twice president of Texas, he once more came into the national consciousness, and John G. Tod wrote from Baltimore that some said that Houston's name and military fame would one day pull the scattered elements of the Democrats together and would make him the president of the United States. Said Tod, "Well, 'we shall see what we shall see.' "[2]

In 1845, in the last days of uncertainty over annexation, Houston left Texas for a visit to Tennessee, stopping en route for a dinner at the old Capitol in Houston. Among the thirty-eight volunteer toasts which featured the occasion, John Fitzgerald toasted the "distinguished guest . . . the sage, the hero and the patriot," with the wish that, should Texas lose its national individuality in the American union, the "same great chief" might "still preside over our destinies."[3] Charles Elliot wrote to Bankhead concerning that trip:

Houston is gone to New Orleans and the *Hermitage* to sound the depths in

[1] James, *Life of Andrew Jackson*, 701.
[2] Tod to Anson Jones, October 25, 1843, Jones, *Republic of Texas*, 262.
[3] *Telegraph and Texas Register*, May 28, 1845.

those quarters, and calculates his chance of running for President in succession to Polk, and I shall think it very wonderful if they do not continue to catch him, and throw him over afterwards, adroit as he is. He is a fellow of infinite resource too, and under the cards he may be working the right way to get.[4]

Consul Kennedy had written to Lord Aberdeen earlier that Democratic organs in the United States were mentioning Houston as a successor to Polk and that Jackson would probably recommend him. The Washington *Globe* was one of the papers that intimated he might be chosen president in the event of annexation.[5]

Jackson would doubtless have made the recommendation, but he was dead by the time Houston reached the Hermitage. There was no death to politics in Tennessee, however, and the Nashville *Union's* account of the barbecue in Houston's honor was quoted by *Niles' Register* as "an amusing item from one of the candidates for congress, strictly characteristic of the man." The *Register* noted that the former president of Texas had "been spoken of as a candidate for the next presidency of the United States."[6] That the candidacy was taken seriously by Texas leaders and that the slight implied in the *Register's* use of the words "amusing item" did not go unnoticed is shown in a letter from Henderson concerning the choice of the first two Texas senators.

For the interest of the state & Houston's *future* interests I wish to see Rusk with him. They are now good friends & Rusk I *know* wishes to see him advanced to the Presidency and when it is seen in the U.S. that the second man of our revolution is the friend and associate of the first—it will do away with the *little* impression which has been made there against him by his enemies.[7]

Two months after Henderson's letter was written, Houston took his seat in the Senate and began his policy of sustaining the Polk administration. In the capital and in Texas his course met with general commendation, and soon after his return for his second session in the Senate, he went for a visit in New York and there received his callers at the Governor's room. James Morgan learned of the New Year's visit and wrote to Samuel Swartwout: "Old Sam & Rusk is or has been with you in N. Y. I learn—depend on it Sam is after the White House!"[8] President

[4] Elliot to Bankhead, June 11, 1845, Ephraim Douglass Adams, *British Diplomatic Correspondence concerning Texas*, 503.

[5] Kennedy to Aberdeen, April 25, 1846, *ibid.*, 479–80; Eugene Irving McCormac, *James K. Polk: A Political Biography*, 357.

[6] *Niles' Register*, LXVII (July 12, 1845), 294.

[7] Henderson to Miller, January 26, 1846, Miller Papers.

[8] Morgan to Swartwout, January 10, 1847, Swartwout Papers.

Polk thought so too. He had welcomed his old Tennessee friend back into the Union and the Democratic fold, but he did not want the return to be at his own expense. When David Kaufman told Polk that Texas was not satisfied with its appointments and Houston was not satisfied with the administration, Polk assured the congressman that Houston had no cause for dissatisfaction and added in his February 1, 1847, note in his diary: "The truth is that Senator Houston desires to be a candidate for the Presidency and probably thinks that I do not throw my official influence into the scale to promote his views."[9]

Texas friends were at work, as were others. Ashbel Smith wrote his old chief that their mutual friend Adrian Terry hoped he was "authorized to speak a word in the right quarters" and added his own commendation: "Your course in the Senate has of course commanded much attention and given universal satisfaction. Your fellow citizens will again call on you to fill the same place whatever your private wishes may be. We are also looking to your being the candidate for the White House."[10] John T. Mills was not of exactly the same opinion. He questioned whether Rusk had really said that Houston was Cass's only recognized opponent for the Democratic nomination and gave as his own judgment that "so much honor is not laid up in store for us."[11]

Houston was keeping in the public eye but was not committing himself. His speech at San Augustine on May 26, 1847, was reported in the New Orleans *Picayune* and picked up by *Niles' Register* with the comment: "General H., as our readers are aware, has been spoken of and written about, as a suitable candidate for the next presidency."[12] There is at least the color of politics in a letter from Houston to Elijah Purdy of New York of June 3, 1847, disclaiming any criticism of Zachary Taylor and insisting that his own opinions on public policy had been determined in accord with what he considered the best interests of the country.[13] Houston's newspaper tilt with Tyler over who got the credit for annexation was also guaranteed to give him more than local publicity. Rusk, acting unofficially as campaign manager, wrote home to San Augustine to express his wishes and to suggest strategy.[14]

John D. McLeod, watching the political pot boil in Austin, wrote Rusk of the chagrin that Houston's nomination would bring to some of his enemies and said that such a move would force John Bull to acknowl-

[9] Quaife, *The Diary of James K. Polk during His Presidency*, III, 364.
[10] Smith to Houston, April 4, 1847, Ashbel Smith Papers.
[11] Mills to Rusk, May 4, 1847, T. J. Rusk Papers.
[12] *Niles' Register*, LXXII (June 5, 1847), 210.
[13] Houston to Purdy, June 3, 1847, *Writings*, V, 12–13.
[14] Rusk to Wallace, October 14, 1847, T. J. Rusk Papers.

edge that the "man with the blanket coat" could both coquette with an English minister and play an effective part in a presidential canvass.[15]

The Democratic Convention of 1848, at which Houston was scheduled to be a delegate, was to meet at Baltimore on May 22. The Senator did some advance canvassing in New York and New England. His New York speech on the boundary of Texas paid joint compliment to Texas *señoritas* and the zeal, ardor, and patriotism of New York Democracy. In March he spoke at Boston and at Norwich and Hartford, Connecticut, and Kaufman reported to Rusk: "Genl. H. has made a tremendously favorable impression throughout New England. The Democracy are everywhere delighted with and love him. At Boston and Norwich where I heard him he spoke in his very happiest vein."[16] Smith commended Houston on the wisdom of his northern tour at the same time that he wrote of abortive Whig attempts at Galveston to get Houston's friends pledged to support Zachary Taylor. Smith had made a Washington's Birthday speech in Galveston, and the *News* correspondent reported that "the Hero of San Jacinto so floated before Smith's vision" that he could not see General Taylor.[17]

As convention time approached, Rusk, who was the working member of the delegation while Houston electioneered, reported from the Washington scene of action: "There is no telling who will be our candidate for President though present appearances seem to point out General Cass with whom I am upon terms of intimacy and friendship. Houston is very anxious to run and I have done all I conveniently could for him, but I fear he will not succeed. It would be better for Texas if we could elect Houston."[18] According to Rusk, both Kaufman and Houston were anxious to make speeches in Congress but were a little hesitant. Houston had his opportunity when he spoke on the Yucatán bill on May 8. It could almost be said that he "protested too much" when, in the speech, he deplored the fact that every Congressional move was colored by its relationship to the presidential election and stated that he would not want to legislate as a senator if senators so far forgot themselves "as to huckster in a Presidential canvass, or render aid to the aspirations of any candidate for that high office."[19]

[15] McLeod to Rusk, November 14, 1847, *ibid.*

[16] Kaufman to Rusk, March 18, 1848, *ibid.* Kaufman was in New England as a member of the official committee from the House to attend the funeral of John Quincy Adams, who died on February 21, 1848. See Rusk to David Rusk, May 7, 1848, David Rusk Papers.

[17] Smith to Houston, March 25, 1848, Ashbel Smith Papers.

[18] Rusk to David Rusk, May 1, 1848, David Rusk Papers.

[19] Speech on Yucatán Bill, May 8, 1848, *Writings*, V, 44.

Ashbel Smith's assistance included a report on the lack of unanimity in Democratic ranks and the formulation of a tariff plank for the Houston platform. For morale he could quote: "Our old friend Radcliff Hudson, now a prosperous manufacturer in Hartford, Conn., is a most staunch and active friend of yours. He said to me that you only need to ride through New England to secure the vote of that section of the country. On the whole things are in admirable trim."[20] As another campaign tactic, Smith wrote for the *Democratic Review* a notice of Charles Edwards Lester's *Sam Houston and His Republic,* that campaign document which Houston had commissioned and edited.[21]

C. A. Harper had an article in the *New Hampshire Patriot* advocating Houston for the presidency but wrote Rusk that several patrons had said that "Houston ought to be satisfied with the vice-Presidency" and that such a solution might do very well.[22] Almost across the continent, F. L. Hatch of the *Texas Banner* at Huntsville chose to take the long view in his prognostication for the home-town candidate: "He is making an immense impression wherever he goes, and his prospects for the Democratic nomination are certainly brightening. Though I can hardly hope that he will get the nomination. My opinion is that Houston will be President of the U. States if he lives ten years longer. He must be. His star is in the ascendant and his destiny is a bright one."[23]

Two days after that gaze into the crystal ball, the Democrats met in Baltimore. On the fourth day of the convention, Houston made what the *Telegraph* called "an excellent speech" on the Mexican War. Lewis Cass received the nomination on the fourth ballot. W. O. Butler of Kentucky was nominated for the vice-presidency. Houston also chose to take the long view and began an energetic campaign in support of the party ticket. Rusk wrote his brother on June 18, 1848, that Houston had been absent for two weeks and that they had nothing in Washington but confusion and electioneering. The next day he reported on Taylor's nomination by the Whigs at Philadelphia on June 7 and added: "Gen'l Houston is off upon another visit to New York. I expect my best policy is to stick to my post."[24]

The New York *Times,* in reporting a "frolicking" speech Houston made in New York City, said that "the Hero of San Jacinto is not much troubled with mauvaise honte" and relayed some of his stories with the

[20] Smith to Houston, late April or early May, 1848, Ashbel Smith Papers.
[21] James, *The Raven,* 362.
[22] Harper to Rusk, May 15, 1848, T. J. Rusk Papers.
[23] Hatch to Miller, May 20, 1848, Miller Papers.
[24] Rusk to David Rusk, June 18 and 19, 1848, David Rusk Papers.

275

opinion that "Gen. Houston would make a first rate comedian should all other trades fail." The Albany *Argus* gave a lengthy account of his Albany speech, repeating one of his stories told in dialect and describing the peals of laughter which it elicited. According to the *Argus*, "his position before the country, his character and career, his fine person and appearance, and his urbane and courteous manner, ensured to him everywhere the popular regard."[25]

Houston accompanied Kaufman to his native state of Pennsylvania, and they spoke at Harrisburg on July 3 and spent Independence Day "addressing the sovereigns" at Carlisle. The Carlisle *Democrat* described the political gathering at Holcomb's Grove, the playing of "Hail to the Chief" to welcome Houston, and the thirteen cheers given before his address, "one of the most happy efforts we have ever heard on such an occasion."[26]

Good speeches and good politics in 1848, according to many Houston admirers, might pay off in 1852. J. G. M. Ramsey of Mecklenburg, Tennessee, so assured Ashbel Smith: "I intended a serious conversation with you [when both were at West Point] & once alluded to it briefly—about Senator Houston for the next race. . . . The South will have the candidate in 1852 & Texas has the first right. Texas, Old Virginia, & Tennessee all claim Houston & we can carry him."[27]

Houston's position on the Compromise of 1850 did not win undivided approval in Texas, but the Boston *Post* commended him for his Union stand, and Radcliff Hudson wrote from Hartford that his conduct in the Senate had won the esteem of all the North and speculated that "for Houston of Texas to take the Ground with Clay, Benton & Webster is all that the friends of Texas wish. We must have a Democratic nomination from the South next & who so soon as old Sam."[28] Providence, Rhode Island, and northern New York State expressed approval too. A Missouri paper called the *Advocate* was still for Cass for president but hoisted its flag for Houston for vice-president for the next election. And the New Orleans *Crescent*, in June, 1850, wrote that if Houston's record as senator gave assurance of his future, he was "destined to a still higher position."[29] F. P. Blair was certain of Houston's desire for the higher position and wrote to Van Buren in midsummer of 1850 that Houston was

[25] *Telegraph and Texas Register*, July 13, August 3, 1848.
[26] *Ibid.*, August 10, 1848; Kaufman to Miller, July 2, 1848, Miller Papers.
[27] Ramsey to Smith, August 8, 1848, Ashbel Smith Papers.
[28] Hudson to Smith, February 7, 1850, *ibid.*
[29] Quoted in *Texas State Gazette*, March 23, June 8, 1850.

"so full of presidential hopes for the great Confederacy" that he would "do anything in his power" to realize that ambition.[30]

To further those hopes, Houston accepted speaking engagements on a variety of subjects, including a temperance speech in Maryland in September, 1850. By the fall of 1850 the Louisville *Courier* was convinced that he stood a better chance for the Democratic nomination than did Cass, Benton, or Buchanan. The New York *Sun*, on October 30, in an editorial entitled "Who Shall Be Our Next President?" could find only one man "fit to unite all the discordant elements of party . . . and lead the nation on triumphantly to higher glory and vaster greatness." For that man the *Sun* declared:

We then propose in the people's name, as the candidate for the next President, General Sam Houston, once Governor of Tennessee, the Father of Texian Independence, twice president of the Texian Republic, now its esteemed, honored, and beloved Senator—the advocate of concession, and the supporter of the peace measures. Who will refuse to rally to the standard of Sam Houston, the true American patriot, the fearless and brave champion of American institutions—a man not influenced by sectional prejudices; who will sustain the honor of the country and the rights of American citizens, under all circumstances—the pupil of the illustrious Andrew Jackson in youth, his bosom friend and councillor in manhood—like him in all the noble qualities that make the great and true man. Such is General Sam Houston, the People's Candidate for the next Presidency.[31]

The *Gazette* listed among other Democratic papers supporting Houston the Louisville *Democrat* and the Louisville *Advertiser,* the Wheeling (Virginia) *Zeitung,* and the *Perry County Democrat* (Pennsylvania). Henderson Yoakum recorded in his journal that papers were talking strongly of Houston possibilities and put in his personal note: "Had many long conversations with him on the subject. He doubtless desires to occupy that high station and believes strongly in his destiny. He is not a man of great reading, but one of the best judges of human nature in the world. We will see."[32] George Lane from Marshall and James Reily from Houston, in letters to Rusk, commended Houston's course and wished success to his nomination.[33]

[30] Blair to Van Buren, July 20, 1850, Van Buren Papers.
[31] Quoted in *Texas State Gazette,* December 7, 1850. See *ibid.,* November 16, 1850, and Rusk to David Rusk, September 1, 1850, David Rusk Papers.
[32] Note of December 18, 1850, Yoakum Papers.
[33] Reily to Rusk, January 8, 1851, and Lane to Rusk, February 3, 1851, T. J. Rusk Papers.

With the uneasy quiet resulting from the 1850 compromise, it was not public policy but party loyalty and play of personalities that were to determine the presidential lottery in 1852. Taylor was dead; Fillmore was not arousing enthusiasm; it looked like a Democratic year. The Democratic leaders, above all, wanted harmony and a "safe" man. W. O. Butler, the vice-presidential candidate in 1848, hoped to get the nod. W. L. Marcy of New York and James Buchanan of Pennsylvania were eager; so were Houston's senatorial colleagues Cass and Douglas. All except Douglas had been in public affairs for years. Campaigning began in 1848, was temporarily pushed into the background by the compromise fight in 1850, and was waged determinedly all through 1851. Early in 1851, A. J. Donelson replaced Thomas Ritchie as editor of the Washington *Union*. F. P. Blair went into the capital from Silver Springs to call on Donelson and pick up political gossip to relay to his friend Van Buren. According to one rumor, a political alliance would make Houston president and Marcy vice-president, but Blair was "mistified to find that none of us can see any high, open, direct road to immediate triumph."[34]

A "Houston Club" organized in Thomaston, Maine, to advance Houston's presidential claims, commended the Texan for his firm and decided support of the Union. The Augusta (Maine) *Age* expressed its preference for Houston and felt that the choice would rest between him and Woodbury. The Newburyport (Massachusetts) *Union* declared that Houston would "unite the democracy, North and South, East and West, more thoroughly than any other candidate."[35] The *Texas Gazette* reported Washington gossip that Democratic politicos were settling upon Cass for president and Houston for vice-president. Donelson was "Houston conscious" again when, as editor of the party organ, he was watching all political straws in the wind. Robert Tyler wrote him that the Philadelphia *Statesman* had fallen into the hands of a set of party hangers-on who professed "to be friends of General Cass, or Houston, but really are for anyone in whose name they may injure Mr. Buchanan." A few weeks earlier, Donelson had written his wife of a New Yorker who said "that Houston can beat Scott or any other opponent in New York!!!"[36]

Houston's correspondence brought him advice and counsel and estimates of the opportunities of other candidates. James Arlington Bennett,

---

[34] Blair to Van Buren, February 25, 1851, Van Buren Papers.
[35] Quoted in *Texas State Gazette*, April 26, July 19, 1851.
[36] Tyler to Donelson, May 4, 1851, and Donelson to Elizabeth Donelson, March 7, 1851, Donelson Papers.

a retired army officer in New York, had volunteered for filibustering in Mexico for Houston in 1844; in 1851 his attention was concentrated on filibustering in Cuba. Narciso López, with the aid of Southern adventurers, made unsuccessful attempts to overthrow Spanish control of the island in 1849, 1850, and 1851, and acquisition of Cuba as a part of imperialist policy and manifest destiny became to many Democrats one of the issues of the 1852 campaign. Houston was opposed to the filibuster movements,[37] but Bennett wrote him that the Cuban question "must be the *issue* on which the democratic candidates will be carried into the presidential chair" and that Houston was the candidate who could carry out the nation's wishes. Several months earlier Bennett had written Houston that Cass and Buchanan followers were pressing Douglas' name in an effort to defeat Houston and urged Houston to come campaigning in New York.[38] Democrats in Hartford were organizing a Houston Club, and E. S. Cleveland sent the Senator the Hartford *Weekly Times*, with the request for news during the Cuban struggle and the hope that they might "in '52 join in the battle cry of 'Houston and Cuba' or 'the Hero of San Jacinto' against the world."[39]

Ashbel Smith was watchful as ever. In London, at the exposition in 1851, he wrote back that in European affairs he was "only a looker on in Venice" but that he had looked into American politics as he had journeyed to New York.

From the moment of leaving Texas to the present time I have profited by every opportunity to learn public sentiment in regard to the next Presidency. Without the shadow of a doubt, public opinion at the North as well as at the South regards you as decidedly the strongest candidate of the Democratic Party; and many Whigs have expressed to me their opinion that you could be elected over any candidate whom they could bring out. . . . There will I suppose be a convention to nominate a candidate as hitherto; I found but one danger, it is the clubbing together of disappointed aspirants to defeat your nomination. Means ought to be taken to secure the attendance of the right sort of men from the several states in the next Convention.[40]

Houston was writing "not one word of politics," or so he assured Nicholas Dean, and to add emphasis: "Well, indeed, I do not talk of

<hr />

[37] Opposing Reaffirmation of the Principles of the Monroe Doctrine, March 2, 1853, *Writings*, V, 416–20; Houston to Bennett, October 18, 1844, *ibid.*, IV, 378–99.

[38] Bennett to Houston, April 3 and September 4, 1851, Domestic Correspondence.

[39] Cleveland to Houston, September 3, 1851, *ibid.*

[40] Smith to Houston, May 9, 1851, Ashbel Smith Papers.

them, I have not written of them, and if you will believe me, I think but little about them!" In answer to Dean's request to know how he could serve the Houston cause, the Senator suggested that he might correspond with such Texans as Henderson Yoakum, Hamilton Stuart, and Ebenezer Allen, but that he himself did not expect to write anything for the public eye. Politics were ripe in Huntsville in July, 1851, but Houston wrote John R. Burke that "I take no part in them."[41]

Illness in the Houston family prevented a projected trip to Dallas to make a speech on August 22, but the *Texas Gazette* of August 30 asserted that the General was not idle, for he did make speeches before the Bible and Temperance societies at Huntsville. He had taken a national stand on temperance when he defended the invitation to admit the Rev. Theobald Mathew to the Senate floor back in December of 1849. The temperance issue was not without its political possibilities and dangers. In February, 1852, Houston was the "orator of the day" at a Grand Temperance Banquet (tickets three dollars each) at Metropolitan Hall in New York. The *Herald* wrote that political movements of the Temperance Alliance in New York and New England had startled the politicians and that the action, spread from state to state, might mean a political party extending all over the Union—at once making Houston "a formidable candidate for the Presidency." The *Herald* felt that the Alliance could not have selected a more proper man.

He has sounded all the depths and shoals and quicksands and snags and sandbars of the waters of destruction. He has been gathered from the gutters . . . and has become a brilliant and shining light among the Sons of Temperance. His case is a living example of the power of an inflexible will in support of a good resolution . . . and the manly fortitude with which he has stuck to the pledge, among all the temptations of Washington, commends him to the applause of all men, of all parties, throughout the Union, and, indeed, all over the civilized world.

The *Herald,* extolling Houston as a military hero greater than Scott, as "sound as a drum" on the Negro question, and "a thousand times more available than a man who has been sober all his life," proclaimed: "The Sons of Temperance are a host—and Sam Houston is their champion."[42] There was political danger in any too definite commitment on any issue. The temperance, or "Holy Alliance," faction wanted to know

---

[41] Houston to Dean, May 8, 1851, and to Burke, July 19, 1851, *Writings,* V, 298-99, 303.

[42] Quoted in *Texas State Gazette,* March 6, 1852.

Houston's opinion of the Maine Liquor Law. The "cold water people," said the Nacogdoches *Chronicle*, "were eager to have him come out in favor of it, and the Tammany Hall folks were determined to drop him if he did so."[43]

With the approach of the presidential campaign, the Washington (Texas) *Ranger* advocated the organization of the Texas Democracy, urging the duty of the party to do its part in the contest whether or not the state furnished the candidate. The *Gazette*, on January 3, 1852, declared that if the state convention nominated Houston and that nomination was ratified by the national convention, he would receive the almost unanimous vote of Texas. The fourth resolution adopted by the state convention of January 8, 1852, was the presentation of Houston to the favorable consideration of the national party with the proviso: "While we would hail his nomination with proud satisfaction, we pledge our warm and hearty support to the nominee of the Democratic National Convention."[44] Washington D. Miller was chairman of the state central committee; Hamilton Stuart was chosen an alternate delegate to the Baltimore Convention. Houston, as a member of the Congressional delegation, was to be a delegate. F. H. Merriman wrote Smith that "if the Old Dragon is a Candidate (which the Lord grant) an alternate will be allowed to fill his seat in the Convention," and added: "The honor of being a Delegate may be something, but their work will be done with the outsiders."[45] A resolution in the Texas House of Representatives to nominate Houston for the presidency passed on January 16, but received twenty-one negative votes. The *Colorado Tribune* at Matagorda noted the action of the convention and the Legislature and commented:

Well! if we mistake not, it has been a hard pill for some of our honorable friends to swallow. But "principles" and not "men" is the cry, so there is no use in the minority struggling against a forlorn hope. It is a mistaken prediction if "Sammiwell's" most arduous advocates don't find in him ere long a few *more principles* than they bargained for.

The *Tribune* condemned the convention as a self-constituted cabal in which not a single states'-rights Democrat had "sufficient manliness to vote against the nomination of General Houston."[46]

[43] "Gen. Houston in New York," Nacogdoches *Chronicle*, March 13, 1852, T. J. Rusk Papers.

[44] Winkler, *Platforms of Political Parties in Texas*, 51.

[45] Merriman to Smith, January 21, 1852, Ashbel Smith Papers.

[46] Winkler, *Platforms of Political Parties in Texas*, 26–27, 26 n.; *Texas State Gazette*, January 17, 1852.

281

The *Item,* a Whig paper which carried as a part of its masthead the words, "Not Willing to Trust Gen. Sam Houston at the White House," was quoted in the *Gazette* but was criticized for dragging in personal prejudice when the action of the convention expressed the wishes of the majority of Texas Democrats. The *Gazette,* as the leading Democratic organ, then edited by H. P. Brewster and J. W. Hampton, carried Houston's name at its masthead as "First Choice of the Democracy of Texas for President" and listed L. D. Evans, Guy M. Bryan, George W. Smyth, and Robert S. Neighbors as candidates for electors. For three or four months the *Gazette* carried a business advertisement of the firm of Sims and Smith at Bastrop combining the presentation of Houston's name for president with a plea that their patrons settle their accounts. Not only did the paper feature reprints of Texas editorials in favor of Houston; it also copied Houston notices from the Augusta *Age* and Saco *Democrat* of Maine, the Providence *Post* of Rhode Island, the West Chester *Democrat* and *Erie County Observer* of Pennsylvania, and the *Warren Journal* of New Jersey. In general they commended Houston for his stand on the compromise, his work for the party, his undoubted patriotism, and his devotion to the principles of civil and religious liberty. Late in February the *Gazette* carried a story of a Houston dinner in Syracuse, New York, in which two of the toasts were: "Sam Houston and Wm. L. Marcy—landmarks of the democratic party of the United States" and "The health and prosperity of Sam Houston—equal to any station—he will adorn the highest."[47]

The *Gazette* also copied from the Hartford (Connecticut) *Times* of February 10, 1852, a letter from Senator Rusk to that paper. Rusk wrote that he was opposed to congressmen's abandoning their legislative duties to participate in political strife but that, since he was afraid in this case his silence might be misinterpreted, he would state "without hesitation" that he preferred his colleague General Houston "to either of the distinguished gentlemen named in connection with the approaching Presidential election."[48] The Nacogdoches *Chronicle* also carried the Rusk letter and an editorial on it: "Nothing can be more gratifying to the Democracy than to witness the two old champions of the republic standing shoulder to shoulder, bearing testimony to the merits of each other, and laboring so energetically to sustain the State for which they have fought and suffered together in days 'lang syne.' "[49]

[47] *Texas State Gazette,* January 17, 31, February 7, 28, 1852.
[48] *Ibid.,* March 13, 1852.
[49] Nacogdoches *Chronicle,* March 13, 1852.

Late in March the *Gazette* took stock of possibilities and found Houston a formidable competitor for the nomination, but noted that even in Texas several Democratic papers showed a preference for Douglas. Across the country Radcliff Hudson was expressing a big "if." "I rather fear that the old Chief will not be first at Baltimore, but if Cass & Douglas run hard against each other as now is the prospect then I think he must be taken up. I think he is the man to beat Scott. The others may be able but I feel doubtful."[50]

And what of the candidate? In October, 1851, he thought fleetingly of his platform, which would be "fit, and 'nice,'" but he had no intention of indicating any of its contents until he could do so "before the nation." To John Houston he complained of unfair treatment by Donelson in the *Union,* which gave more space to Douglas, but he foretold that he would "make 'old Tammany' ring" when he went to New York in January. He was back in the Senate on December 9 and on December 22 spoke against Foote and reaffirmation of the compromise. He denied catering for the presidency or having any petty hankerings after office.[51]

On January 5, 1852, Houston was in the Senate when Louis Kossuth was introduced to congressmen prior to starting on a cross-country tour to secure aid for Hungary in a revolt against Austria. Kossuth was reported to have been much impressed by Houston, but the Senator "was not captivated by his advent" and "played the Indian, and was wary." Kossuth's mission became an issue in the campaign; Southerners generally were hostile to him, but many German-Americans and Irish sympathized with his revolutionary cause. Houston said that he desired liberty for Hungary but did not want to disregard American obligations to other countries. Kossuth's appearance in the Senate wearing a sword offended Houston, as did Kossuth's "pecuniary" motive, for "the dollars, and the contributions, and a splendid retinue, with a body-guard, to march him through the land, were all that he cared about."[52] Houston may have objected to the limelight given the visiting foreigner who so occupied the papers to the exclusion of politicians. On January 10, 1852, Thomas Corwin wrote J. J. Crittenden:

Is Kossuth a candidate for the Presidency? Oh, you should have seen Sam

---

[50] Hudson to Smith, March 29, 1852, Ashbel Smith Papers; *Texas State Gazette,* March 20, 1852.

[51] Houston to John H. Houston, October 11, 1851, *Writings,* V, 316; Speech of December 22, 1851, *ibid.,* 332.

[52] Opposing Reaffirmation of the Principles of the Monroe Doctrine, March 2, 1853, *ibid.,* 416–18.

Houston *last night,* with a red handkerchief hanging down two feet from the
rear of his coat! He looked like the devil with a yard of brimstone on fire
in his rear. All the candidates were there and acted as if they thought themselves second fiddlers to the *great leader* of the orchestra in that *humbug
theatre.*

Civilized men are all *asses.* Your gentleman of God's making, nowadays,
is only to be found in savage life. God help us![53]

Other correspondence contained mention of Houston, much of it
favorable. Charles Sumner wrote John Bigelow on February 3, 1852:

I was won very much by Houston's conversation. With him the anti-
slavery interest would stand better than with any man who seems now among
possibilities. He is really against slavery, and has no prejudice against Free
Soilers. In other respects he is candid, liberal, and honorable. I have been
astonished to find myself so much of his inclining.[54]

F. P. Blair, who had supported Woodbury until the Judge's death in
September, 1851, turned, as did Thomas H. Benton, to support the can-
didacy of Butler of Kentucky. In disillusionment, Blair wrote to Van
Buren on March 2, 1852:

I would certainly rather see the Whigs triumph & have their corrupt
party to fight against in the Government, than our own which put us in condition of Polks & Tylers. . . . But I think we ought to press some pure man as
our candidate, as earnest of our own probity. . . . Butler surrenders—of those
before the public Houston is best—He is certainly now at war with the
Spoilers.[55]

And a congressman from Tennessee, writing of the maneuverings in
Whig ranks to choose a likely candidate and an opportune convention
date, also had commendation for a former congressman from Tennessee:

In respect to Houston, there is but one opinion with friends and foes—all
agree that if he could receive the nomination that he could be elected by a
greater majority than any other person now spoken of in connexion with
the presidency and that he is the only man in our ranks that can defeat Genl.
Scott if he is the candidate of the Whig party.[56]

Ben McCulloch, visiting at the time in the "backwoods of Tennessee,"
said that the state was as usual "on the fence & might be carried for

[53] Mrs. Chapman Coleman (ed.), *The Life of John J. Crittenden, with Selections
from His Correspondence and Speeches,* II, 38.
[54] Pierce, *Memoirs and Letters of Charles Sumner,* III, 278.
[55] Blair to Van Buren, March 2, 1852, Van Buren Papers; Milton, *The Eve of
Conflict,* 82–83.
[56] Andrew Johnson to D. T. Patterson, April 4, 1852, Johnson Papers.

284

Fillmore, but never Scott." As for himself, he hoped the Democratic Convention would make the issue "between them & a *certain Gentleman from Texas.*"[57]

Not all fellow Texans felt the same towards that "certain Gentleman from Texas." Memucan Hunt, in the East on railroad business and also as a visitor at the Military Academy at West Point, wrote back home that either Buchanan or Cass would be the Democratic nominee, for "Houston has no hope—he will only get the vote of Texas—he ranks very low at Washington."[58]

Rusk was also among the Democratic possibilities. Henderson, while assuring Rusk that he would vote for him with pleasure, used the occasion to chastise him verbally for not supporting Calhoun on the Southern Address, and said with remarkable prophecy of other candidates:

I *hate* an office seeker and have no respect for one who shapes his course, not by reason or conviction of right, but by considerations of self interest. I *fear* that Cass & Buchanan are influenced by those considerations—I *believe* that such are the motives which actuate Douglas and I *think* I *know* that such are the motives of Houston's actions. Therefore I cannot & shall not vote for Douglas or Houston & do not believe that I shall vote for either of the other two should either of them be nominated. I have for some time believed that no one of the aspirants would be nominated and I hope they will all be disappointed.[59]

Rusk was on the scene of action and wrote his honest conviction to his brother:

You would be a little astonished at the number and respectability of the men who wish to nominate me but I will not permit myself to think of such a thing. Houston is a little jealous and remarkably anxious. It will nearly kill him if he fails. I mean in good faith and sincerity to press his claims. I think he would run better than any of the other candidates and I am sure it would be better for Texas that he should be President.[60]

"O. P. Q." in the Richmond *Enquirer* advocated Houston's nomination, but Virginia sent an uninstructed delegation to Baltimore. Robert G. Scott of Richmond wrote Houston to question his stand on slavery, and Houston answered that, should he ever be placed in a position where he would have to act in the contingency presented, he would not hesitate to veto any bill which impaired the law protect-

---

[57] McCulloch to Rusk, April 24, 1852, T. J. Rusk Papers.
[58] Hunt to Duval, April 18, 1852, Domestic Correspondence.
[59] Henderson to Rusk, April 23, 1852, T. J. Rusk Papers.
[60] Rusk to David Rusk, May 19, 1852, David Rusk Papers.

ing the constitutional right of the people of the South to the "possession and enjoyment of their slave property."[61] So Houston the politician was giving assurances to Southern slaveowners even while he had the approval of free-soiler Blair and abolitionist Sumner. His mistake was in attempting to be too many things to too many people. Meantime, the *Gazette* was counting noses and deciding that on the first ballot Cass would lead, followed by Buchanan and Douglas, but that the second ballot would be the more important.[62]

The convention assembled on June 1, and balloting began on June 3 after the adoption of the two-thirds rule. On the first ballot the vote was Cass, 116; Buchanan, 93; Marcy, 27; Douglas, 20; King, 13; and Houston, 8. Forty-nine ballots were necessary; the result was the nomination of a dark horse, Franklin Pierce. The highest number of votes that Houston received was fourteen. On the last ballot the vote stood Pierce, 283; Cass, 2; Buchanan, 2; and Houston, 1. North Carolina and Georgia were the first Southern states to swing to Pierce. When the roll call reached Texas, Rusk rose to say that the nomination was acceptable to Texas and that the four Texas votes went unanimously to Pierce. Houston was quoted as saying: "An excellent nomination; it will unite the whole Democracy."[63] And the Democracy worked for Pierce against Scott, the Whig nominee. Of course there were repercussions. Andrew Johnson held that if the Tennessee delegation had worked for Houston, he could have been nominated and elected but that Tennessee sacrificed him in an effort to secure the vice-presidency for Pillow or Brown.[64]

Houston lived up to the prophecy that Donelson had made to Howell Cobb a year before the nomination: "Gen. H. when the time arrives will waive his claims most gracefully, and place himself in the hands of his friends, and campaign it for the nominees of the party."[65] He spoke for the ticket in Pennsylvania and Ohio on his way home from Baltimore, and in Texas expressed confidence of Scott's defeat and electioneered for Pierce and King at Democratic barbecues. At the same time he must have felt keen disappointment and resentment at

[61] Houston to Scott, May 29, 1852, *Writings*, V, 341.
[62] *Texas State Gazette*, May 29, 1852.
[63] *Ibid.*, June 19, July 3, 1852; *Northern Standard*, July 10, 1852.
[64] Johnson to S. Milligan, July 20, 1852, quoted in St. George L. Sioussat, "Tennessee and National Political Parties, 1850–1860," American Historical Association *Annual Report, 1914*, I, 254.
[65] U. B. Phillips (ed.), *The Correspondence of Robert Toombs, Alexander H. Stephens, and Howell Cobb*, Vol. II of American Historical Association *Annual Report, 1911*, 244–45.

the action of conventions, especially conventions which did not reflect the popular choice, and it was small wonder that he was in a mood to seek some other road to his goal—popular nomination or representation of a new party. Meantime he continued in the public eye. On January 8, 1853, he was an official guest when Stephen A. Douglas delivered the oration for the unveiling of Clark Mills's statue of Jackson in Lafayette Square in Washington. The toast offered him on that occasion was: "Gen. Sam Houston, the political creator of a republic; brought into existence by his genius, sustained by his patriotism, and consolidated by his statesmanship; his name and fame shall endure as long as time shall last." The *Gazette* considered the compliment well merited and "the truth of it known and felt by every Texan," and also carried the volunteer toast offered the other Texas senator: "Hon. Thomas J. Rusk of Texas—the distinguished statesman, the wise legislator, and the brave general."[66]

By March, 1853, Houston was angry with Pierce over insufficient patronage and threatened to begin a war on the President with the opening of the next Congress. That session brought the Kansas-Nebraska Bill and Houston's opposition to it which lost him any possible support of Southern Democrats. It also meant the immediate opening of the 1856 presidential campaign. Houston made his last long speech in opposition to the bill in the all-night session of March 3/4, 1854. Two days later Frank Burr wrote to Gideon Welles concerning the Texas Senator:

If Old Sam *should* be lucky enough to get the next nomination, it might be well for me to be here.

I had a long talk with him yesterday. He spoke, among other things, of you —said he had a high opinion of you, and would like, if you were here, to counsel with you on political subjects. As it is, he has conferred (he says) with *no one,* and he is perfectly contented to act out his own judgment. He is as firm, untroubled, light-hearted and even-tempered as he would be on a farm. He sees his points by intuition; but he can also make his propositions and deductions, step by step in detail, with the most exact logical consistency and force. He knows men pretty well—& in most things, he knows them by instinct, apparently; but he is liable to be deceived in some of them by the very generosity and magnanimity of his nature. He is intrinsically a great man. He bears acquaintance and analysis better than any other one I have met with in Washington.

Burr described Houston's impromptu speech of March 3/4 as power-

[66] *Texas State Gazette,* October 16, 23, 1852, February 19, 1853.

287

ful and eloquent—one which made Douglas and Hunter wince—and elaborated on the type of cabinet officials Houston would choose should he be president. Pierce, said Burr, could not let "his Hounds to open on Houston" because Houston had letters written by Pierce in 1852 and 1853 complimenting the Texas Senator.[67]

Houston was in Texas in April and May of 1854. His speech at Houston in defense of his Nebraska vote was described by the *Telegraph* as able and ingenious but as meeting with little sympathy from his hearers, most of whom regarded his course as indefensible or an "unprincipled bid for Northern popularity." The paper did not think that the Nebraska vote would hurt him in Texas, however, and declared:

The fact is, old Sam has beat the little giant at his own game, and to-day would get *two* votes North, for every *one* that the latter would get South, if their names were before a nominating Convention for the Presidency. On the whole, we do not see any good reason for Houston's friends, or his enemies, working themselves into a passion about this Nebraska business.[68]

Guy Bryan would not have agreed about the lack of effect of the speech at home. He visited New York late in the summer and wrote that while Houston did not stand so high as Rusk in the opinion of the Senate he still had influence and had "obtained strength in the North by his Nebraska vote but lost all his strength at home & in [the] South."[69] Hamilton Fish, senator from New York and bitter opponent of the Nebraska Bill, knew that Houston contemplated a visit in New York during the summer; so he queried Moses Grinnell, local leader of the anti-Nebraska organization, on what use could be made of the Texas Senator, but Grinnell answered that the weather was hot and he did not see how any move could be effective on behalf of Houston, especially since "our friends feel well enough, but are slow coaches."[70]

By September, 1854, Texas newspapers began to carry many items on Know-Nothingism, reflecting the growing importance of the party which was developing from the cleavage in both major parties as a result of the Nebraska issue. Many lovers of the Union had been drawn to the "splinter" group by their strong nationalistic principles. Horace Greeley, who had dubbed the Order of the Star Spangled Banner with the Know-Nothing title, drew, in his *Tribune,* the distinction between the healthy element of national feeling in the party and the unhealthy

[67] Burr to Welles, March 6, 1854, Gideon Welles Papers.
[68] Quoted in *Texas State Gazette,* May 13, 1854.
[69] Guy M. Bryan to Austin Bryan, August 2, 1854, Bryan Papers.
[70] Grinnell to Fish, June 25, 1854; Fish to Grinnell, June 26, 1854; and Grinnell to Fish, June 28, 1854, Hamilton Fish Papers.

element of antialien, anti-Catholic prejudice. A sort of natural sympathy among temperance men, antislavery men, Whigs, and Northern Know-Nothings developed into a temporary cohesion.

In the fall elections in 1854, at the high tide of the movement, the Know-Nothings won in Pennsylvania and Massachusetts and joined the anti-Nebraska fusion party to carry the governorship and every Congressional district in Maine. The party elected 9 governors and 104 of the 234 members of the national House of Representatives. In Pierce's own state of New Hampshire the Democratic majority in the House was wiped out, and John P. Hale, Pierce's unrelenting opponent, was sent to the Senate. Edmund Burke, unofficial campaign manager for Pierce in the election of 1852, turned against the President by January, 1854, and helped Houston take his war against Pierce into the enemy's own state. Burke was the orator of the occasion when the Democratic General Committee of New Hampshire met at Concord on October 11, 1854, and nominated Houston as "the people's candidate for the office of the President of the United States to be supported in the election which is to take place in 1856." Burke's address, "To the People of the State of New Hampshire, and of the United States," condemned the Pierce administration and expressed the decision of the New Hampshire committee that the only way to save the Democratic party was the immediate nomination by the people of a distinguished and experienced statesman who could arrest demoralization of the party and consolidate its elements. The address went on to declare that nomination by convention, like nomination by caucus, had become obsolete and that the constitutional right to choose the President must be restored to the people. Burke's sketch of Houston's career was intended to show that as a Union man he would not let the nation be dissevered either by fanaticism or by unjustifiable rebellion. To implement the nomination, San Jacinto clubs were to be organized in every district in the nation.

Burke's speech was used by Lester for the conclusion of his *Life of Sam Houston: The Only Authentic Memoir of Him Ever Published* in a revised version printed by J. C. Derby in New York in 1855. Lester sent Houston a copy of the new edition with a letter reporting frequent conversations with Burke, who had introduced Houston's name throughout New Hampshire "as the most perfect impersonation of the mythical 'Sam.' "[11] Having no political talent within their own fold, the

[11] C. Edwards Lester to Houston, March 28, 1855, Houston Unpublished Correspondence, VI.

nativists were offering bait to men of other camps, and Millard Fillmore and Houston were frequently mentioned. Burke's address in October, 1854, had been to Democrats; by 1855 he was making Houston the personification of Know-Nothingism. The "shift in the wind" may have been in terminology only, but others were curious about a possible Houston shift. Douglas had been met with jeers and burning effigies and indignity in Chicago in September, 1854, when he went home to try to justify his Nebraska Bill to an antislavery constituency. The next month Abraham Lincoln, at Springfield, received a letter from the *Journal* office in Chicago:

Douglas came to town last night pretending to have the ague, & probably cannot be induced to speak here again. Gen. Cass is here & is announced to speak this evening but it will be a very slim crowd. Crittenden of Ky. is also here & has been for several days, & I learn that *Houston* & *Bell* are expected soon. What the movement is, I don't know, perhaps it is all accidental, but it looks to me very much as if there was going to be a shift in the wind.[72]

In Texas, Gail Borden heard rumors of a Houston shift and wrote Ashbel Smith: "Understand that our old friend Sam Houston is a 'Know-Nothing' Baptist. Wonder what Stuart will say. I am glad to learn that the Old Hero has come out on the side of Christianity."[73]

The *Gazette* did not yet associate Houston with Know-Nothingism, but it did take cognizance that he was losing ground while Rusk was gaining universal popularity and influential friends among all parties. Noting the opprobrium which had greeted Douglas in Illinois, the paper pointed to the respect and esteem which greeted Houston in Texas, even though few citizens had approved his course, and took occasion "to mark the contrast between the sober descendants of the pilgrim puritans, and the wild and excitable people of the south."[74]

Houston made several Senate speeches after he got back to Washington in January, 1855, but he was away from his post enough for Rusk to complain: "Houston does little else but electioneer for the Presidency and as usual the work falls on me. The abolitionists are gaining ground within the last few days. They have elected four new senators."[75] Radcliff Hudson apparently thought the electioneering success-

---

[72] Richard L. Wilson to Lincoln, October 20, 1854, from *The Lincoln Papers* (I, 188–89), by David C. Mearns, copyright 1948 by David C. Mearns and reprinted by permission of Doubleday and Company, Inc.

[73] Borden to Smith, December 5, 1854, Ashbel Smith Papers.

[74] *Texas State Gazette*, November 11, 1854.

[75] Rusk to David Rusk, February 10, 1855, David Rusk Papers.

ful, for he wrote that he would not be surprised if Illinois went for Houston. W. W. Leland, another Smith correspondent, was "bound to go his pile on Old Sam," who was the favorite in Ohio and the Middle West and in New York, where all were "up in arms for our friend Houston."[76] New Yorker Preston King balanced Houston's generosity, integrity, shrewdness, good judgment, and self-reliance against his vanity and obstinacy and decided there was "none within the range of possible candidates that I would trust so soon as Houston."[77]

Electioneering took Houston to Boston to make a Washington's Birthday speech at Tremont Temple before the Anti-Slavery Society. His friends tried to warn him that he was making a mistake and handed him a note as he boarded the New York train for Boston. In reply he thanked them for advice but said that he must go on because "to be honest and fear not is the right path." He then expressed his creed: "I would not conceal an honest opinion for the Presidency. If I were [to], I could not enjoy the office, and worse than that, I should blame myself. I know well it is a risk, but it is for the harmony of the Union, if perchance I may benefit it."[78] Knowingly, he took the risk of further antagonizing his own people. He began his Boston speech with the statement that despite his distance from home he was addressing his countrymen and felt confident in delivering sentiments from an honest heart prompted by honest convictions of experience. Identifying himself as a Southern man, he explained the history and economic basis of the slavery institution and made a magnificent plea for the preservation of the Union.[79] The very fact that he had been willing to talk to abolitionists weighed against him in Texas and was not without consequence elsewhere. Leland wrote from New York: "I believe it done him harm by going on to Boston but yet he will come out ahead."[80]

Houston, characteristically, was not trusting his left hand to know what his right hand was doing. While others discussed his chances as a nominee, he went home to make a speech at Nacogdoches, declaring that he was about to retire to private life and interpolating a disclaimer: "I have been accused of catering to the Presidency. Why need I want the Presidency? I have twice been President, and although

[76] Hudson to Smith, February 12, 1855, and Leland to Smith, February 13 and March 26, 1855, Ashbel Smith Papers.
[77] King to Welles, April 23, 1855, Welles Papers.
[78] To Dear General (probably J. A. Bennett), February 20, 1855, *Writings*, VI, 166–67.
[79] *Texas State Gazette*, March 31, May 12, 1855.
[80] Leland to Smith, June 26, 1855, Ashbel Smith Papers.

not on as large a theatre as the U. S., yet the future will show that no President of the United States has ever had the opportunity of doing as much for his country, as I could have done for Texas."[81]

The *Texas Gazette,* on the day after the Nacogdoches talk, listed newspapers supporting him for the 1856 campaign: the *American Watchman* of Lock Haven, Pennsylvania; the *People's Advocate* of New Bloomfield, Pennsylvania; the *State Capital Reporter* of Concord, New Hampshire; the *Gazette* of Lancaster, Ohio; and the *Southern Illinoisan* of Shawneetown. The *Illinoism* had ended an editorial:

That he will be elected President in 1856, we sincerely and candidly believe, and all that is necessary on the part of the people of the United States, to bring about this desirable object, is for them to raise a united voice, and in their might and right say to the political demagogues and political tricksters to stand aside, we know for whom to vote, we know your purpose and occupation—we don't desire your advice—we are determined to manage this canvass for ourselves. "Old Sam" is the man for the crisis—he is the man for the people—we can and will elect him. We say success to the Hero of San Jacinto.[82]

His support of the Know-Nothings in the Texas campaign of 1855 destroyed Houston's last hope of Democratic support in his own state. In August, the *Gazette* played on what had become a familiar theme— the Texas Senator was trying to sell the religious and civil liberties of his former companions for abolition and free-soil votes for the presidency and had deserted the party that had refused to nominate him. But, proclaimed editor John Marshall: "Gen. Houston has not yet, and God knows never will supplant the Pantheon with a toadstool—the old Hickory tree, with a Jonah's gourd of a single night! When he talks of the pulsations of the American heart, we will point to the vote of his own town and that of his own State! The voice of America is the voice of its cherished Democracy."[83]

Houston's rumored break with his party aroused varied reactions. Rusk, whose own name was more and more mentioned for the Democratic nomination, heard from a correspondent in New York: "I would have cheerfully supported Genl. Houston but the Know Nothings claim him as their property, which I am sorry for, as I have always respected Genl. Houston—but am not in favor of Know Nothingism." Radcliff Hudson wrote from Illinois:

[81] Speech at Nacogdoches, May 11, 1855, *Writings,* VI, 183.
[82] Quoted in *Texas State Gazette,* May 12, 1855.
[83] *Ibid.,* August 18, 1855.

292

Is it a fact that Gen. Houston has avowed himself a Know-Nothing? He is a much better judge of parties—but it strikes me he has cast himself once to win & *now* or *never*. I am as ever his strong supporter & Judge Trumbull our newly elected Senator from this state says he is the only democrat that stands any chance. I even think he would carry this state against Douglas himself, as the state is democratic but still anti-Nebraska.[84]

The St. Louis *Republican* accused Houston of "being taken with an itinerating disposition" every time a vote was to be taken in the Senate on a great political question and of delivering "prosy lectures about the Indians, or upon temperance or some other question not calculated to damage his political prospects." Those prospects the paper did not consider bright. "His recent coquetting with the Know Nothing party awfully damaged his reputation with the Democracy, and left him no hope in that quarter; while the recent disasters of the American party in the Southern States . . . leave little hope of preferment growing out of the possible success of that party in the coming election."[85]

In his speech at the Know-Nothing barbecue at Austin, Houston ridiculed the accusation that he had pandered to the favor of abolitionism and courted the presidency. For one thing the office would only bring on new cares and anxieties. The *Gazette* was not impressed, and its sarcastic review of the speech described his reception as cool and formal and promised that the "cold norther" which had accompanied the General to Austin would attend him in his Southern home and whisper to him:

> O will you, will you
> Come to the White House![86]

After a sort of "trial balloon" convention held at Philadelphia in June, 1855, the Know-Nothings lost ground in state after state and had only forty-three members in the House of the Thirty-fourth Congress. The party's national council met in Philadelphia five days before the national nominating convention was scheduled for February 22, 1856. The council quarreled over the slavery issue, as did the convention, most Northerners wishing to postpone naming of a presidential candidate until July. The Southerners and a Northern minority insisted on an immediate nomination.[87] Parson Brownlow of Tennessee had prophesied:

[84] Isaiah Rynders to Rusk, July 6, 1855, T. J. Rusk Papers; Hudson to Smith, September 11, 1855, Ashbel Smith Papers.
[85] Quoted in *Texas State Gazette*, September 22, 1855.
[86] Speech at Austin, November 23, 1855, *Writings*, VI, 223; *Texas State Gazette*, November 24, 1855.
[87] Nevins, *Ordeal of the Union*, II, 467.

"They will nominate beyond all doubt, and whoever they nominate, we will either have to go for, or dispute and divide, which will ensure defeat."[88] Texans were with the North in wishing the convention adjourned until June or July.[89]

The Texas delegates to the national convention included S. W. Sims, J. W. Waddell, Ben Epperson, M. D. Whaley, T. A. Harrison, and E. R. Peck. On February 8, 1856, the Washington *American* wrote that Houston's prospects for the presidency, long obscured, seemed to be gaining, and quoted men from Mississippi and Tennessee as saying that he was the most available man for the American party because of his "power with the masses." There was no mention of Texas in any of the news reports of the convention until February 22, when W. B. Tower of Texas was listed on the Committee on Credentials, but the state had no delegates on the floor. On February 23 that committee listed four delegates from Texas present, one being W. P. Santbaudh. A quarrel over declaration of principles prevented any balloting on candidates until February 25. Various Southerners wanted a declaration condemning antislavery and anti-Nebraska propaganda; Northern delegates refused. On the first ballot, Millard Fillmore, who had never attended a Know-Nothing meeting and was then absent in Europe, received 71 votes. Houston received 6 of the 143 votes cast. The South and New York were satisfied; the Northern men, seventy-one strong, withdrew. On the final ballot Fillmore received 179 votes and Houston 3.

The New York *Tribune* wrote that news of the nomination fell like a wet blanket on Americans in Washington. Had the candidate been the right man, said the *Tribune,* he might have carried New York; but Fillmore, "hackneyed and discarded politician," had no chance at all.[90] A. J. Donelson was nominated for vice-president. Rusk wrote his brother: "We have no news here except that Fillmore and Donelson have been nominated by the Know-Nothings. Houston is disappointed and I think will refuse to support the ticket."[91]

The *Gazette* correspondent in Washington reported to Marshall and Oldham that L. D. Evans did not make the speech he had prepared in favor of Houston because "he did not wish to play the part of riding on the tail of a quarter nag," and that after the first vote "Texas gave Sam the go by." A month later the same correspondent wrote that a general good feeling prevailed between Northern and Southern Know-Nothings,

---

[88] W. G. Brownlow to John Bell, January 15, 1856, John Bell Papers.
[89] Winkler, *Platforms of Political Parties in Texas,* 71.
[90] New York *Daily Tribune,* February 18–27, 1856.
[91] Rusk to David Rusk, February 29, 1856, David Rusk Papers.

with Hale of New Hampshire, Houston of Texas, Seward of New York, and Bell of Tennessee on excellent terms. It was thought, he wrote, that if the election was carried to the House, the Democratic party could be defeated.[92]

The Democrats nominated James Buchanan. James G. Blaine, looking back on the events a quarter of a century later, said that the South refused to present any of its statesmen but gave the Northern Democrats every advantage in "waging a warfare in which the fruits of victory were wholly to be enjoyed by the South." According to Blaine:

If they had wished it, they could have nominated a Southern candidate who was at that moment far stronger than any other man in the Democratic party. . . . All these facts combined—his romantic history, his unflinching steadiness of purpose, his unswerving devotion to the Union—would have made him an irresistibly strong candidate had he been presented. But the very sources of his strength were the sources of his weakness. His nomination would have been a rebuke to every man who had voted for the repeal of the Missouri Compromise, and, rather than submit to that, the Southern Democrats, and Northern Democrats like Pierce and Douglas and Cass, would accept defeat. Victory with Houston would be their condemnation. But in rejecting him they lost in large degree the opportunity to recover the strength and popularity and power of the Democratic party which had all been forfeited by the maladministration of Pierce.[93]

Houston left Congress for a visit home in May, 1856, before the meeting of the Democratic Convention. He had not definitely committed himself on what stand he would take, but the New York *Herald* brought him out as an independent candidate for the presidency. Anti-Houston papers in Texas had a field day in sarcasm. The *Texas Republican* at Marshall declared that he had had to come out "on his own hook" after having failed by following all "popular humbugs, clap-traps, fanaticisms and other isms of the day to court popular favor," and suggested that P. T. Barnum would make him a good running mate. The Dallas *Herald* described Houston as the disappointed dupe of ambition who lived for eight years on the hope of a convention nomination and now sought to set at defiance the established customs of parties because "the rules that regulated these lesser lights are unfitted for this new star of the first magnitude that now pursues its wayward and erratic course through the political heavens." After Houston confided to friends at Nacog-

[92] *Texas State Gazette*, March 22, April 17, 1856.
[93] James G. Blaine, *Twenty Years of Congress: From Lincoln to Garfield. With a Review of the Events Which Led to the Political Revolution of 1860*, I, 124–25.

doches that he was not optimistic about the success of the American party ticket, and assuredly he knew enough of politics not to be confident of its chances, the *Gazette* declared that he had "turned state's evidence against the Know-Nothing party." According to the vitriolic editorial: "No man has ever played a more desperate game for the Presidency than Houston, and none have been more rightfully rebuked by disappointment. He is the last man to talk about 'selfish politicians.' "[94]

On July 12, in a letter to John Hancock, Houston declared that he would support the American nominees for they were good men, the only men in nomination "who do most assuredly claim the cordial support of men who are true-hearted Americans—Democrats and Whigs." He described the Republican platform and principles as sectional, praised Donelson for his love of Union, and said that Fillmore's services had been satisfactory.[95]

The Republicans, at Philadelphia in June, chose John C. Frémont as their nominee. The party's campaign kit contained a booklet called *The Republican Scrap Book*, which included the platform and extracts from various writings to show "the nature and designs of the slave oligarchy." Pages 12 and 13 of the pamphlet were devoted to a section called "Gen. Sam Houston on the Presidency," which was a copy of most of Houston's letter to Hancock but omitted his comments on the Republican party save for the statement that its platform and principles were sectional. Two other pages carried a New York *Post* editorial on Houston entitled "What Makes a Sectional Candidate?"[96] In the opposite camp the *Know-Nothing Almanac and True Americans' Manual for 1856* had an article entitled "Sam Houston on Americanism," quotations from his Independence letter of July 24, 1855.[97]

The Democratic National Committee was also issuing campaign literature expressing its confidence in Buchanan. After Houston, in a speech on August 30, commended the American party because its object was to "cement the Union of the States—to connect them by indissolvable bonds"—and announced that he would acquiesce in the people's mandate, whoever was elected, one of the workers sent a note to Rusk from the Democratic headquarters: "Your Colleague gave us a day or so ago in the Senate a very earnest speech in favor of M. F. and the American

---

[94] *Texas Republican*, May 31, 1856; Dallas *Herald*, May 31, 1856; *Texas State Gazette*, June 7, 1856.

[95] Houston to Hancock, July 21, 1856, *Writings*, VI, 360–61.

[96] *Republican Scrap Book* (1856), in Blair Family Papers.

[97] W. S. Tisdale (ed.), *Know-Nothing Almanac and True Americans' Manual for 1856*, 33.

party. I could but feel a deep regret in seeing him in so mortifying a position."[98]

While at home in the fall of 1856, the Senator made speeches for Fillmore at Huntsville, Nacogdoches, Brenham, and Livingston. On October 20 he wrote Smith, who was speaking for the Democratic ticket, that he was satisfied that "modern Democracy . . . must go to the wall," and said: "I hope that Fremont will not be elected, but if unfortunately such should be our doom, I cannot perceive what worse he can do, than Pierce has done." The week of the national election he wrote Rusk: "I am truly anxious to see you, and not altogether at rest on the subject of [the] Presidential election. I dread the success of the Black Republicans."[99] Buchanan and the Democrats were victorious in 1856. Houston had four more years to dread the success of the "Black Republicans."

During those four years he must also decide on his own future. He would not be sent back to the Senate. Governor he might be, but the same group who opposed him for the Senate would oppose him for the governorship. He talked of retiring and raising sheep, but his family was large and his savings negligible. Besides, that shrewd and active brain was accustomed to deal with national problems, and there was that one unrealized ambition. During those four years his name continued to be newsworthy politically, and in 1860 it was weighed by four political factions for its merit nomination-wise. His own plan, as it evolved, was larger than any faction. He would not run on any platform, but he would be so in demand by the people that he would be chosen outside of any party. The new stage upon which he would enact his moves would be south of the Rio Grande, where he would establish a protectorate over Mexico. His project has been analyzed definitively by Walter P. Webb in his *Texas Rangers*: "To be President of the United States, to be the savior of the Union, and to establish a protectorate over Mexico were the principal features of one grand plan. In this trinity of his ambition, the protectorate over Mexico seems to have been the central figure which supported the other two."[100]

When Houston conceived the idea there is nothing in his papers to indicate. Back in the days of his presidency in Texas, when Washington D. Miller put so many words in the President's mouth, the seed of the protectorate concept may have been planted by a Miller letter. Writing at the time of threatened Mexican invasion in February, 1842,

[98] Walter Lenox to Rusk, September 2, 1856, T. J. Rusk Papers.

[99] Houston to Smith, October 20, 1856, and to Rusk, November 8, 1856, *Writings*, VI, 394–95.

[100] *The Texas Rangers: A Century of Frontier Defense*, 197.

Miller had been youthfully lyrical in his vision of Houston as the "champion of civilization" cutting the "meshes of priestly bigotry and slavish ignorance" in Mexico.[101] Realistic Houston was having none of such an ill-timed idea in 1842. Ultimate and perhaps permanent invasion he may have considered inevitable as a result of what, during the Mexican War, he described as "an instinct in the American people which impels them onward, which will lead them to pervade this continent."[102]

By 1854 that urge of manifest destiny in Texas took a somewhat nebulous form in a secret order known as the "Lone Star of the West," whose members talked mysteriously of "orange groves and vine clad hills" and of the "gem of the Antilles."[103] At the height of Houston's gubernatorial campaign of 1857, the *Gazette* ran an editorial entitled "Members Will Understand," indicating that Houston was a member of the Lone Star association, which he had "prostituted for Know Nothing purposes."[104] After his defeat in that campaign, there was speculation about his political future. A rumor in San Antonio that he would establish residence in Mexico was background for a Paschal editorial in the *Intelligencer* stating that Houston was the "only man who could disarm the jealousies of the North against filibustering" and that the measure of his success would be the number of "adventurous spirits" who might follow him in a "novel voyage up Salt River."[105]

This was a Texas inkling of the Houston idea formally stated on February 16, 1858, when he introduced into the Senate a resolution that the Committee on Foreign Relations investigate the establishment of a protectorate over Mexico, Nicaragua, Costa Rica, Guatemala, Honduras, and San Salvador, "in such form and to such extent as shall be necessary to secure to the people of said States the blessings of good and stable republican government."[106] There was startled reaction at the national level. Henry Wilson of Massachusetts described the resolution as "of a most extraordinary character . . . intended to encourage that spirit of filibustering which has disgraced this country."[107] In April, Houston moved to amend his resolution to confine the proposed protectorate to Mexico, then in the throes of its fourteenth revolution, because the Central American states were in better condition than "our poor, distracted,

---

[101] Miller to Houston, February 16, 1842, Miller Papers.
[102] Speech on Boundary of Texas, March 19, 1848, *Writings*, V, 34.
[103] *Texas State Gazette*, July 1, 1854.
[104] *State Gazette for the Campaign*, July 25, 1857.
[105] *Southern Intelligencer*, September 9, 1857.
[106] Resolution Proposing Protectorate, February 16, 1858, *Writings*, VII, 33–34.
[107] *Congressional Globe*, 35 Cong., 1 sess. (1857/58), 735–36.

adjoining neighbor," with whom "good neighborhood" was "next to an impossibility." In his speech on the substitute proposal Houston outlined the expenditure which would be involved, the expense to be "defrayed by the protected." Five thousand reliable troops would insure the establishment and preservation of internal order, and a good police force would subdue bandits. He related Mexican failure to meet payments due British bondholders and intimated that England would be pleased to have Mexican finances stabilized. He also made a veiled threat to "unfurl again the banner of the 'lone star.' "[108] This Houston brand of secession was described by one of his successors as separation, "not by naked revolution, but through violation of the instrument of union and by virtue of its terms and according to its spirit."[109]

Subsequent efforts to get a vote on his resolution brought rebuke and repartee from other senators. Wilson called the move a "gross insult to Mexico." Hale amused the Senate when he proposed an amendment of his own—"to extend the same inquiries to the Canadas and the other British possessions in our continent." Only Toombs of Georgia concurred, saying that he was prepared to adopt Houston's resolution as national policy. Mason of Virginia, a member of the Foreign Relations Committee, thought the resolution was an indignity to the Latin American states. With such opposition from the Foreign Relations Committee, Houston asked for a committee of seven to serve as "adopted father for his bantling."[110] Failing to secure either the special committee or a vote on his resolution, Houston threatened independent Texas action. Warning that government inaction might cause humane men to undertake the enterprise as a duty to humanity, he asserted that he would not feel restrained "at any age" to "arrest the cruelties on, and to stop the murders of, a defenseless people."[111]

The leopard had not changed his spots, nor Houston his stand, when he was back for the short session of the Thirty-fifth Congress and debating the Pacific railroad bill. Wilson attacked the Gadsden Purchase and the proposed El Paso to San Diego route as a proslavery scheme to conquer Mexico and Central America, and Houston retorted that he would accept the proposition—"take the country, the mines included, and construct the railroad."[112] Minimizing any fear of California's alienation from

---

[108] Favoring a Protectorate over Mexico, April 20, 1858, *Writings*, VII, 84–99.

[109] Charles A. Culberson, "General Sam Houston and Secession," *Scribner's Magazine*, XXXIX (May, 1906), 588–89.

[110] *Congressional Globe*, 35 Cong., 1 sess. (1857/58), Part I, 36, 1891–92.

[111] Concerning a Mexican Protectorate, June 2, 1858, *Writings*, VII, 131.

[112] *Congressional Globe*, 35 Cong., 2 sess. (1858/59), Appendix, 291.

the Union, he conjectured that the Texas border would extend to the city of Mexico by the time California reached it along the Pacific coast "and we shall be harmoniously reunited."[113]

While the Senate was eschewing such blatant expansionism, the newspapers in Houston's own bailiwick were speculating on the protectorate. The Dallas *Herald* opined that Houston or some other gallant spirit must take the lead in regenerating Mexico. The *Intelligencer*, with more "inside" information, took up the theme that London holders of Mexican bonds approved the measure.[114] And apparently the *Intelligencer* was correct. With reservations, the bondholders did approve. On May 26, 1858, they had received a letter from Houston enclosing his speech of April 20 entitled "Favoring a Protectorate over Mexico." They held a meeting on May 28, with David Robertson acting as chairman, and adopted a resolution stating that the meeting desired "to express its unanimous approval of the principles of General Houston's proposal . . . as explained in his printed speech as far as the Mexican bondholders are concerned." Their reservation was a reminder to Houston that the Mexican revenue was pledged and mortgaged for the debt to England and that arrears of interest must be made up out of Mexican general revenue whether Mexico continued as an independent republic or went under the protection of the United States. Robertson was instructed to convey the resolution to Houston and "to communicate generally with him on the subject in reply to his letter." The London *Times* printed the proceedings of the meeting, and the item was carried by the New York *Times* on June 18, 1858.

In speeches of the late summer and early fall of 1858, Houston presented his protectorate plan to Texas audiences as a peculiarly Southern measure which was commended by sagacious statesmen and feared by "timid and time-serving politicians." He predicted that the wisdom of the project would eventually be recognized and that, like the annexation of Texas, it would be taken up by the masses and carried over the heads of politicians.[115] While waiting for that "action of the masses," he declared himself without any definite intentions, writing to Dr. Smith that he had none, "unless he went to Mexico to take a look at the interior of the 'Halls of the Montezumas.'"

That his plans were tentative, while "sick, weary and disgusted" he

[113] Remarks on the Pacific Railroad Bill, January 27, 1859, *Writings*, VII, 223.

[114] Dallas *Herald*, July 10, August 21, 1858; *Southern Intelligencer*, July 14, August 11, 1858.

[115] Speech at Danville, September 11, 1858, *Writings*, VII, 184; Dallas *Herald*, September 1, 1858; *Southern Intelligencer*, October 10, 1858.

faced his last weeks in the Senate, is indicated in a letter revealing his state of indecision to his wife:

At this moment, I need your society and advice more than I have ever done, but as it is not at hand, I will make no decision, whatever, until I can see you on the subject. *In confidence,* I tell you that matter relates to the "Protectorate." I can entertain no proposition, with any pleasure, that even blinks at a temporary separation from you. I hope you will not desire it. And I am sure that you would not be willing, tho' you might consent to it, to separate from any of the children, tho' you might have Sam, Nannie, & Willie with you. You will be able, from what I premise, to form some idea as to the subject on which I wish to see you, & confer with you about.[116]

In his only speech of the 1859 gubernatorial campaign, Houston gave considerable space to the protectorate as a humanitarian project which would secure Texas against Indians on the Mexican border, provide for the reclamation of escaped slaves, achieve American expansion, and "build us up in proud defiance of the rest of the world, a nationality in which freedom exists and strength to maintain it." At the same time he denied that he was a friend of filibustering as the term was popularly understood, and protested that he was opposed to resistance to the laws. He depicted Mexican weakness, gave assurance that the protectorate would be self-supporting, and said that President Buchanan's annual message had sanctioned such a move.[117]

Houston was elected governor in August, 1859, and took office in December. In his inaugural he stated that the restoration of order and the establishment of good government in Mexico were a federal problem, but added a reminder: "Should no change take place in Mexico, restraining their disorders, and should they extend to this side of the Rio Grande, it will demand of the Executive of the State the exercise of its fullest powers, if needful, to protect our citizens, and vindicate the honor of our State."[118]

Mexican disorders at the moment presented a tailor-made opportunity for one who had the inclination and the resources to intervene. The Mexican liberals under Benito Juárez were struggling to overthrow the reactionary government of General Miguel Miramón, and the central government was weakened. At Texas' back door, actually inside that door at Brownsville, the Juan Cortinas war was at its height and offered not only opportunity but excuse. Houston had the inclination; he

[116] Houston to Margaret Lea Houston, January 29, 1859, *Writings*, VII, 225.
[117] Speech at Nacogdoches, July 9, 1859, *ibid.*, 360–63.
[118] Inaugural Address, December 21, 1859, *ibid.*, 383.

thought he knew where he could get the money; he must think in terms of men and ammunition. Webb's analysis of Houston's "grand plan" presents in bold and singularly clear outline the ingenious tactics to get a military force and supplies for that force. The central corps of his troops would be the Texas Rangers plus groups of minutemen raised in the frontier counties. These would be augmented with Indian troops, who would be won by treaty and gift and the old Houston magic. There might be Mexican recruits from the Cortinas followers.

Cortinas had captured Brownsville on September 28, 1859. In October and November he defeated the Brownsville local guard and a force of Texas Rangers under W. G. Tobin and became the champion of the Mexicans of the Rio Grande area. His proclamation of November 23 stated his grievances and indicated that he expected help from Texas, where he said a society had been organized that would devote itself to improving the unhappy condition of Mexican residents. Mexicans of Texas would "repose their lot" under the good sentiments of Governor-elect Houston, who would give them legal protection as soon as he took office.[119] The federal government had moved in the Cortinas affair on November 15, 1859, when General David E. Twiggs had ordered Major S. P. Heintzelman from San Antonio to the Rio Grande "to hunt up Cortinas & his band of marauders & not to follow them into Mexico unless in 'hot pursuit.' "[120] John S. Ford of the Texas Rangers rode in the same buggy in which Heintzelman left San Antonio. Heintzelman soon decided that some Brownsville citizens protested too much, and noted on December 17 that the grand jury's report of disturbances in Cameron County portrayed a lamentable state of affairs along "with much that is buncombe."

On December 27, 1859, six days after Houston's inauguration, Ford's Rangers and Heintzelman's regulars, at Rio Grande City, scattered Cortinas' army and drove its leader into Mexico. The next day Houston issued a proclamation ordering armed bands to disperse and appealing to citizens of the Rio Grande section to cease disorders. On January 2, 1860, he appointed Angel Navarro III and Robert H. Taylor as commissioners to study the disturbances on the river and to muster in or disband Texas troops in accordance with the advice of the United States Army officers in command. The Governor's message to the Legislature on January 13 expressed his confidence in the federal government's ade-

[119] "Difficulties on the Southwest Frontier," *House Exec. Doc. 52* (Serial No. 1050), 36 Cong., 1 sess., 79–82; Webb, *Texas Rangers*, 183.
[120] Samuel Peter Heintzelman Journal, November 15, 1859.

quate control of the situation.[121] Tobin's Rangers had already been mustered out, and the rangers under Ford and John Littleton were placed under Heintzelman's command. With Cortinas' retirement to the interior after the La Bolsa fight, the rangers under Ford and United States Cavalry under Captain George Stoneman continued to scout the border with occasional raids across the river until the arrival of Robert E. Lee to take command. Lee had orders to stop the depredations and, if necessary, to pursue the Mexicans beyond the limits of the United States. Heintzelman, tired of the whole affair and resentful of Lee's expanded authority after his own efforts had actually settled matters, wrote in his journal on April 4 that "if I stay here till Cortinas is caught it will be some time before I leave this frontier; but if only until the troubles are over I could leave now." The next week he had a self-congratulatory entry: "I find that my reports have killed the Governor's plans. I thought that I would be in time for him. He has published a kind of a proclamation. He has also sent a sort of a commission & addressed Col. Lee to know whether the Texas troops will be any longer wanted. I told him no and I suppose that will be the reply."[122]

The Texas Rangers were sent to Goliad for mustering-out orders on March 24, 1860.[123] A month earlier, Houston, acting through Pryor Lea and his brother Albert M. Lea, had sounded out Robert E. Lee on another matter—whether or not he would be "willing to aid . . . to pacificate Mexico," probably in the role of "protector," if Houston became president. Albert M. Lea's report was that Lee would not touch vulgar filibustering and would not make any move against Mexico not in conformity with the law and Constitution. Colonel Lee's own words were: "I have no doubt that arrangements will be made to maintain the rights and peace of Texas, and I hope in conformity to the Constitution and laws of the country. It will give me great pleasure to do all in my power to support both."[124]

Trouble on the Rio Grande was thus potential, not actual, from the beginning of Houston's governorship, but as an international situation it could be used to stimulate national interest. Another basis for appeals to the national government was the unrest on the Indian frontier. Bloody

---

[121] Proclamation of December 28, 1859, Orders to Navarro and Taylor, January 2, 1860, Message to Legislature, January 13, 1860, Writings, VII, 389–90, 395–96, 403–11.

[122] Heintzelman Journal, April 4–16, 1860.

[123] Houston to John S. Ford, March 24, 1860, Writings, VII, 541.

[124] A. M. Lea to Houston, February 24 and April 3, 1860, and Lee to A. M. Lea, March 1, 1860, Governors' Letters.

Indian wars of 1858 and 1859 were partially ended when the Texas reserve Indians were moved north of Red River to Indian Territory, but either those reserve Indians or wild Indians on the northern frontier were making sporadic raids during the early months of the Houston administration. Instead of following his traditional course of posting rangers to intercept the raiders, the Governor adopted an energetic course against them and had a force of over five hundred men on the frontier by the end of March, 1860. In addition, he had ordered a company organized in each of the twenty-three frontier counties, so that his potential force was over eight hundred men. To justify his collection of arms on the frontier and his request for equipment from the federal government, he painted a dark picture of Indian depredations, with Robert E. Lee corroborating the fact that the troops then available were insufficient to guard against the Indians. At the same time that the Governor was directing Middleton T. Johnson on a somewhat haphazard and mismanaged expedition into the Indian country, apparently to keep the rangers organized and on the alert, he was suggesting the establishment of a Texas agency to grant Indian annuities and be the scene of an Indian council which he would attend in April or May, 1860. The federal government would not fall in with his plans.[125]

Washington, even in the tense months leading up to the nominating conventions of 1860, was conscious of the Texas situation, and Houston moved to make the awareness acute. In February he sent Forbes Britton of the Texas Senate with messages to Secretary of War John B. Floyd and President Buchanan. Deploring the situation on the Texas border, Houston wrote that he was trying "to avoid any course which might raise a question as to the propriety of his action" but that in a short time he might have to resort to self-defense to protect his fellow citizens. He wished to defer to action of the national government, but if "matters new and startling" arose, he might have not only to repel aggressions but to adopt measures to prevent the recurrence of similar inroads. Despite her embarrassed financial condition, Texas could muster ten thousand men in thirty days. Could she hope for aid from Washington? Signing the letter to Floyd, Houston penned a briefer one to Ben McCulloch: "There will be stirring times on the Rio Grande ere long. What are you doing? See the President and the Secretary of War." McCulloch's answer was by wire on February 21: "You will soon hear from the government. I am at all times ready to serve Texas."[126]

[125] Webb, *Texas Rangers*, 197–203, 212–13.
[126] Houston to Floyd, February 13, 1860, and to McCulloch, February 13, 1860,

On his arrival in Washington on February 29, Britton went immediately to Secretary Floyd's office and had Houston's message sent in to a council meeting of the War Department. That night the President sent for Britton and asked whether or not Houston intended an invasion of Mexico. Britton's reply was that Houston would make his decision when he got to the frontier and that he was not raising troops for invasion but for defense of Texas, believing that the President would apply such remedies as would render Texas action unnecessary. Buchanan said that he would have to follow the lead of Congress lest a recommendation to the House, where the Republicans had a majority, should defeat the proposed bill for a regiment for Texas defense. Britton continued to importune cabinet members and congressmen and finally asked Floyd if the War Department would use force against Texas troops who might cross the Rio Grande. Floyd's reply was: "No Sir, but I would stand upon this side & clap my hands & holler hurrah."[127]

Ben McCulloch assured the Texas Governor that the government had agreed to concentrate more troops on the Rio Grande but that their orders would be such that "no officer (unless a very bad man) will cross the River in pursuit of the enemy" and that a bill to provide a new regiment for Texas would take a long time to pass."[128] His diagnosis was correct. The regiment had been authorized on April 7, 1858, but no appropriation was made. Finally the Texas delegation got the appropriation tacked on as an amendment to the West Point appropriation bill. The debate in Congress on the measure involved considerable speculation on the relative merits of regulars and Texas Rangers, whether or not Texas really needed assistance, and the extent of Houston's intentions. A. J. Hamilton of Texas, refuting the argument that the complaints of Indian troubles were trumped up to get public money spent in Texas and that Houston had ulterior designs on Mexico, said that Houston wanted the volunteer regiment to be stationed on the northern, not the Mexican, frontier. All efforts were futile, and the regiment bill finally failed late in May, 1860.[129]

Lemuel D. Evans, who had followed the progress of the debate, wrote that Buchanan favored Houston's settling matters on the Rio Grande

---

Writings, VII, 473–74; McCulloch to Houston, February 21, 1860, Governors' Letters.

[127] Britton to Houston, March 3, 1860, Governors' Letters.

[128] McCulloch to Houston, March 4, 1860, *ibid.*

[129] *Congressional Globe*, 36 Cong., 1 sess. (1859/60), Part I, 936–44, 1193–1238; Part II, 1012, 1060–63, 1142–46, 1242–44, 1539, 1783, 1786–1813; Part III, 2309, 2383; Appendix, 241.

and that Houston's "lady friends" in Washington were eager that he "should make a grand *coup de main* . . . upon the Rio Grande immediately."[130]

On March 8, while the West Point bill with its Texas regiment rider was still in the Senate, Houston had wired both the President and the Secretary of War to tender five thousand troops to the government and to ask for immediate shipment to Texas of arms to be used in repelling invasions, whether by Mexicans or Indians. He assured Floyd that he had not ordered any troops to the Rio Grande and that he had made no favorable response to overtures that he take the lead in establishing a protectorate, and to the President he pledged: "I never have nor will I ever perform an official act that is not intended for my Country's advancement and prosperity aside from all selfishness."[131] The acting secretary of war, W. R. Dunkard, gave the government's reply. Additional troops were refused on the grounds that the Cortinas war was ended. Texas might anticipate its next year's allotment of arms, at a cost of some five thousand dollars instead of the arms costing one hundred thousand dollars requested by Houston.[132]

Late in July the Governor did apply to draw in advance the state's quota of arms for the next year and asked for the altered Morse rifles that had been recommended by McCulloch as better adapted for Indian warfare.[133] The rifles would be useful for the militia which had been provided for by the Texas Legislature in February, 1860.[134] The militia was to be divided into thirty-two brigades, each headed by a brigadier general appointed by the Governor until the brigade officers could organize and elect their own commanders. Because of age, family responsibilities, change of residence, or illness, seven of the appointees regretfully declined Houston's commissions. The letters accepting the commissions were virtually a chorus of "On to Mexico!" From Henderson, Webster Flanagan accepted with the hope that there would soon be use for the militia on or beyond the Rio Grande and suggested that a valid excuse to take Mexico would make Houston the president. J. W. Magoffin of Magoffinsville wrote: "Your views in regard to Mexico are perfectly correct."[135]

[130] Evans to Houston, March 19, 1860, Governors' Letters.
[131] Houston to Buchanan, March 8, 1860, and to Floyd, March 8 and 12, 1860, *Writings*, VII, 502, 506, 519–22.
[132] Dunkard to Houston, March 14, 1860, in *Harrison Flag*, April 6, 1860.
[133] Houston to Floyd, July 28, 1860, *Writings*, VIII, 110–11.
[134] H. P. N. Gammel (ed.), *The Laws of Texas, 1822–1897*, IV, 1483–1500.
[135] Answers to Commission, April 23–July 9, 1860, Governors' Letters.

These expressions of his brigadiers were but a few of the statements of approval of his course which Houston received. Every mail brought assurances of support from every part of Texas and from every section of the United States. Joseph L. Hogg wrote from Rusk that he had experienced some hard service in Mexico but was not yet satisfied and would take pleasure in participating in the contemplated campaign.[136] Humphrey Marshall, erstwhile Kentucky congressman and United States minister to China, sent a confidential letter outlining a scheme to make himself a participant in a "grand enterprise" if Houston should once again fabricate a design for empire. That the Mexican move might lead to the presidency, the Kentuckian conceded, as he outlined practical procedure: taking up arms in self-defense when the central government failed to act; crossing the border to create a state of war; establishing law and order in northern Mexico; and either adding "by conquest for our own safety a few more states to the south," or giving "peace to Mexico by Americanizing it all." Marshall predicted military and political success and stated the conditions on which he would participate.[137] It was a "confidential" letter, but Marshall had taken others into his confidence and told Houston that former Senator James Cooper of Pennsylvania would raise a brigade and that Governor Rodman M. Price of New Jersey would probably co-operate. Franklin Pierce received a letter from Washington describing Marshall's proposal and predicting that Old Sam would go ahead and also become a formidable candidate for the presidency.[138]

Along with the offers of volunteers from Ohio, New York, Mississippi, Kentucky, Virginia, Pennsylvania, Illinois, Louisiana, and Georgia, there were other types of offers. R. W. James of New Orleans tendered ten thousand muskets at half-price. Edwin A. Haskins of Philadelphia volunteered a loan of fifty to a hundred thousand dollars because "Mexico must be taken." At Baylor College at Independence the interest was academic. B. H. Carroll had to debate on the affirmative side of the question "Ought the United States to establsih a protectorate over Mexico?" and asked the Governor to send him by return mail his speeches on the subject. Houston's replies, if he made them, are not available,

---

[136] Hogg to Houston, March 28, 1860, *ibid.*
[137] Marshall to Houston, February 25, 1860, Domestic Correspondence.
[138] J. D. Hoover to Pierce, February 25, 1860, Franklin Pierce Papers.
Rodman M. Price (1816–94) was governor of New Jersey in 1853. James Cooper of Philadelphia had other filibustering interests. He was president of a corporation, called the Central American Company, which had backed Henry L. Kinney in his Central American Expedition. See William O. Scroggs, *Filibusters and Financiers: The Story of William Walker and His Associates*, 99.

except in rare instances. To Lyman Morrow of Chicago, who offered troops, he replied that the federal government had taken a hand, so that there was "no necessity for any action on the part of Texas."[139]

To one group, Houston's answer was, "We shall see." This came in a letter to Elkanah Greer, grand commander of the Knights of the Golden Circle, who on February 20 offered the Governor a regiment of one thousand volunteers organized east of the Trinity River and ready for immediate action. An accompanying letter from J. W. Barrett, introducing Greer to Houston, stated the Golden Circle's readiness to sustain the Mexican project and offered Houston the direction of the organization.[140] Activities of the Knights were not confined east of the Trinity. A certain Captain Davis recruited for the group at Fort Belknap in the spring of 1860 and said that one object was to raise a force of twelve thousand men to invade Mexico under Houston's command. The expedition was to be financed by British capitalists, who would pay Houston "a fabulous sum for his work" and then settle an annuity on his wife.[141] Houston's answer to Greer had been neither affirmative nor negative. The state, he said, was bankrupt, so that he had neither arms nor money, and lack of grain and grass en route to the Rio Grande made advance impracticable "at this time."[142]

Between April and August, 1860, there is scant mention of Mexico in Houston's correspondence. The Governor had Sam Jr., who was in school at Bastrop Academy, practicing penmanship by copying his father's letters to the Secretary of War and the Secretary of the Interior. He bought the boy a Mexican sombrero and intimated that he had asked his son's opinion on a proposition that would "involve the welfare of more than forty millions of people."[143] He had not found an opportunity to secure Indian allies, but he had rangers and militia alert and he had encouragement from all sides. He must even have had a prospect of money for arms, for in August he wrote to Ben McCulloch to ascertain *sub rosa* how long it would take the manufacturer to complete from seven to ten thousand of the Morse rifles. With obvious double meaning, he said he wanted one gun to his liking and, if he could get it, would "never try again." He needed to economize because he had a new "pro-

---

[139] Houston Unpublished Correspondence, VII.

[140] Barrett to Houston, February 20, 1860, Governors' Letters.

[141] James Pike, *Scout and Ranger: Being the Personal Adventures of James Pike of the Texas Rangers in 1859–60*, 124.

[142] Houston to Greer, February 29, 1860, *Writings*, VII, 495.

[143] Houston to Sam Houston, Jr., April 14 and 23 and May 15, 1860, *ibid.*, VIII, 12, 27, 55.

tectorate" at home, a son named Temple Lea Houston, born on August 12, 1860. His question to McCulloch, "Who that is a Christian man would not feel interested in his household to provide for it?" sounded like a consideration of that British annuity. All was contingent, however, on a successful meeting of McCulloch, John Hancock, and Colonel Mann with the bondholders in New York, for "if the bond holders cannot be approached, it would take years to raise a reliable force to achieve any glorious result."[144]

Taken by itself, Houston's letter to McCulloch, proclaiming the Mexican project a "mission of mercy and humanity," refutes the argument that the protectorate was for presidential propaganda, for in the letter Houston wrote: "Oh, Ben, on my honor, I forgot to tell you that I am out of the scrape for President. I am arms folded, and will stay so unless some malice is squinted at me." Perhaps he considered the malice inevitable.

If Houston had never conceived and never proposed the protectorate, his national prestige was sufficient to give his name consideration in 1860. During the governor's race in 1859, the *Harrison Flag* pointed out that Houston, not Douglas, had been correct about which party benefited from the Kansas-Nebraska Bill. The paper thought the people would do Houston justice when they found out they had "unintentionally wronged a devoted public servant."[145] The New York *Herald,* on August 18, 1859, declared that if the Democratic party did not avail itself of Houston's personal popularity, he would then be the most available of all men for a National Union party.

His fellow Unionists in Texas cogitated the most advantageous use of that availability. "Leathercoat" Throckmorton wrote Ben Epperson of the Red River country that John H. Reagan was the man for the Senate and that to bring Houston forward for that position would damage his prospects for the presidency. Throckmorton reasoned:

If he fails it is a defeat, and does him up at once. But if he declines in advance and prefers to act as Governor, it takes away the great argument of his opponents—that his only object has been to get back into the Senate. Such a position would leave him free at home, without giving him a chance to go to Washington and by some ill fated movement put his foot into it, as great men often do unawares. Besides it would have a good effect abroad for him to decline Senatorial honor. It would appear like he was not ambitious, and I think would give him many friends.

[144] Houston to McCulloch, August 28, 1860, and to Mann, August 27, 1860, *ibid.,* VIII, 126–28.
[145] *Harrison Flag,* June 29, 1859.

Throckmorton had not decided how best to utilize the advantages of the Unionist victory displayed in Houston's election as governor. If the Democrats were conservative and moderate and chose their best men, the Democratic masses would follow them, but "if the Charleston convention nominates Douglas or any other man as objectionable, then Texas should have a mass convention of the people, adopt a Conservative platform, and put forward our man."[146]

Throckmorton wrote in September. Houston was inaugurated governor on December 21, 1859. On January 13, 1860, he delivered his message to the Legislature, congratulating that body upon the triumph of conservatism. On January 21, he transmitted to the Legislature a message from the Governor of South Carolina accompanied by resolutions from that state asserting the right of secession. Houston appended his own "protest against, and dissent from, the principles enunciated in the resolutions." He denied the constitutionality of secession, proclaimed that only the Constitution and the Union could preserve states' rights, and implored that Texas allay any dangerous sentiment abroad in the land by teaching and cultivating "a more fraternal feeling." He recommended that Texas adopt resolutions dissenting from the assertion of any abstract right of secession and urge upon the people, North and South, "the necessity of cultivating brotherly feeling, observing justice, and attending to their own affairs."[147] Wilds K. Cooke, a former member of the Texas Congress, congratulated Houston on his "manly and patriotic message" and congratulated Texas on having a governor that appreciated the value of the Union. Cooke reported that the general public in Arkansas, Louisiana, and East Texas endorsed Houston's conservative principles and classed him with such statesmen as Washington, Jefferson, and Madison, who believed that "the cement of this union is in the heartblood of every American." Israel B. Bigelow of Brownsville wrote that Houston's message was bound to have a "powerful cooling effect upon many of the plans of our fire eating politicians." Houston's cousin Thomas Carothers, director of the penitentiary at Huntsville and unofficial campaign manager for the Governor, wrote that the South Carolina message had "about caused all *their* banners to be furled" so that the time had come to "hang yours out, upon the outmost walls." A week later Houston heard again from Carothers:

Your South Carolina message has helped all honest public men, to form a

[146] J. W. Throckmorton to Epperson, September 13, 1859, Ben H. Epperson Papers.

[147] Message Transmitting South Carolina Resolutions, *Writings*, VII, 429–41.

just estimate of you. Your . . . policy has familiarized the whole country with your true worth, while a life time devoted to your country's weal, gives to your friends now the right to say, go ahead. We are sure you're right. *I do trust*, we will hear, *very soon* that you are a candidate. I know I'm right about this.[148]

So, never a nominee, Houston was still a candidate. Charles R. Pryor, editor of the Dallas *Herald,* wrote Douglas to request writings on popular sovereignty to run in his paper and posted the "Little Giant" on Texas politics: "We are looking forward with interest to the Charleston Convention, and I think its action will be sustained by the people of Texas, although you may rest assured that Sam Houston will be the Independent Candidate. He is looked upon by the Democracy as more dangerous to our principles than Seward himself."[149] The Democrats were to meet at Charleston in April. Former Whigs and Know-Nothings held a convention at Baltimore in May. After an irreconcilable split at Charleston, the Democrats held delayed conventions at Baltimore and at Richmond in June. Houston's name kept appearing until the last nominee was designated, his friends encouraging him both as a convention nominee and as an independent candidate. He could not but have been influenced by the letters he received. M. H. Beaty thought the only hope for the Union was for the national conservatives to unite upon such a man as Houston, who would be supported by "the hard fisted yeomanry of the country." Thomas Lewelling pointed out the dangers of two Democratic factions in Texas and advised Houston not to leave his old party names and associates.[150]

The first session of the Thirty-sixth Congress opened in December, 1859, with extremists on both sides in control and the South seething over the John Brown raid and H. R. Helper's book, *The Impending Crisis.* There was a two months' battle over the speakership before the Republicans gained control with William Pennington as speaker. The Senate quarreled; threats of secession were made daily. Union meetings were held in the North, and one of them nominated Houston for vice-president. On January 23, 1860, the *Red Land Express* at San Augustine carried an account of a New York mass meeting which nominated Houston for president. Mingled with the advice for independent campaigning was the forlorn hope of some that the national Democratic party

---

[148] Carothers to Houston, March 27 and April 5, 1860; Bigelow to Houston, March 6, 1860; and Cooke to Houston, March 1, 1860, Governors' Letters.

[149] Pryor to Douglas, September 21, 1859, Stephen A. Douglas Papers.

[150] Beaty to Houston, December 20, 1859, and Lewelling to Houston, January 31, 1860, Governors' Letters.

would pick Houston at Charleston. Andrew Plumb, onetime Washington correspondent of the New York *Herald*, was corresponding secretary of the New York Fifth Ward National Democratic Association in 1860. He questioned Houston on his stand on various national problems and said that the conservative tone of his message on the South Carolina resolutions was the admiration of thousands of Northern Democrats, "who would hail with enthusiasm the nomination of the old hero of San Jacinto by the forthcoming National Democratic Convention."[181] Carothers had no such hopes of any Houston movement at Charleston but was sure that his candidate could "beat the nominee of the C. Conv. & the Black Republican to boot," and chafed at Houston's delay in announcing himself when "*the hour* and *the man* are both before the American people."[182]

On March 20, at Buaas Hall in Austin, the "National Democracy" held a mass meeting presided over by N. H. Darnell. A. M. Branch, George McKnight, and D. C. Dickson were among the eight vice-presidents, and E. M. Pease was chairman of the eighteen-member Committee on Resolutions. W. P. Rogers of Huntsville made the opening speech for the man "whose brilliant life awakens so much romantic enthusiasm" with the declaration that he was ready "to follow his standard for a still higher honor, if there could be one superior to that of Governor of the proud state of Texas." The next speaker was Sam Bogart of Collin County, who with "gray locks, thin visage, tall figure and earnest countenance, caused a death like silence before he had uttered a word." Bogart invited "all conservative men of whatever name, who love their country, to unite upon a broad national sentiment." Robert H. Taylor of Fannin County "concluded with a soul-stirring eulogium upon Gen. Houston and the avowal that he was ready to advocate him, as the embodiment of conservatism for the Presidency." Every declaration for "Constitution and the Union" and Houston for the presidency "brought down the house with thundering applause." Judge E. D. Townes ended his speech with "a glance at the Mexican Protectorate and the glorious march of our empire westward under such a leader." An adjourned session of the mass meeting reassembled on March 22 to adopt ten resolutions. The ninth resolution was for support of Houston for the presidency, and the last resolution was for the appointment of a representative in each judicial district to correspond with Houston's friends

---

[181] M. H. Royston to Houston, December 23, 1859, and Plumb to Houston, March 3, 1860, *ibid.*; Lubbock, *Six Decades in Texas*, 297.
[182] Carothers to Houston, March 15, 1860, Governors' Letters.

throughout the nation. Ben Epperson, who made the closing speech, said that he preferred that Houston's choice be made "without the intervention of conventions" and that the people, "the true and genuine Democracy," should choose the man "peculiarly fitted for the emergency," the one "best calculated to calm the troubled waters of sectionalism." The Committee of Correspondence was composed of twenty loyal Union men headed by E. M. Pease.[153]

The Governor was biding his time. His official duties were heavy enough to demand all of his attention, but he was also anxious to see how the wind was blowing before he committed himself. Finally, on March 25, he answered a three-month-old letter from Union men at Galveston asking whether or not he would allow his name to be presented to the Charleston Convention. After pointing out the degeneracy of the convention system and denying that the Democratic party was any longer a national party, he said that he would not consent to have his name submitted to any convention and that he would not accept a nomination procured by "contrivance, trick or management." "If," he declared, "my name should be used in connection with the Presidency, the movement must originate with the people themselves, as well as end with them."[154] Ballinger noted in his diary that "Old Houston" had declined to go before the convention, and Carothers wrote that the answer to the Galveston committee had caused the "organizers" to lose their speech. Among the articulate was John V. Singer of Brownsville, who agreed with the Governor that "corruptions and chicanery of conventions have disgusted the people." J. Thomas Fuller at Sabine Pass wrote that he intended to use his printer's ink for the hero of San Jacinto "while I can write a line or stick a type," and J. D. Logan of the San Antonio *Herald* outlined that paper's plan to work for "the election of the 'Old War-horse' to the White House." Beriah Graham, appointed by Houston as the first head of the State Lunatic Asylum, went east to study institutions for the mentally ill and wrote back that politics constituted the chief topic of conversation and that Houston's name was always mentioned in connection with the next election.[155]

Representative "heroes and patriots" gathered at San Jacinto on April 21, 1860. Isaac L. Hill of Fayette County presided, and among the

---

[153] Democratic Party of Texas, *Proceedings of the Mass Meeting of the National Democracy of Texas.*

[154] Houston to John W. Harris and others, March 25, 1860, *Writings*, VII, 545–54.

[155] Carothers to Houston, April 11, 1860; Singer to Houston, April 18, 1860; Fuller to Houston, March 20, 1860; Logan to Houston, March 28, 1860; and Graham to Houston, April 8, 1860, Governors' Letters.

twenty-three vice-presidents were eight other participants in the Battle of San Jacinto and six soldiers of the Texas Republic. Hill announced that the purpose of the meeting was to commemorate the San Jacinto anniversary and tender to the people of the United States the hero of San Jacinto for the office of chief magistrate. The meeting adopted resolutions of loyalty to the Union and called upon conservative men of all parties in all sections to support Houston as a "true and safe man" who would "arrest the growth of the spirit of disunion."[156]

Reaction was mixed. David G. Burnet rejoiced that Ashbel Smith did not attend the "absurd celebration" and said he could not respect "those who hang on to that false man's skirts merely for the vain hope of political advancement." An old friend of Douglas reported back to Illinois: "General Sam Houston is out in a flaming handbill as a candidate for presidency of the United States. He declares himself the people's candidate, the national democratic candidate, anty convention candidate, anty caucas candidate, anty Duglas candidate, and I hope the Devil's candidate."[157] Harvey H. Allen, of the Committee of Correspondence appointed at San Jacinto, predicted that the movement would cause a sensation and receive support in Tennessee, Kentucky, Arkansas, Pennsylvania, and New York. Nomination of state officers was postponed until reactions could be tested, but the San Jacinto ticket was dispatched to Charleston to reach that city while the Democratic Convention was in session.[158]

Concerning that convention, the New York *Herald* speculated:

The idea is to nominate Douglas, or some other man who will run well at the North, so as to carry the States of New York, Pennsylvania, New Jersey and Connecticut against Seward, and thus prevent his election by the people, and to run Davis in the South against Houston so as to prevent his election by the people. By this arrangement, the election will be thrown into the House of Representatives, where the South, with any two Northern States, can carry it.[159]

When the Southern faction bolted and the Charleston meeting adjourned without making a nomination, Houston's friends were encouraged. John F. McKenny wrote from Goliad: "We have just got news from the Charleston convention. No nomination. This speaks for the

---

[156] Winkler, *Platforms of Political Parties in Texas*, 86.
[157] George Henry to Douglas, April 23, 1860, Douglas Papers; Burnet to Smith, April 30, 1860, Ashbel Smith Papers.
[158] Allen to George W. Smyth, April 22, 1860, Smyth Papers.
[159] New York *Herald*, April 28, 1860.

people's candidate. The people will now take the government out of the hands of trading politicians—newspaper editors. Will you be a candidate? Let me know soon." To a list of goods manufactured at the penitentiary, M. C. Rogers appended a supplementary paragraph on politics: "I find, as expected, that the Charleston Convention have bursted their Doublebarrel Shot Gun and hurt no boddy but themselves. . . . We think Houston stock is looking up. We say Success to the cause and take courage." Far away from Texas, Irwin P. Beadle was hunting a popular subject for a dime novel and proposed a "Life of Saml. Houston" for his series of "books for the millions." He wrote Houston: "It seems to us that the time is ripe for such a publication, while our personal admiration of the subject leads us to make the venture."[100]

On May 9, the National Union Convention assembled at the Presbyterian church in Baltimore, and Murat Halstead described the delegates as in high spirits and confident of their ability "to create a powerful diversion." His report of the first day described John Bell's stock as high but added that "there are many who are anxious to avail themselves of the battle of San Jacinto." Erastus Brooks of the New York *Express* outlined the "Constitution and the laws" as a platform and spoke in behalf of the nomination of Houston, whom Halstead described as "a good old soul, but the most shallow of the shallow politicians who have been engaged for some years in attending to the affairs of our beloved country." A wreck on the Baltimore and Ohio Railroad had delayed the arrival of some twenty members of the convention, including the Texas delegation composed of A. B. Norton, A. M. Gentry, B. H. Epperson, and L. D. Evans. While Brooks was making his Houston presentation, the Texans arrived, headed by Adjutant General Norton, "a man with a beard half a yard long, who was dressed in home-spun and bore a great buckhorn-handle cane." Nominations began about noon on May 10, with the names of John Bell and Edward Everett receiving the most applause. According to Halstead: "When the vote of Texas was called for, her hairy delegate got up and mentioned the battle of San Jacinto, and tried to give peculiar emphasis to the Sam part of Houston's name. But it did not take wonderfully." On the first ballot, Bell received 68½ votes and Housfon 57—3 from Arkansas, 2½ from Connecticut, 5½ from Illinois, ½ from Maryland, 1 from New Jersey, 5 from Ohio, 7½ from Pennsylvania, 4 from Texas, and 28 from New York. James W. Garrard of New York and Norton both made speeches in support

---

[100] McKenny to Houston, May 10, 1860; Rogers to Houston, May 12, 1860; and Beadle to Houston, May 7, 1860, Governors' Letters.

of Houston before the second ballot, on which Houston picked up 12 votes. Bell had 125; the Virginia delegation then cast 13 votes for Bell to give him a majority. Leslie Combs paid high compliment to Houston before changing the Kentucky vote to Bell. Everett was the vice-presidential nominee.[161]

Bell supporters were delighted with the choice of a Southern man "of unquestionable ability, of undoubted fidelity to the Union," and one of them wrote: "If we had taken Genl. Houston we should have failed, not because he is objectionable in either of the above particulars, but because we could not have brought the Conservative Whigs readily into his support." Donelson was not so sure that the correct choice had been made and wrote his wife that Houston was defeated again, "though he was evidently our strongest man for the race." Benefiting from hind sight, Charles March was to write to Franklin Pierce in late March of 1861 that it seemed a pity that Houston had not been nominated instead of Bell as perhaps he might have been elected and have at least postponed the crisis of 1861.[162] That Houston was stronger than Bell was also the opinion of R. D. Rice, a Douglas supporter, who wrote Douglas from Rockland, Maine, to say that Houston's was the only name at Baltimore that could have made the "movement formidable or even reputable in popular estimation." Rice urged that the postponed Democratic Convention at Baltimore declare for Douglas and Houston. "As to Houston," said the New Englander, "he has it is true his peculiarities, and in some things, he may have been erratic—but no man can doubt the honesty of his heart, the purity of his life, or his genuine patriotism. The *people* more than politicians have faith in 'Old Sam,' and will enthusiastically rally in his support."[163] Still another Douglas correspondent solicited the Senator from Illinois to refuse the nomination at Baltimore, wait for a future term, and in 1860 give his influence to Houston or John J. Crittenden.[164]

In Texas, Carothers was not expecting a Houston nomination at Baltimore, but he did anticipate a popular movement strong enough to "drive the Disunion hordes . . . to the Devil" and wrote for Norton of the *Intelligencer* to strike off a hundred campaign broadsides for distribution in

[161] Murat Halstead, *Caucuses of 1860: A History of the National Political Conventions of the Current Presidential Campaign*, 104–20.
[162] A. H. H. Stuart to Blanton Duncan, August 23, 1860, Bell Papers; A. J. Donelson to Elizabeth Donelson, May 11, 1860, Donelson Papers; March to Pierce, March 28, 1861, Pierce Papers.
[163] Rice to Douglas, May 12, 1860, Douglas Papers.
[164] W. D. Brown to Douglas, May 20, 1860, *ibid.*

Huntsville. Jack Davis of Rusk County and James Chandler of Cedar Bayou were writing the Governor that the time was ripe for his announcement as an independent candidate.[165]

Almost a month after his nomination at San Jacinto, Houston finally acknowledged that action in a letter to John H. Manley in which he said that he had never withheld his services from his fellow citizens, declared the proposal of his name at the Constitutional Union Convention unauthorized, and said that he would not consent to have his name submitted at a convention. At the same time Carothers was making contacts with Alabama and Georgia men who might join the Houston forces, was planning campaign literature, and was begging Houston to name the man who should appear on the ticket with him.[166] On May 24, Houston pleased Carothers and placed the Constitutional Union men in an awkward position by writing to D. D. Atchison and J. W. Harris, editors of the *Standard*, that he had decided to respond to the San Jacinto call and consent to let his name "go before the country as the People's Candidate for the Presidency."[167] That his action was anticipated in Virginia is revealed in a letter to Senator Robert M. T. Hunter: "The folly of General Houston in announcing himself a candidate, is another movement that tends to add to the complications, and will have the effect of further distracting the South. I suppose that he will take off Texas, and thus weaken us, to that extent, even if we shall harmonize at Baltimore on a ticket."[168]

Union men in New York were disappointed with Bell's nomination by the Constitutional Unionists. Many of them decided that Houston was a doubtful bet and cast about to determine policy before the meeting of the next state convention.[169] Others decided to go all out for Houston as an independent candidate. On May 29, 1860, New Yorkers, without distinction of party, were invited to meet at Washington's statue in Union Square to respond to the San Jacinto nomination. Texans invited to attend included L. D. Evans, Ben McCulloch, A. J. Hamilton, and John Hemphill.

Rockets were fired, cannon were discharged, Shelton's brass band

---

[165] Carothers to Houston, May 14, 1860; Davis to Houston, May 18, 1860; and Chandler to Houston, May 29, 1860, Governors' Letters.

[166] Carothers to Houston, May 22 and 23, 1860, *ibid.*; Houston to Manley, May 17, 1860, *Writings*, VIII, 58–60.

[167] Houston to Atchison and Harris, May 24, 1860, *Writings*, VIII, 66.

[168] Charles W. Russell to Hunter, May 24, 1860, Charles H. Ambler (ed.), *Correspondence of Robert M. T. Hunter, 1826–1876,* Vol. II of American Historical Association *Annual Report, 1916,* 332.

[169] C. M. Harmon to Stephen A. Douglas, May 28, 1860, Douglas Papers.

helped swell the crowd around the flag-draped platform lighted by torches and Chinese lanterns and bearing a portrait of Houston with the inscription:

FOR PRESIDENT
GEN. SAM HOUSTON
An honest man no party platform needs,
He follows right, and goes where justice leads.

Dr. Stephen Hasbrouck, chairman of the Committee on Arrangements, presided in the absence of Mayor Isaac L. Varian and opened proceedings with a speech in praise of Houston. Campaign songs were distributed, one entitled "Houston and the People." There were resolutions extolling Houston as a man who "has a hold upon the sympathies and confidence of the people possessed by no other living statesman"; proclaiming an independent press and a patriotic people as mightier than caucuses or conventions; and declaring a platform of "the Constitution, the Union, and the laws." Clinton Roosevelt spoke in opposition to the Lincoln nomination at Chicago and put the resolutions to a vote. Dr. Fenelon Hasbrouck, editor of the Westchester County *Highland Democrat*, called for the overthrow of the convention system and submitted an "Address of the Committee on Organization to the Editors of the State," which called upon Union-loving men to organize Houston clubs and choose delegates to a state mass meeting scheduled for July 18, when an electoral ticket would be chosen and a vice-president nominated. D. D. Atchison and J. W. Harris were present to recount the Houston achievements as president of Texas and as United States senator. J. W. Bryce and John McChesney also made speeches, and six other orators were introduced at a supplemental meeting in front of Thorp's Hotel.[19]

In Texas, where organized Democracy was anti-Houston, there was some evidence of a Houston movement. Fourteen counties were represented at a convention at Tyler during a federal court session, and R. F. Mitchell wrote Houston that "we did all for you but *nominate*. You are good for your own state and I believe the entire South, but how will it be in the North? Can any good come out of Nazareth?" E. S. Woods of Galveston, noting the frequency of Houston demonstrations in other areas, hoped that they would "turn the popular eye, both in the North & the South, in the right direction." Even a few Southern eyes were turned to Houston. John J. Flournoy of Athens, Georgia, uncle of Texas

[19] New York *Herald*, May 30, 1860.

Attorney General George M. Flournoy, wrote the Texas Governor that he hoped the postponed Democratic meeting at Baltimore would nominate Houston and Douglas. He urged that Houston have his "San Jacinto neighbors get up small meetings in all the states and run electoral tickets in every state" because he saw in Houston "the finger of God, protecting the Great Republic."[171]

During July, Governor Houston continued to receive letters commending his candidacy. That month he was in Houston and made a speech from the balcony of the Kelly House but made no mention of presidential aspirations, although A. M. Gentry and John H. Manley, who followed him, described the general enthusiasm on his behalf and promised more details at a rally to be held at the Market House the following week. Carothers and J. Carroll Smith were still hopeful and were anxious for news from the New York meeting scheduled for July 18. Reports from Louisiana were encouraging, and Carothers felt that all they needed to do was to get up the electoral ticket, for "there is no man among the candidates can compare popularity among the people with you."[172]

The four candidates nominated by conventions were Douglas, Breckinridge, Lincoln, and Bell. On June 25, 1860, the New York *Herald* ran biographies of the party nominees and added a biography of Houston as the "People's Candidate," with the comment that "his platform is the record of his public life."

By August, the Union men in Texas were still undecided how to vote. Lincoln they must beat; Breckinridge they did not want; Bell they were theoretically committed to; yet Houston seemed stronger than Bell. William P. Ballinger discussed the matter with Bell and Everett men in Galveston and, after a meeting on the night of August 18, recorded in his diary:

We agreed distinctly to a fusion with Douglas & Houston. McKeen [in whose office they met] wanted it understood that if H. or Bell couldn't be elected then the Electors sh'd be at liberty to choose between D. & Breckinridge. And Neill and I advocated that the understanding sh'd be that the electoral vote sh'd be cast for the strongest man to beat Lincoln & Breckinridge—& so it was adopted.[173]

[171] Mitchell to Houston, June 1, 1860; Woods to Houston, June 8, 1860; and Flournoy to Houston, June 7, 1860, Governors' Letters.
[172] Synopsis of a Speech at Houston, July 13, 1860, *Writings*, VIII, 101–103; Carothers to Houston, July 24, 1860, Governors' Letters.
[173] William Pitt Ballinger Diary, August 18, 1860.

Four days before the Galvestonians had decided on fusion, Houston wrote to A. Daly declaring that he would not vote for Lincoln, that he could not vote for Bell, and that he could not support Douglas or Breckinridge except to save his country. He protested before high Heaven that he had no desire to be president and that "nothing but the wisdom of Divine Providence" could "so dispose matters as to advance the wishes" of his friends. He intended to discharge his official duties and husband his strength to meet "if the time comes . . . the subject of Disunion." Four days later the Governor addressed a letter to "Friends in the United States," withdrawing his name as a presidential candidate, lest his remaining longer in the field prove a stumbling block in the way of those desiring harmony. On September 3, he wrote P. T. Richardson opposing the collection of ammunition by the Southern states, declaring that a constitutional remedy for all ills was still available in the federal judiciary, and stating that he had withdrawn from the contest "in support of a Union ticket of all parties to defeat Lincoln."[114]

[114] Houston to Daly, August 14, 1860, and to Richardson, September 3, 1860, *Writings*, VIII, 118–20, 129–30.

For Love of the Union

AT THE END of his senatorial term, Houston
arrived home late in March or early in April
of 1859. The Texas to which he returned was far from placid. Amelia
Barr presented a feminine reaction to the times in Austin.

But early in 1859 changes so great were present, that it was impossible any
longer to ignore them. There were bitter disputes wherever men congregated,
and domestic quarrels over every hearthstone, while feminine friendships
melted away in the heat of passionate arguments so well seasoned with personalities. . . . What really excited them was the question of state rights. They
were furious with the United States Government's interference in their state's
social and domestic arrangements; . . . the last social gathering at my house
was like a political arena. . . .

Robert brought me news from the Capitol every day; and it was as uncertain and changeable as the wind. One day war was inevitable, and Houston

321

was coming from Washington to lead the Unionist party; and perhaps the next day it was the pen, and not the sword that would settle the matter.[1]

On March 30, the *Southern Intelligencer* carried an editorial copied from the San Antonio *Herald* describing a "reactionary feeling in behalf of the Old Hero Patriot" and expressing the hope that the people "are waking up, that the scales are dropping from their eyes, that their great error is coming boldly up to their view and that upon reflection they will remedy the injustice done him and will place him in that position due him for past services." Similarly J. M. Smith of Waco wrote J. W. Latimer of the Dallas *Herald* that a mighty current was flowing in Houston's favor and that even his enemies were admitting that he had redeemed himself by his "masterly efforts and unflinching devotion to the best interests of Texas." Smith urged that Texans who respected talent or loved honor and truth would once more place the Old Chief where he might "continue to stay the tide of *Disunion*, rebuke *Sectionalism*, war upon *Black Republicanism*, and, above all, fearlessly expose corruption in high places, as long as he lives."[2]

The Democratic Convention was set for May 2, 1859, at Houston, and Ballinger wrote that E. M. Pease thought it would probably be a failure and that Houston would be governor if he ran. Houston's brother-in-law reported to Houston's long-time friend: "I think if the old Dragon will run again, that he can make the race this time, the reaction in his favor is wonderful and we shall elect I think our independent candidates."[3] The Texas delegation in the House of Representatives had broken over the secession issue, and the New Orleans *Delta* carried a note that John H. Reagan had denounced "fanaticism" as exemplified by Guy M. Bryan and had "planted himself squarely on the Union platform of Gen. Houston." Early in April the McKinney *Messenger* came out for Houston for governor and Reagan for Congress on a platform of "the Constitution and the Union and devotion to these united with integrity and ability, the true test for office."[4] The San Augustine *Texian* quoted Houston as recommending Reagan as his successor in the Senate because Reagan possessed the three elements of greatness: "genius, integrity, and industry."[5]

---

[1] Amelia E. Barr, *All the Days of My Life: An Autobiography, the Red Leaves of a Human Heart*, 218–19.

[2] *Harrison Flag*, April 8, 1859.

[3] Charles Power to Ashbel Smith, April 1, 1859, Ashbel Smith Papers; William Pitt Ballinger Diary, April 6, 1859.

[4] *Southern Intelligencer*, March 23, April 13, 1859.

[5] Dallas *Herald*, April 17, 1859.

While all Texas speculated and partisan papers chose sides, the Galveston *Civilian* reported that the "veteran warrior and statesman" was contentedly visiting his Cedar Point home, satisfied to retire and possessed of no thought of being a candidate for governor or the Senate. Never failing to support Houston, the *Civilian* also ran a letter from Ben McCulloch to give that veteran ranger's recollections of San Jacinto in answer to James H. Perry's "calumnies of a nutmeg Yankee" against the General. The independent course of George W. Paschal's strongly pro-Union *Southern Intelligencer* aroused bitter criticism from the Houston *Telegraph* and approbation from the Dallas *Herald,* which wrote of Paschal: "Its independent course towards the hero of San Jacinto does not place the editor in a doubtful position in regard to his future conduct; nor is Judge Paschal one of those who think 'that no good man can come out of Nazareth'; the virtues of the old hero he honors with proper respect and his faults he condemns with becoming candor."[*]

On the eve of the convention Paschal wrote Cushing of the *Telegraph* lamenting the imprudences of the Democratic leaders and pointing out the fact that Houston, in the last two years, had "acted like a Democrat." Paschal held that the speech against Watrous was regarded by thousands as sufficient atonement for all Houston's sins and warned his fellow editor that even the Cushing adroit obituary to the memory of Houston might not consign him to a political grave. Runnels was renominated by the Democrats, and Paschal intensified the *Intelligencer's* advocacy of Houston, playing up the Watrous case, carrying J. S. Riley's announcement for the Texas Senate, and calling a rally of National Democrats to be held in Austin. A. J. Hamilton addressed the rally in the federal courtroom in a speech which was "such an one as will tell upon the people" and was followed on the platform by J. M. Swisher, who presented the resolution: "That all freemen who are opposed to the opening of the *African Slave trade, Secession,* and other Disunion issues—all who are friends to the National Democracy . . . express their adherence to the Union—unite with us in electing Genl. Sam Houston for Governor."[']

Then Paschal went outside of the paper to personal correspondence and addressed himself to Ashbel Smith:

The time for a glorious revolution in the cause of National Democracy has

[*] *Ibid.,* May 4, 1859; *Southern Intelligencer,* May 4, 1859.
['] *Southern Intelligencer,* May 11, 25, 1859; Brown, "Annals of Travis County," XIX, 17–18.

come. This is also a time to serve your old and devoted friend Genl. Houston. The Constitution, the Union, the frontier, state reforms, and a large debt of gratitude demand his services. . . . I therefore beg you to throw off any chains which you may feel at that abortion of a convention and to advise Genl. Houston to run. Let us redeem the Democracy. I wish I had time to write my views in full. But you read them in the papers. Help us Ashbel. The people will elect Houston whether he will or not.[8]

Paschal not only put his own views in his editorials. He quoted the *Colorado Citizen* on the fall of the reigning dynasty and the restoration of "primitive, *Union* Democracy"; cited the Jefferson *Gazette* on Houston's political resurrection; clipped a notice from the Crockett *Printer* on the evidence that Reagan's manly qualities had won the old hero's heart; and printed a statement of a Fort Belknap resident that along the frontier, "almost without a dissenting voice, all were clamorous for Houston."[9]

On June 3, 1859, Houston wrote Paschal from Independence that he had yielded his own inclinations to the inclinations of his friends and had "concluded, if elected, to serve the people as the Executive of the State." His principles would be the "Constitution and the Union," for they comprehended "all the old Jackson National Democracy I ever professed, or officially practised."[10] The *Intelligencer* then declared in black-face type: "The Agony Over—SAM HOUSTON IN THE FIELD." The newspaper battle was joined; every plea made by the *Intelligencer,* the *Civilian,* or the *Harrison Flag* on Houston's behalf was answered by the Dallas *Herald,* the *Texas Republican,* the *State Gazette,* and the Galveston *News* with sarcasm and invective.[11]

In contrast with his vocal campaign which covered the state in 1857, Houston made only one speech in the 1859 campaign, an address at Nacogdoches on July 9, which Paschal described as among the best speeches of his life. In it he defended his claim to the name of Democrat, saying that his record showed fewer deviations from the principles of Jefferson and Jackson than that of any other man whose life had been devoted to the public. He condemned the Houston convention, particularly the faction which would have opened the African slave trade. Then, after justifying Texas independence and spirit in "drubbing" him in 1857, he prophesied with telling accuracy the results of secession

[8] Paschal to Smith, May 27, 1859, Ashbel Smith Papers.
[9] *Southern Intelligencer,* May 25, June 1, 1859.
[10] Houston to Paschal, June 3, 1859, *Writings,* VII, 339–40.
[11] Dallas *Herald,* June 15, 22, 29, 1859; *Harrison Flag,* June 24, 1859; *Texas Republican,* July 23, 1859.

and civil war, and outlined the policy which he, as governor, would follow in regard to law enforcement, monopolies, the public domain, and education. He ended, as he had ended so many of those speeches in the Senate, with a plea for Union: "Let me exhort you, then, to stand by the Constitution and the Union. Confide in one another in the hour of danger. Rely upon yourselves when demagogues would mislead you. Maintain those reserved powers which are essential to preserve your liberties against centralization, and they will withstand the shock of centuries."[12]

The chief issue of the campaign was union or disunion; local questions involved the protection of the frontier against Indians and Mexicans, and the reopening of the slave trade. Runnels' Indian policy had alienated the frontier, and although he denied a league with those who wished to open the slave trade, his treatment of the proposition to reopen it was not entirely satisfactory to his party. The *National Intelligencer*, editorializing on the election, wrote:

The State Rights Party of Texas started an unnecessary and disastrous issue. They made the reopening of the African Slave Trade an issue of the election, thus dividing the party. The speeches of the canvass were filled largely with this subject. This was to Houston's advantage; and added to the memories of the past gave him an overwhelming victory over the party that had formerly beaten him by overwhelming odds. The State Rights Party of Texas brought defeat on themselves by making an impracticable and michievous issue.[13]

In 1859, West Texas was not ready to withdraw from the Union in behalf of slavery, nor were western men satisfied with the pre-emption law allowing a settler on the public domain 160 acres of land for every three slaves he owned. Runnels was also charged with extravagance. Houston's victory was a personal triumph and vindication, but he won the election in the west upon the issues that he upheld.[14] The vote was 33,375 for Houston and 27,500 for Runnels. A number of thoughtful Texans, torn between party loyalty and fear of secession, did not cast a ballot. Ballinger, attending the last pre-election rallies in Galveston, said the "bolters" had the larger meetings but the Democrats the more enthusiastic. He tabulated the local results as 403 for Runnels, 307 for Houston, and wrote in his diary: "I did not vote for governor."[15]

[12] Speech at Nacogdoches, July 9, 1859, *Writings*, VII, 343–67.
[13] *National Intelligencer* (Washington, D.C.), August 17, 1859.
[14] C. W. Ramsdell, "The Frontier and Secession," *Studies in Southern History and Politics*, 66, 73; Culberson, "General Sam Houston and Secession," *Scribner's Magazine*, XXXIX (May, 1906), 584–91.
[15] Ballinger Diary, July 22, 30, August 1, 1859.

Ballinger's brother-in-law, Guy M. Bryan, had worked hard for the Democratic ticket and was doubtless in complete agreement with Rutherford B. Hayes, a former college mate, who wrote his condolences:

I do not know what part you took in the late contest for Governor in Texas; but supposing you entertain your former notions about General Houston we probably agree in feeling sorry that the Old Humbug has again risen to the surface. It may be regarded as a proper rounding off of his chequered career by lovers of the romantic, but in any other view it is not agreeable to contemplate.[16]

No Texas paper was as bitter in its reaction to Houston's election as was the Charleston *Mercury.* Judge Edward Bates, Missouri free-soiler and later Lincoln's attorney general, copied for his diary the *Mercury's* pointed abuse of the Texas nominee as a "traitor who ought to fall never to rise again" and "one of the greatest enemies to the South, and most unmitigated demagogues within our borders—a *Southern Free soiler.*"[17]

The defeated candidate wrote "privately and confidentially" to Bryan to urge that he work against the election of Reagan to the Senate, lest "such calamity as his election to the Senate befall the country after that of Houston." The triumph of Houston's "pretended nationalism and Demagogical Union saving doctrines," said Runnels, would "forever prostrate in the State the only two Constitutional States rights men in the state and inflict an irreparable blow upon Southern interests at this time."[18] Reagan was re-elected to the House of Representatives as a regular Democrat, and A. J. Hamilton won a seat as an independent on the Houston ticket. When the Legislature met in 1860, a senator would be appointed to the place vacated by Henderson's death, and Reagan's friends hoped that he would get the post. Reagan himself said that he and the Houston faction were agreed in devotion to the best interests of the country, that he would not oppose the Democratic party, and that he was entirely content for either Houston or George W. Smyth to be sent to the Senate.[19] The same election which made Houston governor sent an overwhelming Democratic majority to the Legislature of Texas. Between the election and the convening of the Legislature, John Brown made his raid on Harpers Ferry on October 16, 1859, and

[16] Hayes to Bryan, September 10, 1859, Charles Richard Williams (ed.), *Diary and Letters of Rutherford Birchard Hayes*, I, 543.

[17] Howard K. Beale (ed.), *The Diary of Edward Bates, 1859–1866*, Vol. IV of American Historical Association *Annual Report, 1930*, 42–43.

[18] H. R. Runnels to Bryan, September 20, 1859, Bryan Papers.

[19] Reagan to William Alexander, October 3, 1859, Reagan Papers.

the resulting fury of antiabolition and radical Southern sentiment made inevitable the choice of fire-eating L. T. Wigfall as Texas senator.

In September, Houston attended barbecues given in his honor at Huntsville and at Montgomery. His correspondence was already heavy with applications for appointment; it was no wonder that he asked Washington D. Miller to take his old post as private secretary. In Austin, Mrs. Robert Barr was anticipating her first view of her hero, described to her by another Austin resident: "You will see him some morning soon, sitting in front of Tong's grocery, looking like a lion, and wearing a Serape Saltillero like a royal mantle. I can't help admiring the man, though I do not like him. In a far-off way he reminds me of Oliver Cromwell."[20]

On December 3, 1859, the thirty-eight managers for the Governor's Inaugural Ball, headed by Sam A. Maverick, issued their invitations for the dance to follow the inauguration on December 21. Criticism and disparagement and partisan animosities continued to be expressed, particularly among some of the legislators, one of whom suggested that the carpet should be removed from the floor of the House for the inaugural since the new governor was accustomed only to the wigwam. Houston must have felt some bitterness about moving his family to the Mansion, when he knew that a resolution on furnishings for the residence had been referred to the Committee on Public Buildings and Grounds after Roger Q. Mills had used the event as an occasion to vent his spleen and say that he saw "no reason why there should be for the Great Mogul of the Know-Nothings such deference and respect."[21]

Because of the chill reception on the part of some members, Houston moved his inaugural address from the House floor to the porch in front of the Capitol. The correspondent of the San Antonio *Herald* was eloquent in his report of the occasion:

The "eagle-eyed, lion hearted" patriot then arose, like one of the patriarchal family. Then burst forth the mighty heart of the people with a great throb; all former applause was weak with that which now made the old capitol building shake to its center. Long and continued was this spontaneous outburst of feeling, while the hero of San Jacinto—the People's choice for Governor stood like a mighty Hercules in their midst,

"The state's whole thunder born to wield
And shake the Senate and the field."

[20] Barr, *All the Days of My Life,* 221.
[21] Culberson, "General Sam Houston and Secession," *Scribner's Magazine,* XXXIX (May, 1906), 585.

The *Herald* described the inaugural address as "replete with practical sense, the pure triumphs of true eloquence, mingled with the rich resources of his mind, and the brilliant flashings of a mighty intellect that could originate as well as execute."[22] Houston began with a plea for legislative co-operation; recommended railroads and other internal improvements, a system of public education, and an adequate frontier defense; and concluded with a condemnation of sectionalism.

The approximately fifteen months of Houston's governorship were months of uncertainty and unrest in state, national, and international affairs. In retrospect, what he projected during those fifteen months is still uncertain, partly because of his habitual reticence about his motives and plans, partly because of the deviousness of his moves in the matter of the protectorate, partly because his every act and motive was suspect and liable to implication and interpretation, however simple or candid it might appear on the surface. The purely domestic problems of executive clemency, direction of the penitentiary, appointment of state officials, railroad charters, the boundary survey, the treasury deficit, and his bitter controversy with State Comptroller Clement R. Johns did not project Houston into the national political scene. The Cortinas affair was settled by federal troops, the regiment bill failed, the frontier forces were called in for lack of funds, and disturbed conditions on the eve of the Civil War prevented effective organization of the militia. Then with Houston's strenuous opposition to secession and to Texas' entry into the Confederate States of America, there was an interval of doubt about what the Governor might do in an effort to keep Texas in the Union and about the possible influence of his attitude on federal action. What his plans were he did not say, and the pieces of the puzzle are not yet all in place. Whatever he planned and why, he loved the Union and he loved Texas, and those loves determined his action, however tortuous his course seemed to become.

In his family life he was a solicitous husband and a proud and devoted father as he enjoyed the longest continuous acquaintance with his children that he had ever known. The summer before he became governor he had spent much of his time at Independence, where the older children were in school, and frequently he made talks in the chapel. After the family moved to Austin, Sam Jr. was sent to Bastrop to board with the James Nicholson family while he attended the Allen Academy. Mrs. Houston continued to suffer from asthma and was expecting another baby; so the Governor devoted much time to caring

---

[22] San Antonio *Daily Herald*, December 27, 1859.

for the other children, getting up at night to shake the fleas from the long underwear of young Andrew Jackson, who had played too long with his dog.[23]

Houston had been in office but a month when he transmitted to the Legislature, South Carolina's resolutions asserting the right of secession. He appended his counterstatement of Texas' satisfaction with the Union as it was and his plea for "urging upon the people of all the States . . . the necessity of cultivating brotherly feeling, observing justice, and attending to their own affairs."[24] Sam Maverick, for one, rejoiced in the Governor's action: "What a blessing it is not to have Runnels here now, aggravating the mischief, as he did all the time he was Governor. Old Sam is the right man for this delicate occasion; for S.C. would be fool enough to go out of the Union, if only she had 3 or 4 states to go with her."[25]

As 1860 moved to the fall election and the Democratic party disintegrated to make a Republican victory inevitable, Houston attended a Union mass meeting in Austin and declared that secession was treason, even if Lincoln were elected, for "the Union is worth more than Mr. Lincoln, and if the battle is to be fought for the Constitution, let us fight it in the Union and for the sake of the Union." The Texas press was not with him. The *Republican* said his speech would bring him nothing but condemnation, and the Dallas *Herald* declared it the "expiring kick (political) of the Old Hero." At Fairfield, Limestone County, citizens adopted resolutions condemning Houston's "sentiment of servility" and hanged L. D. Evans in effigy.[26] Outside of Texas, Houston's attitude was well known. Governor William H. Gist of South Carolina was keeping his legislature in session to call a secession convention as soon as the general election was over, and on October 5, 1860, wrote to all Southern governors except Houston announcing his state's probable secession and asking co-operation.[27] Houston was stumping Texas, speaking at Bastrop, Independence, Navasota, Anderson, Huntsville, Danville, and Cold Spring between October 17 and 29 to argue against disunion. His Thanksgiving Proclamation was a plea "that we may be preserved a United people, free, independent, and prosperous." Fletcher S. Stockdale, representing the opposition, wrote Guy Bryan that "Old

[23] Houston to Sam Houston, Jr., April 7, 1860, *Writings*, VIII, 8.
[24] Message Transmitting Resolutions of South Carolina, *ibid.*, VII, 441.
[25] S. A. Maverick to Mary A. Maverick, February 1, 1860, Samuel A. Maverick Papers.
[26] Speech at Austin, September 22, 1860, *Writings*, VIII, 145–60; *Texas Republican*, November 3, 1860; Dallas *Herald*, November 7, 14, 1860.
[27] Beale, *Diary of Edward Bates*, 102, n. 87.

Sam, and Paschal and Pease and Hamilton *et id. &c.* may take the stump
and shed tears like a crocodile and harp upon the union, these tricks
are stale and no longer win."[28]

As election day approached, reports of incendiary fires, supposedly
the work of abolitionists, caused a wave of hysteria in the state; apprehension of slave insurrections grew, and the Knights of the Golden Circle announced themselves as a secession society. George Bickley, head
of the organization, spoke at Austin on October 24 and defined the object of the association as the fostering and protection of slavery against
all enemies. On November 3 he was at Huntsville, where Thomas Carothers was the leader of the forty-eight men initiated into the order and
where Bickley announced the organization of castles at Austin, La-
Grange, Brenham, Chappel Hill, Houston, and Navasota. Headquarters were at San Antonio, and Bickley promised that if no civil discord
arose after the election to demand action, he would order Texans to
the "scene of action." That scene was Mexico, where more slavery territory could be added to the Union to equalize representation in Congress.[29] Bickley made his speech at Houston on November 8. Two days
before, Lincoln had been elected president. Houston learned the local
results—in favor of Breckinridge—and wrote his son in bitter anguish:

How the State will go, I can't say, but "the Union must be preserved." The
fire eaters got their chunk put out. The price of liberty is blood, and if an attempt is made to destroy our Union, or violate our Constitution, there will be
blood shed to maintain them. The Demons of anarchy must be put down and
destroyed. The miserable Demagogues & Traitors of the land must be silenced,
and set at naught.[30]

That he was driven to considering some drastic step of his own is indicated in a note he dictated on November 9 to be sent to Ed Burleson:
"You will be here [Austin] on some time during tomorrow, *as early
as possible,* with all of the men you can bring, *who are true to the Country* and on whom you can rely in an emergency. When you arrive I
will explain every thing to you." Houston added his own postscript in
pencil: "Dear Colonel, Hurry by all means."[31]

The Lone Star flag was hoisted in Galveston on November 8 and
was soon flying at Houston, Richmond, Huntsville, Gonzales, Navasota,
Waco, and Dallas. Meetings were called to decide upon proper action

[28] *Southern Intelligencer,* October 10, 1860; Thanksgiving Proclamation, October
27, 1860, *Writings,* VIII, 173; Stockdale to Bryan, October 16, 1860, Bryan Papers.
[29] Dallas *Herald,* October 31, November 14, 1860.
[30] Houston to Sam Houston, Jr., November 7, 1860, *Writings,* VIII, 184–85.
[31] Houston to Burleson, November 9, 1860, Edward Burleson Papers.

in the crisis. Reagan wrote O. M. Roberts on November 1, wondering if the Legislature should be convened to call a state convention and whether or not Houston would co-operate in the call or acquiesce in Lincoln's election. If the Governor refused to assemble the Legislature, a call for a convention would place its proponents in opposition to both the state and the federal government. Roberts, on November 25, wrote that Houston was still holding back but was intimating that if he were satisfied that the majority of Texans wanted the Legislature convened, he would resign and let Lieutenant Governor Clark make the call.[32]

Houston was counseling patience—to "wait and see." He advised a young West Point cadet who had volunteered his services to continue his studies because no real cause of disunion existed, and warned that if madness and fanaticism caused secession, then anarchy and confusion and devastation would follow. To a group of citizens who asked his views on the crisis, he wrote that he regretted the election of men whose only claim to the support of the country was their official character but that he felt there was no alternative but to yield to the Constitution. When Lincoln violated the Constitution, that would be the time to revolt, but at the moment there was not more safety out of the Union than in it, so that until Texas was made the victim of "federal wrong," he was for the Union.[33]

According to John S. Ford, the Governor tried indirectly to influence Supreme Court Judges R. T. Wheeler and J. H. Bell to prepare for him a constitutional argument on the doctrine of secession to be issued in a circular which would arrest the secession agitation. Wheeler evaded the issue, and Bell replied that his only objection to secession at the time was one of policy and not of right. The Unionists then took a different tack, which Ford described as "laughable enough, if one could have felt like being amused, at such a time, and on such a subject." They resurrected a statute passed by the Legislature in February, 1858, at the time of the Kansas difficulties, authorizing the Governor to order an election of seven delegates to meet delegates of other Southern states in a convention when such a meeting became necessary "to preserve the equal rights of such States in the Union." On November 28, 1860, Houston sent a copy of the statute to the governors of the Southern states, recommending a consultative convention. He then answered the pleas for calling a special session of the Legislature by saying that

[32] Reagan to Roberts, November 1, 1860, Reagan Papers; Roberts to Reagan, November 25, 1860, Roberts Papers.

[33] Houston to T. L. Rosser, November 17, 1860, and to H. M. Watkins and others, November 20, 1860, Writings, VIII, 192–97, 199–200.

separate Texas action was not necessary until he had received a response from the other states to the request for such a convention.[34]

S. M. Swenson and Tom Green, clerk of the Supreme Court, secured Houston's permission to use the hall of the House of Representatives on December 1 for Judges Bell and Roberts to present their views on the crisis. That same day there was circulated a handbill signed by a number of Harris County citizens, addressed to the Governor and agreeing with his course of consultation and harmonious action by the Southern states. It indicated that at least a few conservative Houston businessmen were not in accord with Ashbel Smith and W. P. Rogers, who had brought a petition to Austin to try to persuade the Governor to join the secession movements. There were isolated examples of others who supported the Houston stand. A. B. Burleson, Ed's cousin, wrote from Bellville:

I want you to see them in Halifax before you convene the legislature—and also you stand square for the Union and the Nation and at the same time the Rights of the South which I and others that know you believe you will do. I find a number of your old acquaintances that are with you and waiting for you to say something before they will follow any man or party of men.[35]

Majority opinion, however, was expressed by the December 5, 1860, editorial in the Dallas *Herald* called "Good News from the Governor," which claimed that he had told the Harris County commissioners that he would not stand in the way of the wishes of the people and would call the Legislature. The *Herald* was in error, perhaps deliberate, for Houston had made no such answer to Smith, Rogers, and Taylor, but he did visit Houston and Galveston on December 7 and 8. At Galveston, conservative Unionists held a meeting to adopt his plan for sending delegates to a consulting convention at Austin. The response to his speech at Houston showed most of his listeners opposed to him and responding to his pleas with "Three Cheers for Yancey." It may have been the speech in Galveston that Thomas North described in his *Five Years in Texas*. Personal friends of the Governor warned him of possible harm which might ensue if he spoke, but Houston said he had seen his friends tremble for his safety before and that he would speak. According to North, "he paralyzed the arm of the mobocrat by his personal presence" and proved it was morally impossible for him to be

---

[34] Memoirs of John Salmon Ford, V, 945–47, 954; Address to the People of Texas, December 3, 1860, *Writings*, VIII, 206–12.

[35] Burleson to Houston, December 5, 1860, Governors' Letters; Memoirs of John Salmon Ford, V, 948–51.

mobbed in Texas.[36] When a reporter from the Galveston *News* finally secured an interview with the Governor, he found him "whittling white pine keepsakes" and could get no written statement, but reported that Houston told him that "he had found Texas in a very bad condition a number of times, out of which he had gotten her, but that she was now old enough to take care of herself, and if she was bent upon her own destruction by secession, he would not go with her . . . but thanked the Lord that he could resign his seat any time he saw proper."[37]

On December 17, the Governor issued the proclamation for a special session of the Legislature to meet on January 21, 1861. W. S. Oldham and Tom Green immediately ordered an extra edition of the *State Gazette* to feature an editorial called "Good News for the People" and then joined the procession which thronged up Congress Avenue to the Governor's Mansion, where Houston spoke from the portico. O. M. Roberts could hear parts of the speech, including the statement that the Governor "would teach the people that he would have his own way; that the people would have to follow him a while." According to the Ford memoirs, when Houston saw the *Gazette* extra with its interpretation of the call of the Legislature, he made some such exclamation as: "The scoundrels! They would contaminate Christ's sermon upon the mount if they could!" South Carolina seceded on December 20. On December 21, Houston and Judge John Hancock were at a meeting at the Capitol to organize a "Union Club," which stood for "Consultation and co-operation of the Southern States to preserve the Union and their rights in it."[38]

It was upon that "Union" basis that Houston, on December 27, issued a proclamation dividing the state into districts for the election, on February 4, 1861, of seven delegates to a convention of the Southern states. His action met the approval of J. W. Throckmorton, who had written to Congressman Reagan that such a Southern convention could call upon the Northern states for a general convention, which could make the adjustments that equal and constitutional rights demanded. When constitutional remedies were exhausted, then dissolution would be the only course.[39] Texas papers, with the exception of Paschal's *Intelligencer,* held a contrary view. The *Texas Republican* said that the

---

[36] Thomas North, *Five Years in Texas; or, What You Did Not Hear during the War from January, 1861, to January, 1866. A Narrative of His Travels, Experiences, and Observations, in Texas and Mexico,* 90–92.

[37] Quoted in *Texas Republican,* December 15, 1860.

[38] Memoirs of John Salmon Ford, V, 958–62.

[39] Throckmorton to Reagan, December 9, 1860, United States War Department Files, Letters Received.

call of the convention for February was intended as a delaying tactic but that fortunately the People's Convention, which would meet to consider secession on January 28, would be simultaneous with the meeting of the Legislature, and that by the end of January the crisis would have so far culminated that there would be no doubt about the course to be pursued. The Dallas *Herald* described Houston's move for the Southern convention as a "puerile effort to mislead the people" and a "flagrant trampling of the law underfoot by the Executive and his toadies."[40]

The Governor's speech at Waco on New Year's Day ended with the statement that he would yield to the decision of the people, but in the event of secession he preferred "a separate Republic of the Lone Star." His hearers gave three cheers for South Carolina, and his friends hastened his departure across the Brazos.[41]

On January 5, J. M. Calhoun, Alabama's commissioner to Texas, was in Austin and wrote the Governor that his state would have a convention on January 7 and was expecting to withdraw from the United States and seek a speedy union with other states of the South. Houston answered that if Alabama boasted of being the first to move for severance of all connection with the federal government, he was proud that Texas had been first to move in the direction of Southern unity and co-operation. Should Texas, in the future, be compelled to provide for her own safety, her interest would lead her to avoid entangling alliances and she would violate no duty to the South if she unfurled her Lone Star. If the Union were dissolved and civil war followed, Texas could "tread the wine press alone." He declared that Texas could not desert conservative men of the North or the border states and hinted again at Texas' manifest destiny:

It will be but natural that her people, feeling that they must look to themselves, . . . will prefer a separate Nationality, to even an equal position in a Confederacy, which may be broken and destroyed at any moment, by the caprice or dissatisfaction of one of its members. Texas has views of expansion not common to many of her sister States. Although an empire within herself, she feels that there is an empire beyond, essential to her security. She will not be content to have the path of her destiny clogged. The same spirit of enterprise that founded a Republic here, will carry her institutions Southward and Westward.[42]

[40] *Texas Republican*, January 5, 1861; Dallas *Herald*, January 9, 1861.
[41] Culberson, "General Sam Houston and Secession," *Scribner's Magazine*, XXXIX (May, 1906), 590.
[42] Houston to Calhoun, January 7, 1861, *Writings*, VIII, 230.

Houston may still have had Mexican conquest in mind, or he may have chosen this method of predicting that when the inevitable break came he would go for Texas independence rather than union with a temporary Southern confederacy. At any rate, his answer made him suspect with both the federal government and the Texas secessionists, who were already planning Southern collaboration. That suspicion was aggravated by his sending a confidential messenger, Ranger Captain John M. Smith, to General Twiggs to ask whether or not the General meant to maintain the property of the federal government or to turn it over to a state officer to prevent its seizure by an unauthorized mob.[43] The day after his letter to Twiggs, Houston delivered his message to the extra session of the Legislature. He summarized his efforts for defense of the frontier and explained how his program had been handicapped by the conflicting provisions in the militia law and the empty state treasury. He portrayed the structure of the federal government as tottering to ruin and Texas faced with abandoning that government or attempting to maintain its constitutional rights within the Union. He pleaded with Texas to take no step without calm deliberation and asked the Legislature to frown upon any attempt of revolutionary leaders to substitute their will for law.[44]

While the Governor was delivering his message, his wife was writing her mother:

Truly the present appearance of things is gloomy enough. . . . General Houston seems cheerful and hopeful through the day, but in the still watches of the night I hear him agonizing in prayer for our distracted country. . . . I cannot shut my eyes to the dangers that threaten us. I know that it is even probable that we may soon be rendered to poverty, but oh, I have such a sweet assurance in my heart that the presence of the Lord will go with us wherever we may go.[45]

[43] Houston to D. E. Twiggs, January 20, 1861, and To the Legislature, January 21, 1861, *ibid.*, 234–52.
According to William Mumford Baker, an unnamed Texas lawyer who acted probably under Houston's commission went to Washington to confer with President Buchanan and urge that he relieve Twiggs of command and appoint Houston in his place. The emissary argued that such action, taken immediately, would prevent secession. Alas for "clerical Buchanan," the lawyer reported, "when I mentioned Houston to him, he turned pale as his cravat." See Baker, "A Pivotal Point," *Lippincott's Magazine*, XXVI (November, 1880), 562.
[44] The Dallas *Herald*, on February 6, 1861, reviewed the message as a "submission document" and reported the Governor's views as "entirely antagonistic" to persons in favor of speedy action by the states.
[45] Margaret Lea Houston to Nancy Lea, January 21, 1861, Houston Unpublished Correspondence, X.

Twiggs had replied to Houston that he hoped that the threatened unauthorized seizure of property would not take place and that he was without instructions from Washington. He sent Houston's letter on to Adjutant General S. Cooper with his fifth plea for instructions on what to do after Texas seceded:

As I do not think anyone in authority desires me to carry on a civil war against Texas, I shall, after secession, if the governor repeats his demand, direct the arms and other property to be turned over to his agents. . . . The troops in this department occupy a line of some twelve hundred miles, and some time will be required to remove them to any place. *I again ask, what disposition is to be made of them?*[46]

That disposition was determined by the Secession Convention, which met on January 28, 1861, one week after the meeting of the Legislature. On the second day a resolution was adopted that it was the sense of the convention that Texas should secede. On the fourth day Houston recognized the legality of the body and assured one of its committees that he would submit to the will of the people as expressed at the ballot box. Roberts, who had been instrumental in calling the convention and acted as its president, wanted to show Houston every courtesy due the chief executive of the state and believed that giving him an opportunity to fall into the movement would thaw opposition to it. He therefore asked J. L. Hogg and W. P. Rogers to induce the Governor to attend the session of February 1, when the secession ordinance was adopted. A preliminary secret conclave had determined that there should be no public discussion, and the most dramatic moments of the day occurred when T. Jefferson Chambers preceded his affirmative vote with a personal remark directed at Houston, and when J. W. Throckmorton rebuked those who hissed his negative vote.[47]

The ordinance was to be submitted to a vote of the electorate on February 23 and, if approved, would take effect on March 2, 1861, the twenty-fifth birthday of Texas and the sixty-eighth of Sam Houston. On February 4 the Committee of Public Safety, headed by John C. Robertson, sent a subcommittee composed of W. P. Rogers, W. S. Oldham, and T. J. Devine to the Governor to outline their plans to seize federal property in the state, even while assuring him that they would not attempt to exercise any power that would conflict with his authority as executive. The committee and the Governor agreed that the executive could not dispose of the property while Texas was still in the

---

[46] United States War Department, *War of the Rebellion*, Series 1, Vol. I, 582.
[47] Memoirs of John Salmon Ford, V, 975–76.

Union and his oath to support the Constitution of the United States was binding. Houston gave assurance that "he never would be instrumental in the shedding of fraternal blood."[48] On that same day the Texas convention elected delegates to the Montgomery, Alabama, convention of the seceded states and adjourned until March 2.

Houston, on February 9, issued a proclamation ordering the election for ratifying or rejecting the secession ordinance. His message to the Legislature on February 6 had stressed the need of appropriations for a state military force to replace the federal force, lest Texas "be subject to the humiliation of dependence on a Government which she has thrown off." This apparent acquiescence to the inevitable drew sarcasm from the Dallas *Herald,* which described Houston as being "converted" and accused him of deserting his "squad of submissionists" while he "threw himself 'weary and heavy laden' with numerous sins upon the mercies of the secession party." Such conversion Houston denied, insisting that he had declared himself for harmony and compromise in order to obtain a fair expression of the will of the people. If the people would bear ruin and civil war, he could bear it with them.[49]

On February 16, Ben McCulloch, acting under orders of the Committee of Public Safety, arranged with General Twiggs for seizure of the United States arsenal and barracks at San Antonio, and the transfer was made on February 18.

The February 23 vote on secession was 46,129 to 14,697 in favor of the ordinance, many Unionists remaining away from the polls and eighteen counties voting against the move. The Secession Convention reassembled and counted the vote, and, on March 4, Houston issued a proclamation that Texas had seceded. That was an inaugural gift for the Black Republican administration that took over in Washington on that day. The next day the convention adopted an ordinance uniting Texas with the Confederate States, and at that point Houston's compliance ceased. Holding that the convention had exhausted its legal powers when it performed its function of submitting the question to a vote of the people, he proposed to recommend to the Legislature, when it reassembled on March 18, the calling of a convention to make requisite changes in the state constitution. To emphasize his point, he had his secretary of state, E. W. Cave, write to L. P. Walker, secretary of war

[48] E. W. Winkler (ed.), *Journal of the Secession Convention,* Appendix II, 399–400.
[49] Dallas *Herald,* February 13, 1861; Extract from Houston Letter, February 20, 1861, *Writings,* VIII, 263–64.

of the Confederate States of America, to deny that Texas was a member of that confederacy and to say that Texas' national pride and dignity did not sanction being annexed to a new government without the state's knowledge or consent.[50]

Houston's letter to the convention committee was received with "stormy disapproval," and the reassembled convention on March 14 adopted an ordinance to provide for the continuance of the existing state government by requiring all state officials to take an oath to support the Confederate States. State officials who were delegates to the convention took the oath on March 15. George W. Chilton was chosen to convey to Houston an order to appear at high noon on Saturday, March 16, 1861, to take the required oath. The Governor had left the executive office, and Chilton delivered the message to the Mansion at eight o'clock in the evening, agreeing to wait for an answer until noon the next day.[51] The oldest Houston daughter, Nancy, then fifteen, described to her son the events in the Mansion after Chilton's departure:

The family had their dinner as usual and when the negro servants had removed the food and soiled dishes, Mrs. Houston brought the family Bible and placed it before the General at the head of the table. The negroes brought in their raw hide bottom chairs from the kitchen and the servants' quarters and arranged themselves along the back wall of the dining room. The General then read a chapter from the Bible, made appropriate remarks, and they all knelt in family prayer as was the usual custom. . . .

After bidding his family good night the General left positive instructions with Mrs. Houston that he must not be disturbed under any circumstances and that no visitors were to be admitted to the mansion. He then went to his bedroom on the upper floor, removed his coat and vest and shoes and remained alone throughout the night during which he did not sleep. Instead he walked the floor of his bedroom and the upper hall in his sock feet, wrestling with his spirit as Jacob wrestled with the angel until the purple dawn of another day shone over the eastern hills. He had come through his Gethsemane, and the die was cast.

When he came down and met Mrs. Houston, he said, "Margaret, I will never do it." That meant that he would not take the oath of allegiance and

---

[50] Winkler, *Journal of the Secession Convention*, 88; Houston to a Committee of the Convention, March 6, 1861, and to Walker, March 13, 1861, *Writings*, VIII, 265–66, 268–71.

[51] Winkler, *Journal of the Secession Convention*, 178–79.

Judge Roberts decided to require Houston's oath on Saturday rather than waiting until Monday, the last day before the Legislature met, in order to prevent any move to embroil the convention and the Legislature. Houston said that Roberts was less gracious than Shylock in demanding his answer in two rather than three days, but Roberts replied that he had no ambition to be considered gracious towards an enemy lying in wait to seize every advantage. See Memoirs of John Salmon Ford, V, 985.

had reconciled himself to be deposed to go into political exile rather than violate his conscience or sacrifice his principles."

The Governor may have spent much of that harrowing night in composing the broadside which he addressed to the people of Texas on March 16, outlining his reasons for refusing his allegiance to the Confederacy but declaring that he would withdraw from his office calmly because he loved Texas "too well to bring civil strife and bloodshed upon her." When the Governor and Cave refused to take the prescribed oath, their offices were declared vacant. William Baker, Presbyterian minister in Austin, himself suspect because of his avowed opposition to secession, said years later:

As I look back into the darkness of those days, the central figure of them all is that of the old governor sitting in his chair in the basement of the capitol . . . sorrowfully meditating what it were best to do. . . . The officer of the gathering up stairs summoned the old man three times to come forward and take the oath of allegiance . . . to the Confederacy. I remember as yesterday the call thrice repeated—"Sam Houston! Sam Houston! Sam Houston!" but the man sat silent, immovable, in his chair below, whittling steadily on."

Edward Clark was sworn in as governor on Monday, March 18, the day that Houston sent his last message to a Texas legislative body. In it he described his acquiescence to the will of the people in accepting secession but decried the usurpation of authority by the convention and the new governor and maintained that all the authority confided in him by the people still remained in his hands."

The governor's decision was his alone, but the private circle of his family was with him, and more than a few consoling letters came in. A. Foster of Hill County deplored the "jack-leg lawyers and half handed understrikers who bemeaned the governor as a traitor." M. C. Rogers, the agent at the penitentiary, predicted dishonor, with the Union dissolved into "fragmentary squads." A. B. Burleson begged Houston to "go for an independent Republic again and play a lone hand." Thomas Carothers complained that the secessionists had placed Texas in such a predicament that the man who loved his country scarcely knew how to act. Even after the election on the secession ordinance, I. C. McAlpin of Cass County asked the Governor "in the name of God and country to never forsake the Union but oppose with your great powers the

---

[52] Address by Temple Houston Morrow, *Senate Journal*, 49 Texas Legislature, reg. sess. (February 27, 1945), 282.

[53] Baker, "A Pivotal Point," *Lippincott's Magazine*, XXVI (November, 1880), 566.

[54] To the People of Texas, March 16, 1861, and To the Legislature, March 18, 1861, *Writings*, VIII, 271–92.

secession move." T. M. Scott of Collin County, after the Governor was deposed, wrote that hundreds of citizens in North Texas approved Houston's course which would "ultimately place your name by the side of those great and good men whose love of country was greater than that of personal aggrandizement." Mrs. Houston's brother-in-law, Charles Power, while approving Houston's motives, warned that since Texas was not able to "go it alone," it would be better to pass quietly into retirement and "let them fight it out," for posterity would give Houston a "page of history which is as much as the greatest can expect." Some solace came from afar. Lydia Howard Sigourney, in Hartford, Connecticut, begged the General to "save Texas for us if you can." Louis Conduel of Morristown, New Jersey, commended his old friend's firmness and urged him to persevere, but Judge Thomas Shankland of New York just advised the Governor to gather his family "and flee out of the land of secession" to New York, where he could have "peace without a revolution and could be interminably amused with the antics of the abolitionists and the strong minded women."[55]

The Governor's family was ordered to vacate the Mansion immediately. Friends helped them pack on March 19 and were still at the Mansion that night when another group of Houston's friends appeared, armed, and told him that they were ready to reinstate him in office. He thanked them for their devotion and loyalty but deplored any move that would precipitate civil strife "merely to keep one poor old man in a position for a few days longer."[56] That expression of his friends was not the only offer to keep him in his position. Lincoln sent at least two messengers to Houston with offers of assistance. In September, some six months after the war had already begun, Houston wrote to Hamilton Stuart and E. W. Cave:

Had I been disposed to involve Texas in civil war, I had it in my power, for I was tendered the aid of seventy thousand men and means to sustain myself in Texas by adhering to the Union; but this I rejected, and in return for the offer, I gave my advice to the Federal Government that I wanted no money, I desired no office, and wished for no troops, but if Mr. Lincoln were wise, and really wished to confer a benefit upon the country, he would evacuate Forts Pickens and Sumter, recall all the Federal troops from Texas, and not take the advice of such men as General Scott, or his administration would be disgraced. Notwithstanding this, when my message was reported to Mr. Lincoln by his own messenger, it appeared from confidential letter-writers in Washington, that he did not believe that his agent had been faithful in the

[55] Miscellaneous letters of February, March, and April, 1861, Governors' Letters.
[56] *Writings*, VIII, 293.

discharge of his trust in reporting my opinion. To this conclusion he was led, no doubt, by . . . charges upon my reputation of abolition and treason to the South. So strong was his belief . . . in these slanders that he immediately resolved to send another messenger and troops to the South."[57]

Lincoln was cognizant of Houston as a strong Unionist who had been frequently mentioned to him as a cabinet possibility. In fact, the Dallas *Herald,* on November 21, 1860, quoted a passenger on the overland stage to the effect that Houston was to be a member of the Lincoln cabinet. The portfolio usually suggested was that of secretary of war. "A Republican" of New Bedford, Massachusetts, made such a suggestion to Lincoln on December 21, 1860, and Josiah Drummond of Portland, Maine, made a similar recommendation to Leonard Swett, who sent the letter on to Lincoln. "All Kentucky" was anonymous in his suggestion of Houston as a Southern conservative, but Francis Blair, Sr., was outspoken in recommendation of Houston as a "true Union man." J. Boree Dods of Brooklyn wrote Lincoln a long letter to depict Houston's availability as a cabinet member whose "independence and true greatness of soul" would prompt him "to burst every party barrier & fly to rescue [his country] from the stormy grasp of revolution." At the same time Dods was asking Houston to recommend Thomas Shankland to Lincoln for a post as naval officer at the Port of New York.[58]

Lincoln would hardly have considered Houston for his cabinet, but that he was earnestly considering the military situation in Texas is indicated by a brief note to William H. Seward, penned at the Willard Hotel three days before the inauguration: "If a successor to Gen. Twiggs is attempted to be appointed, do not allow it to be done."[59]

One of the messengers sent to Texas was Colonel Frederick West Lander. The exact time and circumstances of his mission have not been fully determined, but he was in Washington, D.C., on February 1, 1861, when he resigned his position as superintendent of the Fort Kearney, South Pass, and Honey Lake Wagon Road and offered his services to the government, without compensation, until March 4, the day the Lincoln administration would begin. On the afternoon of February 4, according to a newspaper clipping in the Lander scrapbook, the Colonel called on General Winfield Scott to offer his services to the War Depart-

---

[57] To the Editors of the *Civilian,* September 12, 1861, *ibid.,* VIII, 312.

[58] "Republican" of Maine to Lincoln, in Beale, *Diary of Edward Bates,* 170; "All Kentucky" to Lincoln, December 2, 1860, Lincoln Papers, Reel 11; Blair to Lincoln, January 14, 1861, *ibid.,* Reel 14; Swett to Lincoln, December 13, 1860, *ibid.,* Reel 11; Dods to Lincoln, February 5, 1861, *ibid.,* Reel 16; Dods to Houston, February 11, 1861, Governors' Letters.

[59] Lincoln to Seward, March 1, 1861, Lincoln Papers, Reel 17.

ment. Scott had spent the day preparing instructions for Major Robert Anderson, in command at Fort Sumter.[60] On Sunday afternoon, March 10, Secretary of State Seward sent a note to Lincoln: "Colonel Lander failed to come, but I shall see him this evening, and probably bring him over to see you."[61]

Nineteen days later, eleven days after Houston was deposed as governor, Lander was in Austin, Texas, and wrote to Colonel Charles A. Waite, who had succeeded Twiggs in command at San Antonio, that General Scott's orders to concentrate troops at Indianola for the purpose of giving aid to the Union party in Texas would necessarily fail because of the determination of Governor Houston to protest against such military aid being rendered him. Lander advised Waite to delay for further orders from Washington before making an intrenched camp at Indianola or taking any step which might lead Texas secessionists to imagine that the administration proposed coercion.[62] Houston sent a letter to Waite by the same messenger who bore the Lander communication. Acknowledging intelligence of Waite's orders to concentrate troops to sustain him as governor, Houston wrote:

Allow me most respectfully to decline any such assistance of the United States Government, and to most earnestly protest against the concentration of troops in fortifications in Texas, and request that you remove all such troops out of the State at the very earliest day practicable, or, at any rate, by all means take no action towards hostile movements still [till] further ordered by the Government at Washington City, or particularly of Texas.[63]

On April 1, Waite forwarded the Lander and Houston letters to the War Department, reporting that federal military personnel were in process of leaving Texas and that there had never been any contemplation of collecting troops to sustain the Governor because the Unionists of Texas had no intention of using anything except the press and the ballot box to effect a change in public sentiment.[64] The same day that Lander and Houston wrote to Waite, Lincoln's cabinet was in session in Washington, and Seward was urging that Anderson be instructed to retire from Fort Sumter lest the war begin at that spot. Seward advised: "I would call in Capt. M. C. Meigs forthwith. Aided by his counsel I

[60] Moses Kelly to Lander, February 4, 1861, and clipping "Conference of Military Chiefs," in Frederick West Lander Papers.

[61] Lincoln Papers, Reel 18.

[62] Lander to Waite, March 29, 1861, *War of the Rebellion*, Series 1, Vol. I, 551–52.

[63] Houston to Waite, March 29, 1861, *Writings*, VIII, 294.

[64] Waite to Assistant Adjutant General, April 1, 1861, *War of the Rebellion*, Series 1, Vol. I, 550–51.

would at once and at every cost prepare for a war at Pensacola and Texas, to be taken however only as a consequence of maintaining the possession and authority of the United States."[65]

On April 11, 1861, Lander turned in to the State Department an expense account of $399.35. The day before, the Washington correspondent of the New York *Herald* had written to his paper:

On his [Lander's] return he reported that Governor Houston not only refused to accept military support from the United States government, but desired that President Lincoln should recall the regular troops from Texas. He also reported that Governor Houston urged in the strongest terms the evacuation of Forts Sumter and Pickens, stating that Arkansas would join Texas in secession in the event of coercion. . . . Governor Houston requested to be let alone, and maintained that the union party of the entire South was dead if coercion was once attempted.

This account appeared to President Lincoln so much at variance with what was understood here to be the opinion of Governor Houston, and knowing the political proclivities of the Ambassador ["a distinguished Democrat"], the President immediately dispatched another messenger to Governor Houston.[66]

William Mumford Baker wrote in 1880 a magazine article on Texas called "A Pivotal Point." Nineteen years had passed, and there are statements in the Baker story that are difficult to reconcile with known facts and with what Houston wrote at the time. Because there are so many "irreconcilables" in the Houston career, and because Andrew Jackson Houston, the Governor's second son, aged about seven when the actual events took place, said in 1881 that " 'The Pivotal Point' by W. M. Baker is authentic," the story is included.

Houston, according to Baker, felt that the federal investment in Texas in the form of officers, troops, ammunition, arms, and equipment could be used to resist Texas secession. Failing to have himself appointed to replace Twiggs in command, he secured what he considered a promise from Twiggs not to turn over the federal troops and stores to the secessionists—this sometime in late November or early December. In addition to the federal troops, some eight hundred volunteers in Burnet County awaited Houston's order to move. Lincoln, not yet inaugurated, sent Lander to assure Houston of all the aid he needed the moment the new president took office if Texas could be held in the Union until that time. To secure powder, lead, and food for the intervening weeks, and particularly to get coffee, Houston took S. M. Swenson into his confi-

[65] Mearns, *Lincoln Papers*, II, 498–99.
[66] New York *Herald*, April 11, 1861; clippings and note of expense account in Lander Papers.

dence. Swenson agreed to supply five hundred rations at thirty cents each, and transportation, and went to Houston and Galveston to buy "two hundred and fifty-seven sacks of Rio coffee" and enough "percussion-caps, bacon, rice, and flour to meet the emergency." When Swenson got back to Austin, Houston called him into his office, locked the door, and sobbed with rage that Twiggs was a traitor. Smith had brought Twiggs's letter saying that "*after* secession, if the executive made a demand of the commander of this department," he would receive an answer.

The points that will not jibe are the date of Lander's trip with the offer of assistance from Lincoln and the fact that Houston's letters contain no statement that is in any way tolerant of Lincoln or of the plan to aid Houston with federal troops. Houston wanted command of the forces in Texas, but apparently on his own terms and for his own purposes.[67]

A second messenger sent by Lincoln to Houston was George H. Giddings, a San Antonio merchant, who held the contract for carrying the mail from San Antonio to San Diego by the El Paso route. Giddings was in Washington to see about the renewal of his mail-route contract and was ready to start back to Texas when Postmaster General Blair told him that President Lincoln wanted to see him. The exact date of the interview has not been found, but it was after March 4, probably after Houston's deposition on March 18, and possibly as late as April 12. A scribbled notation on a loose sheet pasted into the Bates diary makes a record of a cabinet council meeting on April 12. "Secy. of War [Cameron] produces letter from Sam Houston—declining the help of U.S. troops, to the commanding officer U.S. in Texas,—till orders from Washington."[68] On that same day the firing began at Fort Sumter, a fact which would rationally place the Lincoln-Giddings interview nearer the end of March than the middle of April. According to Marquis James, Houston was in Georgetown when Giddings brought him the message, sometime between February 23 and March 2, 1861, but Lincoln was not inaugurated until March 4. Rufus C. Burleson's report was that just before Houston was deposed Lincoln sent a special messenger "disguised as a horse trader" with a proposal to send fifty thousand men to Texas. It is not likely, however, that Giddings had to come in disguise, and the identity of Lander was accurately reported in Texas by April 6. Because Lander

[67] Baker, "A Pivotal Point," *Lippincott's Magazine*, XXVI (November, 1880), 559–66; A. J. Houston to Alex Williams, November 14, 1881, printed in Dyersburg (Tennessee) *State Gazette* and copied in *Texas Siftings*, I (December 31, 1881).

[68] Beale, *Diary of Edward Bates*, 182.

was a Democrat and a friend of Scott, Lincoln may well have decided to pick another courier, either before or after he knew definitively of Lander's failure.[69]

As Giddings recalled, Lincoln told him that his object in seeking an interview was to entrust to him a secret message to Governor Houston. Before reading the message, he described it as a confidential and secret letter, known only to the cabinet, and went through the form of swearing Giddings in as a cabinet member. The letter, which was several pages long, after referring to Twiggs's surrender, offered to appoint Houston a major general in the United States Army and authorized him to take full command of government property in Texas and to recruit one hundred thousand men if possible to hold Texas in the Union. If he accepted, the President promised the support of the army and navy and the whole power of the government. Giddings remained in the cabinet session until about midnight and heard Seward prophesy that there would be no war because Humphrey Marshall and others had gone into the border states to hold meetings to arrange for a convention to amend the Constitution. Giddings agreed to take the message to Houston provided that it remain a cabinet secret.[70]

Houston put Lincoln's proposition before four of his Unionist friends: J. W. Throckmorton, George W. Paschal, Ben Epperson, and D. B. Culberson. Epperson wanted to accept the Lincoln offer; the three other men, realizing that secession was inevitable, said that Texas would become the theater of war if such a course were followed and advised against it. So reports the son of one of the Houston confidants. The phrase "secession was inevitable" would seem to place the time of Lincoln's offer of help before February 1, but perhaps Culberson's memory was in error. He did recall that Houston destroyed the Lincoln letter and said that he would take the advice of his friends but that if he had been twenty years younger he would have accepted the proposition.[71]

Paschal, another of the advisers on the occasion, wrote of the incident:

Houston pretty well preserved the secret of the offer sent by President Lincoln to tender him assistance. We must, therefore, pass it by as one of

[69] James, *The Raven*, 410; Georgia J. Burleson, *Life and Writings of Rufus C. Burleson*, 582; Terrell, "Recollections of General Sam Houston," *Southwestern Historical Quarterly*, XVI (1912/13), 134–35; *Southern Intelligencer*, April 27, 1859; Francis White Johnson, *A History of Texas and Texans*, ed. Eugene C. Barker and E. W. Winkler, V, 2385.

[70] Ida M. Tarbell, *The Life of Abraham Lincoln*, II, 69–70.

[71] Culberson, "General Sam Houston and Secession," *Scribner's Magazine*, XXXIX (May, 1906), 586.

those State secrets which resulted in nothing, but behind which Houston might have saved himself and his few Union adherents from much of the odium which was afterward heaped upon them by those who charged the war upon the opposition of the Unionists. But these confidants remained true to their faith, and never asked the publication of facts, which would have shown, at least, a determination to avoid the civil war until it should be forced by the South. Suffice it now to say, the Government offered to go to the assistance of Houston when it was *too late*.[12]

According to Lincoln's biographers:

This refusal is the end of Houston's public career. Without aid he could no longer command sufficient popular support to maintain his authority against local revolution. He was nearly seventy years old; and his advanced age was perhaps the underlying cause of his inability to ride and direct the new political storm.[13]

The necessary secrecy of the Houston-Lincoln exchange confused everybody: the Confederate States government, authorities of the Texas government, and the press. Galveston was jittery about a possible invasion and the reports that federal troops leaving Texas in April, 1861, were suddenly ordered to hold off. Someone at the Capitol in Austin penned an undated memorandum headed "WATCH!" and labeled "about Houston from Balt." It read:

"When it is officially demonstrated that *any one of the 34* states has been invaded by Mexico, the government will forthwith take immediate steps to repel the invaders."

Correspondent N.Y. *Herald* at Washington,
April 3, 1861

U.S. Postmaster Genl. Blair is said to be in receipt of a letter from Gen. Houston, in which the administration is exhorted to maintain the Union at all hazards &c &c.

His suggestions are said to have been discussed in the Cabinet meeting Tuesday last, and that some of the military movements now going on result from them.

Put this and that together and take care of the old man in time.[14]

Charles Power found it hard to listen to the tirades of the Houston enemies and besought Houston to write the *Civilian* stating the nature

---

[12] Paschal, "Last Years of Sam Houston," *Harper's New Monthly Magazine*, XXXII (1865/66), 633.

[13] John G. Nicolay and John Hay, *Abraham Lincoln: A History*, IV, 189.

[14] Undated and unsigned note, Texas State Archives. If the cabinet meeting here mentioned is the one that Giddings attended, his interview with the President came late in March.

of the correspondence with Lincoln and give the lie to those who insinuated that he had been "derelict as a Southern man."[75] Power wrote that he would "not be at all surprised to see Texas made the battleground yet." There were others in the Confederacy of a like mind. Gazaway B. Lamar possibly had not heard of the day-before firing on Fort Sumter when he wrote Howell Cobb on April 13:

I am afraid you will find an elephant in Texas. She will cost more than she is worth, unless old Houston is hanged. And the Indians are so troublesome it will bankrupt the Confederacy to keep them off. And I still incline to the opinion that the Fedl. Govt. are sending most of its forces to Texas under an invitation from old Houston and under the pretext of defending her, but mainly to make war on the Confederacy.[76]

The *Texas Republican* of May 11 carried a *State Gazette* editorial called "Conspiracy against Texas," which stated that the effort to incite civil war in Texas failed only because it turned out to be impracticable. The paper bespoke the humiliation of Texas that there should be an individual among the Texans "whose lust for office and position could have led him into such a wicked scheme." Later during the progress of the war, Houston wryly told Judge Ballinger that files of the *Gazette*, *Telegraph*, and *News* would prove to any Union soldiers that he had been a "better Black Republican for two years past than old Abe himself."[77]

In a speech at Galveston on April 19, and again in his letter to the *Civilian* of September 12, 1861, Houston denied any intrigue with Lincoln, asserting in each case that Lincoln had been misled by the calumnies heaped upon the Governor by the Texas newspapers. Lincoln was to have his own bitter personal knowledge of newspaper opinions, some of which, early in the administration, mentioned Houston. The New York *Times*, on April 3, 1861, carried an editorial called "Wanted—a Policy!" which held that if Lincoln wanted peace he should disarm the fears of war and encourage Union parties in every Southern state and questioned: "Why has SAM HOUSTON, of Texas, been left to fight the battle of the Union alone—without a word of encouragement, or promise of a man or a dollar from the Government at Washington?" For once the *Times* was not omniscient. The Newburyport (Massachusetts) *Daily Herald*, on May 24, 1861, questioned, "Will the Union be preserved?" and delivered the opinion that the tide had turned, that the

[75] Power to Houston, April 16, 1861, Houston Unpublished Correspondence, X.
[76] Lamar to Cobb, April 13, 1861, Phillips, *Correspondence of Robert Toombs, Alexander H. Stephens, and Howell Cobb*, 561.
[77] *Texas Republican*, May 11, 1861; Ballinger Diary, March 9, 1862.

troops moving south would be hailed as deliverers, and so "it will be in every State till the home of Sam Houston is reached, and his bugle notes call the people to duty along the valley of the Rio Grande."[78]

Houston had to bear opprobrium from both directions; the secessionists condemned him as a "submissionist," and even as a traitor who would have placed his state in a position to be subjugated; the Unionists, more especially those outside of Texas who could not comprehend the peculiar local situation, blamed him for indecision. Nicolay and Hay described him as paralyzed by the crisis, with divided purpose and a misguided ambition. James P. Newcomb, a San Antonio newspaper editor who should have had more perception, claimed that, had he "boldly raised the flag of the Union, and called upon the loyal men of the State to stand by him," he could have nipped secession in the bud, but that instead he "sullenly clung to the governor's chair." Horace Greeley, speaking with the voice of authority even when he knew nothing of the Texas situation, wrote that Houston, "had he evinced either principle or courage," could have thwarted conspirators in Texas, who were united and determined, while the Unionists, because of Houston's pusillanimity, "were as sheep without a shepherd."

Charles Anderson, brother of Major Robert Anderson of Fort Sumter fame and a resident of San Antonio, staunchly refuted the Greeley charge, denying that Houston was in any position to thwart conspiracy, declaring that a truer Union man never breathed, and describing Houston as, of all the men he ever knew, perhaps the nearest to being the "man who knew not fear." Recalling Houston's zeal, courage, cunning, self-possession, and the twofold shame that came from unjust and cruel ingratitude from "both traitors and patriots," Anderson denied that Houston had been at fault "either in design or execution" and pointed out that his insistence alone made Texas the sole Southern state that submitted the issue of secession to a vote of the people.[79]

Newcomb conceded that had Houston been twenty years younger

---

[78] Howard Cecil Perkins (ed.), *Northern Editorials on Secession*, II, 664, 842.

[79] Nicolay and Hay, *Abraham Lincoln*, IV, 181; James P. Newcomb, *Secession Times in Texas and Journal of Travel from Texas through Mexico to California*, 9; Greeley, *The American Conflict*, I, 339–40; Charles Anderson, *Texas, Before and on the Eve of the Rebellion*, 11–12.

Houston's son, commenting on the "conflicting and unsatisfactory" statements on Houston and secession, criticized the accounts that questioned his father's ever faltering in devotion to the Union and said they were without valid source. He explained that letters to and from Houston were so suspect that his correspondence with friends had to be "conducted through other members of their respective families." "It is not reasonable to suppose," he said, "that one who bore scars as honorable

he would not have allowed an opportunity "to rescue Texas from disunion pass unimproved," and Paschal wrote of the man whom he had alternately fought and supported politically: "But let it be remembered that Houston was too *old*, and his family too *young*, for him to engage in civil war."[80]

Houston's letter to Waite declining aid from the United States government put the period to his executive action and his life in the state capital. The family moved first to Cedar Point. On the way to the coast Houston, despite threats to his safety, spoke at Brenham to defend his own course and to declare the inevitability of war, "the fearful harvest of conspiracy and revolution." On April 19, 1861, he was at Galveston when he declared that Lincoln had been precipitate and foolish and should have let the South alone. On May 10, at Independence, he said:

> The time has come when a man's section is his country. I stand by mine. All my hopes, my fortunes, are centered in the South. When I see the land for whose defence my blood has been spilt, and the people whose fortunes have been mine through a quarter of a century of toil, threatened with invasion, I can but cast my lot with theirs and await the issue.

His past treatment, just or unjust, he was to forget in an hour that called for unity and all the energies of the people and for fortitude and discipline and submission to law and order.[81]

To his oldest son, eager to join the rush into the Confederate service, he counseled patience until he should be needed to defend Texas. Without forbidding the youth's enlistment, the old General tried to point out the defenseless position of Texas, to which his first allegiance was due, and ended an affectionate father's letter on a poignant note: "Houston is not, nor will be a favorite name in the Confederacy! Thus, you had best keep your duty and your hopes together, and when the Drill is over, come home." Sam Jr. went home only to join the first company that was mustered in the neighborhood, Ashbel Smith's Bayland Guards. The war and the qualities of officers were the chief topics of all conversations and undoubtedly absorbed the attention of a general and the father of a soldier. Houston was in Galveston in February and March of 1862, and Ballinger quoted him as saying that all of the Confederacy's disasters came from poor generalship. Pillow, Price, and Lee he com-

---

as his, could have been made to espouse any cause from fear." See A. J. Houston to Alex Williams, *Texas Siftings*, I (December 31, 1881).

[80] Paschal, "Last Years of Sam Houston," *Harper's New Monthly Magazine*, XXXII (1865/66), 633.

[81] Speeches at Brenham, Galveston, and Independence, *Writings*, VIII, 295–305.

mended. Albert Sidney Johnston was a gentleman but not a general— "merely a good mechanical soldier."[82]

Ashbel Smith wrote from Beaumont on March 13, 1862, that General Louis Hebert had offered Sam Jr. a commission as a second lieutenant and instructor in tactics but that the lad refused to be left at home even for the rank of general. Smith was recommending an appointment to the Confederate War Department. The proud father then wrote to Senator W. S. Oldham, his bitter political opponent of the 1850's, to ask the Confederate congressman's patronage in securing a commission for his son. Two days later, April 7, 1862, Sam Jr. was injured at Shiloh.[83]

The father had put aside old animosities. Margaret Houston had probably never harbored any against Mrs. Anson Jones. The mothers were united in their fears as rumors flew that young Sam Houston was dead and Charles Elliot Jones was injured. A letter from Jim Hageman to his mother reporting that Sam was a prisoner and that Charles had only a flesh wound in the arm was passed on to Mrs. Jones and from her to Mrs. Houston, who returned it with the note: "I heard on yesterday, that you had received a letter from your son Charles. If it is true, I congratulate you and rejoice with you sincerely. My heart is still crushed with anguish and suspense."[84]

However much General Houston may have approved General Hebert's commendation of his son, he had no tolerance for Hebert's proclamation of martial law in Texas in May, 1862. To that effect he wrote to Governor Francis R. Lubbock and to S. M. Swenson, protesting the suspension of the Bill of Rights and the triumph of military over civil law. Worry over young Sam was aggravated by the fact that he himself, despite his support of the Southern cause from the time of his retirement from office, was still an object of suspicion. He disclaimed too much resentment of the provost marshal's questioning of movements in the Houston household and interrogation of the Houston children. As he wrote to Swenson: "The reasons which I gave against secession and

[82] Houston to Sam Houston, Jr., May 22 and July 23, 1861, *ibid.*, 306, 308–309.
[83] Smith to Houston, March 13, 1862, Governors' Letters; Houston to Oldham, April 5, 1862, *Writings*, VIII, 315–16.
[84] Margaret Hageman to Mary Jones, May 1(?), 1862, and Margaret Lea Houston to Mary Jones, May 6 and 15, 1862, Anson Jones Papers.
On the battlefield at Shiloh, Sam Houston, Jr., was attended by a Union chaplain. Upon ascertaining his name, the chaplain, one of the ministers whose right of petition General Houston had championed in 1854, nursed the young soldier until he was sent to St. Louis and imprisonment at Camp Douglas. Sam Jr. was exchanged and sent home in the fall of 1862; later, as a lieutenant, he saw service in the Louisiana campaigns. See Temple Houston Morrow, "Bullet Marks Psalm in Bible Given Sam Houston, Jr., by Mother," Dallas *Morning News*, March 5, 1939.

the predictions which I made are still brought up in the minds of my enemies and they cannot believe in my hearty support of the cause which is now of life and death to us all."[85]

The Houston family income was derived chiefly from supplying firewood for Galveston. When the federal blockade cut off the island in the fall of 1862, the family left for Huntsville. The old General led the wagon containing his household furnishings into Brenham on November 1 and ran into a local meeting called to discuss measures against those who refused to take Confederate currency. Houston hobbled to the Washington County courthouse for one more speech. He told of advising Governor Lubbock not to send any more men out of the state and berated Lincoln's appointment of A. J. Hamilton as military governor of the state "to mark his contempt for the people of Texas." Houston lingered in Washington County for about a month waiting for better weather for the move on to Huntsville. From Independence he wrote Ashbel Smith to protest that "another man ought not to leave Texas": "If Texas is lost & ruined, what would the Confederacy be without her? She has been its *van* and *rear* guard. Oh, that our Governor would rise from his *lair* and shake the dew drops from his mane!!! And say, 'by the Constitution I am the Sovereign of a Sovereign State,—*the people look to me to save it, and they will sustain me in its salvation.*'"

When General John B. Magruder and his "cotton-clads" recaptured Galveston on New Year's Day of 1863, the old General wrote his congratulations and his wish that Magruder might "be enabled to carry out the regeneration of Texas." A letter to W. S. Oldham to congratulate him on his free-trade stand and his opposition to the conscript law also indicated continuing interest in governmental policy.[86]

Despite Houston's frequent illness and his age, there were those in Texas who still thought that his interest in government was an active one looking to his own participation. In April of 1862, Ballinger fought a local political battle, determined to "secure Galveston against Houston influence, which however, I consider only imaginary." In March of 1863, Ballinger confided to his diary that he suspected Houston was in Galveston "to survey the field for governer." On May 4 he wrote, "*On dit* that old Houston will run against Peter Gray for Congress." Guy Bryan was convinced that Houston would run if he thought he could win and that he would be supported by the "dissatisfied, disaffected, and dis-

[85] Houston to Lubbock, August 9, 1862, and to Swenson, August 14, 1862, *Writings*, VIII, 316–22.

[86] Houston to Smith, November 18, 1862; to Magruder, January 7, 1863; and to Oldham, February 24, 1863, *ibid.*, 323–26.

loyal."[87] About a month after Bryan so wrote to Jefferson Davis, Charles Power wrote Houston to report a general change in sentiment and his opinion that the people would call the old hero for governor because even old opponents were strong for him, including Guy Bryan, who had said, *"You would be the best man if you could be trusted."*[88]

The man was as enigmatic at seventy as he had been at forty. His speech at Houston on March 18, 1863, while mentioning his age and infirmity and acknowledging his broken dream of empire and the destructability of the Union, pledged his all for the success of the Southern cause and declared his belief that the Southern people were equal to their destiny. Ballinger described the speech as commonplace and flat and commented that Houston steered clear of all offense. The General's voice was weak, and he looked feeble when he spoke in Houston, but his sarcasm was biting as ever when he wrote G. Robinson of the Huntsville *Item* on May 27, 1863, to say that he had noticed the "agonizing distress of some of the presses of Texas" relative to his potentialities as a gubernatorial candidate and was "disposed to relieve them from their painful apprehension." He had, for months, he said, invariably declared that he would not permit his name to be used as a candidate and ended his letter: "A man of three score years and ten, as I am, ought, at least, be exempt from the charge of ambition, even if he should be charged with having loved his country but too well."[89]

In February, 1863, Mrs. Houston had written one of her younger sons that his father would probably scold about his leaving school without permission and running up a store account, but asked him not to be too sensitive, for the time would come soon enough when he would have no one to admonish him when he did wrong. The General made his will at Huntsville on April 2, 1863, appointing his wife and Thomas Gibbs, Thomas Carothers, J. Carroll Smith, and Anthony M. Branch as his executors. He was ill at the time, but two weeks later wrote his daughter Nannie comments on Confederate generals and pertinent advice on how to avoid the appearance of being involved in a "love scrape." He was quite sick again on April 15, but by early May he was in Houston and Galveston and went on to Sour Lake, hoping that the springs there would benefit his health. In July he made the trip back home to Huntsville for the last time. His last conversations concerning the war and the

---

[87] Bryan to Davis, March 9, 1863, Dunbar Rowland (ed.), *Jefferson Davis, Constitutionalist: His Letters, Papers and Speeches,* V, 442–44.

[88] Power to Houston, April 14, 1863, Houston Unpublished Correspondence, XI.

[89] Ballinger Diary, March 18, 1863; Speech at Houston, March 18, 1863, and Houston to Robinson, May 27, 1863, *Writings,* VIII, 327–39, 346–47.

Union were with federal prisoners at the penitentiary. After a five weeks' illness, he died of pneumonia on July 26, 1863.[90]

Three days later, E. H. Cushing, who had fought Houston on every political issue, wrote for his *Tri-Weekly Telegraph* an editorial on the passing of "one of the great men of the age." The editor voiced the yet unanswered question, "What were the springs of action in his mind?" and expressed an appreciation of a powerful personality and a remarkable career. "He has not always been right, nor has he always been successful, but he has always kept the impress of his mind upon the times in which he has acted," said Cushing. Houston's greatness lay not in his virtue nor in his generosity of heart, but in his power over men—"in the certain power of discovering the springs of human action, a thorough knowledge of human nature, and an ability to use this knowledge." The editorial ended:

We pity the heart that could now conceive evil of him. His noble qualities will ever stand out clear before the people.

So, let us shed tears in his memory, tears that are due to one who has filled so much of our affections. Let the whole people bury him with whatever of unkindness they had for him. Let his monument be in the hearts of those who people the land to which his later years were devoted. Let his name be sacredly cherished by Texans, as a debt not less to his distinguished services than to their own honor of which he was always so jealous and so proud.

Swante Palm was the recorder and E. M. Pease the chairman of the committee of York Rite Masons of Colorado Encampment which, on August 1, adopted the resolutions upon the death of Sir Knight Sam Houston. The encampment wore a badge of mourning for thirty days and sent to the family a copy of the resolutions:

While we deeply mourn his loss, we contemplate with proud satisfaction his character as a patriot and a soldier, under whose guidance Texas achieved her independence of Mexico; and his qualities as a statesman, under whose wise and prudent counsel our citizens were ever protected in all those rights and privileges for the security of which governments are instituted. Full of years and honors he has gone to the tomb, but, in his love and devotion to his country, he has left us an example that will cause his memory to be ever cherished and revered.[91]

[90] Margaret Lea Houston to one of her sons, February 6, 1863, and to Houston, June 8, 1863, Houston Unpublished Correspondence, XI; Arthur James Fremantle, *Three Months in the Southern States: April–June, 1863,* 68–69; A. J. H. Duganne, *Camps and Prisons: Twenty Months in the Department of the Gulf,* 254.

[91] Houston Unpublished Correspondence, XI.

The news of Houston's death was received over Texas with profound sorrow, but the troubled conditions of war times prevented any official recognition of the hero of San Jacinto until the meeting of the Reconstruction Constitutional Convention in 1866. A. J. Hamilton then wrote Mrs. Houston that the convention had adopted resolutions of respect in honor of the Governor and had passed an ordinance appropriating money to pay to her the Governor's salary for his unexpired term.[92]

The spring of 1866 also saw the publication of Paschal's article on Houston, an article written partially to pay tribute to his friend and partially to answer the question so often asked outside of Texas: "Is Sam Houston still living?" Paschal's knowledge of Houston and his examination of the Houston materials led him to "certain safe conclusions": that everything Houston ever said in a state paper was well said; that in the darkest hours he dared to speak and vote his sentiments regardless of political and personal consequences, consulting no guide but the best interests of his country; and that in every official station he was scrupulously honest. Paschal's own conclusion was: "Faults he had, and who has not? But he possessed transcendent virtues. To have loved the Union living and dying would cover a multitude of political sins."

In 1831, Tocqueville regarded Houston as an "unpleasant consequence of popular sovereignty" and an example of "how far wrong the people can go." Whether or not he would have been of the same opinion in 1863 one does not know, but the great French traveler and political philosopher ended his study of *Democracy in America* with a comment which is singularly applicable to Houston: "Providence has not created mankind entirely independent or entirely free. It is true that around every man a fatal circle is traced beyond which he cannot pass; but within the wide verge of that circle he is powerful and free." Houston chafed at his encirclement, but few men in American history have done more to widen their circle of political activity than he, and within his circle he was singularly powerful in accomplishment and independent in thought. He branded his mark on Texas and left an indelible trace in the pages of the nation's history.

[92] Hamilton to Margaret Lea Houston, April 16, 1866, Executive Records, Register Book 281, p. 179, Texas State Archives.

Hamilton was directed by the convention to procure a full-length picture of Houston to be hung in the House of Representatives. He asked Mrs. Houston's advice on the picture to be used and told her that he knew of a good portrait in New York.

Bibliography

Bibliography

PRIMARY SOURCES

Manuscript

Baker, Moseley. Letter from General Moseley Baker to General Sam Houston, October, 1844. Typescript, Archives Collection, University of Texas Library.

Ballinger, William Pitt. Diary. Typescript, Archives Collection, University of Texas Library.

Bell, John. Papers. Library of Congress.

Berkeley, Lewis. Papers. Alderman Library, University of Virginia.

Blair Family Papers. Library of Congress.

Brown, Frank. "Annals of Travis County and the City of Austin from the Earliest Times to the Close of 1875." Typescript, Archives Collection, University of Texas Library.

Bryan, Guy M. Papers. Archives Collection, University of Texas Library.

Burleson, Edward. Papers. Archives Collection, University of Texas Library.

Burnet, David G. Papers. Archives Collection, University of Texas Library.

Domestic Correspondence. Archives, Texas State Library.

Donelson, Andrew Jackson. Papers. Library of Congress.

357

Douglas, Stephen A. Papers. University of Chicago Library.

Duerr, Christian F. Diary, 1834–44. Baylor University Library. Typescript, Archives Collection, University of Texas Library.

Epperson, Ben H. Papers. Archives Collection, University of Texas Library.

Fillmore, Millard. Papers. Buffalo Historical Society, Buffalo, New York.

Fish, Hamilton. Papers. Library of Congress.

Ford, John Salmon. Memoirs. Typescript, Archives Collection, University of Texas Library.

Governors' Letters. Archives, Texas State Library.

Heintzelman, Samuel Peter. Papers and Journal, 1856–60. Library of Congress.

Houston, Sam. Biographical File. Barker History Center, University of Texas Library.

———. Papers. Library of Congress. Microfilm, University of Texas Library.

———. Unpublished Correspondence. Twelve typescript volumes (copies of scattered original letters). Archives Collection, University of Texas Library.

Jackson, Andrew. Papers. Series I and II, Library of Congress. Microfilm, University of Texas Library.

Johnson, Andrew. Papers. Library of Congress.

Johnston, William Preston and Albert Sidney. Papers. Tilton Memorial Library, Tulane University of Louisiana.

Jones, Anson. Papers. Archives Collection, University of Texas Library.

Lander, Frederick West. Papers. Library of Congress.

Lincoln, Abraham and Robert Todd. Papers. Library of Congress. Microfilm, University of Texas Library.

Maury, Matthew. Papers. Alderman Library, University of Virginia. Owned by Mrs. Kenneth H. Adams, of Delray, Florida. Photostatic copy of entry for June, 1831, Archives Collection, University of Texas Library.

Maverick, Samuel A. Papers. Archives Collection, University of Texas Library.

Miller, Washington D. Papers. Archives, Texas State Library.

Monroe, James. Papers. Library of Congress.

Nacogdoches Archives. Typescripts, Archives Collection, University of Texas Library.

Perry, James F. Papers. Archives Collection, University of Texas Library.

Pierce, Franklin. Papers. Library of Congress.

Polk, James K. Papers. Library of Congress.

Reagan, John H. Papers. Archives, Texas State Library. Typescripts, Archives Collection, University of Texas Library.

Roberts, Oran M. Papers. Archives Collection, University of Texas Library.

Roosevelt, Franklin D. Papers. Roosevelt Memorial Library, Hyde Park, New York.

Rusk, David. Papers. Stephen F. Austin State College, Nacogdoches, Texas. Typescripts, Archives Collection, University of Texas Library.

Rusk, Thomas Jefferson. Papers. Archives Collection, University of Texas Library.

Smith, Ashbel. Papers. Archives Collection, University of Texas Library.

Smyth, George W. Papers. Archives Collection, University of Texas Library.

Society of Tammany of the Columbian Order. Constitution and Roll of Members, 1789–1916. Photostat, Division of Manuscripts, New York Public Library.

Starr, James Harper. Papers. Archives Collection, University of Texas Library.

Swartwout, Samuel. Papers. Archives Collection, University of Texas Library.

Taylor, John. Papers. Duke University Library.

Travis, William Barret. Diary, August 20, 1833–June 26, 1834. Typescript copied from original in James Harper Starr Papers. Archives Collection, University of Texas Library.

United States War Department. Files. Letters Received. National Archives.

Van Buren, Martin. Papers. Library of Congress.

Wade, S. C. Papers. Duke University Library.

Walker, Robert J. Papers. Library of Congress.

Welles, Gideon. Papers. Library of Congress.

Yoakum, Henderson. Papers. Archives Collection, University of Texas Library.

Printed

Adams, Charles Francis (ed.). *Memoirs of John Quincy Adams, Comprising Portions of His Diary from 1795 to 1848*. Philadelphia, J. B. Lippincott and Company, 1874–77. 12 vols.

Adams, Ephraim Douglass. *British Diplomatic Correspondence concerning the Republic of Texas, 1838–1846*. Austin, Texas State Historical Association, 1917.

Adams, John Quincy. *Speech of John Quincy Adams . . . on the Freedom of Speech and Debate*. Washington, Gales and Seaton, 1838.

Ambler, Charles H. (ed.). *Correspondence of Robert M. T. Hunter, 1826–1876*, Vol. II of American Historical Association *Annual Report, 1916*. Washington, Government Printing Office, 1918.

Anderson, Charles. *Texas, Before and on the Eve of the Rebellion.* . . . Cincinnati, Peter G. Thomson, 1884.

Barker, Eugene C. (ed.). *The Austin Papers*, III. Austin, University of Texas Press, 1927.

Barr, Amelia E. *All the Days of My Life: An Autobiography, the Red Leaves of a Human Heart*. New York, D. Appleton and Company, 1913.

Bassett, John Spencer (ed.). *Correspondence of Andrew Jackson*. Washington, Carnegie Institution of Washington, 1926–35. 7 vols.

Beale, Howard K. (ed.). *The Diary of Edward Bates, 1859–1866*, Vol. IV of American Historical Association *Annual Report, 1930*. Washington, Government Printing Office, 1933.

Benton, Thomas Hart. *Thirty Years' View; or, A History of the Working of the American Government for Thirty Years, from 1820 to 1850*. New York, D. Appleton and Company, 1854–56. 2 vols.

Boucher, Chauncey S., and Robert P. Brooks (eds.). *Correspondence Addressed to John C. Calhoun, 1837–1849*, Sixteenth Report of the Historical

Manuscripts Commission, pp. 125–533 of American Historical Association *Annual Report, 1929.* Washington, Government Printing Office, 1930.

Congressional Globe, 29 Cong., 1 and 2 sess.; 33 Cong., 1 sess., Part I; 35 Cong., 1 and 2 sess.; 36 Cong., 1 sess., Parts I, II, III, and Appendix.

Correspondence between Col. Anthony Butler and Gen. Sam Houston. N.d.

Democratic Party of Texas. National Democracy of Texas. *Proceedings of the Mass Meeting of the National Democracy of Texas.* Austin, Southern Intelligencer Office, 1860.

Duganne, A. J. H. *Camps and Prisons: Twenty Months in the Department of the Gulf.* New York, J. P. Robens, 1865.

Featherstonhaugh, G. W. *Excursion through the Slave States, from Washington on the Potomac to the Frontier of Mexico.* London, John Murray, 1844. 2 vols.

Fremantle, Arthur James. *Three Months in the Southern States: April–June, 1863.* New York, John Bradburn, 1864.

Frizzell, John (comp.). *Proceedings of the Most Worthy Grand Lodge, F. and A.M., of the State of Tennessee, from Its Organization.* Nashville, Southern Methodist Publishing House, 1873.

Fulton, Maurice Garland (ed.). *Diary and Letters of Josiah Gregg.* Norman, University of Oklahoma Press, 1941–44. 2 vols.

Gammel, H. P. N. (ed.). *The Laws of Texas, 1822–1897.* Austin, Gammel Book Company, 1898. 10 vols.

General Convention of 1833. *Constitution or Form of Government of the State of Texas.* New Orleans, Office of the Commercial Bulletin, 1833.

Gray, William Fairfax. *From Virginia to Texas, 1835: Diary of Col. Wm. F. Gray Giving Details of His Journey to Texas and Return in 1835–1836 and Second Journey to Texas in 1837.* Houston, Gray, Dillaye and Company, 1909.

Gulick, C. A., Jr., and others (eds.). *The Papers of Mirabeau Buonaparte Lamar.* Austin, VonBoeckmann-Jones, 1921–27. 6 vols.

Jameson, J. Franklin (ed.). *Correspondence of John C. Calhoun,* Vol. II of American Historical Association *Annual Report, 1899.* Washington, Government Printing Office, 1900.

Jones, Anson. *Memoranda and Official Correspondence Relating to the Republic of Texas, Its History and Annexation, Including a Brief Autobiography of the Author.* New York, D. Appleton and Company, 1859.

Lubbock, Francis Richard. *Six Decades in Texas; or, Memoirs of Francis Richard Lubbock, Governor of Texas in War Time, 1861–63: A Personal Experience in Business, War, and Politics.* Ed. C. W. Raines. Austin, Ben C. Jones and Company, 1900.

Manford, Erasmus. *Twenty-five Years in the West.* Chicago, Erasmus Manford, 1875. Rev. ed.

Nevins, Allan (ed.). *Polk: The Diary of a President, 1845–1849.* New York, Longmans, Green and Company, 1929.

Newcomb, James P. *Sketch of Secession Times in Texas and Journal of Travel from Texas through Mexico to California.* San Francisco, privately printed, 1863.

North, Thomas. *Five Years in Texas; or, What You Did Not Hear during the War from January, 1861, to January, 1866. A Narrative of His Travels, Experiences, and Observations, in Texas and Mexico.* Cincinnati, Elm Street Printing Company, 1871.

Perkins, Howard Cecil (ed.). *Northern Editorials on Secession.* New York, D. Appleton–Century Company, 1942. 2 vols.

Phillips, U. B. (ed.). *The Correspondence of Robert Toombs, Alexander H. Stephens, and Howell Cobb,* Vol. II of American Historical Association *Annual Report, 1911.* Washington, Government Printing Office, 1913.

Pierce, Edward L. *Memoirs and Letters of Charles Sumner.* Boston, Roberts Brothers, 1877–93. 4 vols.

Pike, James. *Scout and Ranger: Being the Personal Adventures of James Pike of the Texas Rangers in 1859–60.* Princeton, Princeton University Press, 1932. Reprinted from the edition of 1865 in "Narratives of the Trans Mississippi Frontier."

Quaife, M. M. (ed.). *The Diary of James K. Polk during His Presidency, 1845 to 1849.* Chicago, A. C. McClurg and Company, 1910. 4 vols.

Register of Debates in Congress, Comprising the Leading Debates and Incidents of the Second Session of the Eighteenth Congress. Washington, Gales and Seaton, 1825.

Reynolds, John. *My Own Times, Embracing Also the History of My Life.* Belleville, Illinois, B. H. Perryman and H. L. Davison, 1855.

Richardson, James D. (comp.). *Messages and Papers of the Presidents.* Washington, Government Printing Office, 1896–99. 10 vols.

Rowland, Dunbar (ed.). *Jefferson Davis, Constitutionalist: His Letters, Papers and Speeches.* Jackson, Mississippi Department of Archives and History, 1923. 10 vols.

Smith, Ashbel. *Reminiscences of the Texas Republic.* "Historical Society of Galveston Series," No. 1, December 16, 1875. Galveston, 1876.

Smither, Harriet (ed.). *Journals of the Sixth Congress of the Republic of Texas.* Austin, VonBoeckmann-Jones, 1940–45. 3 vols.

Tisdale, W. S. (ed.). *Know-Nothing Almanac and True Americans' Manual for 1856.* New York, DeWitt and Davenport, 1856.

United States Congress. "Difficulties on the Southwest Frontier," *House Exec. Doc. 52* (Serial No. 1050), 36 Cong., 1 sess.

————. *Senate Journal* (Serial No. 657), 32 Cong., 2 sess.

United States War Department. *War of the Rebellion.* Series 1, Vol I. Washington, Government Printing Office, 1900.

Van Tyne, C. H. (ed.). *The Letters of Daniel Webster, from Documents Owned Principally by the New Hampshire Historical Society.* New York, McClure, Phillips and Company, 1902.

Williams, Amelia W., and Eugene C. Barker (eds.). *The Writings of Sam Houston.* Austin, University of Texas Press, 1938–43. 8 vols.

Williams, Charles Richard (ed.). *Diary and Letters of Rutherford Birchard Hayes.* Columbus, Ohio State Archaeological and Historical Society, 1922–26. 5 vols.

Winkler, E. W. (ed.). *Journal of the Secession Convention of Texas, 1861.* Austin, Austin Printing Company, 1912.

———— (ed.). *Platforms of Political Parties in Texas.* University of Texas *Bulletin No. 53.* Austin, 1916.

———— (ed.). *Secret Journals of the Senate, Republic of Texas, 1836–1845.* Austin, Austin Printing Company, 1911.

SECONDARY SOURCES

Manuscript

Arthur, D. C. "The San Augustine Collection in the Library of Texas Technological College." M.A. thesis, Texas Technological College, 1931.

Catterton, Conn D. "The Political Campaigns of the Republic of Texas of 1841 and 1844." M.A. thesis, University of Texas, 1935.

Covington, Nina. "The Presidential Campaigns of the Republic of Texas of 1836 and 1838." M.A. thesis, University of Texas, 1929.

Crocket, George L. Notes. Archives, Texas State Library.

Jennings, Vivian. "History of Sam Houston's Governorship of Texas." M.A. thesis, University of Texas, 1934.

Stenberg, Richard R. "American Imperialism in the Southwest, 1800–1837." Ph.D. dissertation, University of Texas, 1932.

Yager, Hope. "The Archive War in Texas." M.A. thesis, University of Texas, 1939.

Printed—Books

Acheson, Sam. *35,000 Days in Texas: A History of the Dallas News and Its Forbears.* New York, Macmillan Company, 1938.

Adams, Ephraim Douglass. *British Interests and Activities in Texas, 1838–1846.* Baltimore, Johns Hopkins Press, 1910.

Allen, O. F. *The City of Houston from Wilderness to Wonder.* Temple, Texas, privately printed, 1936.

Ambler, Charles H. (ed.). *The Life and Diary of John Floyd.* Richmond, Richmond Press, 1918.

Barker, Eugene C. *The Life of Stephen F. Austin, Founder of Texas, 1793–1836: A Chapter in the Westward Movement of the Anglo-American People.* Nashville, Cokesbury Press, 1926.

Bassett, John Spencer. *The Life of Andrew Jackson.* New York, Macmillan Company, 1916.

Bill, Alfred Hoyt. *Rehearsal for Conflict: The War with Mexico, 1846–1848.* New York, Alfred A. Knopf, 1947.

Blaine, James G. *Twenty Years of Congress: From Lincoln to Garfield. With a Review of the Events Which Led to the Political Revolution of 1860.* Norwich, Connecticut, Henry Bill Publishing Company, 1884–86. 2 vols.

Bruce, Henry. *Life of General Houston.* New York, Dodd, Mead, and Company, 1891.

Buell, Augustus C. *History of Andrew Jackson: Pioneer, Patriot, Soldier, Politician, President.* New York, Charles Scribner's Sons, 1904.

Burleson, Georgia J. (comp.). *The Life and Writings of Rufus C. Burleson, D.D., Ll.D., Containing a Biography of Dr. Burleson by Harry Haynes.* [Waco?], 1901.

Campbell, Tom W. *Two Fighters and Two Fines: Sketches of the Lives of Matthew Lyon and Andrew Jackson.* Little Rock, Pioneer Publishing Company, 1941.

Claiborne, J. F. H. *Life and Correspondence of John A. Quitman.* New York, Harper and Brothers, 1860. 2 vols.

———. *Mississippi, as a Province, Territory and State, with Biographical Notices of Eminent Citizens.* Jackson, Power and Barksdale, 1880.

Coleman, Mrs. Chapman (ed.). *The Life of John J. Crittenden, with Selections from His Correspondence and Speeches.* Philadelphia, J. B. Lippincott and Company, 1871. 2 vols.

Corbin, Diana Fontaine Maury (comp.). *A Life of Matthew Fontaine Maury.* London, Sampson Low, Marston, Searle, and Rivington, 1888.

Crane, William Carey. *Life and Select Literary Remains of Sam Houston of Texas.* Philadelphia, J. B. Lippincott and Company, 1884.

Cranfill, J. B. *From Memory: Reminiscences, Recitals, and Gleanings from a Bustling and Busy Life.* Nashville, Broadman Press, 1937.

Curtis, George Ticknor. *Life of James Buchanan.* New York, Harper and Brothers, 1883. 2 vols.

Davis, Varina Howell. *Jefferson Davis, Ex-President of the Confederate States of America: A Memoir by His Wife.* New York, Belford Company, 1890. 2 vols.

Foreman, Grant. *Indians and Pioneers: The Story of the American Southwest before 1830.* New Haven, Yale University Press, 1930.

———. *Pioneer Days in the Early Southwest.* Cleveland, Arthur H. Clark Company, 1926.

Freeman, Douglas Southall. *R. E. Lee: A Biography.* New York, Charles Scribner's Sons, 1934–35. 4 vols.

Gambrell, Herbert. *Anson Jones, the Last President of Texas.* Garden City, Doubleday and Company, 1948.

Greeley, Horace. *The American Conflict: A History of the Great Rebellion in the United States of America, 1860–64.* Hartford, O. D. Case and Company, 1865–67. 2 vols.

Guild, Josephus Conn. *Old Times in Tennessee, with Historical, Personal, and Political Scraps and Sketches.* Nashville, Tavel, Eastman, and Howell, 1878.

Halstead, Murat. *Caucuses of 1860: A History of the National Political Conventions of the Current Presidential Campaign.* Columbus, Follett, Foster and Company, 1860.

Hamersly, Thomas H. S. *Complete Regular Army Register of the United States for One Hundred Years, 1779–1879.* Washington, T. H. S. Hamersly, 1880.

Hamilton, James A. *Reminiscences of James A. Hamilton; or, Men and Events, at Home and Abroad, during Three Quarters of a Century.* New York, Charles Scribner and Company, 1869.

Hawkins, Walace. *The Case of John C. Watrous, United States Judge for Texas.* Dallas, University Press, 1950.

Hill, Jim Dan. *The Texas Navy in Forgotten Battles and Shirtsleeve Diplomacy.* Chicago, University of Chicago Press, 1937.

Hobby, A. M. *Life and Times of David G. Burnet, First President of the Republic of Texas.* Galveston, Galveston News Office, 1871.

Hogan, William Ransom. *The Texas Republic: A Social and Economic History.* Norman, University of Oklahoma Press, 1946.

Horn, Stanley F. *The Hermitage, Home of Old Hickory.* Richmond, Garrett and Massie, 1938.

Houston, Samuel Rutherford. *Brief Biographical Accounts of Many Members of the Houston Family.* Cincinnati, Elm Street Printing Company, 1882.

James, Marquis. *The Life of Andrew Jackson.* New York, Bobbs–Merrill, 1938.

———. *The Raven: A Biography of Sam Houston.* New York, Blue Ribbon Books, 1929.

Johnson, Francis White. *A History of Texas and Texans.* Ed. Eugene C. Barker and E. W. Winkler. Chicago, American Historical Society, 1914. 5 vols.

Kemp, Louis Wiltz. *The Signers of the Texas Declaration of Independence.* Houston, Anson Jones Press, 1944.

Lester, C. Edwards. *Life and Achievements of Sam Houston, Hero and Statesman.* New York, Hurst and Company, 1883.

———. *The Life of Sam Houston: The Only Authentic Memoir of Him Ever Published.* New York, J. C. Derby, 1855.

Ludlow, N. M. *Dramatic Life as I Found It: A Record of Personal Experience, with an Account of the Rise and Progress of the Drama in the West and South.* St. Louis, G. I. Jones and Company, 1880.

McCormac, Eugene Irving. *James K. Polk: A Political Biography.* Berkeley, University of California Press, 1922.

Mayo, Robert. *Political Sketches of Eight Years in Washington.* Baltimore, Fielding Lucas, Jr., 1839.

Mearns, David C. *The Lincoln Papers: The Story of the Collection with Selections to July 4, 1861.* Garden City, Doubleday and Company, 1948. 2 vols.

Merriam, Lucius Salisbury. *Higher Education in Tennessee.* Bureau of Education Circular of Information No. 5, 1893. Washington, Government Printing Office, 1893.

Miller, Edmund T. *A Financial History of Texas.* Austin, University of Texas Bulletin No. 37. Austin, A. C. Baldwin and Sons, 1916.

Milton, George Fort. *The Eve of Conflict: Stephen A. Douglas and the Needless War.* Boston, Houghton Mifflin Company, 1934.

364

Moore, John Trotwood (ed.). *Tennessee, the Volunteer State*. Chicago, S. J. Clarke Publishing Company, 1923. 4 vols.

Morrell, Z. N. *Flowers and Fruits in the Wilderness; or, Forty-six Years in Texas and Two Winters in Honduras*. Dallas, W. G. Scarff and Company, 1886. 4th ed.

Morrow, Temple Houston, "Address by Temple Houston Morrow," *Senate Journal*, 49 Texas Legislature, reg. sess., February 27, 1945.

Morton, Oren F. *A History of Rockbridge County, Virginia*. Staunton, Mc-Clure Company, 1920.

Nevins, Allan. *Ordeal of the Union*. New York, Charles Scribner's Sons, 1947. 2 vols.

Nicolay, John G., and John Hay. *Abraham Lincoln: A History*. New York, Century Company, 1890. 10 vols.

Niles' Register. Baltimore, Washington, and Philadelphia, 1811–49.

Parks, Joseph Howard. *Felix Grundy, Champion of Democracy*. Baton Rouge, Louisiana State University Press, 1940.

Parton, James. *Life of Andrew Jackson*. Boston, Houghton Mifflin Company, 1885. 3 vols.

Phelan, James. *History of Tennessee: The Making of a State*. Boston, Houghton Mifflin Company, 1889.

Pierson, George Wilson. *Tocqueville and Beaumont in America*. New York, Oxford University Press, 1938.

Ramsdell, C. W. "The Frontier and Secession," in *Studies in Southern History and Politics*. New York, Columbia University Press, 1914.

Ray, Worth S. *Austin Colony Pioneers*. Austin, privately printed, 1949.

Richardson, Rupert Norval. *Texas, the Lone Star State*. New York, Prentice-Hall, 1943.

Rives, George Lockhart. *The United States and Mexico*. New York, Charles Scribner's Sons, 1913. 2 vols.

Scroggs, William O. *Filibusters and Financiers: The Story of William Walker and His Associates*. New York, Macmillan Company, 1916.

Sioussat, St. George L. "Tennessee and National Political Parties, 1850–1860," in American Historical Association *Annual Report, 1914*, I. Washington, Government Printing Office, 1916.

Smith, Justin H. *The Annexation of Texas*. New York, Barnes and Noble, 1941.

Smith, William Ernest. *The Francis Preston Blair Family in Politics*. New York, Macmillan Company, 1933. 2 vols.

Statues of Sam Houston and Stephen F. Austin—Erected in Statuary Hall of the Capitol Building at Washington. Proceedings in the House of Representatives on the occasion of the reception and acceptance of the statues from the state of Texas. Washington, Government Printing Office, 1905.

Steen, Ralph W. *History of Texas*. Austin, Steck Company, 1939.

Strecker, John K. *Chronicles of George Barnard*. Baylor University *Bulletin*. Waco, September, 1928.

Tarbell, Ida M. *The Life of Abraham Lincoln*. New York, Macmillan Company, 1928. 2 vols.

Texas. Attorney General's Office. *United States* v. *Texas.* Brief for the State of Texas in Opposition to Motion for Judgment.

Tocqueville, Alexis de. *Democracy in America.* Henry Reeve translation as revised by Francis Bowen and edited by Phillips Bradley. New York, Alfred A. Knopf, 1945. 2 vols.

Wallis, Jonnie Lockhart, and Laurance L. Hill. *Sixty Years on the Brazos: The Life and Letters of Dr. John Washington Lockhart.* Los Angeles, privately printed, 1930.

Webb, Walter Prescott. *The Texas Rangers: A Century of Frontier Defense.* Boston, Houghton Mifflin Company, 1935.

Williams, Alfred M. *Sam Houston and the War of Independence in Texas.* Boston, Houghton Mifflin Company, 1893.

Williams, Elgin. *The Animating Pursuits of Speculation: Land Traffic in the Annexation of Texas.* New York, Columbia University Press, 1949.

Wise, Henry A. *Seven Decades of the Union: The Humanities and Materialism.* Philadelphia, J. B. Lippincott and Company, 1872.

Yoakum, Henderson. *History of Texas, from Its First Settlement in 1685 to Its Annexation to the United States in 1846.* New York, J. S. Redfield, 1855. 2 vols.

Printed—Articles

Baker, William Mumford. "A Pivotal Point," *Lippincott's Magazine,* XXVI (November, 1880).

Barker, Eugene C. "The Annexation of Texas," *Southwestern Historical Quarterly,* L (1946/47).

———. "The Private Papers of Anthony Butler," *The Nation,* June 15, 1911.

Courtenay, Walter Rowe. "The Tennessee Sesquicentennial Sermon: God Walked These Hills," *Tennessee Historical Quarterly,* V (1946).

Culberson, Charles A. "General Sam Houston and Secession," *Scribner's Magazine,* XXXIX (May, 1906).

Golden, Gabriel Hawkins. "William Carroll and His Administration, Tennessee's Business Governor," *Tennessee Historical Magazine,* IX (April, 1925).

Harris, Dilue. "Reminiscences of Mrs. Dilue Harris," *Quarterly of the Texas State Historical Association,* VII (1903/1904).

Henderson, Mary Virginia. "Minor Empresario Contracts for the Colonization of Texas, 1825–1834," *Southwestern Historical Quarterly,* XXXII (1928/29).

"Historical News and Notices," *Tennessee Historical Quarterly,* V (1946).

"Historical Sketch of Washington County," *The American Sketch Book,* IV (1878). Austin, Texas Capital Print.

Horn, Stanley F. (ed.). "Holdings of the Tennessee Historical Society," *Tennessee Historical Quarterly,* III (1944).

"Letters of James K. Polk to Andrew J. Donelson, 1843–1848," *Tennessee Historical Magazine,* III (March, 1917).

Lewis, Sarah Elizabeth. "Digest of Congressional Action on the Annexation of Texas, December, 1844, to March, 1845," *Southwestern Historical Quarterly*, L (1946/47).

Miles, Guy. "The Tennessee Antiquarian Society and the West," *East Tennessee Historical Society Publications, No. 18* (1946).

Moore, Powell. "The Political Background of the Revolt against Jackson in Tennessee," *East Tennessee Historical Society Publications, No. 4* (January, 1932).

Parks, James H. (ed.). "Letter Describes Andrew Jackson's Last Hours," *Tennessee Historical Quarterly*, VI (1947).

Parks, Norman L. "The Career of John Bell as Congressman from Tennessee, 1827–1841," *Tennessee Historical Quarterly*, I (1942).

Paschal, George W. "Last Years of Sam Houston," *Harper's New Monthly Magazine*, XXXII (1865/66).

Powell, Fred Wilbur. "Hall Jackson Kelley, Prophet of Oregon," *Quarterly of Oregon Historical Society*, XVIII (March, 1917).

Red, W. S. "Allen's Reminiscences of Texas, 1838–1842," *Southwestern Historical Quarterly*, XVIII (1914/15).

Rowland, Kate Mason. "General John Thomson Mason," *Quarterly of the Texas State Historical Association*, XI (1907/1908).

"Selected Letters, 1844–1845, from the Donelson Papers," *Tennessee Historical Magazine*, III (June, 1917).

Smith, Culver H. "Andrew Jackson, Post Obitum," *Tennessee Historical Quarterly*, IV (1945)

Smither, Harriet (ed.). "Diary of Adolphus Sterne," *Southwestern Historical Quarterly*, XXX–XXXVIII (1926–35).

———. "English Abolitionism and the Annexation of Texas," *Southwestern Historical Quarterly*, XXXII (1928/29)

Steen, Ralph W. "Analysis of the Work of the General Council, 1835–1836," *Southwestern Historical Quarterly*, XLI (1937/38).

Stenberg, Richard R. "Jackson's Neches Claim, 1829–1836," *Southwestern Historical Quarterly*, XXXIX (1935/36).

———. "The Texas Schemes of Jackson and Houston," *Southwestern Social Science Quarterly*, XV (1934/35).

Terrell, A. W. "Recollections of General Sam Houston," *Southwestern Historical Quarterly*, XVI (1912/13).

Texas Siftings, I, 1881.

Thrall, Homer S. "Sam Houston," *Round Table*, IV (July, 1892).

Printed—Newspapers

Austin *City Gazette*, 1839, 1842.
Austin *Daily Bulletin*, 1841.
Cincinnati *Daily Commercial*, 1856.
Dallas *Herald*, 1855–61.
Dallas *News*, 1892.

Galveston *News*, 1856.
Harrison Flag (Marshall), 1859.
LaGrange *Intelligencer*, 1844–45.
Morning Star (Houston), 1841.
National Intelligencer (Washington, D.C.), 1859.
New York *Herald*, 1860–61.
New York *Times*, 1858.
New York *Tribune*, 1846–50.
San Antonio *Daily Herald*, 1859.
Southern Intelligencer (Austin), 1856–60.
Telegraph and Texas Register (San Felipe, Harrisburg, Columbia, Houston), 1835–50.
Temple *Times*, 1909.
Texas Monument (LaGrange), 1850.
Texas National Register (Washington-on-the-Brazos), 1846.
Texas Republican (Marshall), 1852, 1859.
Texas Sentinel (Austin), 1840–41.
Texas State Gazette (Austin), 1849–56.

Index

Index

Houston, Nancy Elizabeth: birth, 179; writes to father, 233; tells of Houston's refusal to take oath, 338–39; father advises, 352; mentioned, 204, 224

Houston, Sam. To early manhood: birth and parentage, 5; removal to Tennessee, 6; life with the Cherokee Indians, 5; education, 5, 6; schoolteacher, 6; early military career, 6, 7, 8; subagent to Cherokees, 8; study of law, 8; member of Dramatic Club of Nashville, 8; admitted to the bar, 9; elected attorney general, 9; appointed adjutant general, 9; major general of Tennessee Militia, 9

—. In Tennessee politics: advocates Jackson for president, 10; Congressman from Tennessee, 10, 11, 12, 13; speeches in Congress (on Greek independence, 10, at end of first term, 12, on Congress of Panama, 13, on West Point Board of Visitors, 14, on patronage, 15); duel with William A. White, 14; deals with Southard, 15; inaugural as governor of Tennessee, 16; governor of Tennessee, 15, 16–17, 18, 19; message to Tennessee Legislature, 1827, 16–17; resigns as governor of Tennessee, 20, 21; leaves Tennessee, 23; see also Jackson, Andrew; Tennessee

—. In exile: refuge with the Cherokees, 24, 26, 29; adviser on Indian affairs, 24, 25, 28, 35; project for Columbia River colony, 29; painted as Marius, 30; quarrel with Stanbery, 31, 33, 34; accused of ration fraud, 34

—. Removal to Texas: interest in Texas, 35; objectives in Texas, 37, 38, 39, 40, 41, 42, 48, 50, 51, 52, 55; plans for going to Texas, 42, 43, 44, 45, 47, 48, 50; prophecy on future of Texas, 1834, 49; first trip to Texas, 56; land grants, 56, 61; delegate to convention of 1833, 57; law practice in Texas, 61

—. During Texas Revolution: criticized for retreat, 40, 68, 69, 267; chairman of mass meeting at Nacogdoches, 62; in command of Nacogdoches troops, 62; delegate to Consultation, 63; major general of Texas

Army, 63, 64, 67; elected to convention of 1836, 66; treats with Cherokees, 66; opposes Matamoros Expedition, 66; Battle of San Jacinto, 69–70

—. During Republic of Texas, 1836–45: in New Orleans for medical care, 71, 72; agent for land business, 72; elected president of Texas, 75, 76; army problems and policy, 77, 82; first inaugural, 79, 118; policy on Santa Anna, 84; foreign policy, 84–86; valedictory as president, 92–93, 113; return to law practice, 93; visit to U.S., 1839, 93–95; representative in Fourth Congress, 95, 99; attack on Lamar Indian policy, 96; on Cherokee Land Bill, 100; elected president, 1841–43, 101; second inaugural, 102–103; moves government to Houston, 104; messages to Congress, 1842, 105; vetoes war bill, 106; disclaims further responsibility for archives, 108; policy criticized, 109, 110; message on foreign affairs, 1844, 128–29; speeches on annexation, 145, 155; speech on temperance, 155, 277; speech defending administration, 164; endorses Jones for president, 112; visits U.S., 155–57; elected delegate to convention of 1845, 157; concern over U.S. opinion of him, 159; see also annexation; Archive War

—. United States senator: elected senator, 115, 160, 163, 166, 168, 169; speech on Yucatán, 156, 189, 274; speeches on Oregon, 156, 168, 173–74, 191; party alignment, 164; duties of, 169, 176, 194–95, 218–19, 222, 234, 235, 246–47, 257, 258; Mexican War, 172, 175, 176, 181–82; speech on course in Congress, 179; debates bill to organize new army corps, 181; relations with Polk, 182–83, 272; speeches on boundary, 183, 197–98, 206; re-elected, 185–87; at Democratic National Convention, 1848, 190, 275; vote on Oregon, 191; memorial on territory acquired from Mexico, 193; refusal to sign Southern Address, 194; conduct of Senate, 194; defends Father Mathew, 201; favors Compromise of